O9-BUC-265

Abortion and the Politics of Motherhood

California Series on
Social Choice and Political Economy

Edited by Brian Barry and Samuel L. Popkin

ABORTION AND THE POLITICS OF MOTHERHOOD

Kristin Luker

UNIVERSITY OF CALIFORNIA PRESS

Berkeley Los Angeles London

University of California Press
Berkeley and Los Angeles, California

University of California Press, Ltd.
London, England

Library of Congress Cataloging in Publication Data

Luker, Kristin.
Abortion and the politics of motherhood.
(California series on social choice and political economy)
Bibliography: p.
Includes index.
1. Abortion—United States. 2. Abortion—Political aspects—United States. 3. Pro-life movement—United States. 4. Motherhood—United States—Moral and ethical aspects. I. Title. II. Series.
HQ767.5.U5L84 1984 363.4′6′0973 83–47849
ISBN 0–520–04314–6

Printed in the United States of America

1 2 3 4 5 6 7 8 9

To James Wester Luker
and Bess Littlefield Luker

And Lucile Wester
and Virginia Wester Howe

Contents

Foreword

How do people decide whether to regard fetuses as the single-celled creatures they once were or as the babies they will become?

Kristin Luker's book explains why the opposing positions in the abortion debate are held with such fervor and why the issue of the appropriate legal status of abortion has become such a divisive one in American society. On the basis of extensive interviews with activists on both sides of this issue, Dr. Luker shows how positions on abortion depend on broader commitments and, in particular, on contrasting views of the place of motherhood in a woman's life.

This book's contribution to the understanding of contemporary society is apparent; its place in the California Series on Social Choice and Political Economy may be less so. The books in this series are concerned with connections between individual choices and social outcomes. We welcome Dr. Luker's book because it gives content to an idea frequently stated but rarely worked out in convincing detail: that our understanding of moral choices is illuminated by an examination of their social setting. Her analysis of how technological and social changes have combined to create a new moral agenda in politics also helps to explain how people decide to participate in movements that are based on moral issues.

Scholars interested in applying models of decision making to social movements have generally concentrated on issues or movements where people attach no value to participation in the movement for its own sake. That is, studies have emphasized situations in which contributions to a movement are viewed purely as costs, and where individuals consider their contributions solely in terms of their own ultimate benefits. In contrast, participation in the movement for or against abortion is viewed as having value irrespective of whether that participation affects the ultimate outcome of the struggle. Dr. Luker shows that the outcome of the debate over the constitutionality and social validation of abortion may affect activists' senses of identity and esteem. To both pro-choice and pro-life activists, the Supreme Court decision on abortion was important not so much for its practical consequences (Dr. Luker is studying activists in California, where abortion was already legal before the 1973 Supreme Court decision) as for the increased legitimacy they felt the decision accorded to abortion and the lifestyle it facilitates. Lifestyles require validation and support, and the pro-choice and right-to-life movements provide milieux that uphold starkly contrasting lifestyles based on widely divergent views of motherhood.

There are also intimate relationships, Dr. Luker shows, between medical technology, social roles, and the attractiveness of movements furthering moral values. The abortion issue, for example, is affected by changes in our technical ability to detect pregnancy. Once improved technology verifies with certainty whether a woman is pregnant, looking the other way when medicines are used to bring on menses becomes less easy. The development of the contraceptive pill also directly affects the emergence of abortion as a mass issue. The pill, along with easier and safer abortion, enables women to schedule pregnancy and therefore to subordinate childbearing to an entire life plan.

These developments in technology, along with the emergence of opportunities for women in nearly all sectors of American life, have led to the emergence of a new, highly prestigious social role—the career woman. A woman can now live a life of status and glamour without children, even without marriage. The validation of such a life trajectory has led to a perceived devaluation of the roles of mother and wife. The major social significance of this change has been the creation of a chasm between women who have options outside the family and women who do not.

Those not intimately involved with the history of abortion or the history of women's issues may be surprised to discover that abortion was as prevalent in America at certain times in the nineteenth century as it is today. Why, then, has abortion become a mass issue for the first time in our own era? Luker argues that abortion is a widespread issue today because of women's increased ability to incorporate children and marriage into a long-term career plan. A hundred years ago, one issue—the status of the fetus—dominated the abortion controversy. Today, there are two issues: the status of the fetus and the status of motherhood in American society. The modern debate over abortion taps not only attitudes about the sanctity of life but also deep-seated feelings about the place women should occupy in society and about what the proper family structure should be.

Dr. Luker's comparison of women in the pro-choice and pro-life movements makes clear that the moral status of the fetus is not a trivial issue. Beyond concern with the fetus, however, those committed to either side in the abortion controversy are deeply convinced that its resolution is a key to resolving a whole set of struggles about the distribution of careers and jobs in America. The pro-choice women see the ability to plan childbearing as necessary to fulfilling their potential as human beings. The pro-life women, in contrast, view pregnancy and childrearing as central to the lives of all women. The right-to-life movement is an attempt to form a moral cartel to use state power to define the social role of women. Dr. Luker shows that this movement represents an attempt not just to protect the fetus but also an attempt to ensure that family is a higher priority than career among women and that women whose work is within the home are not accorded lower prestige than women whose work is all or partly outside the home. Dr. Luker is one of the first scholars to investigate the rise of movements that seek to put the power of the state behind moral positions. In so doing, she helps us understand the importance to many people of the validation of their moral outlook by legitimating political institutions.

Brian Barry
Samuel L. Popkin

Preface

Some very large proportion of the people who open this book will have already made up their minds on the abortion issue. They will have opened it because they search for new ammunition to confront their opposition or to persuade the uncommitted. They will have opened it because they want to monitor what is being written about abortion these days. These latter will read the first few pages, trying to determine which side I am really on. If I have done my job well, both sides will soon conclude that I have been unduly generous with the opposition and unfairly critical of themselves. They will become annoyed and perhaps outraged as they read things that they know to be simply and completely wrong.

The question of which side I am on came up frequently in the course of writing this book. Ironically, people on both sides soon came to assume that I was by natural inclination on their side. That perception was based on a certain kind of truth. This book was written to explore my own feelings about an enormously complicated topic. While the militants on both sides would have us believe that the abortion debate is actually very simple, such simplicity is both a necessity and a luxury for them. A necessity because we must believe that the things about which we are passionate are either clearly good or clearly bad. But because the belief in simplicity reduces any possibility of dialogue or learning or coming to terms with real human dilemmas, it is a luxury that neither society nor the debate itself can afford.

The voices in this book are those of the people most intimately committed to the conflict over abortion. Throughout the text, in their own words, men and women who have chosen to become active—and in some cases prodigiously active—in outlawing abortion or, conversely, in keeping it legal and freely available—articulate what it is about abortion that captures them.

The book is based on the premise that the abortion debate is a terribly important one, whose meaning and implications will not be fully understood for a long time. Yet it is a first attempt to begin to outline how the debate came into being, what it means, and who has chosen to be on the different sides. Because the abortion debate draws on deep—and often unconscious—beliefs and feelings about, and experiences with, such things as children, families, sex, religion, and the basic natures of individuals—men and women—reactions to it are profound and powerful. This book was written in an attempt to understand where the profundity—and the power—of the debate comes from.

Acknowledgments

A book like this is simultaneously one of the most individual of products and one of the most collective. While an author has the ultimate responsibility for the journey of a thousand crossroads that finally results in a book, this particular author has been blessed with unusually good company along the way. A number of people have generously given time, money, moral support, good ideas, and tough criticism, above and beyond even the expectations of good colleagueship. This part of the book allows me to thank some of those without whom it is quite literally true that I could not have finished (and in some cases even begun) the journey.

First, I am indebted to those courageous souls who were willing to take a chance on furthering a most controversial project. It is no secret that it took some faith and fortitude for foundations to risk money on a research topic that was certain to offend someone and, if I have done my job well, should offend a great many people. Hope Aldrich, the Commonwealth Fund, and the Ford Foundation were willing to take that risk, and I am very grateful. By the same token, Joan Dunlop was in a very real sense the godmother of this book; without her help and support all along it might never have come into being.

As a place that actively supports intellectual endeavor, the University of California has been everything a scholar could wish. It generously supported this work, both by awarding me a Junior Faculty Career Development Award and by grants from the Committee on Research. Moreover, UC San Diego has one of the finest research libraries it has ever been my pleasure to enter. Anita Schiller, Susan Galloway, and Sharon Anderson, reference librarians at Central Library, and Jackie Doyle, a reference librarian at the Biomedical

Library, not only helped me find the unfindable but educated me along the way, and they were just the most visible members of a group of fine professionals who make research more bearable.

My colleagues here and elsewhere were stalwart supporters during the times of high stress and good critics and advisers all the time. I am indebted to Bennett Berger, Chandra Mukerji, Leonard Ross, Karen Paige, Gail Lapidus, Martin Schapiro, David Laitin, Joseph Gusfield, and Jacqueline Wiseman. I am especially indebted to Charles Nathanson, Peter Cowhey, Sam Popkin, and the much-missed Diane Horowitz, all of whom let me talk this book out to them over a period of five years. Sam Popkin was an exigent but supportive series editor, Gene Tanke taught me about writing with his careful copyediting, and Grant Barnes was all that one could wish a supervising editor to be.

I was privileged during this research to have assistants who put much more energy and commitment into their work than their paychecks would reveal. Kathleen Murphy Mallinger, Judith Liu, Judith Greenberg, and Paula Rosenstein gave enormous amounts of themselves to this project and were friends as well as colleagues.

Finally, this book is the product of modern computer technology, both in terms of the analysis of the background characteristics of abortion activists interviewed in the course of the study and in terms of the word processing that produced the manuscript. Mike O'Hagan, Rick Accurso, and Jerry Fitzsimmons regularly rescued me from the whims and mysteries of this technology and did so with unfailing tact, good humor, and a bemused sense of the abilities of computers to drive mere humans beyond the brink. Debra O'Hagan helped wrestle the manuscript into submission, in her usual calm and competent way.

In short, I have been gifted with good friends, good colleagues, and the generous support of institutions during the writing of this book. I have been very lucky indeed.

1

Introduction

In two short decades, the issue of abortion has moved from the fringes of public concern to center stage. By now, no level of American political life has escaped a confrontation with it. Adoption of the federal budget has been delayed several times over the past decade while Congress has debated the issue.[1] The same kinds of delays have confronted state legislatures across the country. Even on the local level, once-sleepy school boards have become tumultuous when asked to consider the place of abortion in sex education curricula, and zoning boards have split over whether an abortion clinic should be permitted to operate in a community.[2]

What is it about abortion—of all the myriad moral issues we face daily—that makes it so troubling, so hard to deal with in reasoned tones? This question becomes even more difficult to answer when we recall just how recent the abortion debate really is. Although the nineteenth century had its own "right-to-life" movement (which will be explored in this book), for most of our century, abortion was simply not discussed in polite company. As recently as twenty years ago, although abortion existed as a very real *private* dilemma, as a *public* phenomenon it was of interest only to a few scattered reformers, theologians, and public health physicians.

Much as the slavery question once did, the abortion issue polarizes. Some abortion clinics have been attacked by arsonists; others have suffered minor sabotage, such as the injection of epoxy glues into the doorknobs of locked doors.[3] Most dramatically, in 1982 the director of an abortion clinic and his wife were kidnapped, allegedly by people who opposed abortion.[4] On a less melodramatic level, the abortion activists I interviewed in the course of researching this book frequently broke into tears of rage and grief when speaking of their feelings on the subject.

Why is the debate so bitter, so emotional? Part of the answer is simple: the two sides share almost no common premises and very little common language. For example, those who oppose abortion usually begin by stipulating that since the embryo* is an unborn child, abortion is morally equivalent to murder. But for those who accept abortion, this initial stipulation is exactly what is problematic; from their point of view, the embryo has the capacity to become a child but it is not a child yet, and it therefore belongs in a very different moral category. Thus, one side begins with a given that the other side finds highly debatable, that the embryo is the moral equivalent of the child it will become.

Early in the process of becoming involved in the abortion issue, people on each side (pro-life and pro-choice) often feel compelled to "share the faith" or to "enlighten" their opposition. In most cases, they rehearse those details about embryonic life that have led them to believe that the embryo is self-evidently either a "baby" or a "fetus." Most of them, however, reached their conclusion about the nature of the embryo very early in their lives; they are unable to see why the data they find so convincing are not equally compelling to someone who was brought up with a very different view of the embryo. If things go further, tempers often flare. A pro-life person can confound a pro-choice attacker by simply stating that it is obvious that the embryo is a baby, pointing out its very evident similarities to a newborn child and brushing aside its evident dissimilarities. Conversely, a pro-choice person can enrage a pro-life person by admitting that although the embryo is human (it is not, after all, some other species) and alive (it is not, after all, dead), this nevertheless does not prove that the embryo is "a human life"—in any case not a "meaningful" human life.

* In political movements, language becomes politicized: a choice of words is a choice of sides. In referring to the form of life that exists between conception and birth, to use either the word *fetus* or the word *baby* is to make a political judgment; in pursuit of neutrality, I will use the term *embryo*, even though it is technically inaccurate. Similarly, I will refer to people as *pro-abortion* and *anti-abortion* activists, although each side finds this general description of its activities much too limited. I will also call the two sides the *pro-life* (or *right-to-life*) and *pro-choice* movements, although each side is emphatic that the label used by the other is a mockery of what it is really up to.

For people who are deeply involved in the abortion issue, these differences of opinion, and the inability to have anything resembling a dialogue about them, are not serious problems. They dismiss those who disagree with them as being either ignorant of the facts or perversely unwilling to admit the truth when it is presented to them. More negatively, they see their most committed opponents as bigots, as people so deeply in thrall to some other interests (the Catholic church, or feminism, or "utilitarianism") that they are unable to think freely about the abortion issue. It should be clear that such explanations preclude any real understanding of why people differ on this issue.

And that, quite simply, is the purpose of this book: to discover how people come to differ in their feelings about the rightness or wrongness of abortion. By way of exploring the question, we shall present a number of arguments about abortion. It is important to make these arguments explicit at the outset, not only because they support the whole logic of the rest of the book, but also because they are bound to upset, offend, and vex those on both sides of the issue.

The first and most important argument is that *the moral status of the embryo has always been ambiguous*. Though both sides turn to history and philosophy and law to buttress their argument that the embryo is or is not a baby, none of these disciplines gives any evidence that can prove the status of the embryo "beyond a reasonable doubt." With respect to history, for example, it is true that the early Christian church denounced abortion (along with other barriers to procreation, such as contraception, homosexuality, or surgical sterilization); but it is also true that the church's sanctions against abortion were almost never as severe as the penalties for the murder of an adult person. Moreover, throughout most of the history of Western Christianity, abortion early in pregnancy, though verbally chastized, was often legally ignored.[5] In philosophy, too, the status of the embryo has been ambiguous. For most of the last two thousand years, the embryo, like a child or a woman, was not considered a legal person. And in harmony with the theories of embryology in vogue until the nineteenth century, most philosophers did not call it a "natural" person. (Even here, there was dispute. The Greek Pythagoreans assumed that the embryo *was* a natural person, but the Stoics did not.) Finally, in Anglo-American common law it is certainly true that embryos have certain legal rights—the right to inherit property, for example. But it is equally true that the embryo must generally be born alive in order to benefit from them. Thus, these rights are not invested in the embryo per se but are held in trust, as it were, until the embryo becomes a newborn child.[6]

In short, philosophy, law, and history only confirm something we already knew about embryos, that they are located on a continuum that stretches from a single sex cell (an egg or a sperm) to a newborn human infant. All that these disciplines can tell us is that sometimes embryos are treated as the babies they will become while at other times they are treated as the primitive single-celled creatures they once were.

Until recently, there has been very little pressure to clarify this state of events, no need to determine, once and for all, where on this continuum an embryo "belongs." Until the mid-nineteenth century, what went on during pregnancy was in large part simply mysterious. In fact, until fifty years ago it was impossible even to diagnose pregnancy with any degree of reliability until "quickening," the point at which the woman can feel the embryo move within her, an event that occurs during the fifth or sixth month of pregnancy. Until at least 1850, the act of inducing an abortion was itself a rather haphazard affair based primarily on herbal medicines. Because these medicines were difficult to prepare in accurate doses and were typically quite poisonous to the woman herself, abortion was unreliable, probably excruciatingly unpleasant, and often fatal. The arrival of the curette on the gynecological scene in the 1880s probably made abortions more effective, but this technological "advance" brought with it new dangers of perforation and infection. Until the invention of antibiotics in the twentieth century, therefore, most abortions were ineffective or lethal.

But this ambiguity about the status of the embryo reflects more than the limits of medical knowledge and the dangers of abortion as a medical procedure. It is important to remember that for most of its history, the United States has been a rural, agrarian country and that such countries generally place a very high value on the birth of children. In addition, the United States was a frontier country where land was plentiful, and inexpensive land is usually associated with high fertility. In fact, during the country's early history, the birthrate was among the highest in the world, on a par with those modern-day Third World countries that we now think of as having "exploding" populations.[7]

In order for the status of the embryo to become a major public issue, therefore, there are a number of preconditions. For example, people today have not only a theory of prenatal development but also direct visual "evidence" of the embryo in the form of intrauterine photographs. Anesthesia, antiseptics, the vacuum curette, and antibiotics have made abortion relatively painless, almost 100 percent effective, and much less physically threatening to the woman involved than bearing her pregnancy to term.[8] Similarly, the United States has become an urban, industrial society with birthrates that have gone from among the highest in the world to among the lowest. Of course, these changes do not in themselves explain why abortion has become a major issue in the last twenty years. But they do explain why the status of the embryo could have remained ambiguous for so long. When the embryo was invisible, when pregnancy did not officially exist until the fifth or sixth month, when fertility was highly valued, and when abortion was unpleasant, dangerous, and often ineffective, there were few pressures to define the status of either the embryo or abortion.

Most people active in the abortion debate today will take offense at this first argument, that the status of the embryo has always been ambiguous. Partisans on each side of the issue can point to articles, monographs, and "facts" that "prove" that the embryo has always (or almost always) been accorded the social and legal attributes they favor. This leads to our second major argument: *the abortion debate is not about "facts" but about how to weigh, measure, and assess facts*. For example, both sides agree that embryos have heartbeats by approximately the twenty-fourth day of pregnancy but that they do not breathe until birth. They cannot agree, however, about what these facts mean. For those on the pro-life side, it is important that embryos have heartbeats. They consider the lack of respiration unimportant and argue that in any case it will occur in time. For pro-choice people, the converse is true: because embryos do not breathe until birth, and all babies breathe, the presence of a heartbeat is merely an indicator that a baby may eventually be born, and until then the embryo is something else, namely, a fetus. The two sides therefore examine exactly the same set of "facts" but come to diametrically opposed conclusions about them.

The third argument we shall make is that *the debate about abortion is a debate about personhood*. Whether the embryo is a fetus or a baby is important because virtually all of us agree that babies are persons and that persons have what our eighteenth-century ancestors called "inalienable rights"—basic rights that cannot as a rule be lost, sold, or given away. Perhaps the most precious inalienable right is the right to not have one's life ended except by due process of law.[9] If the embryo is a baby—and hence a person—then to end its life deliberately, except under very extraordinary circumstances, is something akin to murder. However, if it is not a baby but rather a fetus, then whatever rights it has are more similar to those of the fertilized egg it once was than to the baby it may become; to end its life is therefore something closer on the moral scale to contraception than to murder.

The technological advances of modern medical science have created an urgent need for Americans to arrive at some reasonably explicit decision rules about what it takes to be a full-fledged member of the human community. Before these technological advances, persons were conventionally thought of as having a group of attributes that necessarily functioned together. People had heartbeats, respiration, and brainwaves, and the failure of one meant the failure of the others in short order. Now, however, with the rapid proliferation of new medical technologies, a person missing one of these attributes can be kept alive indefinitely. Because the demand for medical services is potentially inexhaustible, as Victor Fuchs has argued, those concerned with the costs of medical care have begun a debate about who should receive the benefit of scarce medical resources.[10] For reasons we shall explore at length, once a debate such as this ceases to be merely a technical one concerned only with which patient is most likely to recover, it raises terribly difficult philosophical questions. These "bioethical" questions, as they are usually called, have become pressing because so many individuals are now equally entitled to medical care: if modern technology is applied, they are all equally likely to recover. Thus, some participants in the bioethical debate have begun to discuss the moral status of patients. They argue, in effect, that certain kinds of injuries (such as "brain death") prevent a person from being an active member of the social community and therefore make him or her less of a person.[11]

Thus, abortion is simply the most visible (and perhaps most accessible) place for ordinary Americans to grapple with the philosophical issue of personhood. Determining the morality of abortion depends upon determining whether or not the embryo is a full-fledged person. And this effort, in turn, calls on different assumptions about what are the important boundary markers of personhood.

It is particularly relevant that the debate on personhood—whether it occurs in the broader context of bioethics or in the narrower context of abortion—is a debate about *the allocation of scarce resources.*

Abortion is therefore one of the few questions on which ordinary people have presumed to make judgments about bioethics. Perhaps because pregnancy is such a common experience in all corners of the social world, people have firsthand ideas and feelings about it and are less willing to defer to experts. But the fact that people use everyday language to talk about the abortion issue should not obscure a basic point: part of what makes the abortion issue so heated is that people do in fact see it as related to these larger issues. The people interviewed for this book understand clearly enough that the way in which personhood is defined in the case of abortion is related to the way in which it is defined in the cases of heart transplants and kidney dialysis. They also understand that the issue of personhood is intimately related to decisions about who will get scarce resources—a point that leads directly to our next argument.

The fourth argument to be made is this: *the abortion issue is emotionally charged because new political constituencies—primarily women—have vested social interests in whether the embryo is defined as a baby or as a fetus*. Although both sides can fairly claim to be altruistic—the pro-choice side on behalf of women (especially poor women) who need safe, clean, legal abortions, and the pro-life side on behalf of unborn babies—their involvements also reflect personal vested interests. To be sure, these interests are not crassly materialistic: no one enters the abortion debate with an eye to fame and riches. They are deeper, broader, and more subtle. People see in the abortion issue a simultaneously pragmatic, symbolic, and emotional representation of states of social reality—states that they find reassuring or threatening. With respect to the issue of personhood, for example, the different location of pro-life and pro-choice people in the social environment predisposes them to use different traditions of moral discourse in thinking about the issue and to perceive different definitions of personhood as more moral or less moral. The view that personhood is basically social in nature, which implies that some individuals have a less compelling claim than others on scarce resources, is perceived quite differently by persons who expect to have access to those resources and persons who have reason to fear that they may be denied such access.

Participants in the abortion debate, therefore, are defending a *world view*—a notion of what they see as sacred and important—as well as a view of the embryo. Concretely, a decision about the moral status of the embryo is an implicit statement about the role of children and women in modern American society. If the status of the embryo has always been ambiguous, as argued here, then to attribute personhood to the embryo is to make the social statement that pregnancy is valuable and that women should subordinate other parts of their lives to that central aspect of their social and biological selves. Conversely, if the embryo is held to be a fetus, then it becomes socially permissible for women to subordinate their reproductive roles to other roles, particularly in the paid labor force. As this book will demonstrate, the past twenty years have seen the emergence of two very different constituencies of women, two groups that have different experiences in the world and different resources with which to confront it. Whenever a decision about the status of the embryo, and therefore about abortion, is set forth, it enhances the resources held by one group and devalues the resources held by the other.

The outcome of the debate about personhood will affect all of us. On the broadest scale, individuals in this generation have witnessed tremendous technological change with respect to life and death, which the abortion issue touches closely. On a more personal scale, women of this generation have lived through massive social changes that have shaped (and been shaped by) the abortion issue. A thorough study of the abortion debate, therefore, must look at the most critical and rarely examined parts of social life: the meaning of life and death, the meaning of parenthood, the role of sexuality, what is "natural" for men and women, and how morality is formed and experienced.

The first part of this book offers an account of how the abortion debate came into being; it demonstrates that the way in which the issue was framed in the nineteenth century fundamentally determined how it would be framed in the twentieth. The second half of the book examines why persons active in the abortion debate think and feel as they do and how their thoughts and feelings are related to the larger fabric of their lives. In this respect, much of this book is a sociology of knowledge. It argues that how people align themselves in the abortion debate depends in part upon the social worlds in which they live. To be sure, their positions on this issue are rarely a straightforward reflection of their "interests." More typically, an individual's reaction to abortion draws on social, psychological, symbolic, and moral resources, as she or he tries to fit abortion into a larger world view.

The first part of the book, which describes the history of thinking on abortion and its evolution as an issue of public policy, is based primarily on a variety of historical records. Abortion in America emerged as a public issue for the first time in the nineteenth century, and materials from that era—books, medical journals, newspapers, and persuasive literature—have been used to document the origin and meaning of that first debate. Chapter Two therefore discusses the emergence of what might be thought of as the first "right-to-life" movement. The resolution of that first debate resulted in the disappearance of abortion as a moral issue of public concern and its reemergence as a technical issue managed by physicians. Chapter Three documents the "century of silence" that surrounded abortion once it had become medicalized. Chapter Four examines how the medical control of abortion eventually broke down, in large part because of technological changes within the medical profession itself.

The second part of the book, which deals with how people active in the present-day debate think about and deal with the abortion issue, is based primarily on verbatim transcriptions of extensive interviews with highly committed activists, those people who are most deeply involved in the debate. These are the people who do the concrete, sustained political work of the debate in order to bring law and public opinion on abortion into line with their own values. Though it is true that they are not representative of the broad panoply of American thought or belief on abortion—because they are so politically energetic in defense of their views—their beliefs and values predominantly shape the debate. At least one person from every major pro-life and pro-choice group in the state of California was interviewed for this book so that comparisons between the two sides could be based on intensive data. (In fact, the research also included comparative interviews with abortion activists in six other states.) The advantages and drawbacks of this case-study approach and the technical details about the selection of interviewees are discussed in Appendix One.

Therefore, Chapter Five uses excerpts from these interviews with abortion activists to explore the reemergence of abortion as a political and moral issue; it documents the rise of a new constituency in the abortion debate, a group of people who began to talk of legal abortion as a woman's *right*. Chapter Six documents how a second constituency emerged in response to that claim, by making the counterclaim that a woman's right to abortion was outweighed by another right, the embryo's right to life. Chapter Seven shows how beliefs about abortion are intimately tied to the two very different world views of the pro-life and the pro-choice activists; their beliefs about abortion are intimately connected to their attitudes toward children, sexuality, parenthood, the proper role of women, and the like. Chapter Eight examines who these new activists on each side were and why abortion in this new context aroused such passionate and emotional commitments. Chapter Nine speculates about the future of the debate.

Given the arguments this book makes about the history and meaning of the abortion controversy in America, one thing is clear: the abortion debate is likely to remain bitter and divisive for years to come. Beliefs about the rightness or wrongness of abortion both represent and illuminate our most cherished beliefs about the world, about motherhood, and about what it means to be human. It should not surprise us that these views admit of very little compromise.

2

Medicine and Morality in the Nineteenth Century

SURPRISING AS it may seem, the view that abortion is murder is a relatively recent belief in American history. To be sure, there has always been a school of thought, extending back at least to the Pythagoreans of ancient Greece, that holds that abortion is wrong because the embryo is the moral equivalent of the child it will become. Equally ancient however is the belief articulated by the Stoics: that although embryos have some of the rights of already-born children (and these rights may increase over the course of the pregnancy), embryos are of a different moral order, and thus to end their existence by an abortion is not tantamount to murder.[1]

Perhaps the most interesting thing about these two perspectives (which have coexisted over the last two thousand years) is the fact that modern-day subscribers to the first point of view—that abortion is always murder—have been remarkably successful in America at persuading even opponents that their view is the more ancient and the more prevalent one. Their success in this effort is the product of an unusual set of events that occurred in the nineteenth century, events I call the first "right-to-life" movement. After a brief review of the history of abortion prior to the nineteenth century, this chapter will be dedicated to examining that first anti-abortion movement, which so decisively shaped the modern debate on abortion in America. Those readers interested in exploring in more detail the early history of abortion (or examining the claims made here about that history) can consult a number of excellent works on the topic.[2]

In the Roman Empire, abortion was so frequent and widespread that it was remarked upon by a number of authors. Ovid, Juvenal, and Seneca all noted the existence of abortion, and the natural historian Pliny listed prescriptions for drugs that would accomplish it. Legal regulation of abortion in the Roman Empire, however, was virtually nonexistent. Roman law explicitly held that the "child in the belly of its mother" was not a person, and hence abortion was not murder. After the beginning of the Christian era, such legal regulation of abortion as existed in the Roman Empire was designed primarily to protect the rights of fathers rather than the rights of embryos.[3]

Similarly, although early Christians were actively pro-natalist and their rhetoric denounced abortion, contraception, homosexuality, and castration as all being morally equivalent to murder, the legal and moral treatment of these acts—and particularly the treatment of abortion—was never consistent with the rhetoric.[4] For instance, induced abortion is ignored in the most central Judeo-Christian writings: it is not mentioned in the Christian or the Jewish Bible, or in the Jewish Mishnah or Talmud.* Abortion, it is true, was denounced in early Christian writings such as the Didache and by early Christian authors such as Clement of Alexandria, Tertullian, and St. Basil. But church councils, such as those of Elvira and Ancyra, which were called to specify the legal groundwork for Christian communities, outlined penalties only for those women who committed abortion after a sexual crime such as adultery or prostitution. Most importantly, perhaps, from the third century A.D. onward, Christian thought was divided as

* Opponents of abortion sometimes argue that the Bible does express disapproval of abortion in Exodus 21:22–23. In fact, what is mentioned there is accidental miscarriage. The text says that when two men are fighting and they strike a pregnant woman, "causing the fruit of her womb to depart," they may be liable for a capital offense, depending on whether "mischief" has occurred. It is not clear what is meant by "mischief"; the Hebrew word it stands for ("ason") occurs only one other time in the Bible. Nor is induced abortion covered in the Talmud; for information on abortion in Jewish law, see David Feldman, *Birth Control in Jewish Law*, p. 255. The only related text in the Mishnah says that during a difficult delivery, an embryo may be dismembered until "the greater part" of it is born; only when the "greater part" has been born does Jewish law hold that the embryo is a person, and "we do not set aside one life for another"; see Immanuel Jakobovits, *Jewish Medical Ethics*, p. 184.

to whether early abortion—the abortion of an "unformed" embryo—was in fact murder.* Different sources of church teachings and laws simply did not agree on the penalties for abortion or on whether early abortion is wrong.[5]

In the year 1100 A.D., this debate was clarified, but hardly in the direction of making abortion at all times unequivocally murder. Ivo of Chartres, a prominent church scholar, condemned abortion but held that abortion of the "unformed" embryo was not homicide, and his work was the beginning of a new consensus. Fifty years later Gratian, in a work which became the basis of canon law for the next seven hundred years, reiterated this stand.[6]

The "formation" of an embryo (sometimes known as "animation" or "vivification") was held to happen at forty days for a male embryo and at eighty days for a female embryo; the canonist Roger Huser argues that in questions of ambiguity the embryo was considered female. In this connection it is important to remember an intriguing fact of human embryology: *all* embryos start out morphologically female and remain so until the sixth week of pregnancy; and they continue to *appear* female to the naked eye until at least the fourth month of pregnancy.[7] In practice, then, Gratian's rulings, which remained intact until the nineteenth century, meant that even Catholic moral theology and canon law—which were, in effect, the moral and legal standard for the Western world until the coming of the Reformation and secular courts—did not treat what we would now call first trimester abortions as murder.[8] (And given the difficulty in ascertaining when pregnancy actually began, in practice this toleration must have included later abortions as well.)

Nineteenth-century America, therefore, did not inherit an unqualified opposition to abortion, which John Noonan has called an "almost absolute value in history."[9] On the contrary, American legal and moral practice at the beginning of the nineteenth century was quite consistent with the preceding Catholic canon law: early abortions were legally

* The distinction between the formed and the unformed embryo, which drew on Aristotelian beliefs about pregnancy, was first introduced in the Septuagint, the Greek translation of the Bible. Though rejected by some (e.g., St. Basil), it was formally entered into legal and theological arguments by Tertullian in *De Anima*, where abortion was held to be murder only if the embryo was formed; later this holding was ratified by Jerome, Ivo of Chartres, and Gratian. For an overview of the development of Christian thinking in this area, see Noonan, *Contraception*, pp. 10–12; Huser, *The Crime of Abortion*, p. 18; and Grisez, *Abortion*, pp. 137–55.

ignored and only late abortions could be prosecuted. (In fact, there is some disagreement as to whether or not even late abortions were ever prosecuted under the common law tradition.)[10]

Ironically, then, the much-maligned 1973 Supreme Court decision on abortion, *Roe* v. *Wade*, which divided the legal regulation of abortion by trimesters, was much more in line with the traditional treatment of abortion than most Americans appreciate. But that in itself is an interesting fact. The brief history of abortion just outlined, as well as the Supreme Court decision, seems very much at odds with what many Americans—and not only those with pro-life sympathies—have believed: that until recently, abortion was always treated both popularly and legally as the moral equivalent of murder.

This chapter will argue that such a pervasive misapprehension about the historical status of abortion is due in large part to the effects of the first "right-to-life" movement in the United States, which took place approximately between 1850 and 1890. This movement, composed primarily of physicians, made what was in the context a novel claim: that abortion at all periods of pregnancy was murder. In view of the success of this first movement, there is a further irony in the fact that when we look closely at the circumstances and behavior of these nineteenth-century physicians, we find that even most of them were not certain that abortion was really murder and that their opposition to abortion was based on more complicated motives than a desire to protect embryonic life.

The Origins of the First Right-to-Life Movement

At the opening of the nineteenth century, no statute laws governed abortion in America. What minimal legal regulation existed was inherited from English common law tradition that abortion undertaken before quickening was at worst a misdemeanor. *Quickening*, as that term was understood in the nineteenth century, was the period in pregnancy when a woman felt fetal movement; though it varies from woman to woman (and even from pregnancy to pregnancy in the same woman), it generally occurs between the fourth and the sixth month of pregnancy. Consequently, in nineteenth-century America, as in medieval Europe, first trimester abortions, and a goodly number of second trimester abortions as well, faced little legal regulation. Practically speaking, the difficulty of determining when conception had occurred, combined with the fact that the only person who could reliably tell when the pregnancy had "quickened" was the pregnant woman herself, meant that even this minimal regulation was probably infrequent. In 1809, when the Massachusetts State Supreme Court dismissed an indictment for abortion because the prosecution had not reliably proved that the woman was "quick with child," it was simply reiterating traditional common law standards.[11]

In contrast, by 1900 every state in the Union had passed a law forbidding the use of drugs or instruments to procure abortion at *any* stage of pregnancy, "unless the same be necessary to save the woman's life." Not only were those who performed an abortion liable for a felony (usually manslaughter or second degree homicide), but in many states, the aborted woman herself faced the possibility of criminal prosecution, still another departure from the tolerant common law tradition in existence at the beginning of the century.[12]

Many cultural themes and social struggles lie behind the transition from an abortion climate that was remarkably open and unrestricted to one that restricted abortions (at least in principle) to those necessary to save the life of the mother. The second half of the nineteenth century, when the bulk of American abortion laws were written, saw profound changes in the social order, and these provided the foundation for dramatic changes in the status of abortion. Between 1850 and 1900, for example, the population changed from one that was primarily rural and agricultural to one that was urban and industrial, and birth rates fell accordingly, declining from an estimated average completed fertility for whites of 7.04 births per woman in 1800 to an average of 3.56 births in 1900. The "great wave" of American immigration occurred in this period, as did the first feminist movement.

The intricate relationships between social roles, moral values, and medical technologies that were associated with changing patterns of fertility simultaneously became both the cause and the product of demographic strains—strains between rural and urban dwellers; between native-born "Yankees" and immigrants; between the masses and the elites; and possibly between men and women.[13]

But within this complex background against which the first American debate on abortion emerged, we can trace a more direct social struggle. The most visible interest group agitating for more restrictive abortion laws was composed of elite or "regular" physicians, who actively petitioned state legislatures to pass anti-abortion laws and undertook through popular writings a campaign to change public opinion on abortion. The efforts of these physicians were probably the single most important influence in bringing about nineteenth-century anti-abortion laws. (Ironically, a century later it would be physicians who would play a central role in overturning these same laws.) Even more important is the fact that nineteenth-century physicians opposed abortion as part of an effort to achieve other political and social goals, and this led them to frame their opposition to abortion in particular ways. In turn, the way they framed the issue would cast a very long shadow over rounds of the debate yet to come.

The Background of Mobilization

Before we can understand the role of physicians in the abortion debate of one hundred years ago, we must recognize that our modern-day assumptions about both the nature of medicine and the nature of abortion in the nineteenth century are likely to be quite wrong.

Physicians in the nineteenth century

Modern observers accustomed to thinking of the medical profession as prestigious, technically effective, and highly paid are sometimes shocked to learn that it was none of those things in the nineteenth century. On the contrary, much of its history during that century was an uphill struggle to attain just those attributes. Whereas European physicians entered the modern era with at least the legacy of well-defined guild structures—structures that took responsibility for teaching, maintained the right to determine who could practice, and exercised some control over the conduct and craft of the profession—American physicians did not. Because of its history as a colony, the United States attracted few guild-trained physicians, and consequently a formal guild structure never developed. Healing in this country started out primarily as a domestic rather than a professional skill (women and slaves often developed considerable local reputations as healers), and therefore anyone who claimed medical talent could practice—and for the most part could practice outside of any institutional controls of the sort that existed in Europe.[14]

It is true that some early colonies did establish different fee structures for "trained" as opposed to "folk" doctors, but these regulations were not supported by "enabling" legislation. "Trained" physicians had the right to charge more, but there were no regulatory mechanisms by which they could enforce their higher fees or, more importantly, deny others the right to practice medicine. From the earliest days of the medical profession in this country, therefore, physicians wanted effective licensing laws that would do for them what the guild structures had done for their European colleagues, namely, restrict the competition.[15]

In the early part of the nineteenth century, the fate of trained physicians became even worse. What few regulations had existed in the colonial period were swept away in the era of Jacksonian democracy, and medical practice became one vast free market. Moreover, during the second quarter of the century, deep doctrinal divisions appeared within the ranks of trained physicians themselves. For the first third of the century, physicians had depended on a model of illness that called upon the use of drastic medical treatments such as bleeding or the administration of harsh laxatives and emetics. By the 1850s, a new group of physicians (including such luminaries as Oliver Wendell Holmes) rejected the use of this "heroic armamentarium" and earned for themselves the sobriquet of "therapeutic nihilists" inasmuch as they seemed to argue that anything a physician could do was probably ineffective and might be dangerous as well.[16]

Two other developments during the course of the century kept the social and professional status of medicine low. First, as the effectiveness of "heroic" medicine was called into question by some physicians themselves, there was a proliferation of healers who advocated new models of treatment. Thomsonians, botanics, and homeopaths among others all developed "sects" of healing and claimed the title of doctor for themselves. These nineteenth-century sectarians flourished, perhaps in part because they tended to support relatively mild forms of treatment (baths, natural diets) instead of the "heroic" measures used by many doctors. Thus, regular physicians (those who had some semblance of formal training and who subscribed to the dominant medical model) found themselves in increasing competition with the sectarians, whom they considered quacks.[17]

Concurrent with the emergence of the sectarians, there was an explosion of new medical schools: an estimated four hundred new ones opened during the course of the century.[18] Unlike modern-day medical schools, whose strict admission standards are legendary, the majority of these schools were proprietary. Like modern-day vocational schools, they were open to all who could pay their fees, and precisely because they depended upon fees to survive, they were reluctant to fail anyone who could be counted on to pay tuition regularly.[19]

Members of the regular medical profession were therefore caught in a dilemma. In order to upgrade the profession's status, they had to upgrade not only the standards of practice but also the education and qualifications of those who wished to practice. However, the prerequisite to such an upgrading—the restriction of the title of "doctor" to only the best and the best-trained physicians—was difficult to meet because of the lack of licensing laws. Physicians faced the paradox that they could not obtain licensing laws until they were "better" than the competition, but becoming "better" depended on having licensing laws. The way in which physicians solved this problem was to bring them to the center of the abortion debate in America.

Abortion in nineteenth-century America

With respect to abortion, as with respect to physicians, modern-day stereotypes about the nineteenth century can easily lead us astray. Contrary to our assumptions about "Victorian morality," the available evidence suggests that abortions were frequent. To be sure, some of these abortions may have been disguised (or rationalized) by those who sought them. Early in the century, a dominant therapeutic model saw the human body as an "intake-outflow" system and disease as the result of some disturbance in the regular production of secretions.[20] Prominent among medical concerns, therefore, was "blocked" or "obstructed" menstruation, and the nineteenth-century pharmacopoeia contained numerous emmenagogues designed to "bring down the courses," that is, to reestablish menstruation.[21] However, since the primary cause of "menstrual obstruction" in a healthy and sexually active woman was probably pregnancy, at least some of these emmenagogues must have been used with the intent to cause an abortion. Especially in the absence of accurate pregnancy tests, these drugs could be used in good faith by physicians and women alike, but the frequent warnings that these same drugs should not be used by "married ladies" because they would cause miscarriage made their alternative uses quite clear.[22]

Similarly, newspaper advertisements for patent medicines designed to bring on "suppressed menses" were common during the era; according to a number of sources, such advertisements appeared even in church newspapers.[23] Discreet advertisements for "clinics for ladies" where menstrual irregularities "from whatever cause" could be treated (and where confidentiality and even private off-street entrances were carefully noted in the advertisement itself) were common. A typical example is an 1873 San Francisco advertisement for a "doctress" specializing in "female irregularities":

> Doctress A. M. Hoffman, 4422 Folsom St. between 10th and 11th, 30 years experience; has her diploma of the highest school of Germany, will thoroughly treat all Diseases of Women and Children; She would intimate to Ladies suffering from Uterine Disorders that she has a sure specific for female irregularities. All communcations strictly confidential. She has lately added a first-class Lying In Hospital where patients can receive the best of medical attendance. Terms moderate.[24]

As the noted medical historian Richard Shryock has observed: "One of the most striking and common forms of quack advertising in the United States was that of abortifacient drugs; a fact which seems hardly consistent with our notion of Victorian propriety. . . . The common form of the 'ads' was something of this sort: 'Dr. ——'s Female Pills, one dollar a box, with full directions. Married ladies should not use them. Sent by mail.' " Shryock validates a commonly heard complaint by noting: "Similar announcements and other quack appeals filled not only the daily and weekly papers, but the 'family newspapers' and even the religious press."[25]

Aside from the use of these emmenagogues to bring on "delayed" menstruation, various attempts were made during this period to estimate the frequency of induced abortion as we now understand it. These estimates were primarily the work of physicians who wanted to convince the public that abortion was a problem of great magnitude, and so their estimates must be treated cautiously. Nonetheless, estimates from differing sources yield roughly comparable results. An Ohio medical investigation concluded that one-third of all "live births" (*sic*) ended in induced abortion. Dr. Horatio Storer, one of the most visible anti-abortionists of the era, estimated that there was one abortion for every four pregnancies; a survey of Michigan physicians found between 17 and 34 percent of all pregnancies ending in abortion; and an 1871 American Medical Association committee concluded that 20 percent of all pregnancies were deliberately aborted.[26] (As a point of comparison, modern estimates since the legalization of abortion in America in 1973 suggest that there is one abortion for every three live births.)[27] In 1864 the grand jury of the city and state of New York expressed its concern about the increasing frequency of abortion, and in 1869 the Presbyterian General Assembly was moved to condemn "unscriptural views of marriage" and, in particular, abortion and infanticide.[28] Even European travelers commented on how frequent abortion was in the United States.[29] Contemporary observers such as these were in unanimous agreement that the women who engaged in abortion did not believe they were doing anything wrong. The common law tradition, they argued, led women to feel that abortion before quickening was morally blameless, only slightly different from preventing a conception in the first place.

Physicians and abortion

In the second half of the nineteenth century abortion began to emerge as a social problem: newspapers began to run accounts of women who had died from "criminal abortions," although whether this fact reflects more abortions, more lethal abortions, or simply more awareness is not clear.[30] Most prominently, physicians became involved, arguing that abortion was both morally wrong and medically dangerous.

The membership of the American Medical Association (AMA), founded in 1847 to upgrade and protect the interests of the profession, was deeply divided on many issues. But by 1859 it was able to pass a resolution condemning induced abortion and urging state legislatures to pass laws forbidding it; in 1860, Henry Miller, the president-elect of the association, devoted much of his presidential address to attacking abortion; and in 1864 the AMA established a prize to be awarded to the best anti-abortion book written for the lay public. Slowly, physicians responded to the AMA's call and began to lobby in state legislatures for laws forbidding abortion.[31]

Meanwhile, a number of physicians who took the AMA's directive to heart began to publish books designed to convince the public that abortion was a medical and a moral wrong. Most of these men were elite "regular" physicians and associated with university-based medical schools. The prolific anti-abortionist Horatio Storer, for example, was the son of a Harvard Medical School professor and was himself destined to become the vice-president of the AMA. In 1868 he published *Criminal Abortion* (with Franklin Fiske Heard), having published *Why Not? A Book for Every Woman* in 1866 and *Is It I? A Book for Every Man* in 1867. Hugh Hodge, a professor of the diseases of women and children at the University of Pennsylvania, published *Foeticide, or Criminal Abortion* in 1869. Ely Van de Warker, the president of the Gynecological Society of Boston, published "The Detection of Criminal Abortion" in the society's medical journal and later reprinted it as a monograph for the general public in 1872.

Medical societies also began to undertake investigations of the problem of abortion, and several of them published their findings for the benefit of other physicians and the general public.[32] In all, scholarship on the nineteenth-century abortion debate has been hard-pressed to find any other group of anti-abortion activists as central and visible as physicians.[33]

Why should nineteenth-century physicians have become so involved with the question of abortion? The physicians themselves gave two related explanations for their activities, and these explanations have been taken at face value ever since. First, they argued, they were compelled to address the abortion question because American women were committing a moral crime based on ignorance about the proper value of embryonic life. According to these physicians, women sought abortions because the doctrine of quickening led them to believe that the embryo was not alive, and therefore aborting it was perfectly proper. Second, they argued, they were obliged to act in order to save women from their own ignorance because only physicians were in possession of new scientific evidence which demonstrated beyond a shadow of a doubt that the embryo was a child from conception onward.

The physicians were probably right in their belief that American women did not consider abortion—particularly early abortion—to be morally wrong. As we have shown at the beginning of this chapter, that attitude would have been consistent with a long moral and legal tradition. But the core of the physicians' claim—the assertions that women practiced abortion because they were ignorant of the biological facts of pregnancy and that physicians were opposed to it because they were in possession of new scientific evidence—had no solid basis in fact.

Physicians claimed that women (and the public at large) did not know that the embryo was alive because they subscribed to the "outmoded" doctrine of quickening; but whether this meant that women were ignorant of the "facts" of pregnancy is another question. Andrew Nebinger, a member of the Pennsylvania State Medical Society, was charged with the task of surveying "all the regular physicians in practice" in Philadelphia on the practice of "criminal abortion." He cited as typical a physician who said:

> I have been shocked beyond measure by having proposals made to me to procure abortion by women of education and respectable position in society, and who were even professors of religion in some cases. They were in all instances married women, but their idea generally was that the foetus is not alive, but only has, one might say, a capacity for living, and hence that, to destroy it was not homicide, and hardly more criminal than to prevent conception.[34]

Hugh Hodge expanded on this theme:

> Married women, also, from the fear of labor, from indisposition to have the care, the expense, or the trouble of children, or some other motive equally trifling and degrading, have solicited that the embryo should be destroyed by their medical attendant. And when such individuals are informed of the nature of their transaction, there is an expression of real or pretended surprise that any one should deem the act improper. . . . This low estimate of the importance of fetal life is by no means restricted to the ignorant, or to the lower classes of society. Educated, refined, and fashionable women—yea, in many instances, women whose moral character is, in other respects, without reproach; mothers who are devoted, with an ardent and self-denying affection, to the children who already constitute their family—are perfectly indifferent regarding the foetus in utero.[35]

Ely Van de Warker agreed: "There are laws, which if enforced, will check this trade [in abortion]. These laws are not enforced, and I think for this reason: I am forced to believe, that in relation to this crime there exists a moral obliquity in all ranks of society."[36]

This stand had an important advantage for physicians. It meant that the American women who practiced abortion (and who were generally thought to be members of the "better classes") could be defined as *inadvertent* murderesses, persons led astray because they believed in the doctrine of quickening.[37] Thus, a physician could condemn the "sin" without the necessity of condemning the "sinner." When Winslow Ayer, a medical school professor from Michigan, asserted that women sinned because they were ignorant of the physiology of gestation, he neatly outlined how the physicians' claim allowed them to accuse and absolve women at the same time: "The *crime* [of abortion] is wholly inconsistent with the purity of woman's nature, and revolting to her moral sentiments. It is generally the act of those who know not what they do."[38]

The actual evidence, however, suggests that the American public had long since been exposed to the basic physiological facts about pregnancy. Certainly, ordinary people had access to the general *idea* that pregnancy represented, at least on the physiological level, a continuous process. A home medical book published in 1817 for a popular audience (and dedicated to "the Wives of the Ministers of the Gospel of the United States") gave the following information, which was not substantially at variance with what the physicians were arguing:

> Thus the contents of the pregnant womb, formed in miniature at conception, are the child, the waters, the membranes holding them, the navel cord, and the afterbirth. . . . Seven days after conception, parts of the child are distinguishable to the naked eye . . . [and] the head and trunk may be easily distinguished. Fifteen days after conception, the head and most prominent features of the face are apparent. The nose resembles a small elevated thread . . . two black points represent the eyes. At one month, the young, called the fetus, is an inch in length. . . . All parts of the face may be seen, the body is visible, the haunches and belly are prominent, the hands and legs are formed; the fingers and toes are divided; the skin is thin and transparent. . . . At the end of six weeks . . . the form is more perfect, only the head is larger in proportion. . . . About this time the motion of the heart is visible. . . . It is at the fourth month that the mother feels the motion of the child within, which is called quickening. . . . This motion is the only infallible symptom of pregnancy; and generally terminates the [previous] unpleasant sickness and disease.[39]

Similarly, a "lady's medical guide" published fifteen years later asserts: "[The womb's] function is to receive the first rudiments of the fetus, and to assist in the full development of all its parts, until it attains that state of perfection, in which it is destined to enter into the world, and form a new living being."[40]

It is difficult today to ascertain how popular these particular "lady's guides" were; we know only that the nineteenth century, like the twentieth, had its "popular health movement" and that books like these proliferated.[41] What can be proved, however, is that the American public did not suffer from the ignorance imputed to it. For at least sixty years *prior* to the emergence of the physicians' crusade against abortion, Americans had been exposed to the idea that abortion *at any period* of pregnancy was wrong. Dr. Buchan's *Domestic Medicine*, a book reprinted so often that it was the nineteenth century's equivalent of Dr. Spock's *Baby and Child Care*, was unusual in that it forcefully opposed abortion as early as 1797. In the course of discussing "involuntary abortion" (miscarriage) in the second month of pregnancy, long before quickening, the American edition of *Domestic Medicine* appended the following aside against induced abortion:

> Every woman who procures an abortion does it at the hazard of her life; yet there are not a few who run this risk, merely to prevent the trouble of bearing and bringing up children. It is surely a most unnatural crime, and cannot, even in the most abandoned, be viewed without horror, but in the decent matron it is still more unpardonable. Those wretches who daily advertise their assistance to women in this business, deserve, in my opinion, the most severe of all human punishments.[42]

No distinctions about quickening were proposed, and the context makes it clear that for Buchan, pregnancy was one unbroken, continuous process.

Although physicians after the middle of the century began to claim "new scientific evidence" to back up their assertion that what had been a minority view in Buchan's day was now the "scientifically correct" view, upon inspection this "new evidence" is remarkably general. In fact, the period during which the physicians began to organize against abortion (approximately 1850 to 1870) witnessed no major advances in the understanding of embryology; the real breakthroughs had come much earlier. The notion that pregnancy is a biologically continuous process had been asserted in a widely read American textbook, *Burns' Obstetrical Works*, as early as 1809.* By that date, the debates be-

* This work made explicit the same point that the "regulars" were trying to claim as *new* fifty years later:

> I must remark, that many people at least pretend to view attempts to excite abortion as different from murder, upon the principle that the embryo is not possessed of life, in the common acceptation of the word. It undoubtedly can neither think nor act; but upon the same reasoning, we should conclude it to be innocent to kill the child in the birth. Whoever prevents life from continuing, until it arrives at perfection, is certainly as culpable as if he had taken it after that had been accomplished.

tween the ovists and the animalculists had been virtually resolved, and few educated medical people remained to be convinced that pregnancy was anything but continuous. By 1817, Christian Pander had described the three layers of what he had named the blastoderm and had demonstrated how various organs and systems develop from each of the three layers. Another popular textbook published in 1819 showed a woodcut of a developing embryo in utero.[43] The more detailed discoveries about pregnancy made later in the century—the exact role and structure of the human ovum and the exact mechanics of the process of fertilization—were in the nature of technical additions to a generally accepted principle and were in any event made many years after American physicians mobilized against abortion.[44] They came to be used as *evidence* in the debate about abortion, but it is hardly the case that their emergence on the scene *caused* the debate.

When examined closely, therefore, neither part of the physicians' claim was, strictly speaking, true. Women (and the general public) knew that pregnancy was a *biologically* continuous process from beginning to end, and physicians were not in possession of remarkable new scientific discoveries to use to prove the case.

Both popular and medical writings of the period suggest that for many years prior to the first "right-to-life" movement, the nineteenth-century public agreed with the anti-abortion physicians' belief that pregnancy was, biologically speaking, a continuous process that led to the birth of a child. Where they disagreed was upon the *moral* implications of these biological facts. The public did not consider the embryo "not alive" in the biological sense, as the anti-abortion physicians asserted. Rather, public (and much medical) opinion seems to have been that embryos were, morally speaking, simply not *as alive* as the mother, at least until quickening—and sometimes later than that, if

---

Burns did not disapprove of all abortions (and neither did his colleagues later in the century, as I shall show). This same passage continues:

> I do not, however, wish from this observation, to be understood as in any way disapproving of those necessary attempts which are occasionally made to procure premature labor, or even abortion, when the safety of the mother demands this interference, or when we can thus give the child a chance of living, who otherwise would have none. (John Burns, *Burns' Obstetrical Works*, pp. 34–35.)

The extent to which Burns's books—the obstetrical treatise and his *Midwifery* (1810)—were relied upon by American physicians is documented in Irving Cutter and Henry Viets, *A Short History of Midwifery*, p. 210.

the pregnancy threatened the life of the woman. Indeed, the same home medical book that contained the detailed descriptions of intra-uterine life noted earlier had this to say about uterine hemorrhage or "flooding":

> When the flooding returns, in great degree, in spite of all efforts to prevent [it], the women becoming extremely pallid, showing excessive loss of blood, but one remedy is left, and that is to produce an immediate abortion. Unless the danger be very pressing, the advice or direction of a physician should be taken before the destruction of the child. *It should, however, always be remembered that the life of the child is not to be compared with that of the mother* [emphasis added].[45]

This preference for maternal life over embryonic life reflects standard medical practice, at least according to textbooks in use at the time. William Dewees, the author of a classic obstetrical textbook published in 1826 and reprinted nine times over the next twenty-five years, denounced abortion when practiced by women, yet quoted approvingly the traditional notion that the life of the child was "incomparably small" when pitted against that of its mother. Similarly, Gunning Bedford, another well-respected obstetrical expert whose work was reprinted eight times, argued in favor of abortion: "Without the operation, two lives would certainly be sacrificed, while, with it, it is more than probable that one would be saved." Charles Meigs, the author of another much-reprinted obstetrical textbook, agreed: "Whenever a clear indication for the sacrifice of the tender embryo exists, no evil is done in procuring the greater good of the mother; on the contrary, the act by which it is destroyed is as purely good as the saving of a man's life. The lesser, in morals, must yield to the greater; the lesser is always included in the greater."[46]

What the anti-abortion physicians achieved, therefore, was a subtle transformation of the grounds of the debate. By asserting that women had abortions because they were ignorant of scientific knowledge, doctors shifted the focus of the debate from moral *values* to empirical *facts*. But judging by the available evidence, the public, the medical profession in general, and the anti-abortion physicians in particular were *not* at odds with one another over the facts about what went on during pregnancy. With greater or lesser degrees of detail, all seem to have drawn on relatively widely available and popularly accepted beliefs about the development of the embryo. Popular (and legal) acceptance of abortion was not based on ignorance of "the facts," as physicians asserted, but on *a different moral evaluation of the facts*.

Motives for Mobilization

Thus, the question remains: why, in the middle of the nineteenth century, did some physicians become active anti-abortionists? James Mohr, in a pioneering work on this topic, argues that the proliferation of healers in the nineteenth century created a competition for status and clients. The "regular" physicians, who tended to be both wealthier and better educated than members of other medical sects, therefore sought to distinguish themselves both scientifically and socially from competing practitioners. Support of anti-abortion activity was admirably suited to this need. By taking an anti-abortion stand, regular physicians could lay claim to superior scientific knowledge, based on the latest research developments and theories (usually from abroad) to buttress their claim that pregnancy was continuous and that any intervention in it was immoral.[47] At the same time, they could claim to be following the Hippocratic Oath, which contains a clause proscribing at least one form of abortion practice.* The abortion issue thus gave them a way of demonstrating that they were both more scientifically knowledgeable and more morally rigorous than their competitors.

Mohr suggests that there were several more practical reasons why regular physicians should have opposed abortion. On the one hand, outlawing abortion would remove a lucrative source of income from competitors they called "quacks" and perhaps remove that temptation from the path of the "regulars" as well. In addition, the "regulars" were predominantly white, upper-income, and native-born; as such, they belonged to precisely the same group that was thought to harbor the primary users of abortion. As a result, they were likely to be con-

* In fact, the Hippocratic Oath originally outlawed only a "pessary to produce abortion." See W. H. S. Jones, *The Doctor's Oath*, p. 11. Edelstein argues that Hippocrates (more properly the "Hippocratic school") was the forerunner of our modern-day holistic health practitioners. As such, what in large part was being rejected in this passage was the use of drugs rather than specifically the act of abortion ("Hippocratic Oath," pp. 18–38.) Although the Oath also forbids surgery ("I will not use the knife . . ."), American regulars chose to conveniently overlook that part. Thus, it is more likely that the regulars opposed abortion not because the Oath did but rather because both their opposition to abortion and their adoption of the Hippocratic Oath were simultaneous aspects of their attempts to professionalize.

cerned both about the depopulation of their group in the face of mounting immigration (and the higher fertility of immigrants) and about "betrayal" by their own women (because abortion required less male control and approval than the other available forms of birth control).[48]

More broadly, Mohr argues that nineteenth-century physicians had a firm ideological belief that abortion was in fact murder. He asserts that they tended to place an absolute value on human life and that having established to their own satisfaction that abortion represented the loss of human life, abortion became included in this more general value.[49] The historian Carl Degler has made much the same argument: "Seen against the broad canvas of humanitarian thought and practice in Western society from the seventeenth to the twentieth century, the expansion of the definition of life to include the whole career of the fetus rather than only the months after quickening is quite consistent. It is in line with a number of movements to reduce cruelty and to expand the concept of sanctity of life."[50]

It is certainly true, as Mohr claims, that the mobilization of American physicians against abortion took place in the context of a profound dilemma within the medical profession, a dilemma produced by the lack of a traditional guild structure, the proliferation of competing medical sects and dissension within the ranks of the regulars themselves. Physicians wanted to upgrade their profession by obtaining licensing laws that would restrict medical practice to only the best and the best-trained among them. But lacking such licensing laws and given the ease with which one could become even a "trained" physician by attending one of the proliferating "proprietary" medical schools, regular physicians had no way of proving that they were any better than their competitors.

Nineteenth-century physicians needed to be "better" than their competition in order to persuade the public that licensing laws were not simply a self-serving "restraint of trade," designed only to raise the price of a doctor's bill by eliminating the competition. (The "restraint of trade" complaint arose routinely whenever regular physicians pressed for licensing laws.) But they could not be "better" until they had licensing laws that would purge their own numbers of the inadequate or the incompetent.

As we know, regular physicians succeeded in their campaign for licensing laws. More than almost any other profession, medicine now rigorously exercises the right to control who shall enter the profession, how they shall practice, and how competitors will be treated; its nineteenth-century stand against abortion contributed substantially to this ultimate success. It is in the context of this drive for professionalization that the political activity of American physicians against abortion must be understood. When examined closely in this context, their actual behavior raises serious doubts about whether they had, as Mohr and Degler claim, an unparalleled commitment to the "sanctity of life" of the embryo.

The traditional explanation of how one group of medical practitioners in America, the regulars, successfully strove for and obtained the attributes that we now associate with modern medicine (and that, incidentally, squeezed out the competition) emphasizes the dimension of training. Until quite recently, most histories of medicine (whether written by physicians or social scientists) attribute this success to the superior education and understanding of the regulars and to their adoption of a new way of looking at the problem of disease, namely, "the scientific method." In this viewpoint, the regulars triumphed because they were "scientific" in contrast to their "unscientific" competitors.[51] On the other hand, recent studies of medical professionalization have tended to focus on another dimension, on what Charles Rosenberg has called the "sordid realities of the marketplace."[52] This approach emphasizes the fact that regular physicians (and in particular those who *organized* on behalf of the regulars) tended to be of a higher social status than their sectarian competitors and tended to cater primarily to an upper-class clientele. The expenses of a medical education—especially when it was combined, as it often was for elite physicians, with a tour of study at a European university—tended to restrict the ranks of the regulars to the well-to-do.[53] Notwithstanding the generally higher level of education among regulars, however, the actual content of the medical training they received was problematic. For much of the century, medical education was extremely informal, and by the latter part of the century, an increasing part of it, even for regulars, took place in proprietary schools that were very close to being "diploma mills."[54]

Since most medical historians agree that regular physicians began to mobilize for licensing laws that would restrict competing practitioners *before* they could convincingly demonstrate that they were better healers in practice, writers in this second school have tended to see the success of the regulars as more frankly political. They argue that because the regulars were largely members of the elite, they were able to use their class standing and educational credentials to argue that they were "better" than the sectarians and the doctors trained by apprenticeship.[55]

As is often the case, the full truth probably lies somewhere between the view of the first school, which stresses the improvement of technical understanding among physicians, and the view of the second, which stresses their use of political rather than technical skills. Anyone who reads nineteenth-century medical textbooks cannot fail to be impressed by the explosion of knowledge that occurred in the last third of the century. Consider gynecology, for example. In 1830 textbooks prescribed long lists of seemingly interchangeable herbs for a vaguely defined malady called "chlorosis," which appears to have no modern-day counterpart; yet by 1885 physicians could undertake major gynecological surgery with some cautious expectation that the patient might survive.[56] The gynecological textbooks of the 1880s illustrate the dawning of antisepsis, anesthesia, and bacteriology; they are replete with engravings, which for the first time began to teach physicians about the human body from cell theory to gross anatomy.[57] In a real sense, medicine in the 1880s was closer to our own era than it was to the medicine of a mere forty years before.

Nonetheless, it is also true, as the second school of thought argues, that regular physicians had begun to mobilize politically *before* this explosion of new knowledge had effectively taken place. The AMA, for example, was founded in 1847, before many of these technical accomplishments were made and long before physicians were able to translate these accomplishments into better survival rates for their patients. At best it can be argued that the drive for professionalization was concurrent with scientific progress; it is virtually impossible to argue, as the first school did, that professionalization was the *product* of such progress. Finally, it may be argued that until the level of scientific progress is dramatically higher than it was during the nineteenth century, the ordinary consumer cannot differentiate between a "scientific" practitioner and a folk healer. Given the standard of living in the nineteenth century and the relatively primitive (though rapidly improving) state of medical knowledge, it remains to be demonstrated whether the average person would have been able to rank varieties of practitioners by effectiveness.[58]

By the middle of the nineteenth century, therefore, American physicians had few if any of the formal attributes of a profession. The predominance of proprietary medical schools combined with the virtual absence of any form of licensing meant that the regulars could control neither entry into the profession nor the performance of those who claimed healing capacities. With the possible exceptions of the thermometer, the stethoscope, and the forceps, the technological tools of modern medicine were yet to come; and lacking the means of professional control, regular physicians were hard put to keep even those simple instruments out of the hands of the competition.[59] Because they could offer no direct, easily observable, and dramatic proof of their superiority, regular physicians were forced to make an indirect, *symbolic* claim about their status. By becoming visible activists on an issue such as abortion, they could claim both *moral stature* (as a high-minded, self-regulating group of professionals) and *technical expertise* (derived from their superior training).

Therefore, the physicians' choice of abortion as the focus of their moral crusade was carefully calculated. Abortion, and only abortion, could enable them to make symbolic claims about their status. Unlike the other medico-moral issues of the time—alcoholism, slavery, venereal disease, and prostitution—only abortion gave physicians the opportunity to claim to be saving human lives.[60] Given the primitive nature of medical practice, persuading the public that embryos were human lives and then persuading state legislatures to protect these lives by outlawing abortion may have been one of the few life-saving projects actually available to physicians.

Physicians, therefore, had to exaggerate the differences between themselves and the lay public. Anti-abortion physicians had to claim that women placed *no* value on embryonic life whereas they themselves ranked the embryo as a full human life, namely, as a baby. But these two positions, when combined, created an unresolvable paradox for physicians, a paradox that would haunt the abortion debate until the present day.

If the embryo is a full human life, as these physicians claimed, then abortion can never be morally right, even when undertaken to save the life of the mother; the Western tradition does not permit even physicians to "set aside one life for another," as the Jewish Mishnah puts it.[61] The only logical moral position was that of Bishop Kenrick of Philadelphia, who declared with respect to abortion in 1841 that two deaths were better than one murder.[62]

But if abortion is never morally right, then nineteenth-century physicians had no grounds for claiming it as a medical issue that required their *professional* regulation. Once they had alerted Americans to the "fact" that abortion was murder, the logical move would have been to turn the issue over to their "competition"—clergymen who would deal with its moral consequences and lawyers who would deal with its legal consequences. Ironically, what the physicians did, in effect, was to simultaneously claim both an *absolute* right to life for the embryo (by claiming that abortion is always murder) and a *conditional* one (by claiming that doctors have a right to declare some abortions "necessary").

Physicians could not give up either half of the paradox. In order to claim that doctors as professionals were sufficiently prestigious and upright to be trusted with arbitrating the sacred boundary between life and death, they had to claim both that the embryo was a life and that physicians could sometimes sacrifice that life. Once this claim about abortion was successful, doctors could then be professionally and socially on a par with the traditional "gentlemen's professions" of the clergy and the law. (Nor was this dimension of the debate hidden from nineteenth-century anti-abortion physicians. As one of them noted: "The opinions of medical men on [abortion] regulate public sentiment, govern the tribunals of justice, and influence even the minds of the mental philosopher and the scrutinizing theologian."[63]) On the other side of the paradox, however, the logic of the physicians' need to upgrade their status meant that they could not simply advocate the elimination of all abortions. They sought instead *to regulate* abortions, thereby serving their own professional goals.

If these regular doctors were as actively opposed to abortion as their public rhetoric suggested, we would expect the result of their efforts to be laws that either forbade abortions entirely or, at the very least, carefully defined the few kinds of abortions that could take place. On the other hand, if physicians were trying to both *create* and *control* a moral problem at the same time, we would expect laws that would forbid nonphysicians to perform abortions but would give physicians a great deal of legal discretion to perform abortions when they wanted to—a discretion hard to reconcile with their public contention that abortion was always murder.

And, in fact, an inspection of most nineteenth-century state laws suggests that this latter course was the one taken. By 1900 only six states did not include a "therapeutic exception" in their abortion laws, a clause stating that any abortion undertaken by or on the advice of a physician to preserve the life of the mother was legal. These laws in effect gave physicians almost unlimited discretion in deciding when an abortion was necessary. Only ten of these state laws specified that the physician must consult with another physician before performing the operation; two specifically stated that *regular* physicians must make the decision; and Maryland stipulated that a "respectable" physician was required. No mechanism was set up for reviewing "medical judgment," and, further, none of these laws described exactly what constituted a threat to life. For example, must the threat be immediate or can it be long term? Similarly, they did not specify the confidence level needed. Must the pregnancy be an unquestionable threat to maternal life, or could the threat be only probable? Finally, two of these laws specified that a doctor's "bona fide" intent to save the life of a woman was sufficient to justify abortion.[64]

There is further evidence that physicians wanted to create a category of "justifiable" abortion and to make themselves the custodians of it. Some anti-abortion physicians actually opposed legislative attempts to tighten or spell out what exactly was entailed in the therapeutic exception. Even some of the most ardent anti-abortion activists tended to feel, on balance, that it was better to tolerate some abuse in the practice of abortion than to put too tight a rein on the medical profession. The same Hugh Hodge whose *Foeticide* was an often-cited tract of the movement wrote in his textbook on obstetrics that although abortion was "one of those unnatural and horrible violations of divine laws," restriction of the medical practice of abortion should not be condoned,

> for such objections apply to all operations in surgery, and we cannot argue against the use of a good agent because it may be abused. Neither should it be regarded as an objection that the accoucheur may be requested to induce abortion in the same woman in several successive pregnancies; for he cannot allow the female to perish under his eye when the means of preserving her life is in his power.[65]

In short, the opposition of the regulars to abortion could become quite tempered when it appeared that abortion could be suppressed only at the cost of increased social and legislative control of the medical profession.

Nineteenth-century anti-abortionist literature, gynecology textbooks, and articles in medical journals indicate still another important consequence of the physicians' paradox: the terms chosen to define physician boundaries—"saving the life" of the woman—were perhaps deliberately vague. The word *life* may mean physical life in the narrow sense of the word (life or death), or it may mean the social, emotional, and intellectual life of a woman in the broad sense (style of life). Thus, "saving the life" of the mother may mean saving her only from imminent death, or it may mean protecting the process and quality of her daily life.

Physicians were willing to induce (and in their writings to advocate inducing) abortions under both of these definitions of the term *life*. Not only were cardiac disease, "consumption," and pernicious vomiting causes for abortion, so also were "neurasthenia" (an all-purpose diagnosis for complaints from "high-strung" women) and many other complaints that would compromise the woman's life in the broader sense of the word. The range of acceptable grounds for abortion is demonstrated by T. Gaillard Thomas, an outstanding obstetrician-gynecologist and a strong anti-abortionist. He believed that abortion was indicated when pregnancy would "destroy the life or intellect, or permanently ruin the health of the mother."[66] Even Horatio Storer, in many ways the most prominent anti-abortionist of his day, subscribed to a broad view of what "saving the life" of a woman entailed. While arguing that the decision to induce an abortion is a weighty one and must always be taken in consultation with colleagues, his list of indications for abortion includes other considerations besides strict preservation of maternal life, notably what would later be called health and "fetal" indications:

> There are other instances that might be cited, cases of dangerous organic disease, as cancer of the womb, in which, however improbable it might seem, pregnancy does occasionally occur; *cases of insanity, of epilepsy, or of other mental lesion, where there is fear of transmitting the malady* to a line of offspring; cases of general ill health, where there is perhaps a chance of the patient becoming an invalid for life [emphasis added].[67]

All the available evidence suggests, therefore, that rhetoric notwithstanding, nineteenth-century anti-abortion physicians who were successful in securing the first statute laws prohibiting abortion never believed that embryos had an absolute right to life. Instead, like most of those around them (and indeed, like most Americans of the present day), they believed that although embryos had rights, these rights were subordinate to the life of the mother, in both the broad *and* the narrow sense.

The important difference between the nineteenth-century physicians' stand and the previous public and legal toleration for abortion does not lie in a radically new view of the nature of the embryo or of its rights. To be sure, on the rhetorical level, these physicians had made an almost unprecedented claim—that the embryo's right to life was absolute so that abortion at any period of pregnancy was murder. In practice, however, physicians agreed that the embryo's rights were in fact conditional. What was at the core of their movement, therefore, was a *reallocation* of social responsibility for assessing the conditional rights of the embryo against the woman's right to life, both narrowly and broadly defined. From the late nineteenth century until the late 1960s, it was doctors, not women, who held the right to make that assessment.

Consequences of the Physicians' Crusade

The medicalization of the abortion decision had important implications for physicians, for women, and for the debate itself. With respect to physicians, once this first anti-abortion movement was successful, statute laws prohibited all abortions except those performed by (or on the advice of) physicians. But, as we have noted, none of these laws specified *how* physicians were to go about ascertaining that an abortion in any given case was medically necessary (except, of course, by conferring with a colleague).

Medical societies logically could (and later did) exclude members who flagrantly applied a set of abortion criteria not shared by the majority of their colleagues, but on the whole they were forced to interpret most practices as being "in good faith." Most gynecology textbooks suggested that a cautious practitioner would confer with at least one colleague to make sure that there was agreement on the "indications" for a proposed abortion.* As a result, some women whose "cost-accounting" of the value of embryonic life was widely at variance with

* In fact, this was standard procedure in this and in other medical undertakings even before the physicians began their crusade. For a classic obstetrical textbook that makes this point, see Dewees, *Diseases of Females*, p. 192.

that of the medical profession (e.g., women who sought abortions exclusively for birth control) were undoubtedly denied abortions. For others, however, the very success of the medical profession in claiming exclusive responsibility for abortion meant that if a reasonably plausible medical indication for abortion could be presented to a sympathetic physician, neither the medical society nor any other authority was likely to intervene.

The removal of the abortion decision from public scrutiny by defining it as a question of "medical judgment," combined with the semantic ambiguity built into the phrase "to save the life of the mother," meant that a wide range of practices on abortion could be undertaken in good faith. Broadly speaking, doctors and their women patients agreed in principle that abortions should be done when necessary. They appear to have disagreed only over what conditions and circumstances constituted a necessary reason for abortion. Undoubtedly there were physicians who followed the implications of the public rhetoric and seldom or never induced abortions. On the other hand, the existence of various problems of pregnancy (cardiac problems, renal problems, diabetes, toxemia of pregnancy, vomiting), which we now consider minor but which were virtually untreatable at the time, when combined with an awareness that childbirth could be a very real risk to life, probably meant that at least some physicians would induce abortions. The upper-income woman who knew her family doctor quite well, who had some semblance of a physical reason to avoid childbirth, and whose motivations for abortion did not fundamentally offend the values of the physician may have had little difficulty in obtaining an abortion in this era.

More pragmatically, there are reasons to believe that having the medical profession nominally control abortion would not have had much impact on what women and their husbands were actually doing, especially during the early years of the anti-abortion crusade. It is the point of this chapter that physicians were claiming abortion as part of a strategy of enhancing their own professional status and control. But not until the very last years of the century, at the earliest, was that status or control very real. Thus, the existence of laws on the books that stated that abortions were illegal unless performed by regular physicians to preserve the life of the woman may not have made much difference in any individual woman's life—for two reasons.

First, much of medical practice still took place in the home, and formal medical attention was something that many Americans sought only *in extremis*. Thus, it is plausible that there existed a "female culture"—handed down from mother to daughter or passed around by relatives and friends—of drugs, techniques, and instruments that might be used to bring on an abortion.[68] The possible effectiveness of these techniques will be considered later; the point here is that it is quite possible that many women thought of abortion as something to be accomplished by home remedies rather than by formal medical attention.

Second, physicians may have had strong incentives to be open-minded about determining which abortions were medically necessary. Despite the success of the anti-abortion campaign, effective licensing laws for doctors were not in effect until after the turn of the century. Regular physicians, although their status was rising during the last quarter of the century, still had to compete in a relatively open market for patients. Portraying themselves as "women's friends," physicians who turned away *all* their patients' requests for abortion had to face the possibility that those patients might seek out another practitioner who would be more understanding and that these patients might not be willing to relinquish such a sympathetic supporter afterward. (Then, as now, women constituted a significant portion of the medical clientele, both by themselves and as decision-makers for other members of the family, notably children.) Given the competition for clients, an ideology that physicians were the protectors of women, and some ambiguity about the indications for abortion, one can easily imagine situations in which physicians would be willing to give their women patients the abortions they wanted, under the rubric of saving their lives.

It is true, of course, that by the last quarter of the century physician-provided abortions held the promise of being more effective than abortions produced at home, although whether or not this was true depended on geographic location, as well as the professional training and the skill of the person providing the abortion. "Folk remedies" and patent medicines available to women for producing abortion were mostly herbal in nature, consisting of materials such as aloes, apiol (parsley), black hellebore, savin (juniper), tansy, pennyroyal, rue, "Peruvian bark" (quinine), and ergot. Most of these herbs are cathartics or laxatives, and some may have stimulated abortions, perhaps by means of gastric upset. While large-scale pharmacological studies of these herbs are lacking, some of them do appear to have some degree of abortifacient activity, but their effectiveness was undoubtedly far from 100 percent.[69] (Problems about their reliability were compounded by the fact that obtaining exact dosages from plant material is hard to do, and since many of these herbs are poisonous in large doses, it was hard to determine effective but nonlethal doses.)

In contrast, as humoralistic theories of medicine declined, physicians became more willing to enter the major body cavities through surgery; and by the latter part of the nineteenth century, physicians had begun to induce abortion by the use of probes and sounds, uterine lavage, breaking the amniotic membrane, and dilating the cervix.[70] Cervical dilation was often accomplished either by hand or by "sea tents" (laminaria), which have been rediscovered in the last few years for the practice of abortion.* Hegar dilators were invented in 1879 (although the principle was known as early as 1832), and an improved curette was introduced in France in 1872. Thus, dilation and curettage was a practical reality by the last quarter of the nineteenth century.[71]

It must be noted, however, that although physician-induced abortions were more effective, they may also have been more often lethal. Puerperal fever was the scourge of nineteenth-century obstetrics, and abortion, like childbirth, makes women vulnerable to puerperal fever by creating sites for infection within the uterus. Like their European counterparts, American obstetrical practitioners were at first skeptical of theories that suggested that they themselves could be sources of infection to the women whom they treated, and they were slow to implement antiseptic technique based simply on epidemiological evidence.† By the late 1880s, obstetrical textbooks had begun to recommend the use of antiseptic techniques for abortions as well as for deliveries; but as Richard Wertz and Dorothy Wertz point out, these techniques were not always used with unrelenting vigor, and puerperal fever remained a danger well into the twentieth century.[72] In the absence of antibiotics, puerperal fever was quite likely to be fatal.

* Ironically, Storer was one of the earliest to popularize the "sea tent" or "elm tent" for abortion, illustrating once again the paradoxical nature of the physicians' attitudes toward abortions; see Horatio Storer, "Elm Tents for the Dilatation of the Cervix Uteri" (1855).

† Oliver Wendell Holmes in his famous 1843 essay had described the empirical pattern of puerperal fever; Semmelweis in 1848 had described preventive measures. Holmes issued a second monograph in 1855 on the causes and prevention of this terrible scourge of childbirth. The same Hugh Hodge who was so active in the anti-abortion movement, however, together with Charles Meigs, another prominent physician, rejected Holmes's findings, and the incorporation of this information into medical practice was delayed.

In actual practice, the contradiction between the two efforts by physicians—to convince the public that abortion was murder and to make this newly created moral issue one in which medical judgment was necessary—had consequences that were to shape the abortion debate for the next one hundred years. Because doctors successfully asserted professional control over the issue, a major part of it disappeared from view. There continued to be concern about women who performed abortions on themselves, and the newly defined criminal abortionists were prosecuted; but, in general, physicians made their decisions on abortion without public scrutiny. The medical profession certainly may have prosecuted gross violators of community norms, but the very fact that these had become *professional* norms meant that their nuances were hidden from social view.

Meanwhile, the ideological sleight of hand performed by the physicians left its imprint on the debate for the ensuing century. Because the profession had successfully achieved the right to handle this thorny public issue within the confines of its own domain—because in effect the American public accepted the profession's claim that it was capable of juggling the conflicting rights of the abortion decision—the physician's paradox disappeared from view. Thus, both "strict" and "liberal" constructionists—the inheritors, in other words, of both the neo-Pythagorean view that the embryo is a baby and the Stoic view that it is not—could rest assured that the issue had been turned over to a morally rigorous and self-evidently upstanding profession, which in turn would make wise decisions. The intrinsic conflict between the two interpretations was therefore hidden from view: partisans of each interpretation could feel confident that theirs was the dominant one—that all abortion was murder or that physicians could, should, and would do abortions when the circumstances warranted. As a result, abortion as a major social, political, and ethical issue could disappear beneath the cloak of an emerging profession's claims, there to rest quietly for almost a century.

3

The Century of Silence

By the end of the nineteenth century, the success of the first "right-to-life" movement meant that abortion had become a medical rather than a moral issue. For almost a century, the philosophical issue involved—whether or not the embryo is a full human person—was obscured by the fact that physicians made almost all "official" decisions on abortion.

Although this new state of affairs had its opponents, controversy on abortion was remarkably low-key for the better part of a century. Some observers, particularly those concerned with maternal and child health, worried about the public health problems inherent in the criminal abortions now being performed by amateurs. Between 1900 and 1960 a number of conferences, medical journal articles, and monographs were addressed in whole or part to the problem of criminal abortion.[1]

At the same time, the passage of abortion laws, which held that physicians could perform abortions to preserve the life of the mother but did not spell out how physicians were to make this discrimination, meant that the medical literature was filled with scholarly debates attempting to clarify precisely which "indications" merited abortion.[2] Despite the fact that these debates in medical journals show very little agreement about when to perform an abortion, this issue was limited for all practical purposes to scholarly exchange. Between 1890—when anti-abortion laws finally became a standard part of statute law throughout the United States—and the late 1950s, both the public and the medical profession accepted these laws as a legitimate part of American life. Few serious attempts were made to overturn them.*

In the late 1950s, however, both professionals and lay people began to agitate for changes in abortion laws, and their calls for change were heeded. In 1967, Colorado, North Carolina, and California passed new laws on abortion, and by the eve of the 1973 Supreme Court decision on abortion almost a third of the states had formally "liberalized" their abortion laws.[3] The term *liberalization*, however, is something of a misnomer: many of these new laws simply gave explicit legal recognition to abortion policies already in place. The 1973 Supreme Court decision, of course, overturned both these new reform laws and the older nineteenth-century laws still on the books in most states and returned at least early abortion to the status it had held before the first "right-to-life" movement, namely, one unregulated by legal authority.

These events raise two related questions. First, what accounts for the remarkable political and social quiescence that surrounded abortion for seventy years? This period of acceptance is all the more intriguing because it stretched across the Great Depression—when American fertility reached a historic low, when the burdens of unintended pregnancies must have been very high, and when by many accounts the practice of illegal abortion flourished.[4] Even the Depression, which gave rise to the most profound social and political change this country has seen, failed to create a movement to liberalize or repeal abortion laws.

Conversely, given this remarkable period of quiet on the abortion question, how can one account for the emergence in the 1960s of a nationwide movement that put abortion back on the legal and political agenda? To put it more dramatically, how (and why) did abortion, a topic barred from the American political arena for so many years, become an issue that now routinely confronts presidential aspirants and is an issue on which almost everyone has an opinion?

Briefly, this chapter will argue that abortion was not a public or social issue for most of its history because medical "ownership" of abor-

* This assertion is based on a content analysis of all articles on abortion written between 1890 and 1960 and indexed under that heading in three sources: *Readers' Guide to Periodical Literature*, the *Index Medicus*, and three large California newspapers of that time, the *Los Angeles Times*, the *San Francisco Chronicle*, and the *San Diego Union*. These three sources showed nothing resembling a political movement aimed at changing abortion laws, although there were scattered articles and books calling for abortion reform.

tion as a phenomenon served to undercut potential opposition from all other quarters. But the continued status of abortion as primarily a *medical* problem (rather than a moral, ethical, religious, social, legal, or economic problem) depended on the ability (and willingness) of physicians to present a united front against the "outside world" of nonphysicians. This chapter will examine how the united front of physicians rested on a set of specific historical and technological factors and how these factors changed over the course of the twentieth century.

The Period of Quiescence

Having made the paradoxical claim both that abortion was murder *and* that doctors had the right to perform abortions, physicians took advantage of a number of historical forces to consolidate their position. In the short run, these forces—a complex intermeshing of political, social, technological, and structural issues—enhanced their control over abortion. But over the course of the twentieth century, these same forces would drive at least some physicians into the vanguard of a movement aimed at overturning the abortion laws passed by their nineteenth-century predecessors.

The public and abortion

For both ideological and practical reasons, once the medical profession had sought and claimed the right to make abortion decisions, its very success precluded "outsiders" from exercising much control. With respect to the ideological dimension, for example, it must be appreciated how beautifully constructed the nineteenth-century physicians' argument was. By defining the debate as being between two opponents—women, who felt that embryos were not alive, and doctors, who knew that they were—physicians effectively precluded any further discussion of the moral meaning of the embryo. Moreover, by making the issue one of female ignorance versus technical knowledge available only to physicians, the doctors moved the grounds of the argument from one of values (how to assess the moral claims of the embryo) to one of "fact" (the physiological status of the embryo) and thus onto a ground where they had considerable resources.

The most important fact about the medical profession's claim to control abortion, therefore, was that they had *transformed the grounds of the debate*. Although physicians framed the issue itself as a moral one (in their persuasive literature they referred to it as "antenatal infanticide"), they framed their own claim to it as a professional and technical one. Only physicians using their medical skills, they argued, could determine when the continuation of a pregnancy would threaten the life of a woman—just as only physicians could define what was meant by the "life" of the woman.

To be sure, this is in one sense a moral claim. It tacitly argues that physicians are sufficiently trustworthy to be charged with the transcendent task of weighing the competing life-and-death rights of two parties; and, indeed, it was precisely this moral dimension that made abortion so attractive to physicians as a cause. But the moral claim was based on technical expertise. Unlike members of the clergy, who based their claims to the sacred sphere of life on personal characteristics (they had a "vocation," a "calling," from the Almighty), physicians based their claim to decision-making rights in abortion cases on technical characteristics: only a trained doctor could tell when an abortion was "medically needed."

Once the issue was constructed in this way, it is not surprising that other potentially interested parties—notably ministers, lawyers, and women—were prevented from challenging physicians for the right to control abortion. Physicians could denigrate the clergy, for example, as being merely theoretical speculators in the matter.[5] Given the growing prestige of science after the last quarter of the nineteenth century, the clergy would have been hard put to use religion to challenge medical science on the issue of abortion.

Similarly, there is no evidence that the legal profession ever systematically challenged physicians for control of abortion during this period. Again, this makes sense. As the physicians had constructed the issue, there was a clear division of labor: physicians examined those women who wanted abortions and, using their medical expertise, decided which abortions were "medically necessary." All other abortions became, by definition, "criminal" abortions, which were clearly under the purview of the legal profession. Lawyers could not hope to challenge doctors on their medical decision-making, and this division of labor respected the boundaries of both professions quite neatly.

It is even easier to understand why women—the group most directly affected—failed to make any sustained challenges to the medical profession's control over abortion until the 1960s. Warren Sanderson has argued that the dramatic decline in the American birth rate between 1800 and 1900 simply could not have occurred without recourse to abortion.[6] And according to the nineteenth-century physicians who opposed it, it was used most frequently by women of the "better classes." Part of the answer why these upper-class women, for whom abortion was such a critical part of the fertility controls available to them, did not protest the medical profession's claim is certainly the pragmatic one noted in the previous chapter. The logic of medical judgment meant that at least some women could probably still get the abortions they wanted from physicians, and these abortions had at least the promise of being more effective than the "home remedies" women had previously relied upon. More critically, however, there were important ideological reasons why women could not effectively campaign against medical control of abortion.

Once abortion decsion-making was defined as technical, women—like the clergy and lawyers—had neither the skills nor the credentials to challenge doctors. But the handicap women faced in confronting doctors on abortion was even more fundamental than a lack of technical expertise. Once physicians had made their rhetorical claim that an embryo was a full human life (a claim they ignored in practice), women were excluded as decision-makers. In a decision situation newly conceptualized as pitting the rights of a woman against the rights of an embryo, *women were defined as self-interested parties whose vested interests in the outcome made them incapable of reaching an "objective" decision.* In other words, physicians presented themselves as the only group capable of making the decisions that would "objectively" weigh the needs of women against the value of embryonic life. Women, by virtue of being affected by abortions, were now ideologically excluded from any control in the decision-making surrounding those abortions.

Once the clergy, lawyers, and women were precluded from any effective challenge to medical control of abortion, public acceptance of the technical basis of their claim gave doctors unquestioned legitimacy in the area of abortion. The durability of this legitimacy has been remarkable. Even today, those Americans who advocate a constitutional amendment (or any law) prohibiting abortion except to preserve the life of the woman believe that the limited amount of decision-making involved should be restricted to doctors. But both opponents and supporters of abortion have reason to fear the return of complete medical hegemony, however unlikely such resurrection may be. As this chapter will document, the very logic of physician control of abortion inevitably prevents any systematic regulation of it.

The medical profession and abortion

Just as nonphysicians (women, the clergy, and lawyers) were constrained from challenging medical decision-making on abortion, a number of factors have historically kept physicians themselves from exerting anything resembling close control over one another. Once abortion decisions had been made exclusively a matter of medical judgment, individual physicians were placed under the enormous burden of interpreting the meaning of "good faith." It became difficult for individual doctors to argue that physicians should *never* perform abortions, for that would be to say that abortion was not an appropriate field for medical decision-making in the first place. Similarly, any physician who raised questions about the abortion practices of colleagues was in fact raising questions not about moral standards but about *technical competence*—and physicians have been remarkably unwilling to publicly challenge the technical expertise of their colleagues.[7]

The medical profession's control of abortion therefore gave rise to a wide variety of practices surrounding when, how, and how often an individual physician would perform an abortion. The doctrine of medical judgment required that each demand for abortion be considered as an individual case; and since the grounds upon which decisions were made were ostensibly *technical* ones, two women with very similar cases might well have different outcomes in their search for a therapeutic abortion (i.e., one performed by a physician). In short, the doctrine of medical judgment permitted a considerable degree of arbitrariness in the decision.

The existing data on therapeutic abortions performed between 1900 and 1960 make the point. They are entirely consistent with the logic that physicians could and did use a wide range of criteria, more or less haphazardly. Even in places as public as hospitals, available data suggest that physician discretion was very wide indeed. (And it is important to recall that prior to World War II a substantial number of abortions probably occurred in the less public settings of homes and physicians' consulting rooms.)[8] Thus, the woman who had the good luck (or good information) to encounter a "liberal" physician in a liberal hospital had a good chance of getting her abortion, but a woman with less luck (or information) was in a different situation. Judging from the available data on the ratio of abortions to deliveries between 1926 and 1960, the chance of getting a therapeutic abortion seems to have been almost random: abortions became neither easier nor harder to obtain over time; no geographic area had a monopoly on abortion; and abortion in the most liberal settings was *fifty-five* times more frequent than in the most conservative settings.[9] Only in fantasy could this variation be attributed to "objective" differences in the pregnancies of women who sought abortions in the various settings. Rather, the doctrine of medical judgment permitted physicians to use an almost unimaginably wide range of criteria for deciding upon an abortion, *and neither the public nor individual physicians appear to have been very troubled by the discrepancies*.

Equally interesting in terms of how the issue was to be constructed later, medical control of abortion also permitted a wide range of *beliefs* about abortion. Although the "strict constructionists" (those who accepted abortion only to preserve the physical life of the woman) were to argue beginning in the late 1960s that abortions had previously been performed only to prevent the death of the woman, a content analysis of articles on abortion in the *Index Medicus* demonstrates quite clearly that during the period 1900–1960 physicians were willing to perform abortions (and report them in national journals) for indications that certainly did not fit a strict constructionist view.

Whether national medical journals (*Journal of the American Medical Association*, *American Journal of Obstetrics and Gynecology*) or regional journals (*California Medicine*) are examined, it is quite clear that twentieth-century physicians continued to be vague as to whether preserving maternal life meant preserving strictly biological life or whether it meant preserving the quality of life in the broader, more social sense of the word. When physicians discussed the legitimate grounds for abortion in the period between 1890 and 1950, they frequently assumed that abortions to preserve the health of the woman (including her mental health) were acceptable, as were abortions in cases of rape or incest or when there was a likelihood of what would later be called "fetal deformity."[10] As one physician noted, describing abortions performed at the hospital where he practiced: "It must be admitted that, while the majority of these therapeutic abortions were done to *preserve the mother's health*, to *prolong her life*, and to *prevent serious and permanent injury*, under the direction of at least two practitioners of medicine, the life of the mother was not always threatened imminently" (emphasis added).[11] The question of imminent danger to a woman's life raised here seems almost irrelevant, considering how broadly the term *danger* has already been defined. The above 1946 quote, from the most prestigious obstetrical journal of the era, makes quite clear that physicians were not limiting themselves to the preservation of *life* but were considering the preservation of *health*, broadly defined, as well.

This wide range of medical beliefs about what constitutes valid grounds for abortion is similarly illustrated in a 1930 survey of sixty-two practicing physicians in the southern United States. Although the number of responses is small and the overall response rate is unknown, it is interesting to note, nonetheless, that ten of these sixty-two doctors in what is generally thought of as one of the more conservative regions of the United States approved of abortion "for social reasons to prevent disgrace," another six approved abortions "for economic reasons, poverty," twenty-two approved "for health reasons, life not involved," thirty-six approved for rape, and twenty-one "for dominant hereditary taint in both parents." One physician out of the sixty-two, representing the far end of the continuum, did not approve of abortion even to save the life of the mother. In other words, a majority of these southern doctors approved of abortion following rape; substantial minorities approved of abortion for health and for fetal reasons; and one out of ten approved for strictly economic and social reasons. Not one of these indications is within a strict construction of the law since none can be argued to present a clear threat to the physical life of the mother.[12]

Medical control of abortion as an issue meant that neither "outsiders" (the lay public, other professionals) nor "insiders" (other physicians) were likely to question the exclusive right of physicians to perform abortions or their individual interpretations of that right. Until the late 1950s, therefore, any debate about abortion was primarily a *technical* one among physicians, and the moral issues that were later to play such a central role in the debate were largely relegated to the background.

Public attitudes toward abortion

Because physicians were willing to document their beliefs and practices, it has been possible to begin to reconstruct their views on abortion. For all of the reasons explored so far, however, it is almost impossibly difficult to take a sounding of *public* opinion toward abortion during this period. Public opinion polls as we know them did not exist for all practical purposes until just before World War II.[13] Apparently, no nationwide poll on abortion was taken until the 1960s. Indeed, a public opinion poll on therapeutic abortion would have been something of an anomaly during this period, given the existing definition of it as an exclusively medical problem. It would have been as implausible as asking the American public today about its opinions on the efficacy of coronary bypass operations. By the same token, once medical control of abortion was complete, all other abortions were by definition "criminal," and open and frank discussion of criminal activities in public was likely to be uncommon.

Surveys of popular literature confirm the lack of public discussion about the issue in this period. There were scattered calls for abortion reform and occasional articles about the dangers of criminal abortion. The legalization of abortion in the Soviet Union in the late 1920s provoked a number of American articles, some urging that America follow Russia's lead and others arguing for emphatic rejection of it.[14] But overall the popular writings on abortion were like those on other "social problems"—low-key, informative, and far from effective at stirring public passions. In short, there was so little formal "public opinion" on abortion between 1890 and 1960 that making any kind of generalization about it would be foolhardy.

The scattered data we can glean from this period, however, should warn us against too quick an assumption that abortion is merely a "modern" problem, the product of the "sexual revolution" and the pill. For example, the lack of public discussion about abortion should not make us believe that abortion did not exist. As noted, the medical literature makes it clear that therapeutic abortion, performed for a wide variety of reasons and with a stunning range of frequencies, was common; and other data suggest that for at least some parts of the American public, illegal or "criminal" abortion—although not openly discussed—was an accepted part of reproductive life.

Perhaps the most comprehensive data on induced abortion for the twentieth century, found in the Kinsey Report, show that between one in five and one in four women who had ever been married had aborted a pregnancy; moreover, almost 90 percent of the premarital pregnancies reported in that study were ended by abortions, most of them illegal.[15] Other smaller studies have also reported high levels of abortion (mostly illegal), though none uses a random sample and each is nonrepresentative in some important way. Taussig, for example, sampling 1,241 pregnancies, reported a ratio of one abortion per 3.28 live births. Marie Kopp, using 10,000 records from the birth control center founded by Margaret Sanger, reported 7,677 induced abortions in 38,985 pregnancies or a one-to-five ratio. A Chicago study of 104 lower-income Jewish women found 47 percent of them reporting the use of induced abortion to control their fertility, while a national study of predominantly upper- and upper-middle-class women found approximately 10 percent who had ended a pregnancy with what the researcher called an "artificial" (i.e., induced) abortion. Similarly, a study of low-income women attending a clinic in New York found that 12 percent of the Catholic women, 14 percent of the Protestants, and 13 percent of the Jewish women reported the use of induced abortion; other research from New York City, Cincinnati, Baltimore, Minneapolis, Newark, and Philadelphia found women reporting that they deliberated ending between 5 and 22 percent of their pregnancies by abortion.[16]

By the same token, maternal mortality figures give a very indirect measure of the extent of abortions. A fifteen-state survey of maternal deaths made in 1927 and 1928 revealed that of the 7,537 women who died from pregnancy-related causes, 794 of them, or slightly more than 10 percent, had died from the results of a self-induced abortion. In a similar ten-year Philadelphia study, abortions (both self-induced and abortionist-induced) accounted for 20 percent of all maternal mortality.[17]

The continued existence of popular support for abortion should not be surprising. As noted in the previous chapter, until the last part of the nineteenth century, family newspapers carried discreet advertisements about where women could get private treatments for "menstrual blockages" from whatever cause. In another uncanny echo of the present day, abortion opponents in the nineteenth century railed against the enormous financial success of Madame Restell, New York's most prominent abortionist. But whereas the advertisers in family newspapers (and Madame Restell) were simply providing what was then a legal service, the passage of state anti-abortion laws (and the federal Comstock Law, which prohibited sending information or equipment about either contraception or abortion through the mails) made non-physician providers of abortion by definition criminal abortionists.

Why did women seek criminal abortions? And what do the criminal abortions they sought tell us about popular attitudes toward abortion in either its therapeutic or its criminal form? In answer to the first, women probably sought illegal abortions for three reasons. The first reason was money: professional medical care was expensive until the advent of widespread medical insurance after the 1960s. Because we take for granted the existence of readily available, affordable medical care by a licensed physician, we tend to forget that such care was, until recently, for all practical purposes available only for the well-to-do in urban areas.[18] For some large sectors of the population, and for many medical problems besides abortion, care by a licensed physician was out of the question for much of the century.

A second reason derives from the erratic nature of therapeutic abortion practice: women and their husbands could not easily predict when physicians would consent to perform abortions, and thus could not know when they should approach a physician. As physicians became more and more successful as professionals, their incentives to restrict abortions—to act as "gatekeepers"—increased. After 1910, when competing practitioners were squeezed out by licensing laws, physicians could begin to be more stringent in their abortion decision-making without fearing the loss of clients to the competition.[19] Also, as doctors became more technically competent and reduced the ranks of the competition, there were fewer bona fide "competitors" for women to go to, and women were forced into the clientele of amateur abortionists.

Illustrative figures prove the point. While estimating the "demand" for abortions between 1890 and 1960 is impossible (common sense suggests that events such as the Depression must have affected the ebb and flow of how many women wanted abortions), it is possible to come up with some very inexact guesses as to the range of the demand for abortion and to show that physicians by the 1920s and 1930s were simply not meeting that demand. To use very crude estimates to prove a point, there is apparently one abortion for every four live births in the

United States at the present time, and in some states there is one abortion for every three live births.[20] Interestingly enough, nineteenth-century estimates of the ratio were in this same range: some observers thought that there was one abortion for every four live births, others that there was one abortion for every five live births.[21] If we assume, for the sake of argument, that between them these two sets of estimates give a very rough indication of "demand" for abortion in the first half of this century, then figures for even the most liberal hospital in its most liberal period suggest that doctors operating in hospitals could have answered only a fraction of the demand. For example, using the more conservative estimate of one abortion for every five live births and the most liberal hospital in the period (Bellevue, in the period 1935–1945), the demand could have been met only by *fourteen* out-of-hospital abortions for every in-hospital abortion. Such a ratio is at least plausible. When one looks at the most conservative hospital in the table, however, (Ohio State University Hospital in 1959), there would have been *768* out-of-hospital abortions for every in-hospital abortion—a ratio that seems quite improbable. Even in a midrange hospital (Los Angeles County in the period 1941–1945), there would have been seventy-one out-of-hospital abortions for every in-hospital one, which still seems improbable.

Although some authorities, like Taussig, may be right in their assumption that doctors did a great many abortions in the woman's home (or perhaps in the physician's office), the gap between the demand for abortion and the available figures on the hospital supply is significant. Taken together with the available evidence on how arbitrary physician decisions on abortions performed in hospitals were, this suggests that women and their husbands did not ask doctors for abortions because they had no way of predicting ahead of time which physicians would do abortions for which reasons and were therefore forced to turn to criminal abortionists.

There is a third and more speculative reason why women may have sought illegal abortions. Since the advent of the contraceptive pill and the intrauterine device (IUD), we have come to assume that fertility-related matters are within the purview of the family doctor. But for most of the first half of the twentieth century, fertility control was a domestic, "home-made" affair, not at all within the province of physicians. For most of this period, coitus interruptus, the rhythm method, and over-the-counter condoms were probably the primary sources of contraception.* With the social climate defined until the 1930s by the Comstock Law, fertility control was a private, not a public, practice.

The same may have been true of how at least some women thought about abortion, notwithstanding the physicians' claim of abortion as a medical matter. Scattered evidence suggests that women often tried to buy nonprescription preparations in pharmacies or by mail order to induce abortion in the privacy of their own homes. Similarly, the toll of self-induced abortions suggests that for some women, abortion was always something of a "do-it-yourself" project.[22] Finally, it has been claimed, throughout the history of abortion in America, that there is an underground female network for sharing the names of abortionists and the techniques of abortion and that such information is often passed down from mother to daughter. Even after the physicians' campaign had taken place, an observer could complain in 1892:

> [Abortion is a] sin of such delicacy that people affect to be shocked when it is publicly alluded to, and yet a sin which is practiced, applauded and commended so widely in private, that even children are not ignorant of its prevalence among their elders. [It is a sin in which] in many cases, daughters are deliberately nurtured and trained, so that when opportunity is presented for its practice, the conscience is so stultified and suborned by long training and familiarity with its hellish and poisonous consequences, that it is committed without compunction.[23]

What is not clear (and may never be) is whether women sought illegal abortion because they believed that physicians would not help them, because they asked physicians for help and were rejected, or because what Philippe Ariès calls their "mentalité" about abortion included the belief that abortion, like contraception, was not an appropriate topic to bring to a physician.[24]

Only two things are clear about illegal abortions: at least some

* As late as 1965, for example, when one out of every four white Americans and one out of every five black Americans were using the pill, 19 percent of whites and 16 percent of blacks were still using the condom; 7 percent of whites and 22 percent of blacks were still using douching; 6 percent of whites and 4 percent of blacks were using coitus interruptus; and 14 percent of whites and 2 percent of blacks were using the rhythm method. In other words, as recently as two decades ago, even after high-technology forms of fertility control were available, almost half of all Americans were still using nonprescription, over-the-counter, or "home-based" methods of contraception. See U.S. Bureau of the Census, "Fertility Indicators: 1970," p. 53 (Table 32).

women had them, and despite the success of the first "right-to-life" movement, many American women (and perhaps some men) were far from persuaded that they were immoral. In an echo of the earlier commentator who argued that abortions were "practiced, applauded, and commended" in private, Frederick Taussig wrote in 1936:

> We are amazed at the frankness with which decent women discuss this matter [induced abortion] among themselves or with their physician. Every physician will testify that it is without any feeling of guilt that most women speak of induced abortions in the consultation room. The most striking evidence of the attitude of the public is the fact that, even when positive evidence of guilt is brought in the trial of an abortionist, he is rarely punished by the jury before whom the case is tried.[25]

In much the same way, the author of the 1941 Indianapolis study, the first large-scale modern attitude survey on contraception and fertility, noted: "Our interviewers were told by three or four cooperating wives in the neighborhood, 'Say, you ought to see Mrs. So-and-So, she has paid enough money for abortions to buy a house.' "[26]

Taussig's comment that juries would not convict accused abortionists was made by other observers as well. At the 1921 meeting of the American Obstetrical and Gynecological Society, a Mr. Oakley, the public prosecutor for the city of St. Louis, was challenged to show any conviction of either a doctor or a midwife for criminal abortion. He could not but "cynically said that juries would not convict, as there was always at least one man of the twelve afraid that his own wife had trafficked with the particular abortionist on trial."[27]

This unwillingness to convict abortionists was apparently a fairly widespread pattern, as suggested by data on the fates of those charged with doing abortions. In Alabama in the period 1894 to 1932, for example, there were forty indictments and five convictions; in Arkansas between 1921 and 1932, twenty-seven indictments and nine convictions; in Massachusetts between 1849 and 1858, thirty-two indictments and one conviction; in Michigan between 1893 and 1932, 156 indictments and forty convictions; in Minnesota between 1911 and 1930, 100 indictments and thirty-one convictions; and in Utah between 1896 and 1932, seventeen indictments and three convictions.[28] By the same token, convicted abortionists were often dealt with leniently. A statistical analysis of all 111 convictions for abortion in New York County between 1925 and 1950 (about four convictions per year) indicates that 44 percent of those convicted were given probation. This is all the more remarkable when it is realized that 55 percent of these prosecutions were brought about because of a woman who was sufficiently ill after the abortion to arouse public notice and that in 10 percent of the cases the woman had died as a result of the abortion.[29]

In summary, we may say that in the late nineteenth and early twentieth centuries, public attitudes toward abortion conformed to a characteristically Victorian way of handling sexual matters. On the public level, abortion was rarely discussed. (Whether this was because it was associated with sexuality and reproduction or whether it was publicly assumed to be a sin in itself is not clear.) On the private level, however, people drew a distinction between what was *moral* and what was *proper*, or at least proper for public discussion. In intimate circles or in the privacy of the medical consulting room, women may have been very frank about their abortion experiences, and abortion, in certain circles, could be accepted as a normal fact of life. But the "medicalization" of abortion and the concurrent creation of "criminal" abortions outside the pale of polite discussion acted together to do for individuals what the doctrine of medical judgment did for physicians, namely, obscure deep divisions in public attitudes about the morality (in contrast to the propriety) of abortions.

Pressures for Change

The ability of the medical profession to forestall challenges on the matter of abortion was based on an important precondition: medical science had to be ambiguous enough, technically speaking, for physicians to tolerate the wide range of practices we have described. So long as *some* abortions were necessary to preserve the physical life of the woman, few physicians were willing or able, for the reasons already outlined, to take on the task of clearly defining which abortions were truly "justified."

The progress of medical science itself began to change this situation. One clear trend, which emerged as early as the 1920s and intensified after World War II, was the decline of the strictly physical categories that had served as the major indications for therapeutic abortion.[30] Between the two world wars, medical science made large strides in eliminating or discovering new treatments for conditions that had previously threatened maternal health. For example, tuberculosis, once a common indication for abortion, was virtually eliminated. Improvements in cardiology meant that even serious cardiovascular and renal disease no longer implied the necessity for ending a pregnancy; by 1936, physicians could confidently assert that a woman with only one kidney could be safely managed to a live birth. Perhaps most dramatically, the invention of intravenous glucose feeding and anti-nausea drugs eliminated pernicious vomiting of pregnancy (hyperemesis gravidarum), which in some settings had been considered the most frequent indication for abortion.[31]

As a consequence of these large-scale medical changes, the indications for abortion tended to shift away from the more clearly medical into the psychiatric and social; proportionally fewer abortions were performed to preserve physical life, and proportionally more were performed to preserve mental health and the quality of life. While, as we have seen, the use of medical criteria did not entirely fit the letter of the law, the increasing invocation of psychiatric criteria created a new set of problems. Originally, abortions on psychiatric grounds were said to be justified because a woman might commit suicide if she were not given an abortion; abortions given for this reason thus nominally conformed to the rhetoric of "preserving the life of the woman." Later research suggested that suicide was rare among pregnant women.[32] Next, it was debated in the literature whether a woman might suffer a postpartum schizophrenic episode should she not be aborted.[33] The occurrence of such episodes was subsequently shown to be so rare that the criterion was useless, and in any case was not in accordance with a strict interpretation of the law.

The improvements in medical and obstetrical care therefore planted the seeds of a crisis within the medical profession. So long as some abortions *could* save the physical lives of women, professional pressures kept "strict constructionists" from watching their colleagues (at least those in good standing) very closely to see that their abortions actually *did* save lives. But as abortions necessary to save lives became a medical rarity, one pillar of the medical profession's support for abortion began to crack. The "strict constuctionists" began to look forward to the day when abortions would never need to be performed. But neither they nor their "broad constructionist" colleagues fully appreciated just how deep the divisions between them really were. The claims of the medical profession to manage abortions, the doctrine of medical judgment, and the rhetoric of preserving the life of the woman had all served to obscure the fact that two very different notions of the word *life* and two very different beliefs about the moral status of the embryo had existed concurrently. Both strict and broad constructionists believed themselves to be in the majority, but the progress of medical science was bringing them closer to the day when their professional differences would become public ones.

These emerging differences between the two sides led the profession to adopt what now seems, in retrospect, a delaying tactic: the establishment, beginning in the 1950s, of therapeutic abortion boards in hospitals. These boards usually consisted of internists, obstetrician-gynecologists, and psychiatrists and often excluded the physician of the woman whose abortion was being considered. It seems plausible to assume that these panels were designed in part to provide individual physicians with institutional support so that opponents of any given abortion decision would have to challenge an entire hospital rather than a single doctor. The hospital boards, however, soon created problems of their own.

One immediate effect of the boards was to restrict access to abortion. In an effort to choose cases that would be most defensible, only those cases acceptable to all doctors on the board were approved. In one university hospital, for example, an average of eleven therapeutic abortions per year had been performed between 1930 and 1949; but in the year following the establishment of the board, only a single abortion was performed. Other hospitals reported similar results.[34] In fact, restricting access may have been one of the goals of such boards. For example, there appears to have been a trend to require sterilization as a concomitant to granting the abortion, on the grounds that if *this* pregnancy were a threat to the woman's health, subsequent pregnancies would also be a threat. Such a requirement may have had a rational basis when the threats to women's lives were largely physical and irreversible; but its continued (and apparently *increased*) use in conjunction with psychosocial criteria suggests that it was used at least in part for deterrent purposes.[35]

These therapeutic abortion boards also brought forth another more fundamental problem—and one that would probably reemerge if the United States should once again pass legislation forbidding abortion except to save the life of the woman. As Guido Calabresi and Phillip Bobbitt have pointed out, there are only a finite number of ways in which institutions can make what they call "tragic choices."[36] The therapeutic abortion board system claimed to be what Calabresi and Bobbitt would call a "criteria" system—a system that serves anyone who meets the criteria (in this case, that the pregnancy threatens her life). But when there is no consensus about how to assess the criteria—as there increasingly was not in the 1950s and undoubtedly would not be today—there is an almost irresistible pull to degrade the system, to convert it into some other kind of system.

There is considerable evidence that this is exactly what happened in the 1950s. Some hospitals turned their therapeutic abortion boards into quota systems, where only a given number of abortions proportional to the number of live births could be performed.[37] A case could be turned down simply because the month's quota had already been exceeded. At the same time, these boards also tended to become market systems, in which women with wealth, information, and medical advocates were far more likely to be granted abortions than their poorer, less well-informed, and less well-connected peers.[38]

Questions of inherent fairness aside, the therapeutic abortion boards in the 1950s were presenting themselves as something they simply could not be, given the emerging differences of opinion within the profession. As they degenerated from criteria systems into systems based on quotas and markets, their legitimacy became increasingly problematic both inside and outside the medical profession. This failure of legitimacy began to give rise to new feelings of discontent. As therapeutic abortion boards became perceived as more and more unworkable and unfair, physicians began to cast about for other resolutions of the dilemma. And the search for new resolutions was hampered by at least two important social developments: the changing locale of medical practice and the emergence of an institutionalized "strict constructionist" view of abortion.

Over the course of the century, the site of medical care—particularly for minor surgical procedures such as early abortion—moved from the home and the consulting room to the hospital. The trend accelerated dramatically after World War II. In 1900, for example, only an estimated 5 percent of all births occurred in hospitals, and by 1930, the figure was still probably under a third of all births.[39] In 1936 Taussig could cautiously advise physicians to perform abortions in the hospital for fear of uterine perforation, but he could also add an illustration demonstrating how to adapt a kitchen table so that an emergency abortion could be done at home. He writes that "abortions done by the patients or in the patient's home where no record whatsoever is available for medical inspection" were "innumerable," and that seems plausible in a setting where hospital stays were still a rarity for large segments of the American public.[40] The movement out of the home and into the hospital brought much greater public overview to many medical processes. When the decision-making process leading to an abortion and the abortion itself were performed in the woman's home, the phrase "between a woman and her doctor" (and probably her husband as well) was still a social reality. When that social reality began to fade, with the involvement of other people, widely varying interpretations of when an abortion is justified came into public view. The more public abortions became, the more opportunities for conflict arose.

The other critical factor that helped transform the emerging medical differences of opinion into a social problem was the emergence of an institutionally based "strict constructionist" view of abortion. Throughout this period, medical (and presumably public) opinions on abortion, ranging from the very strict (that abortions are never permissible) to the very liberal (that abortions are permissible to save the "life or health of the mother" broadly construed) *were mostly undiscussed*. How individuals sorted themselves out on this issue was undoubtedly a product (as it is today) of general overall conservatism or liberalism, previous experiences, personal history, and that general category known as "values." During this period, however, abortion and contraception emerged as special moral issues for Catholics. For Catholic laymen and physicians as well as priests and nuns, there existed a clear moral teaching on these issues, as opposed to the more diffuse religious teachings of other religious groups, and this fact was to have its own chain of social consequences.[41]

It is important to be careful in documenting the development of this teaching and its effects on individuals and the social order because in recent years partisans of abortion law reform or repeal have tended to categorize their opponents as merely instruments of the "Catholic hierarchy." Historically and at present, this view is not tenable. However, the emergence of an *institutionally* based "strict constructionist" view on abortion played an important role in the development of the debate, and it cannot be discounted.

The earliest American Catholic stand on abortion was that of Francis B. Kenrick, the bishop of Philadelphia, who in 1841 declared that there were no "therapeutic" indications for abortion. Two deaths, in his view, were better than one murder.[42] This is consistent with nineteenth-century Catholic moral theology, which began to forbid abortion during all periods of pregnancy. In 1869 Pope Pius IX, in reworking the teaching on abortion, stipulated excommunication as the penalty for anyone who successfully procured an abortion.* He thus abandoned the distinction between the animate and inanimate embryo (or between early and late abortion), which had been maintained virtually intact from the Decretals of Gratian in the twelfth century and certainly since Pope Gregory IX in 1234.[43]

The church (which did not have to confront the competing ideological imperatives that faced nineteenth-century American doctors) now found abortion without exception morally wrong. Between 1884 and 1902, the Congregation of the Inquisition (later called the Holy Office and now called the Congregation for the Doctrine of the Faith) specifically addressed a number of issues surrounding therapeutic abortions. In 1884, it held that craniotomy (the crushing of the embryonic skull to end an impossibly difficult labor) was not permissible; in 1889 any operation that directly killed the embryo was outlawed; and in 1902 surgery for the removal of an ectopic embryo (an embryo implanted outside the womb) was also forbidden. In 1917, the formal codification of the canon law held that anyone procuring the abortion of a "human fetus" was to be excommunicated; and separate canons explicitly included the abortion-seeking woman and the physician undertaking the operation. Since then, formal Catholic pronouncements have only served to reiterate this stand. Pope Pius XI explicitly spoke to the issue in 1930, in his address "Casti Connubi"; and Pius XII—in 1944, 1948, and again in 1951 in the "Address to the Italian Midwives"—emphatically rejected therapeutic exceptions. Pope John XXIII ratified this position, as did the Second Vatican Council and Pope Paul VI.[44]

This uniform and unconditional opposition to abortion, even to therapeutic abortion, must be understood in light of the church's long development of a theory of marriage and sexuality. This theory, which is both complex and subtle, is still under debate in some details, but

* An interesting sidelight on the 1869 teaching is that debate continued within the church until 1917 as to whether the penalty of excommunication applied to either the woman herself or to the physician performing the operation, as opposed to the person who "procured" the abortion (Huser, *Crime of Abortion*, pp. 139–48). The 1917 revision of canon law held (in Canon 2350) that all who successfully procured an abortion, specifically including the woman herself, were automatically excommunicated (Grisez, *Abortion*, p. 180).

official doctrine follows a general outline. First, natural law implies that a human function, such as sexuality, must be used for the purpose for which it was created. To do otherwise is to misuse that function, which has both spiritual and worldly consequences. In terms of sexuality, the function of intercourse is to create children. Consequently, masturbation, surgical sterilization, the use of contraceptives, and abortion are all morally wrong because they serve to "frustrate" the natural function. In recent years, the church has acknowledged that intercourse plays other roles in the lives of married people (sex among unmarried people, unless they are trying to have a child, is by definition aimed at frustrating the natural function); but these other roles are deemed secondary to the primary one of creating the next generation.[45] In Catholic moral theology, the use of the "rhythm" method is not contradictory, as some non-Catholics feel, because it implies *refraining* from using the sexual capacities during times that are likely to be fertile; this is defined as morally different from using those same capacities in the presence of "artificial" contraceptives, which will ensure that conception does not take place. Finally, the present Catholic position on when life begins means that abortion in all cases implies the death of a full human being so that abortion belongs to a qualitatively different moral order from activities that merely "frustrate" reproduction.

Because these views are thought to be located in the natural order of things, the church argues that they are applicable to everyone, Catholic or not. But even were this logical implication not to exist, it is difficult to imagine a state of affairs where people who believe that certain activities are both morally and socially damaging should not denounce those activities when they see them in progress all around them.

Nineteenth-century abortion laws were by no means passed in response to Catholic concerns. If anything, they were passed in response to feelings *against* Catholics, in particular their higher fertility rates.* At that time, public opinion widely diverged on the moral meaning of abortion. The statute laws passed in the nineteenth century, which held that abortion was permissible to save the "life" of the mother and the concurrent appropriation of the problem of abortion by the medical

* Although nineteenth-century anti-abortionists admired the unwillingness of a largely Catholic immigrant population to use abortion, it was feared that they would "possess New England," as Brevard Sinclair put it in 1892, because native-born Protestant women were using abortion so frequently (*Crowning Sin of the Age*, p. 17).

profession meant that society had effectively hidden from public scrutiny its conflicts about what actually constitutes the "life" of the woman. As noted, at least some doctors were consistently open about performing abortions for indications that were legal only if the broad construction of the word "life" was used. As the process of abortion decision-making became more public, doctors grew concerned about the possibility that differences in interpretation might lead to lawsuits; and more liberal doctors objected to what they saw as the "unfairness" of the policies instituted by hospitals to protect themselves from accusations of performing "too many" abortions. Doctors (and to some extent other professionals concerned with the problem of illegal abortion) began to advocate clarification of the laws.

It is in this context that the official institutional stance of the Catholic church became important. By the early twentieth century, from the standpoint of its coherent body of teaching against all abortions, the church's tacit toleration of abortions to save the physical life of the mother was already a considerable compromise. Although Catholic hospitals were forbidden to undertake abortions, there is no evidence that the church actively opposed officially sanctioned medical abortions in non-Catholic hospitals. In part, this may have been due to the relative invisibility of such abortions; the logic of "professional control" and the social status of most doctors would have tended to make the number of abortions (and the indications for them) known only to a few.

However, the church *was* willing to take a public stand on the issue of birth control. As birth control became more publicly visible and public attitudes began to change, officials of the church were willing to testify when these issues were publicly debated. For example, a roster of official Catholic spokespersons opposed a bill to delete contraceptives from the Federal Comstock Law (which forbade sending contraceptive devices or information through the mails).[46] Abortion was far less publicly visible than contraception and thus produced fewer official reactions. Papal pronouncements on the topic have been noted; on the state and local level, scattered discussions prior to the 1960s on abortion law reform generally aroused little public interest. But the mere existence of an institutionally based "strict constructionist" view, when tied to an integrated theory of human sexual and moral behavior, meant that when conflicts between strict and broad constructionists became apparent, strict constructionists who were also Catholics were likely to see the newly revealed difference of opinion as a substantial threat to their ethical views. In short, when abortion began to lose its status as a technical medical issue because of changes in the nature of medical practice, the institutional position of the Catholic church encouraged consideration of it as a moral issue.

The Finkbine Case

Most well-read people today recognize the name of Karen Ann Quinlan, a young woman with "brain death" whose parents requested permission to have her life-support systems removed.* The "Quinlan case" of 1975 became a shorthand way of referring to the problem of using heroic measures to sustain life when the prognosis for recovery is very poor and also served to bring that general social issue to the attention of a wide audience, relatively few of whom had ever been confronted by it before. Abortion had its own Karen Ann Quinlan. Her name was Sherri Finkbine, and, in several interviews with me, it became clear that her case revealed the differences of opinion between "strict" and "broad" constructionists and brought the moral issues of abortion before the public in a dramatic fashion.

Sherri Finkbine was married and the mother of four children under seven; she was expecting her fifth in 1962 when she discovered that the sleeping pill she had been using was Thalidomide. This drug, which her husband had picked up on a European vacation some months before, had been the focus of an intense but little publicized struggle within the U.S. Food and Drug Administration because reports from Europe had suggested that it had a very high teratogenic (embryo-deforming) potential.[47] Early in Finkbine's pregnancy, reports began to filter into American newspapers about babies born in England, Germany, and Belgium (where Thalidomide had not been banned) with extensive and crippling deformities. Legs, arms, and hands seemed particularly vulnerable in utero to the effects of Thalidomide, and a characteristic syndrome of deformities in the newborn was linked with maternal use of the drug during pregnancy.

Finkbine, whose job in the media made her a well-informed person, began to worry about the sleeping pill she had been taking and decided

* The first story on Karen Ann Quinlan appeared in the *New York Times*, Sept. 14, 1975, p. 44. Over the next five months, the *Times* ran a total of fifty-four more stories on Quinlan.

to call her obstetrician-gynecologist. He was soothing and said she probably had nothing to worry about, but he took down the brand name of the pills and suggested that she come in on Friday to discuss it further. On Friday, he had the worst possible news for her: not only was the drug indeed Thalidomide, but it was the strongest possible dosage. The odds for deformity, in his mind at least, were very high. With relatively little discussion he firmly suggested a therapeutic abortion. As Finkbine recalls it: "In talking it over with my [obstetrician], he said, 'Sherri, if you were my own wife and we two had four small children, and you really wanted a fifth child, I'd say start again next month under better odds.' " Finkbine was sufficiently naive to ask if the abortion could be performed at Our Lady Hospital (a Catholic institution) where her last baby had been born. Her physician suggested a local public hospital instead and booked her into the operating room for 8 A.M. the following Monday morning. He asked her to write a letter to the hospital's three-member therapeutic abortion board but assued her that it was only a formality.

Had matters remained there, Sherri Finkbine would never have become famous. She would have quietly had her abortion on Monday morning, like countless thousands of others before her—a woman whose physician decides that her case represents a clear and unambiguous indication for abortion, feels confident that the local medical community will agree, and therefore induces an abortion that was not technically legal only if the strict construction of the law in that particular state were followed, namely, that her own physical life was threatened.

But matters were not to rest there. Finkbine was no abortion radical (and despite her later experiences, never became one). As a married woman with small children, she felt that abortions should be undertaken only when necessary; she simply believed that in her case abortion was both necessary and morally correct. But she was upset that she had been able to obtain and unknowingly take a drug that had destroyed her pregnancy, and she felt compelled to warn other people. The Air National Guard in her area had recently been airlifted to Europe to deal with the Berlin Wall crisis, and Finkbine feared that if her husband had brought Thalidomide back from Europe, the pregnancies of the wives of the National Guardsmen might also be at risk. On Sunday, the day before her scheduled abortion, she called a friend who worked for the local newspaper and told her story. The friend promised to withhold her name, but Monday morning's paper had a front-page, black-bordered headline: "Baby-Deforming Drug May Cost Woman Her Child Here." Within hours of the paper's appearance, her scheduled abortion was canceled. The ambiguity in the law between saving her life broadly considered and saving her physical life had been called to the public's attention, and some integration of the different views was called for. On Thursday, her physician asked for a court order to perform the abortion; she and her husband were named in the legal request and immediately became public figures.

The reaction was instantaneous and almost overwhelming. Wire services picked up the story, and Finkbine and her husband were deluged with reporters. Thousands of letters, cards, and phone calls came in. A few of these made death threats against her and her children, and the FBI was brought in to protect her. Some of the reporters who interviewed her made suggestions: she should go to Japan, she should go to Sweden, she should stay and fight the court case. As the pressure mounted, she decided that she simply wanted it over. She and her husband applied for visas to Japan but were mysteriously turned down, probably because the Japanese government was wary about importing a moral dilemma of international proportions. Finally, she and her husband were permitted to go to Sweden, where a panel of medical experts examined her to see if she qualified for an abortion under what was a relatively restricted abortion law. (Though all the Scandinavian countries formally considered social, economic, and fetal circumstances in deciding whether or not to perform abortions, approval was by no means automatic.) Her request was granted, and early in the fourth month of her pregnancy she had an abortion. As she came out of the anesthetic, the obstetrician told her that the embryo was so seriously deformed it would never have survived.

Upon returning home, Finkbine faced the consequences of having become a public figure of powerful symbolic importance to many people. She lost her job, and the calls and letters continued for some time. On a personal level, her story is one of irony, tragedy, bad timing, and fate. She was an ordinary woman who found herself in the wrong place at the wrong time. But as a case study, her story illustrates a number of important points already made in this chapter.

Finkbine's physician believed that the probability of her giving birth to a seriously deformed child was in itself sufficient indication for an abortion, and the evidence suggests that his view was shared by everyone who participated in the decision before it "went public." It is worth noting that this physician was not Finkbine's long-time family doctor. For reasons irrelevant to her case, she had changed physicians after the birth of her last child and had seen this practitioner only two or three times before. Thus, it cannot be said that he was a trusted family friend who was willing to "take a chance" for a patient of long standing. Besides, the case was apparently perceived as presenting little or no risk. No prolonged or complicated review procedures were thought necessary; the physician was able to schedule her into an operating room for an abortion on the next working day.

By medical standards, then, Finkbine fit into the values of "middle-of-the-road" physicians on this issue. She was married and the mother of several children; she wanted an abortion only for this pregnancy, which was in any event clearly damaged; and she was likely to try to become pregnant again soon. In no way did her case present "deviant" features that might have muddied the waters. For the physician who accepted anything except a rigid "strict constructionist" view of the law, Sherri Finkbine's pregnancy presented an unimpeachable case for abortion.

If the procedural casualness with which the abortion of Sherri Finkbine was decided upon and planned demonstrates the extent to which the physician, the hospital, and Finkbine herself assumed that their views and values on the matter were shared, then the furor and outrage that followed public disclosure of the case demonstrates the extent to which "strict constructionists" felt that their view of the moral order was under assault. Both extremes on the continuum had assumed that their views were representative of public opinion; the case of Sherri Finkbine demonstrated how great their differences really were. Each side began to mobilize support for claiming that its own view of abortion was in fact the common one, the historically correct one, and the morally proper one.

To some extent, that mobilization had already begun to occur; the Finkbine case merely accelerated a process already in motion. In 1959, the American Law Institute had proposed a Model Penal Code that would have written into the abortion law the considerations some doctors were already using: the mental health of the mother, rape or incest, and fetal deformity; and in 1961, a year before the Finkbine case, California legislators were already considering a reform law similar in principle to this model. But with the Finkbine case, what had been a trickle of public interest in the issue of abortion became a torrent.

4

Abortion Reform: The Professionals' Dilemma

As THE control of abortion by physicians eroded, the consensus on the meaning of abortion eroded as well. Agreement among physicians that they alone should decide when to perform abortions depended upon the existence of a continuum of reasons for performing abortions. As "preserving the life of the woman" in the physical sense of the word became a medical rarity, the continuum collapsed and the consensus broke down. For the first time since the nineteenth century, medical technology—in this case, advances in obstetrical science—set the stage for abortion to reemerge as a political and moral issue.

This reemergence took place in two stages. In the first stage, considered in this chapter, discussions of abortion were restricted to small, well-defined groups of elite professionals: public health officials, crusading attorneys, and prominent physicians. In the second stage, described in Chapter Five, abortion moved into its present status as a "women's issue." This chapter will argue that the small groups of elite professionals who supported "liberalization" of abortion laws were as successful as they were precisely because the issue had *not* yet been defined as a "women's issue." When the debate was restricted to professionals, the philosophical issues that had been obscured for so long were still minor themes in the discussion; therefore, those outside these professional circles who had a moral opposition to liberalized abortion remained in large part an unawakened constituency. Similarly, within the ranks of professionals, those who were morally opposed to abortion were constrained from making that opposition more active by ties of professionalism and colleagueship. Thus, although the moral dimensions of abortion—and consequently the passions involved—became somewhat more prominent in the early days of the abortion reform movement, especially compared with the preceding "century of silence," abortion was still far from the major moral issue it was to become once the public (and in particular, women) became involved. As long as the moral issues remained largely latent (i.e., when the abortion debate had not yet become "symbolic"), those active in the debate had both a willingness to compromise and room to do so.

This view of how slowly morality became an issue in the abortion debate is admittedly counterintuitive. Once a phenomenon becomes an issue and then a cause, there is a strong temptation to project the present backward into the past, to experience the issue as having always been defined in the way that it is now. In the case of abortion, given that now it has become one of the central moral dilemmas of our time, it is particularly hard to imagine that it took at least a decade for the moral dimensions of the debate to come to the fore.

In order to document this assertion, the chapters that follow will focus in detail on the events in California, one of the first states to liberalize its abortion law (in 1967). The national events and forces described in previous chapters were certainly at work in the processes recounted here. But looking at how they operated in one state reveals the richness of the social tapestry underlying the general process whereby abortion came to be a great issue of the times.[1]

The Beginnings of Reform in California

In 1960, the state law in California regarding abortion was typical of mid-nineteenth-century anti-abortion laws. First passed in 1849 as part of the general territorial penal code and later formally entered in 1872 as California Penal Code section 274, California's abortion law held that anyone who provided any drug or instrument to procure the miscarriage of a woman "unless the same is necessary to preserve her life" was liable to imprisonment for not less than two nor more than five years. Subsequent amendments to the law made even the attempt to produce abortion illegal, including attempts made on nonpregnant women, and set penalties for the separate crime of soliciting abortion. Case law upheld these provisions so that neither the pregnancy of the woman nor the success of the abortion was necessary for the crime to have taken place. Case law also reaffirmed the special status of physicians: in 1940 the court held that the burden of proof was on the state to prove that an abortion performed by a physician was *not* necessary, and in 1959 it held that in order to justify abortion, a threat to the woman's life need only be reasonably foreseeable, not imminent.[2]

Until the end of the 1950s, the abortion situation in California was much like the general one outlined in the previous chapter: no one seems to have paid much attention to the philosophical issues involved; medical abortions took place with little or no public overview; and public interest in the issue was limited to the occasional news report detailing the arrest of an illegal abortion ring. (In 1960, three large newspapers in the state ran a total of six articles on illegal abortion—hardly a torrent.)[3] It is true that professionals had been concerned about the problem of illegal abortion in California since at least the 1930s, but their reaction recalls what Mark Twain said about the weather—everybody talked about it but nobody did anything about it.

The first attempts to rewrite the California law on abortion date back to 1959. In that year, Herbert Packer and Ralph Gampell, a lawyer and a lawyer-physician, respectively, published an article in the *Stanford Law Review* reporting the results of a survey they had undertaken in twenty-six representative California hospitals, excluding those opposed to abortion in principle (i.e., Catholic hospitals).[4] The survey consisted of two parts. The first part was a factual one, designed to ascertain how many therapeutic abortions were actually undertaken and the decision-making mechanisms involved. In the second part, the responding hospitals were asked to assess whether abortion would be "justifiable" in each of eleven hypothetical cases presented as vignettes. In the judgment of the authors, who for purposes of argument subscribed to a "strict-constructionist" view of the law, two of these eleven cases were clearly legal, two were doubtful, and seven were clearly illegal—four fetal injury cases, a rape case, a "psychiatric" case, and a "socioeconomic" case (a woman with five children whose husband was unable to work).

Whatever the construction of the law used by Packer and Gampell, the results of their survey demonstrated quite clearly that in California, as in the rest of the nation, "strict" and "broad" constructions of the law were employed side by side under the doctrine of "medical judgment." For example, incidence figures in the twenty-six hospitals surveyed ranged from one therapeutic abortion for each 126 live births to *no* therapeutic abortions per 7,615 live births. Further, each of the seven cases that the authors considered clearly illegal was considered acceptable by at least one of the hospitals surveyed. Perhaps not coincidentally, the authors also found that in the previous ten years there had been a dramatic increase in the creation of therapeutic abortion committees in hospitals, an indication that physicians in California, as elsewhere, were beginning to try to deal with the divergencies between "strict" and "broad" constructions of the abortion law.[5]

The content of this article did not guarantee it much impact; after all, similar articles could have been written about the sporadic application of drug laws, sex laws, or even the death penalty.[6] But in this case, a path for political action was already being cleared. In 1959 the American Law Institute (ALI), a national nonprofit organization whose goal was to "rationalize" legal process, had drafted a model statute that approved abortion in cases where it was necessary to protect the life and health of the mother (including her mental health), in cases of rape and incest, and in cases where there was a probability of congenital defects appearing in the embryo.[7] In other words, the model statute specifically provided legal permission for performing the sorts of abortions that the Packer and Gampell study, as well as others, had shown California physicians to be performing anyway.[8] Upon reading the article, a young lawyer in the state attorney general's office prevailed upon an old friend, now an assemblyman, to carry a version of the ALI bill into the 1961 session of the state legislature. That assemblyman, John Knox, described in an interview with me his decision to do so:

> I was a freshman legislator in January of 1961, when [my friend] talked to me about getting an abortion reform bill introduced. At that time, to the best of my knowledge . . . nobody had introduced such a bill anywhere in the country. . . . It was quite a thing. Although I was a freshman legislator, and probably *because* I was a freshman, I didn't know any better. But it really struck a note with me. As a very impressionable teenager, particularly in those days when you didn't get very much information about the facts of life or biology or anything else, I'd read an

> article in *Collier's* about a woman in Colorado who had been raped by a mentally defective person who had escaped from some institution, and was being forced to bear the child. And I just thought that was outrageous. It made a very deep impression on me at the time. So when [my friend] asked me to do this, that sort of brought that experience back to my mind, and I thought about it, and really decided without talking to anyone, particularly my normal advisers, and decided to go ahead with it. I did remember mentioning it to Senator George Miller. He was kind of my mentor at the time—he was on the Rules Committee of the Senate, he's a very devout Catholic. I mentioned to George that I was thinking of introducing an abortion reform bill. He said, "Have you ever met Cardinal MacIntyre?" And I said no. He said, "You're about to."

As a result of his sponsorship of the bill in 1961, Knox "took a lot of heat":

> Well, then the next session came up in 1963, and I had some old friends who were very angry with me. I didn't change my view in the matter, but I was preached against in the 1962 election from virtually every Catholic pulpit in town and received some very angry letters from priests. But it didn't seem to affect the election results all that much . . . [because I] won fairly handily. I ran ahead of Pat Brown, who was running for reelection for governor, so I must have done fairly well. . . . The next year, 1963, the decision had to be made, well, what are we going to do now? And I had some reluctance, not that I was personally afraid of it, but I just didn't like [offending] some very close friends of mine, including Senator Miller, who were literally hurt by the thing. I mean, physically, they were very upset.

When a new freshman legislator from Beverly Hills, Anthony Beilenson, asked if he could carry the bill during the next session, Knox agreed and turned over all his files to him. The issue had come to Beilenson's attention at a dinner party where a woman (who also worked in the state attorney general's office) had spoken to him about the need for the Knox bill or a bill like it. A few years before, a young law partner of his had written a prize-winning essay arguing for abortion reform.[9] Like Knox, Beilenson was new in the legislature and looking for good causes, but he was by no means a committed advocate for abortion on demand:

> I had no prior concern . . . that I can recall about abortion. I don't think I was interested in family planning, which since [then] has been my principal long-term interest as a legislator. . . . [But] it didn't take a lot

> of persuasion to make it completely obvious to me, as I think it did to a lot of people at the time, that we weren't talking about abortion on demand, we were talking about cases of rape or incest or where continuation [of the pregnancy] . . . involved substantial risk to the mother's physical or mental health. In the cases of that sort, it was just clearly barbaric and wrong that women couldn't have access to decent medical care. I think it probably got the law passed relatively quickly—[the fact] that the existing state of the law was barbaric or archaic, not moderate.

These quotations about the early history of the Therapeutic Abortion Act (also known as the Beilenson bill), from interviews undertaken for this book, demonstrate several important points about the climate in which abortion reform began to grow.

First, abortion was taken up as an issue primarily by people who were members of professional elites. Packer was on the faculty of the Stanford Law School and Gampell was a specialist in forensic medicine; and the persons who first brought the issue to the attention of Assemblyman Knox and then Assemblyman Beilenson were professionals affiliated with the state attorney general's office.

Next, the critical early participants in the reform movement did not see the issue as explosive or highly charged. It is hard to imagine today that even a freshman legislator such as Assemblyman Knox would not realize that a bill to liberalize abortion would be deeply offensive to a political mentor who was a "very devout Catholic." Knox's account of his actions makes it clear that he did not see Catholic opposition as a threat to his political career, and he says he decided to hand the issue over to Assemblyman Beilenson because his support of the bill had caused *personal* stress to his friend and mentor, who was "literally hurt by the thing."

Perhaps the most telling evidence of how low-key the issue was lies in the fact that both Knox and Beilenson were *freshmen* legislators. As other researchers have noted, young politicians typically seek to make a name for themselves by supporting causes that are new but not dangerously controversial.[10] Beilenson has made much the same point himself. When asked why, as a busy young legislator, he came to choose the abortion issue among the many competing for his attention, he answered: "I was a new person, I had no agenda. . . . I carried a few bills for the City of Los Angeles my first year, but as a freshman member of the state assembly, I didn't have a large or even a moderate-sized legislative agenda. I wasn't terribly busy, certainly not . . . in terms of my own legislation." Thus, for Beilenson, like Knox, the abortion reform bill, while it undeniably had opposition (it passed in the California Senate, 48 to 30) was "touchy" only because it was connected with a general social taboo concerning sexuality and was thought to be offensive to one religious group—not because it was political dynamite.

Perhaps the single most interesting thing about both the assemblymen involved—as well as Packer and Gampell, whose article started it all—is their tacit assumption that the law, as then written and then interpreted, was a "strict constructionist" law. For example, all four assumed that abortions after rape, for fetal indication, or when there is substantial risk to the mother's health were not only not legal but also not available, hence creating the need for a new law. But the Packer and Gampell article itself had proved that a substantial segment of medical opinion perceived these very same abortions as "justifiable." And data from medical journals suggest that abortions for these reasons were performed with some regularity.[11] Thus the paradox: these abortions were illegal (and therefore unavailable) only if the law were strictly and narrowly interpreted. But the data are clear that a strict construction of the law was only *one* of a number of possible interpretations then in use in the medical community.

So why did Packer and Gampell and later Knox and Beilenson—all in one way or another abortion "liberals"—tacitly subscribe to the belief that a new law was needed because a strict construction of the existing law precluded the kinds of abortions they felt were both necessary and proper?

The answer, in brief, is that all four were responding to a need being experienced within some sections of the medical community. For exactly the reasons outlined in Chapter Three, a difference of principle was brewing among physicians. As abortions to preserve the physical life of the woman became increasingly rare, "strict constructionists" began to argue that their interpretation of the law was the only legitimate one. "Broad constructionists," whose beliefs and practices had been protected by the professional consensus that abortion was a medical issue that only doctors could rule on, now faced the possibility that their medical colleagues would disagree with them, not on technical grounds, as previously, but on moral grounds. These abortion liberals began to feel the need to have their views explicitly written into law rather than be tacitly taken for granted.

Constituencies for Reform

Once the abortion reform bill began to be discussed among small groups of interested elites, a number of different constituencies emerged from among them to press for abortion reform. Their beliefs found expression in a critical series of public hearings on the issue between 1961 and 1964. After the abortion reform bill was first introduced in 1961, its sponsor, Knox, took it "on the road" in 1962 and held public hearings on it in the southern part of the state. Two years later in 1964, Beilenson did the same with his new version of the bill, holding hearings in both the southern and northern parts of the state. An analysis of the transcripts of those public hearings, combined with interviews with the surviving participants, will give us a picture of the emerging interest groups and will show how the definition of the issue began to change. The essential point still holds: with the exception of a small group of people interested in repealing *all* abortion laws (about whom more in the next chapter), the persons who appeared at these hearings *on both sides* were predominantly members of professional elites.

The problem of illegal abortion

The first group to be mobilized into the abortion reform movement were those people who had long been concerned about the problem of illegal abortion. In essence, the passage of section 274 of the California Penal Code in 1872 had served to create two categories of abortion: therapeutic (or "justifiable") abortion (undertaken to preserve a woman's life) and criminal abortion. Our interviews suggest that the boundaries between the two remained relatively clear until the 1950s. If an abortion was performed by a "reputable" physician in good standing in the community, who consulted with colleagues about the indications for the abortion, and performed it in an "above-board" fashion from motives that were seen as "humanitarian" rather than commercial, that abortion was very likely to be defined as therapeutic. If criminal abortions were therefore those performed in secret by unlicensed persons out of commercial motives, it is not surprising that they presented their own set of medical hazards.

In the 1962 hearings on the Knox bill, Theodore Montgomery, M.D., of the State Department of Public Health, testified on the preliminary results of a joint study on maternal mortality conducted by the

California Medical Association and the State Department of Public Health. Of 515 known cases of maternal mortality (deaths occurring within ninety days of the termination of a pregnancy), seventy deaths or 14 percent were attributed to criminal or self-induced abortions. Moreover, since the figure of 515 deaths included deaths from *any* cause (such as an automobile accident), the actual percentage of abortion deaths would have been higher. In 1959, Montgomery argued, abortion deaths from illegal abortions accounted for one-third of all maternal deaths.[12]

There is a considerable irony here. Reformers were becoming more vocal about the problems of criminal abortion at a time when criminal abortion was probably becoming *less* lethal to women. Largely because of the increasing use of antibiotic drugs, overall maternal mortality had been steadily declining for many years and had begun to drop dramatically after World War II. For example, between 1915 and 1919 there were 727.9 maternal deaths nationwide per 100,000 live births. In 1945, by contrast, there were only 207.2 such deaths, and by 1960 there were only thirty-seven maternal deaths per 100,000 live births.[13]

Even assuming that these figures do not include a number of women whose deaths from illegal abortion were ascribed to something else, the overall numbers are still small. Montgomery's seventy deaths from illegal abortion, for example, represent less than one-fifth the number of women killed in automobile accidents in California in that same year.[14] Thus, it was not the sheer magnitude of the loss of maternal life (which was in any event declining) that was of concern to the reformers; it was the *meaning* of those lives.

There are several reasons why the deaths of these women came to be seen as a tragic and pressing social problem. First, deaths from criminal abortions were unevenly distributed: poor women died more often. When there is a demand for a product or a service that is nominally illegal but morally acceptable to some "patrons," a black market emerges. Black markets—whether in illegal drugs, Prohibition era alcohol, or abortion—tend to be what economists call "wealth-sensitive": well-to-do people can usually get a "better" or at least a safer product. On the other hand, since it is hard to get reliable information in a black market, it is difficult for normal market forces to squeeze out dishonest or dangerous producers. As a result, people risk being blinded by "bathtub gin" (as happened during Prohibition), or poisoned by additives such as strychnine in their illegal drugs, or disabled or killed by faulty medical procedure during illegal abortions. Since there is little "quality control," anyone who engages in these black market activities faces such risks; but because the markets are wealth-sensitive, poor people face the risks more often.

Second, because both competition and comparison shopping are rare, black markets are highly profitable. And when a highly profitable but nominally illegal service exists, it often creates problems of police and judicial corruption. Reformers argue, for example, that when there is little or no public outrage about abortion, gambling, or prostitution, the enforcement of existing laws against them becomes expensive, arbitrary, and selective. It is expensive because citizens injured in pursuit of such services are reluctant to help the police and, in fact, may continue to support the black market by their patronage. It is arbitrary because the vigor of enforcement is discretionary and can therefore be "political"; the tolerance of crime that would be implied by the idea of an occasional "crackdown" on murder or robbery is abhorrent to us, but we accept "crackdowns" on illegal abortion, gambling, or prostitution as laudable. It is selective because when a "crackdown" occurs, it seldom falls evenly upon all those who have engaged in the nominally illegal activity; it is likely to fall only on those whom the police wish to punish for other reasons.[15]

Finally, and perhaps most subtly, reformers argue that laws that are commonly broken cause *moral* damage. They argue that the very frequency of the forbidden behavior—be it gambling, prostitution, or drug dealing—indicates a lack of moral consensus that these activities are, in fact, immoral. But as many reformers concede, this is a delicate argument. They do not argue simply that these "crimes" are frequent (for, after all, so are grand theft and murder); their main point is that the moral consensus that agrees that murder is wrong does not surround these other activities. Laws that are not taken seriously, they argue, tempt people to lose respect for the law as an institution.

Since the 1930s, then, in California as in the United States as a whole, a small number of professionals had argued that the "costs" of the nineteenth-century laws on abortion were too high, in both humanitarian and pragmatic terms, and that these laws were unfair and unworkable. These spokespersons became more active throughout the state in the late 1950s and early 1960s.

Thus, when hearings were held in 1962 on the first version of Knox's bill, which would have modified California law in the direction of the ALI's Model Penal Code, those testifying in favor of the bill included two lawyers associated with various district attorney's offices in the state (one of whom was Beilenson's former law partner); a psychiatrist who had written extensively on the problems of abortion; two physicians representing the two largest obstetrical-gynecological associations in the state; and a physician representing the State Department of Public Health. With the exception of the two obstetricians, all of these proponents of the new bill spoke primarily about the problem of *criminal* abortion.

It is important to remember that although such pragmatic calls for reform are directed at all "victimless crimes"—alchohol and drug abuse, gambling, prostitution, and various sexual activities—they rarely produce significant change. Without the mobilization of actively concerned interest groups, such "good government" proposals for a more "rational" treatment of crimes against morality seldom get beyond the stage of public rhetoric.

The problem of therapeutic abortion

The eventual success of the abortion reform bill was brought about by the emergence of a second constituency, a group of people (also primarily professionals) concerned with the problem of therapeutic abortion. When different definitions of morality are in conflict, one way of reducing tensions is to "buy off" some of the demands of the opposing groups in socially acceptable ways. This effort requires no deep philosophical reconsideration of the laws; it requires only an acknowledgment of the concerns and commitments of each side. For example, government-sponsored gambling (off-track betting or lotteries) and government-run methadone clinics acknowledge that some people believe that gambling is a matter of personal choice and that drug addiction is a medical problem. Both governmental responses give a degree of support to these views but stop short of completely legalizing betting and heroin use. By definition, this sort of compromise cannot meet all the demands of one party, for to do so would be to raise fundamental moral questions. But that is precisely what makes it workable.

This is one way of describing the historical working compromise on abortion that existed prior to the reform movements of the 1960s. The presence of a strict law satisfied those who wanted to believe that virtually all abortions should be outlawed whereas the much broader interpretation of the law in actual medical practice satisfied those who felt that embryos were only potential persons and that embryonic rights were far less compelling than the rights of mothers. Since the fundamental ideological differences between the two views were hidden from the public (to be weighed in individual cases by individual doctors), this form of compromise worked reasonably well for many years.

It is therefore of great historical importance that in the early 1960s the efforts of the first reform constituency—the persons concerned with the problems of illegal abortion—came to be supported by a more actively involved interest group whose stake in the issue was more direct. This new group, prefigured by the two obstetricians who testified at the 1962 hearings, was composed of physicians who saw the ideological consensus within the medical profession breaking down and sought to have explicit new ground rules on abortion spelled out.

The consensus was being broken down by several forces. First, and probably foremost, was the improvement in obstetrical science, which by the 1950s had virtually eliminated the need to perform abortions simply in order to save the life of the mother. In California, as elsewhere, abortions were usually undertaken because of psychiatric indications. For reasons outlined in the previous chapter, once the "cover" of strictly medical conditions began to evaporate, physicians began to make abortion decisions that were perceived by their colleagues and the general public alike as less "technical" than moral.

As the medical indications for abortion began to disappear, what had been an issue of *boundaries* (how to decide when an abortion was "medically necessary") then became an issue of *moral principle* (how did one weigh the life of the embryo against the life of the woman? And in both cases, exactly what kind of "life" was at issue—did life mean physical life only, or did it mean social life as well?). As a result, once the physical indications for abortion were no longer the prominent ones, even "reputable" physicians began to disagree among themselves about what constituted a "justifiable" abortion. Here is how one physician, who became one of the earliest and most prominent abortion law reformers of the early 1960s, described the situation in the 1950s:

> I wasn't really interested in reshaping the law; *I considered what I was doing was acting within the law then*. You have to realize we lived in an entirely different legal climate then. . . . There were malpractice, illegal activity, and professional liability aspects, but [they were] relatively rare. It would have to be that somebody died [in an abortion] under most unusual circumstances. Doctors were not being sued like they are now, but there was always the rumbling in the background—"if the district attorney hears about this, we might be faced with criminal charges." . . . When we'd consult [our lawyers] and say, "We think this patient should be aborted, but we don't know if this is life-threatening or not," they'd say, "Well, you might be sued." You don't know anything about the disease and its relation to pregnancy. What effect does the pregnancy have on the disease? What effect does the disease have on the pregnancy? And so we would go ahead on the basis that it was a life-threatening disease or situation. But [such cases] were rare, you might have one or two in the hospital in a year, and it took a great deal of work to accumulate even six or eight cases. But there was always the implication in the background that the district attorney, if he decided to make an issue of this, it could be a legal problem because even the district attorney couldn't interpret the law.

As this statement suggests, the early physician-activists were primarily interested in securing legal backing for what they were already doing. They were in effect already using a "broad construction" of the law, which they believed was accepted by their colleagues as ethical; they wanted their decision-making rights explicitly written into law, just to be on the safe side.

Subsequent events in California brought public attention to these issues and mobilized a substantial number of California physicians into a far more activist stance. The first of these events, in 1962, was the previously noted case of Sherri Finkbine, the housewife who discovered she had taken Thalidomide in the early days of her pregnancy and requested an abortion. As noted in Chapter Three, her request might very well have been quietly granted had she not inadvertently "gone public" with her case before the operation was performed. Media coverage of the case was extensive: both AP and UPI picked the story up, the *New York Times* ran a series of articles on it, and representative newspapers in California eventually wrote an average of eleven articles each on it.[16] The Finkbine case forced people to define exactly what circumstances *in principle* constituted legitimate grounds for abortion, and it forced doctors to define exactly what they were doing when they were performing an abortion. Under this pressure to set guidelines, the deep cleavages between "strict constructionists" and "broad constructionists" emerged.

"Strict constructionists" had always assumed that abortions were being performed only when the physical life of the mother was at risk, and they referred (and continue to refer) to the wording of the various state laws to validate their claims. Although for them an abortion always meant the death of a full (albeit unborn) person, they were willing to turn a blind eye when they thought that this not-yet-born person was being sacrificed "in a good cause," namely, to preserve the life of its mother—even though in practice, as we have seen, the guidelines for such a decision could be very loose indeed. Our interviews suggest that "strict constructionists" thought that abortions were rare, that the vast majority of them represented relatively clear-cut cases where either the embryo or the mother or both would have had to be sacrificed, and that doctors on the whole could be relied upon to weigh the death of this unborn person against the fact that the mother's death would not only preclude any further births but might hurt her already existing family in tragic ways. More to the point, until the Finkbine case the issue was simply not very salient to those physicians opposed in principle to abortion. In part, their very opposition to it seems to have shielded them from an awareness of the reasoning implied in the decisions to undertake a therapeutic abortion; as a practical matter, they were unlikely to have been asked to become involved in any of the decision-making surrounding abortion. Further, they had confidence in their medical colleagues. They may have felt that some doctors were "stretching" things a bit, but the fundamental value differences that were later to emerge were still buried under collegial relations, and no one seems to have felt any pressing need to clarify the differences of opinion.

To "broad constructionists," the moral reasoning inherent in the Finkbine case was self-evident. Their goal was to safeguard health, and health to them meant normality. When the chances were high (and no one ever specified exactly what probabilities were "high") that an embryo would be born with severe handicaps and hence be "abnormal," it was clear to them that it was ethically preferable to end the life of a potential person rather than force a "real" (born) person to live a life of diminished capacities. The costs of bringing a damaged child into the world—costs to the child itself, to its family, and to its community—were seen to be so high as to make abortion the obvious moral choice.

"Strict constructionists," however, found the Finkbine case deeply disturbing. They had been willing to tolerate a situation where what they thought of as being the life of one person (an embryo) was sacrificed to save the life of another (a woman). But it posed enormous logical (as well as ethical) problems to argue that an individual must be sacrificed for its own good. *The fundamental disagreement about whether or not an embryo represented a "real" person or merely a potential person, a disagreement that had existed beneath the surface for at least a hundred years, was finally forced into the open by the Finkbine case.* More subtly, the Finkbine case touched on themes that would become more clearly articulated later: the moral meaning of "handicap," the role of intervention and control in human life, and the larger question of what qualities individuals (including handicapped individuals) must have in order to be considered "fully" human. The dilemma of abortion in cases of a "damaged" embryo (known variously as "fetal" or "eugenic" indications) found "strict" and "broad" constructionists facing each other across a chasm.

With the advent of the Finkbine case and the awareness that others both inside and outside the profession did not share their values, liberal (and even middle-of-the-road) physicians began to feel that they had to agitate in order to have the grounds for such abortions written explicitly into law. The assertion that abortions for fetal indications could be justified because having a handicapped child would drive a woman into psychosis, a weak argument to begin with, became increasingly hard to uphold against the arguments of newly mobilized "strict constructionists." Before Finkbine, both sides could assume that they shared the same basic values and were only debating questions of implementation. After Finkbine, it was clear that fundamental differences existed, and neither side could expect the "opposition" to trust the assertion that if left unregulated, abortions would be done "correctly."

Had the Finkbine case merely come and gone, at the very least it would have made some key physicians aware that the supposed professional consensus about abortion was in fact no consensus at all. But other events soon presented the dilemma again. In 1964–1965, California suffered an epidemic of rubella, commonly known as German measles. This childhood disease, usually no more than a minor nuisance even in adults, had been increasingly documented since the 1940s as capable of inflicting prenatal injuries when contracted by the mother in the first sixteen weeks of pregnancy. Present-day abortion activists debate the frequency and severity of such injuries, but the classic obstetrical textbook in use during the epidemic under discussion asserted that the probability of deformity was 30 percent and that the deformities were typically major—blindness, deafness, serious mental retardation, cardiac problems, and the like.[17] In fact, abortion was performed relatively often for rubella after the Australian epidemiological studies of 1941 made clear the correlation between the disease and infant deformity. In a number of different settings, abortions for rubella accounted for as many as 10 to 20 percent of all abortions performed.[18] With the onset of the California rubella epidemic, a pattern of performing abortions for rubella was already in place. One activist physician, who by 1962 was both a clinical instructor at a large teaching hospital and past-president of a professional medical association, noted:

> Rubella then was established as damaging a certain amount of babies and was accepted, I think, by most ethical physicians as a reason for terminating a pregnancy regardless of legal reform. And the mechanisms were set up in hospitals where a committee would review a case. "She has rubella, she doesn't want this baby and she's going to go crazy if she has it, she can't raise a deformed, defective baby"—all these things [were considered]. . . . I'm talking about large hospitals, teaching institutions, and large community hospitals.

Thus, practitioners like this one, believing that abortions in the case of rubella were good medical practice and assuming that most of their colleagues would agree, became increasingly aware that they were performing abortions that might not be strictly within the letter of the law, given the presence of a newly mobilized "strict constructionist" constituency that might be willing to argue the issue on principled grounds.

Liberal physicians in elite hospitals (teaching hospitals, university-affiliated hospitals) continued to perform such abortions, but they increasingly began to feel that they might be in some need of legal protection. Informally, and later formally, they began to approach the state legislature.

Because of these changes within the medical profession, in the

1964 interim hearings called to study the new therapeutic abortion bill, the bulk of those testifying in support of the bill were now concerned about the dilemmas of "reputable" physicians. In contrast to the 1962 hearings, where criminal abortion had been the dominant theme, only six of the twenty-five supporters of the reform bill mentioned criminal abortion, and a number of them did so only in passing. Far more typical was a physician who supported the bill because it would relieve the medical profession of "a nearly intolerable burden of social responsibility."[19]

Our interviews suggest that key medical professionals believed there was general support—both public and professional—for the idea that clear evidence of fetal abnormality was a legitimate indication for abortion. And in part, they were right: a Gallup poll taken just after the Finkbine case showed that over half of those surveyed thought that Sherri Finkbine had made the right decision (32 percent disagreed and 16 percent had no opinion).[20] These physicians reported that the attorney general had informally assured them that law enforcement officials were much too busy dealing with illegal abortionists to worry about subtle borderline cases occurring in bona fide medical practice, but their awareness of an ideological opposition made them nervous. Although they dismissed this opposition as religious in nature (and therefore not "medically valid"), they did not want to practice what later came to be called "defensive medicine." More to the point, once it had been called to their attention that they might not be in compliance with the strict letter of the law and once they had become aware that *there was no unanimity within the medical profession*, calls to bring the state law more in line with mainstream practice became more frequent.*

The 1964 hearings, therefore, represented the convergence of a number of interests. Those testifying in favor of the bill included some of the "pragmatic reformers" concerned with illegal abortion who had been present at the 1962 hearings. Religious groups in favor of a more

* Similar strategies can be seen in current controversies among physicians about when to "pull the plug" on terminally ill patients. It is clear that physicians have been making these decisions for decades with little in the way of commentary from their colleagues. This is because until recently, "pulling the plug," like abortion, was seen as a technical, not a moral, decision. Once seen as a moral decision, however, physicians become willing to confront one another in public, and one can confidently expect the creation of ethics boards, like therapeutic abortion boards, to spread the accountability, followed in turn by calls for a uniform law that will define physician responsibility. If the abortion debate is any guide, however, such strategies will not effectively contain the controversy over the long run.

liberal abortion law were represented by a rabbi, a representative of the state's Episcopal bishop, and a Unitarian minister. Among the new groups represented were the American Association of University Women, the Humanists, and a group dedicated to repealing all abortion laws (which we shall discuss in the next chapter). Finally, there were moderate civic groups such as the California Junior Chamber of Commerce (Jaycees). In describing how state delegates at the Junior Chamber of Commerce convention came to support the bill by an 80 percent margin, its representative noted:

> The reasons for the vote [to support the Beilenson bill] were not the reasons of experts, but those of ordinary citizens, most of them family men. Primarily, the Jaycees believe that the important question of whether or not to continue a pregnancy to term in difficult situations such as rape, incest, or danger to the physical or mental health of mother or child should be left to the judgment and religious beliefs of the individuals involved. The Thalidomide cases were very much in mind.[21]

As it continues, this particular testimony demonstrates how physicians had begun informally to rally support for the new law. In the case of the Jaycees, a physician on their Governmental Affairs Committee had urged them to debate the issue. The presence of the Jaycees at this hearing demonstrates both that physicians were active in mobilizing community groups in support of the new bill and that the basic logic of the "broad constructionist" view among physicians was in large part acceptable to such middle-of-the-road groups as the Jaycees.

The array of testimony *against* the bill in these 1964 hearings further convinced the pro-reform activists that the opposition was in large part religious. In the northern part of the state, the opposition was exclusively from Catholic organizations, including the St. Thomas More Society, the Guild of Catholic Psychiatrists, the Catholic Physicians Guild, the Catholic Parent-Teacher Groups, and the California Council of Catholic Hospitals. In the southern part of the state, opposition was more diverse, but it did include two Catholic organizations, a statement from a Lutheran minister, a similar statement from a Congregational minister, and a number of statements from Catholic physicians.[22]

In contrast, the assorted group of professionals who turned out to testify in favor of the bill represented the confluence of the two previously mentioned constituencies for reform. Some wanted clarification of the legal status of certain kinds of abortions—those done for health reasons, rape, and fetal indications. Others—represented by public health professionals, lawyers, the Chamber of Commerce, and the American Association of University Women—had a long-standing concern with illegal abortion. Finally, there were the first hints of what would become a mass movement on abortion: ordinary citizens, mostly women, who opposed all abortion laws in principle.

Their joint presence at the 1964 hearings served to mobilize these various groups into formal political activity. In part they were moved and persuaded by each other's testimony. More importantly, the hearings allowed the two major reform constituencies to "cross-pollinate": in later hearings and writing the physicians would speak more forcefully about the issues of illegal abortion, and those concerned with illegal abortion would begin to discuss the problems of vagueness in indications for legal abortions. The recognition that they had interests in common (and more subtly, an opposition in common) mobilized a feeling that "common sense" and "science" would have to organize to show the state legislature that although "religious dogmatists" might be loud in their opposition to formal abortion reform, most citizens (and most elites) supported it. Consequently, a meeting was called through the auspices of the dean of the School of Public Health at a local university, and a group of lawyers, physicians, social workers, and public health professionals formed a working committee, eventually to be christened the California Committee on Therapeutic Abortion (CCTA). Thus was born the first formal organization aimed at passage of a *reformed* abortion law.

The members of CCTA resembled those of a typical "blue-ribbon" group. It included lawyers who would later be judges, physicians who were and would become heads of departments in major universities, and representatives from many of the local colleges and universities, law schools, and medical schools. Most had advanced degrees, and most had attended Ivy League universities or their West Coast equivalents. Not surprisingly, they chose to pursue an elite strategy in trying to get the law reformed. As one of the founders of CCTA put it:

> This is the way it worked. A small group of distinguished physicians drafted and revised and finalized a statement on abortion and the problems of illegal abortion; it said why the law constituted a barrier to good health care, was inequitable and illegal and unconstitutional, and was ill advised and dangerous and shocking for a civilized society. And then that statement, with the names of the initial signers, was sent to a large

> number of physicians in the state. [Similar statements were sent to] lawyers, ministers, social workers, and sociologists. I guess there were four statements in all, and there were thousands of signatures.

Thus the diverse members of CCTA had a common goal, that of getting the Beilenson bill passed. Their logic was simple: California's nineteenth-century abortion law had become unfair and restrictive *now that a mobilized strict constructionist constituency could be expected to press its case*. In particular, after the Finkbine case, the abortion reformers were able to demonstrate that abortion in cases that demanded some degree of public support—in particular, cases of rape, cases where the pregnancy would threaten the health rather than the life of the mother, and cases of fetal damage—could be prohibited if a strict construction of the law were followed; and with the 1872 law on the books, such a construction was theoretically possible at any time.

New Pressures for Reform

Neither the 1961 nor 1964 version of the abortion reform law was able to get out of committee. The hearings on the bill had brought together those concerned about illegal abortion and those concerned about the rise of a "strict constructionist" group and thereby led to the founding of CCTA in order to press for abortion reform. Subsequently, however, an event occurred that served to mobilize even more physicians into the cause and to move the bill closer to passage.

As we have seen, the "strict" and "broad" constructions of abortion law had been able to coexist in apparent harmony for almost a century. In adjusting to the discrepancy between the two views, the medical profession made an interesting sociological accommodation. Since there was not (and could not be) any agreement upon how and when to perform an abortion, a consensus was reached on *who* should perform an abortion, namely, a licensed physician. Surviving activists on both sides of the issue concur that prior to 1960, most physicians had a tacit agreement about what constituted a "legitimate" abortion. Almost by definition, if the characteristics of the practitioner and the conditions of practice were "reputable," then the abortion was "justifiable." As one activist obstetrician-gynecologist noted:

> Anything that was done in hospital surroundings with plenty of consultants and was recorded as such, the district attorneys technically could prosecute . . . but they were not interested . . . because they had their

> hands full with criminal abortions. They did want to know about M.D.'s who were making a living doing abortions in their offices—that was clearly a different mode.

Another activist obstetrician was asked this question: "When there was a difference of medical judgment, how did you differentiate in your own mind between a 'reputable' practitioner and someone who was doing something a little 'shady'? What were the benchmarks?" The answer was as follows:

> I would think they were the standard benchmarks that label any reputable practitioner. . . . He was a member of the county medical society, he was recognized by his colleagues as an ethical practitioner, he belonged to a hospital staff. . . . The person who did not have these qualifications . . . and whom we heard was doing abortions, was the one who was the back-alley abortionist.

This informal distinction between what "reputable" and other physicians did in the matter of abortion meant that there was an on-going process of negotiation. If a "reputable" practitioner did an abortion openly, then to challenge the grounds on which that decision was made would have entailed taking on not only the original physician but the consultants and the hospital (and perhaps the professional norms of self-regulation) as well. "Reputable" physicians could therefore count on a layer of institutional and professional support for "above-board" abortions. Conversely, in order to maintain that professional and institutional support, they could accept only those cases that were reasonably likely to be approved by their colleagues. And they were forced to make private estimates of community sentiment as well.

In 1966, this informal understanding of what constituted a legal abortion was torn apart. As we have noted, many "broad constructionist" physicians had assumed that abortions done after maternal exposure to rubella were perfectly ethical, and many physicians had performed such abortions, though with an increasing uneasiness in the light of the emerging "strict constructionist" view. But according to our interviews, in 1966, at a public hearing called to discuss this issue, the head of the California State Board of Medical Examiners was heard to publicly threaten that the board would "get" any physician who performed abortions for maternal exposure to rubella. The head of the board, a physician, was self-evidently a "strict constructionist." He was always referred to by others in interviews as "a devout Catholic" and was later one of the founders of the pro-life movement in California. Shortly after the public hearing, the board did indeed charge seven physicians with performing illegal abortions on patients exposed to rubella.

What was so upsetting about this act from the point of view of many physicians who had previously chosen not to get involved was that the seven physicians, all men, were in the elite rank of the profession and *had all subscribed to the tacit rules for "legitimate" abortion.* They were on the teaching faculty of perhaps the most prestigious medical school in the state; they were clearly well-respected physicians; all of the abortions in question had been performed in an open and "above-board" fashion; and each physician had asked for medical consultation with other colleagues before performing the abortions. Indeed, the openness of their procedures is indicated by the fact that the head of the board had discovered these abortions in a search of medical records, a search prompted by a story about these physicians in *Life* magazine.

This event shook the "broad constructionists" within the medical community. Many, even when being interviewed well over ten years later, bristled at the memory of the event. To them, the head of the Board of Medical Examiners had broken the cardinal rule of medicine: he had singled out reputable colleagues, who had been performing in accordance with the accepted *technical* criteria of the profession, and had accused them of *moral* turpitude. Moreover, for reasons to be explored shortly, they considered his construction of the law to be a "religious" one, hence illegitimate.

Thus, ironically, the anti-abortion head of the Board of Medical Examiners may have been the abortion law reformers' best friend. Physicians throughout the state and across the country rallied to send money and support to their threatened colleagues and to support a reformed abortion law. Some 2,000 physicians formed a nationwide support group, which included the deans of most of the major medical schools in the country.

To be sure, the reaction to the prosecution of "reputable" physicians' activities was skillfully shaped by CCTA, the organized pressure group founded in 1964. But without the clear evidence provided by the Board of Medical Examiners that CCTA's basic contention was correct—that with the 1872 law still on the books, a "strict construction" of the law could be invoked at any time—CCTA's road to the statehouse might very well have been considerably longer.

When the elites concerned with illegal abortions were joined by the elites concerned with therapeutic abortions and both were supported by a new grass-roots movement (to be examined in the next chapter), there was wide-ranging support for the new reform law. Groups ranging from the American Association of University Women to the Young Republicans supported it. As the reformers pursued their strategy of convincing fellow professionals that the old law was open to arbitrary challenge on religious grounds, these professionals were persuaded that some change in the law was necessary. In short order, between 1964 and 1967, the American Medical Association, the American Bar Association, the American Academy of Pediatrics, the California Medical Association, the California Bar Association, and numerous other groups threw their support behind abortion reform. On the grass-roots level as well, abortion was being discussed with increasing frequency, and legislators could perceive, however dimly, that "public opinion" was becoming favorable to some change in the abortion laws. With what was perceived as a groundswell of public support, the bill to change abortion laws was reported out of committee in 1967 and voted on. A mere six years after its first proposal, a variation of the "Scandinavian type" of "middle-way" law was passed. Though it did not permit abortion on demand, it offered considerable protection to the medical profession. It provided that an abortion was legal when it was done by a qualified medical doctor, in a hospital certified by the American Hospital Association, and when it was done to prevent mental or physical damage to the woman.*

In what might seem an ironic outcome given the history of the bill, California's Governor Ronald Reagan made it clear that he would veto the proposed law unless its reference to "fetal indications" was deleted.† Thus the point which in many ways had catalyzed the whole

* The new bill permitted a physician to "aid, assist, or attempt" an abortion if that abortion took place in an accredited hospital, the hospital's therapeutic abortion board having determined that the pregnancy would "gravely impair" the physical or mental health of the woman. It also permitted abortions when the pregnancy was the product of rape or incest or when the woman was the victim of statutory rape *and* below the age of fifteen. Specific sections outlined the procedures whereby the district attorney had to be notified in these cases of "felonious intercourse"; other sections mandated the size of therapeutic abortion boards and decreed that there needed to be unanimous consent if the board consisted of fewer than three members (*California State Senate Bill No. 462*, Sacramento, Ca.).

† Although the "fetal indications" clause existed in the ALI Model Penal Code version and in all three of the earlier versions of the Beilenson bill, Governor Reagan

movement for revision was apparently abandoned at the last moment. However, interviews with a number of the surviving principals suggest another interpretation. As noted earlier, from the late nineteenth century to the 1960s, an informal accommodation existed whereby no one got everything they wanted on the issue of abortion, but everyone got something. Under the new law, the medical profession was permitted to perform most of the abortions they wanted to with very little social control. Abortions of married women, or of women who had been raped, or whose embryos had some physical problem (in short, abortions that did not raise troubling questions of sexual morality) could often be performed, even though they were not consonant with the strict letter of the law; and "strict constructionists" could be satisfied with a nominally strict law to which most people paid lip service.

The Finkbine case (followed by the rubella cases) had upset the accommodation whereby all parties thought they agreed on the ground rules. Given this interpretation, then, the governor's decision to veto the new law unless the fetal indications clause was dropped can be seen as an attempt to generate a new modus vivendi because the fetal indications clause was the single most offensive clause to those holding to a "strict constructionist" view. In all other cases, the tacit or explicit argument is that the embryo is being sacrificed for some "greater good." While in some of these cases the "greater good" might seem inconsistent with a belief that the embryo represents a full human person, the fetal indication is the only one where logically a less valuable meaning of the embryo would be written into law. Had the governor signed the Beilenson bill into law as it was originally written, *it would have brought the thorny issue of personhood explicitly into the debate*.

By insisting that the fetal indications for abortion be dropped, this

---

called a press conference on Mar. 9, 1967, saying that he had reservations about the lack of a clause requiring residence and about the fetal indications clause. Beilenson removed the fetal indications clause, but Reagan called another press conference on June 13, 1967, just before the legislature was to vote; he raised a number of objections and again mentioned the dilemma of fetal indications. Several surviving legislators argue that this was a clumsy attempt by Reagan, then a first-term governor, to affect the vote then pending. By breaching the rules of legislative courtesy (Beilenson had already amended the bill in order to gain the governor's support), Reagan may have turned the tide in favor of the bill in the state legislature. Reagan having gone on to other things and the abortion issue still being an exquisitely sensitive one, no one seems willing (or able) to describe how he came to have these reservations and who educated him on the issue to begin with. For another account of these events, see Jain and Hughes, *California Abortion Act, 1967*.

issue was temporarily sidestepped. In so doing, the grounds for a new compromise were laid. The actual wording of the new law was sufficiently liberal that most of the doctors we interviewed said they were confident they could in fact do abortions in rubella and Thalidomide cases. They would simply argue that raising a disabled child created physical and mental risks for the mother, and they could point to a substantial body of support for liberalized abortion to forestall any potential conflict. Once "mental health" of the mother had been written into the bill, the "broad constructionists" felt they had ample room to cover the case of the congenitally damaged embryo.

The new law also mollified "strict constructionists." Although the grounds for abortion had been broadened considerably, the deletion of the fetal indications clause meant that they had not been forced to concede the *principle*. Although many more abortions were likely to be performed, in each of them a physician was obliged to weigh the life of the embryo against the life of the mother. Strictly speaking, of course, some of the weighing of lives embodied in this new law was not entirely logical; for example, permitting abortion in cases of statutory rape meant that what strict constructionists insisted was a full human life could be sacrificed merely because its mother was under the age of consent when it was conceived. But deletion of the fetal indications clause meant that the *principle* that the other side was working from—that an embryo is not a person but merely a potential person—had not been formally written into law.

Up to now, the abortion debate in California had been pursued primarily in narrow institutional channels governed by tacit rules about the political process. Had it continued to be limited chiefly to professionals, it is quite likely that the debate would have ended here. Like the debates over illegal gambling or methadone treatment for heroin addiction, it would have become a restricted discussion among professionals with competing interests and ideologies about implementation of a law. A new compromise would have emerged, a new equilibrium in which mutually opposing forces held each other more or less in check.

But this did not happen. Even as professional elites were courting the state legislature, a public, grass-roots movement was gathering strength. Its participants were not satisfied with the new, somewhat broader law that worked primarily to protect physicians. They wanted something fundamentally different, and they were prepared to work for it. More to the point, they were prepared to do what no one else to date had been willing or able to do. By making a claim that women had a *right* to abortion, they challenged the medical profession's control of the abortion decision. In so doing, they brought to the surface the philosophical issues that had remained latent for so long: the value and meaning of the embryo.

5

Women and the Right to Abortion

PRIOR TO 1967, the abortion debate in California was conducted in a spirit of compromise and civility; professional men and women tied to one another by bonds of colleagueship and sociability endeavored to create a new compromise on abortion that they envisioned would provide the basis for a second century of calm. But their efforts failed. Within a very short time, intense passions and moral concerns became central to the debate. A group of women who valued motherhood, but *valued it on their own timetable*, began to make a new claim, one that had never surfaced in the abortion debate before this, that abortion was a woman's *right*. Most significantly, they argued that this right to abortion was essential to their right to equality—the right to be treated as individuals rather than as potential mothers. In this chapter we shall consider how women, as a self-conscious interest group, came to cast the abortion debate in an entirely new framework.

As we have seen, women as individuals were amply represented in the elite groups that supported the Beilenson bill; women who were lawyers, public health officials, and physicians argued forcefully and effectively that the 1872 law was oppressive and unfair. But two critical points about those women must be kept in mind. First, with very few exceptions, they were, like their male colleagues, professionals who had been trained in and were affiliated with elite institutions. Second, their arguments in favor of the bill were virtually indistinguishable from those of their male peers. Like their male colleagues, they argued that the old California law created problems with both criminal and therapeutic abortions, and they argued that certain kinds of abortions, such as those undertaken to safeguard the health of the woman, or to terminate pregnancy after rape or incest, or in cases of fetal deformity, deserved the explicit protection of the law. The language of a *right* to abortion, however, was not to be found in their claim.

Notwithstanding the efforts of these individual women in the cause of reform, women in general were not seen as contributors to the passage of the Beilenson bill. The reaction of state legislators of the 1960s, when asked what role women had played in securing passage of the Beilenson bill, could best be epitomized as a blank stare. All of them could name individual women who had been active in the reform group California Committee on Therapeutic Abortion (CCTA), but none of them believed that women *as a constituency* were central to the issue. Only our tendency to project the present onto the past makes this surprising. What we have come to think of as "the women's movement," for all its dramatic and pervasive influence on American life, is a very recent phenomenon, dating from the late 1960s or the early 1970s.[1]

The emergence of women as a self-conscious interest group that claimed abortion as a right marked a new and fundamentally different stage in the abortion debate. Although its origins can be traced back to 1961, this interest group was only a nascent force when much of the debate on the Beilenson bill took place. Its full effect came only after 1967, in the period leading up to the Supreme Court decision of 1973.

Through 1967, physicians and most other interested parties had every reason to believe that the new Therapeutic Abortion Act would simply clarify the legal basis on which abortions could be performed; by explicitly authorizing "broad construction" of the 1872 law, which many doctors were already using in practice anyway, it would mean very little change in the status quo. Senator Beilenson, for example, estimated that under the provisions of the new law, there would be only a very modest increase over the number of therapeutic abortions then being legally performed.[2] As both the bill's author and its physician supporters seem to have understood it, the Therapeutic Abortion Act created what might be thought of as a Scandinavian-type "middle-way" abortion law: abortions could be performed for reasons that went beyond simply protecting the physical life of the woman, but physicians would continue to exercise substantial control over abortions, and far from all abortion requests would be granted. Although the new law would clarify the medical profession's management of abortion, few thought it would challenge either the fact of that management or the social status of abortion itself.

Things did not turn out that way. In 1968, the first full year under the new law, 5,018 abortions were performed. In the next year, however, the number of abortions tripled, to 15,952. The following year that number itself quadrupled, and 65,369 abortions were performed. In 1971 it almost doubled again, and 116,749 abortions were performed. In 1972 the rate stabilized at a little over 100,000 abortions a year and has remained at that level to the present. In four short years, therefore, the number of abortions sought and performed in California increased by *2,000 percent*. Moreover, by 1970 it was becoming apparent that what had been proposed as a "middle-way" solution had in fact become "abortion on demand." It is possible that the mechanisms of medical review (and psychiatric review in the case of those using the "mental health" criterion) may have been sufficiently cumbersome and expensive to discourage some women from applying for an abortion in the first place; but by late 1970, of all women who applied for an abortion, 99.2 percent were granted one. By 1971 abortion was as frequent as it would ever become in California, and one out of every three pregnancies was ended by a legal abortion.[3]

These figures compel us to an important conclusion. The ending of one out of every three pregnancies by an induced abortion and, more strikingly, the granting of an abortion to over 99 percent of all the women who wanted one bespeak the fact that for the first time in over a century, medical control of abortion was becoming nothing more than a legal fiction. By 1971, women in California had abortions because they wanted them, not because physicians agreed that they could have them.

These changes ushered in a new era in the abortion debate. For the first time since the physicians' crusade of the nineteenth century, a substantial number of citizens agreed, at least in practice, that women, not doctors, should decide when an abortion is necessary. To understand how abortion ceased to be a technical, medical issue and became a "women's issue" of great moral significance, we must understand the rise of a new constituency in the debate and the basis of its claim that women have a right to control their own bodies.

A New Constituency, a New Issue

Throughout the 1960s, while abortion law reformers were mobilizing support for the Beilenson bill, another group was mobilizing on behalf of a new cause: the *repeal* of all abortion laws. Abortion, they said, should be of concern only to the woman herself; physicians and other "authorities" had no right to intervene. Those who wanted the *reform* of abortion laws wanted something narrow and clear-cut. They wanted the state legislature to pass the Beilenson bill, and they wanted to demonstrate to the legislature that respectable members of the professions (and the public) supported this change. In short, they advocated a more "rational" regulation of the problem of abortion. Those who wanted total *repeal* of abortion laws, however, wanted something else. They wanted to redefine how abortion decisions should be made and who should make them; they wanted, in fact, to redefine the ground rules on abortion that had held sway for a century.

Like many of the phenomena of the larger women's movement of which abortion became a part, the drive for total repeal of abortion laws was carried forward by many evanescent organizations that formed for one "action" and then disbanded, fairly spontaneous public activities such as demonstrations, "speak-outs," and "street theaters." Although these activities were undoubtedly instrumental in changing the public climate, they left few records and are difficult to study after the fact. As a practical matter, therefore, we have been constrained to study the one formal organization, founded in 1961, that did visible and sustained work for the repeal of all abortion laws. But it should be kept in mind that this is an artificially well-ordered way of studying a movement that was in many ways spontaneous, amorphous, and intermittent.*

* This highlights the difference between studying "social movements," which are conveniently represented by formal organizations designed to pursue their goals consistently over long periods of time, and studying "collective behavior," such as riots and spontaneous demonstrations. Any study of the changing social and legal climate with respect to civil rights in the 1960s, for example, could not look simply at the formal social movement represented by organizations such as the NAACP, SNCC, CORE, and the like but would have to examine spontaneous events such as urban, inner-city riots. This study perforce focuses on the formal social movement to change abortion laws, but it is important to recall that to the extent that a demand for legal abortion was part of the larger women's movement, it was also represented by incidents of collective behavior, which also helped shape public opinion.

The group opposed to all abortion laws originated among persons who had read about the first abortion reform bill (the Knox bill) in 1961 and organized a petition campaign in support of it. One of these individuals soon discovered that she had deep reservations about the Knox bill and the Beilenson bill that followed it:

> [Knox] was very courageous I guess, but as a recipient of the dictums of that law, I felt it was just absolutely degrading. I mean it was just wrenching to read it, and the same with the Beilenson bill. And Beilenson was a very humanitarian person and he did a lot of good things, and he's still in there pitching. . . . But when I read their proposed laws I thought, My God, women are really just cattle in this country.

Not only did the Beilenson bill begin to seem ideologically offensive to this new group, it came to be seen as bad political strategy as well. As another member put it: "[Beilenson] was a good friend, but we couldn't get him to say the word *repeal*, they only wanted reform. Well, there's nothing to set back a good cause like a little tiny reform. You know, they reform a little bit and then they sit on their duffs for ten years saying 'What do you girls want now?' We didn't want a reform, we wanted repeal." (As these two quotations suggest, the relationship between those supporting repeal and those supporting reform was a complicated one. To the extent that the repealers were in fact a separate constituency, they were often impatient (and worse) with the elite professionals whose goals were more limited. To the extent that both sides wanted *some* change, however, they often made common cause.)

After the failure of the Knox bill, the repealers realized not only that some change was possible but also that the kinds of reform then under consideration in the state legislature were simply not satisfactory to them. They put together an organization they called the Society for Humane Abortions (SHA) and set out to change public opinion on abortion. From their own accounts and the accounts of others who were involved in the cause of reform, it is possible to discern a number of important features that distinguished the repealers from the reform activists and enabled them to become a vital force in eventually changing the social (and political) perception of abortion.

First, and most centrally, they began to use the language of *rights* in talking about women and abortion. One of the first women recruited to SHA put it quite directly:

> When we talk about women's rights, we can get all the rights in the world—the right to vote, the right to go to school—and none of them means a doggone thing if we don't own the flesh we stand in, if we can't control what happens to us, if the whole course of our lives can be changed by somebody else that can get us pregnant by accident, or by deceit, or by force. So I consider the right to elective abortion, whether you dream of doing it or not, is the cornerstone of the women's movement. . . . It's been a common denominator of the women's movement because without that right, we'd have about as many rights as the cow in the pasture that's taken to the bull once a year. You could give her all those rights, too, but they wouldn't mean anything; if you can't control your own body you can't control your future, to the degree that any of us can control futures.

Next, by their leafletting, abortion teach-ins, and petitions they accomplished something both subtle and profound: they made the "unspeakable" speakable and thus cleared the way for public dialogue about women's rights to abortion. Especially in the early years, they found that asking people to sign a petition to repeal abortion laws was slow business because people needed to think and talk about the issue. As one SHA founder said: "I had to plan on spending a whole afternoon to maybe find out what about four or five people thought. It took almost a full hour for a person to . . . think over [and discuss] all sorts of things and come out with some kind of a comment [before] maybe they'd sign the petition." Another early SHA activist reported:

> We started a series of lectures, we titled them "do-it-yourself abortion lectures." Of course they were not how to do-it-yourself abortion lectures, they were very, very careful. We went through the material with doctors and attorneys to make certain that we didn't hurt anybody; but we were determined that the only way you can break through a thing like this is to make people talk about it. Of course it was very, very illegal at that time, what we were doing. Even giving information [about abortion] was a felony.

For reasons explored in Chapter Two, in the early 1960s even persons with pro-choice sympathies seldom spoke of abortion outside intimate settings. This was not, as pro-life people sometimes think, because these people saw it as intrinsically immoral but rather because it was associated with sexuality generally. Just as even today contraceptives are not advertised on television and commercials for euphemistically named "feminine products" can be seen only on late-night television, abortion in those days was like reproduction and menstruation—very real facts of life but not something to be discussed in polite company. What SHA was doing was making it acceptable for people to discuss whether or not some change in the law was needed and, equally important, to discuss the moral basis for such a change.

The SHA activists addressed themselves to "the people" rather than to the professionals courted by CCTA. They spoke on late-night television and radio talk shows, and they gave public lectures in which they described what they saw as the hypocrisy and bias of abortion laws. And the public responded: after every talk they were flooded with letters and telephone calls from people who agreed with them and wanted to join up. As one of them put it: "We didn't sell anyone anything, we didn't have to. It was a terrible need, and all you had to do was start the conversation and people would just come from everywhere. It was an idea that had come into its own, I guess." Thus, SHA began to create a mass movement that was prepared to think critically about all abortion laws, not just the reforms proposed by elites. In short, it laid the groundwork for a new way of thinking about abortion.

Finally, SHA began to take direct action by engaging in civil disobedience. Once having defined abortion as a right, they began to declare openly that they would help women exercise this right by referring them to illegal abortionists, primarily in Mexico, whom they had inspected for cleanliness and respectability. They were both defiant and openly political about their plans. For a considerable period of time, some SHA members would not give a woman a referral until she had written a letter to her legislator urging the repeal of abortion laws. To women in need of an abortion (as well as to the illegal abortionists) this stand was a startling one. Women were being told that abortion was their *right*, and abortionists were told that the referrals they received represented a principled act of moral defiance.*

In each of these activities, the women in SHA fundamentally challenged the legitimacy of the existing way of dealing with abortion, which was to treat it as a medical issue to be resolved by doctors. For the first time, they claimed it should be dealt with by women on behalf

* Not surprisingly, referrals to illegal abortionists by women who thought of themselves as engaging in civil disobedience created no little consternation among the illegal abortionists themselves. These women engaged in "white glove" inspections of the illegal clinics, urged women to report back to them about how they had been treated, and were scandalized by offers of kickbacks. For abortionists who had grown accustomed to living outside the law, this intrusion of high-minded supervision was unsettling.

of women. It is true, of course, that since the early nineteenth century abortion opponents had claimed that women were wont to band together in a feminine conspiracy to pass on abortion information behind the backs of men and "moral" society. But the women in SHA were a far cry from the stereotype of Victorian women passing on abortion secrets behind closed doors. They and their scattered male supporters were not covertly conspiring to break laws that they accepted as fundamentally legitimate. In their own minds, they were much closer to their compatriots who had "sat in" in Alabama to protest Jim Crow laws or had marched on Washington to protest an unfair (but legal) draft. (Ironically, of course, one can see the women's movement on abortion as an attempt to move things closer to earlier nineteenth-century practice, when abortion was a private and domestic matter, rather than a public and social one.)

This stance was clearly revolutionary. Since the mid-nineteenth century, physicians had successfully argued that abortion was such a weighty decision that only a professional, a doctor, could be trusted to handle it "objectively." In the 1960s women began to claim that no man (including most physicians of the time) could make an "objective" decision on abortion, and, further, only the woman herself could legitimately decide whether or not an abortion was "necessary." A new era had begun.

SHA based its political (and moral) arguments on the assertion that there were *no* claims in the abortion situation that could compete with the claims of the pregnant woman. In other words, the interests of other parties were secondary compared with the interests of the woman involved, so secondary, indeed, that they had no right to be formally represented in any decision-making procedure. SHA acknowledged that there might be times when the abortion decision entailed the weighing of competing interests but insisted that only the woman herself was entitled to do the weighing. According to its logic, any abortion law whatsoever (except for minor regulations of the kind surrounding any surgical procedure) would be inherently unfair. For if the interests of the woman herself were so compelling that only she was the legitimate judge of what was the right decision in the situation, who needed laws?

It could be argued that all this is simply a complicated way of restating the slogan that "women have a right to their own bodies." But that argument overlooks precisely what is most important about the situation. Until SHA was organized, women seemed willing to live with a situation in which their right to control their own bodies was defined as only one of several competing rights, such as the rights of a husband (or whoever was the father of the embryo), the right of the state to regulate sexual morality by regulating the consequences of sexual intercourse, and the right of the state to control the production of potential citizens. It may very well be true that women were not happy about sharing their right to control their own bodies with various competing claims; but the interesting fact remains that until SHA was formed, they did not choose to exert organized political pressure on their own behalf. The abortion law reformers took it for granted that there were competing interests in the abortion decision and that some regulation of these competing interests was necessary; they wanted the boundaries of the regulations drawn a little differently and, more to the point, more explicitly. Those who were active in SHA, however, denied that any legitimate competing interests existed and were therefore opposed in principle to any regulation.

Consciousness-Raising

What the Society for Humane Abortion was trying to do by its public speaking, leafletting, and abortion lectures can be summarized in the term "consciousness-raising." This term has become so familiar that it is easy to overlook its profound social and political implications. What it implies is that people can be made to experience as problematic events or situations which they had previously accepted without complaint. It carries within it the belief that it is not necessarily the objective conditions of life that cause people to make social change but an individual's *subjective* experience of those conditions. Moreover, it assumes that people's subjective assessments can be changed by exposing them to new information—by deliberately "raising their consciousness."

The actual process whereby women were able to raise the consciousness of other women about the legitimacy of laws on abortion, however, suggests that the interplay between objective conditions and subjective realities is considerably more complex than this rationalistic description would imply.

The fact is that the women who became active on abortion, whether in the reform movement *or* the repeal movement, did not become mobilized into political activity simply by being exposed to the objective problems associated with the traditional way of treating abortion in America. Rather, for every woman we interviewed, abortion activism was the result of having her "consciousness raised."

This process of consciousness-raising affected both those women who wanted reform (CCTA) and those who wanted repeal (SHA). We shall see that once the women in SHA, who wanted no abortion laws whatsoever, made the claim that women had a *right* to abortion, the two groups became less readily distinguishable from each other; it became more important that the women reformers were *women* than that they were *reformers*. Once exposed to the new definition of the issue, the reform women (in contrast to their male physician peers) became converted to the political goal of repeal.

This convergence could occur in part because women in both groups shared personal experiences with the problems of abortion. Indeed, illegal abortion had been a stark fact of their reproductive lives. Not all of them had experienced an illegal abortion themselves, but the twenty-one surviving women reform activists and the eight surviving women repeal activists reported thirty-four illegal abortions that they had had, were aware of, had participated in, or had arranged. Some were the abortions of friends, sisters, and mothers. Without a control group it would be difficult to tell if these women eventually became abortion activists because of their individual illegal experiences or because knowledge of illegal abortion was simply a "typical" part of the life of most women. In any event, two things are clear: illegal abortion was a fact of life for these particular women, and exposure to illegal abortion in itself had not been sufficient to mobilize them in an effort to change abortion laws.

A woman who later became a reform activist gave the following history of exposure to illegal abortion:

> My mother told me, as I was growing up, how in the 1920s she took women to illegal abortionists in New York, and that made a big impression on me. [In 1947] when I was a freshman in college, my roommate became pregnant . . . and needed to have an illegal abortion and I helped her through that to an extent, but not as much in retrospect as I would have liked.

Subsequently:

> [A few years later] my sister married a doctor who had this technique

for mechanical induction, which we used to give out to people, which consisted of riding a bicycle until exhaustion and taking purgatives and treacle enemas and quinine pills or something like that. . . . in my early twenties, I became pregnant myself. I was wearing a cervical cap which didn't work . . . so I started searching for an illegal abortionist myself, and that was quite a revealing experience.

This story, though more detailed (and more extended in time) than that of the average pro-abortion activist, was by no means unusual, as suggested by these reports from three different women:

In 1943, my father helped my sister get her first abortion. I'm really proud of my father. . . . He went to one of his business associates and said, "Look, I've gotten a woman pregnant, where can I get help?" because he didn't want to reveal who it was that he was helping. I always thought that took a lot of guts, because he's a very moral person, and in his whole married life I'm sure he never had an affair with anyone . . . although I'm sure he was a rather gay young blade before that.

I knew about abortions among friends and relatives. I knew that my father-in-law, who was a doctor, was often approached by others, because he was a very humane person, to make referrals. And he did, he had the names of responsible illegal abortionists. . . .

After I was married and had two children, I was using a method of birth control that my doctor had recommended, but it didn't work and I got pregnant again. I told him I didn't want to be pregnant. He was a general practitioner, and he said, "I can't do anything about it, but talk to my nurse." So I talked to his nurse—a very knowledgeable woman who'd been a supervisor in a local hospital for almost ten years and knew what was going on in the world—and she gave me the names of three doctors over the border.

Another woman active in the repeal movement recounted this experience, which took place when she was a young teenager during the latter years of the Depression:

[With] my first baby . . . I had a very, very hard labor, three days, and I could hear people coming into the room saying, "Is she dead yet?" Well, I didn't die, of course, but my little girl weighed five pounds and she was terribly jaundiced and her little head was mashed in and black from all that pounding on her, and so the doctor told me, after I left the hospital, not to have another baby. He said, "If you do, you'll die, you'll just never deliver another child." But he didn't tell me how not

> to . . . so of course without contraception, without any knowledge about what to do, in three months I was pregnant again. I went back to him and he was very, very rough with me, very annoyed, possibly because he hadn't been paid yet. That was back in the hard times. He said, "I told you not to get pregnant," and I said, "You didn't tell me how not to." And he said, "I don't know whether I can do anything for you or not, but I'll try to." So I went out of there and I was scared. I didn't know what to do, I had this tiny little bit of a baby, and nobody but me to take care of it, and you know, babies having babies is tough. I was working in a drugstore—and had already gone back to work from the other pregnancy—and I told one of the young women who worked in the tea room with me. She was older than I was, and she said, "Well, you can have an abortion." And I said, "How? Where?" She told me about a woman in Center City, outside of Hampton, a Cuban woman named Madame Anita, so I went out to see her and she said she would do it for fifty dollars.

Some women reported abortions where the issue of legality was carefully avoided:

> Just before I got married, I got pregnant again, and had an abortion with a gynecologist in Pacific City. My sister said, "If you want an abortion go to him and say this thing, and he'll do it." So I went to him and said I had had a miscarriage and that doctors in the city told me that if I continued to have some bleeding or other problems I should probably have a D & C [dilation and curettage]. So I went to this doctor and told him that, and he examined me, and since I was probably ten to twelve weeks pregnant, it would have been very obvious to him that I was pregnant. He had me come to his office on a Saturday morning and did a D & C, which was not customary. But we never talked about the fact that he was doing an abortion. He didn't and I didn't, though we both knew exactly what was happening.

Finally, even women in this group who did not have direct experience with illegal abortions reported being keenly aware of the problem. For example:

> I guess I was aware of it as a college student because there were illegal abortions that were within my ken at the time. Then I was aware of it in the 1950s, when I was living in Geneva, Switzerland, because women were coming from England to Geneva to get abortions because abortions were fairly available for a price in private clinics in Geneva. I was aware of the problems of decision and the agony a woman faced when she had an unwanted pregnancy.

What these stories demonstrate is the point made in Chapter Three, that it is hard to generalize about "illegal abortion in America." Depending on the era, the age of the woman involved, her social milieu, the experiences of her friends and relatives, and simple chance, arranging an illegal abortion could be either quite difficult or relatively easy. Note also the variety of abortion experiences that even this small group of people provides: there were self-induced abortions, abortions provided by physicians across the border, abortions provided by physicians under ambiguous circumstances, and abortions performed by openly nonmedical people such as Madame Anita.

The black market aspects of illegal abortion, combined with the fact that a pregnant woman seeking an abortion has only a very short period of time in which to find it, meant that it was hard to predict who would succeed in finding an abortion (and what kind). For example, a woman who was married to a physician was unsuccessful in her search for an illegal abortionist, although she was later able to find one for a friend. (Being the wife of a physician made her particularly fearful of using a nonmedical abortionist.) In contrast, a young college student reported relatively little trouble: "I had several friends helping me through it, it was definitely accepted; I think it was quite a big underground."

Given the fact that illegal abortions constituted a black market and black markets have difficulty forcing out unscrupulous or unskilled practitioners, the illegal abortions reported by those we interviewed were painful in every sense of the word. Here are two examples:

> I went over and she put a cervical pack in me. I guess we all know what cervical packs are now, but then I had no idea what she'd done. She was a kindly lady, a big, black motherly lady, and she said you go home and wait. Well, I was too scared and too young to ask any questions, so I went back to work and about three days later I was running a fever you wouldn't believe. It must have been 102, and I was just staggering around with pains in my tummy. . . . That evening we had a dinner engagement with my husband's older sister and I knew something was wrong, so I got up from the dinner table and went into her bathroom and sat down on the stool and had these terrible grinding pains and I looked down and saw some kind of little bony limb protruding out. Well, as the kids say now, I just freaked out. . . . I didn't really myself quite know what was happening, and I didn't have anything to work with, so I grabbed toilet paper and stuffed everything back up inside of myself like

> a tampax. I came out and grabbed my coat and put it around me and said, "I'm awfully sick and I have to go home." My husband said, "I'll take you," but I said, "No, you stay and have dinner, I'm going home." I went out and got a taxi. [The abortionist's house] wasn't too far from town, and I had just enough money to pay [the taxi driver] to the nickel. I went around to the side of the house in the dark and knocked on the door. She let me in, and I was crying and I was feverish. There was a little table there and she put me on it and said, "Now wait a minute and I'll take care of you." And she started working on me and I was crying and she came and I will remember this till the day I die, she came and put her arms around me on the table like that, and she said, "Honey, did you think it was so easy to be a woman?"

> At noon we went back [to the abortionist] and he told my husband to wait in the waiting room. I went with him through his office and we went out the back door of his office into this huge room—it was a big, empty warehouse. In one corner there was an examining table with a cupboard where his instruments were and a screen around it and a restroom in the corner. And he said to lie down on the table, and then he said, "Now you have to be very quiet because I can't have anyone in the neighborhood hear you scream." So, with no anesthesia, [and twelve weeks pregnant] I had a D & C. It seemed like it took forever. It hurt terribly. I bit my lip and clenched my fists; fortunately I have no fingernails, or I'm sure they would have gone right through my hands. It seemed like it would never end, and it was *terribly* painful. I suppose it took ten minutes, but it felt like two hours. When he finished he said to sit up . . . and he took the bucket and dumped it in the toilet and came back. And he gave me a teeny, teeny piece of paper with the name of an antibiotic written on it. "Now whatever you do, no matter if you start hemorrhaging or feel faint, no matter what happens, don't let anyone examine you on this side of the border. If you have a problem, go somewhere on the other side of the border." So, of course, I was sure I was going to start hemorrhaging any minute. That really scared me. So I went out and told my husband, and we got into the car. I can still see him sitting there with his knuckles white on the steering wheel and me sitting up looking healthy so no one would examine me. We didn't go to the pharmacy, we went back across the border and to our doctor. I didn't have any later problems, but that was an experience I don't want anyone to have to go through. It was humiliating, frightening. . . .

Remarkable as it may seem, none of these women became politically active—in either the reform or the repeal movement—as a direct result of their experiences with illegal abortion. They may have thought the situation was unfair, and they would have been among the first to say how painful the personal consequences of illegality were, but *none of them questioned the status quo*. Not one of them left her experience with illegal abortion vowing not to rest until such wicked and barbaric laws had been abolished. For example, the woman who found herself in the midst of miscarrying in the bathroom of her sister-in-law's house said:

> I was too young to realize it was a law, I just knew doctors wouldn't do it. I certainly wasn't politically motivated. I was too young and too ignorant to know about politics. I was saving my life and taking care of my [first] child. . . . If I died, who was going to take care of my baby? . . . But I didn't have a vendetta at that time, and I didn't say I'm going to rush out and fight this condition. I put it in the back of my memory, and I solved my problem with my husband by leaving him.

When asked if she still felt any outrage about her experience, she said: "Only with the doctor and his attitude."

A woman who spoke of her sister's abortion struck the same chord:

> At the time, I was thinking much more about [my sister]—what was her personal reaction, was her health all right, was there any danger that she wouldn't be able to bear children later—all those things which were much more personally oriented than politically oriented. [I didn't think] why don't they change those laws, or it's unfair that she had to go through this. I must have [thought] that's the way things are, and this is the way you have to do them—although I'm sure I was aware . . . that if you do something that's illegal, it can be dirty, it can be unsterile, it can be done by somebody who's not skillful, and so forth.

Still another woman, when asked if she thought it legitimate that there were laws against abortion at the time of her own illegal abortion, said:

> No, I wouldn't say I thought it was legitimate . . . but I don't think I was questioning. I mean that seems odd now, but I just wanted to get myself through, I wasn't looking at the big picture. . . . I have no recollection of being bitter in a feminist sense. . . . There wasn't this whole framework of understanding it—how wrong it was that [abortion] wasn't available.

All these comments make a similar point. These people, who later became so active in changing abortion laws, had considerable personal experience with illegal abortion in one way or another and had seen or suffered the experiences of the illegality of abortion, yet none of them was directly "radicalized" by the experience itself. For all of them, the issues surrounding illegal abortion had to do with their individual problems of getting through the maze of illegality rather than challenging the fact of that illegality itself. They worried about pragmatic things: getting killed or injured, being inadvertently sterilized, getting arrested, failing to find an abortionist, but *they did not question the legitimacy of the laws that had driven them into such a situation*. Virtually all of them had been directly confronted with what they saw as the evils of illegal abortion, yet their urge to right this wrong remained dormant until the 1960s when they had their consciousness raised. How can one account for this, given the vivid and painful nature of their experiences?

Women activists themselves often account for it by saying that they were too busy or that they didn't have the resources to challenge abortion laws. But this is not an entirely satisfying explanation. When the movement to change abortion laws actually occurred, it drew on the energies of busy people of all ages and occupations; it seems fair to say that given the right circumstances, people make the time and find the resources. These activists also suggest that they did not become involved earlier because abortion was not something that could be discussed in polite company. That is, because abortion was taboo, women found it hard to admit that they had had abortions, and therefore found it hard to talk about the issue, and therefore could not come up with a different definition of the situation. One activist made the point most clearly:

> I told my sister I was pregnant, and she's the one who told me [about getting an illegal abortion]. I had the feeling that she had probably had one, too, but we didn't talk about that. And that was part of the whole thing. What did women in the community do? Nobody talked about it. Each one of us thought that we were a separate little person who was the only one who had ever done such a thing.

But interestingly enough, the taboo on abortion seemed to be more connected with sexuality than with the problem of whether abortion implied the taking of a human life. We must remember that the public claim that the embryo had a right to life did not become a central part of the abortion debate until later, after women had begun to claim a *right* to abortion. The way in which the issue had been defined until then enabled these activists to make a subtle but important distinction:

> [Abortion was] illegal but not immoral. . . . I don't remember anyone raising that as an issue. It was dangerous, and you were a little outré to be looking around for one or talking about it; it was like an admission of sexuality, although I was married at the time. But I don't recall anyone saying you're killing a baby or anything like that.

Another said: "I don't think I ever had any moral feeling about abortion. . . . When I was growing up, you just didn't talk about it. Nobody talked about it. It just wasn't part of the conversation. It was a word you didn't say in public."

The association of abortion with sexuality, in a context where sexuality was tabooed, did the same thing on the popular level that the claim of "medical expertise" had done on the medical level: it obscured the latent philosophical conflict. As we have seen, some physicians thought that an embryo was a full human person and some did not, but the claims of medical decision-making about therapeutic abortion hid these differences of opinion from most people. Our interviews suggest that rules of "politeness" served the same function on the level of public attitudes. The women whose views we are examining in this chapter assumed that the embryo was only a potential person and that most people shared their values. In fact, many others disagreed. But since abortion was connected with sexuality (especially premarital sexuality) and public discussions of sexuality were taboo, these philosophical differences remained hidden.

What changed? The pro-abortion women we have been quoting tell us that they had previously thought of abortion only in personal terms—will I be hurt, will I be sterilized, can I find a "good, clean" illegal abortionist—rather than in political terms—women have a right to abortions. As one of them said, the present "framework of understanding" did not exist. But how did that framework emerge in the early 1960s? To borrow a phrase from later in the movement, how (and why) did "the personal become political"?

The Social Sources of Abortion Activism

There seem to have been several interlocking reasons why these women came to redefine their own experiences in a way that made the claim of a right to abortion seem obvious to them. First, there were changes in the social situation concerning abortion in the 1960s. Second, there were people, like the founders of SHA, who encouraged public discussion of abortion in a new language, the language of women's rights. Third, and perhaps most subtly, there were structural factors in these women's lives which made them especially receptive to this new language of rights.

Changes in the social situation

The way was paved for a new era in the abortion debate as soon as physicians began to disagree among themselves about abortion. Once there came to be an obvious difference of opinion among physicians about the moral status of abortion rather than the technical grounds for it, the control of abortion was open to new claims. It is not surprising that after one group of physicians (the "broad constructionists") asked state legislature to make *some* changes in the law, other interest groups were encouraged to press their demands. In other words, it is conceivable that the public movement on abortion might never have been successful had physicians not sought to amend the law that gave them the right to control abortion in the first place. Had the medical profession been able to maintain its consensus that abortion was an appropriate enterprise for physicians (and only physicians) and had it not sought legal sanction for one interpretation of the law, nonprofessionals might have had little luck with their claim that abortion was a *woman*'s right.

Perhaps the point can be made in yet another way, by comparing the success of the abortion reform activists with the relative failure of those who claim that control over the experience of childbirth is a woman's right. Despite considerable public discussion by feminists about the need for women to seize control of labor and delivery, the fact remains that for the overwhelming majority of pregnancies, physicians have the upper hand when it comes to decision-making.[4] Managing pregnancy, birth, and delivery continues to be almost unanimously claimed by the medical profession as a *technical* enterprise. However much the physician may wish to please a pregnant woman, the physician can still claim to be the possessor of technical information beyond the ken of the lay person and must therefore be the ultimate decision-maker "for the patient's own good."

Thus before abortion could become a "women's issue," the medical profession had to give up or lose its claim to technical control over abortion. As soon as some physicians were willing to publicly criticize the practice of colleagues on grounds of principle, the legitimate control over abortion by physicians was at an end, and the field was cleared for new contenders.

Ideological forces

This was the context in which the activities of the women in SHA became so important. The rhetoric of liberal physicians in support of the Beilenson bill was a signal to interested groups that physicians were no longer in agreement about their control over abortion and that there was room for change. However much women as a group may have wanted to seek control over abortion, they were largely without influence until they took up the new tactics introduced by groups like SHA across the United States: civil disobedience, public speaking to any group that would listen, and, most important, use of the rhetoric that women had a right to abortion. These tactics transformed the debate. Now women who wanted abortions were no longer victims, a less-than-legitimate group of rule breakers who wanted the rules changed simply because they had "gotten caught." Rather, they were women who were crusading for a basic civil right—the right of a woman to "own the flesh she stands in," as one of them had put it.

It was of central importance that by the time physicians began to visibly relinquish their control over abortion, SHA's "consciousness-raising" activities throughout the state had created a group of women ready to accept a new "definition of the situation." They were no longer interested in simply expanding the legal grounds on which doctors could perform abortions. They wanted to make women, not doctors, the ultimate decision-makers about abortion.

Structural forces

As we have noted, state legislators active in 1967 did not see the claim that abortion is a woman's right as particularly relevant to the debate surrounding California's new abortion law. How did this claim become such a central part of the debate? Why did increasing numbers of women (and men) come to accept it?

To explore this question, it will be necessary to go outside the interviews and examine some large-scale structural forces in American society that were changing profoundly at this time. Once we understand these changes, it will be possible to understand the revolutionary claim that women were making: that women, not physicians, are the only legitimate and appropriate decision-makers on abortion.

Examining these large-scale structural changes is necessary because most pro-choice women we interviewed found the idea that women have a right to abortion so obvious—once they encountered it—that they could not imagine ever having thought otherwise. But as shown earlier, they all did: they all had some kind of experience with illegal abortion, and they did not think it obvious that free legal abortion was their right; they merely worried about getting killed, arrested, or inadvertently sterilized. They lacked what one of them called "a framework of understanding."

Several social changes have been stereotyped as "reasons" for both "the women's movement" and its support of the repeal of all abortion laws. There is some truth in each of them—but only some. For example, a "sexual revolution" is often said to have given rise to both feminism in general and support for abortion in particular. It is true that sexual mores were changing in this period and that more women were having sex before marriage. But it is also true that premarital sex had been increasing for almost a century and that this period saw only an acceleration of a trend.*

By the same token, it is often argued that the birth control pill is responsible for much of the women's rights movement. It is true that the pill had become the most commonly used marital contraceptive by 1965, and it had probably become a favorite method of birth control among unmarried women as well.[5] The pill (and later the IUD) gave American women, for the first time, a highly effective birth control method that could be used outside the context of sexual intercourse. There are no formal studies on the matter, but the existence of a form of birth control that permitted women to approach sexual encounters with almost the same degree of sexual freedom as men cannot be underestimated. On the other hand, we must remember that the found-

* The Kinsey Report showed that the following percentages of women had had premarital sex by age twenty: 8 percent in 1920; 18 percent in 1920–1929; 25 percent in 1930–1939; 21 percent in 1940–1949 (computed from Alfred Kinsey, *Sexual Behavior in the Human Female*, Table 84). By comparison, Zelnick and Kantner found 46 percent of teenaged women they surveyed in 1976 had been premaritally sexually active.

ers of SHA had begun to argue for women's rights to abortion by 1961, long before use of the pill had become widespread.

Perhaps the pill played a more indirect role in encouraging support for abortion. Mariano Requena has found that in Latin America the introduction of more effective contraception led to an *increase* in the abortion rate. He argues that after couples have made a commitment to lower fertility, they are less willing to tolerate mistakes when they occur. In the United States, therefore, one could assume that the availability of the pill—a virtually 100 percent effective contraceptive—would have created a population of people who had made important life commitments that depended on very high levels of fertility control.[6] But many of the highly educated women who joined the movement against abortion laws were diaphragm users, and the pill is only marginally more effective than the diaphragm when the latter is used conscientiously.* (Of course, a very small change in effectiveness may mean a very large change in psychic state if the change represents the difference between getting pregnant or not.) Thus the pill itself may have had some subtle role in encouraging support for abortions, but it seems unlikely that it was directly responsible for the fervor—and the moral claims—that women brought to the debate in favor of abortion.

Finally, it is sometimes argued that the 1960s and 1970s provided a uniquely hospitable climate for intense social arousal and mobilization in all sorts of causes, and the pro-choice cause was only one of them. As the civil rights movement, the antiwar movement, the women's movement, and the gay liberation movement suggest, the "climate" for social change was indeed favorable.[7] But once women became mobilized as an interest group, the fact that the climate was favorable to political mobilization does not explain why they chose to make the right to abortion a central claim.

The right to abortion, after all, was not always a central tenet of the feminist movement. Indeed, such a definition of it is relatively recent. As noted in Chapter Two, women in the "first wave" of feminism, the women's suffrage movement, did not make this claim, even though the practice of abortion was part of the social setting of the period. (By the

* The diaphragm when used with spermicidal jelly has an estimated 2–3 percent failure rate; the pill has a method failure rate of 0 percent and a user failure rate of 2 percent. Thus, moving from a consistently used diaphragm to the pill would not have meant a major *statistical* change in the risk of pregnancy. See *Family Planning Handbook for Doctors* (London: International Planned Parenthood Federation, 1974); and Jones and Jones, *Novak's Textbook of Gynecology*.

same token—and improbable as it may seem to those not actively involved in the present-day abortion debate—a relatively small group called Feminists for Life now argues that abortion is opposed to everything feminism stands for, especially the championing of the rights of the weak and socially dispossessed, including the embryo.) Although many people may believe that belief in the right to abortion is an intrinsic part of feminism, the genesis of such a belief needs to be explained.

The reasons why so many women took up the language of women's rights, and eventually insisted on nothing less than abortion on demand, may be found in certain profound and even revolutionary structural changes that American women as a group faced in the 1960s and 1970s. Before that time, American society, like most others, expected adult men and women to play distinctly different roles. Men were expected to work in the paid labor force for most of their adult lives, and women were expected to devote their adult years to the care and nurturance of a family. Even as recently as 1950, a major textbook on marriage and the family noted that although it was very difficult to predict what a man would be doing at the age of twenty-four, one could predict what a woman would be doing at that age with virtual certainty. It could be argued that this was not only a *description* but a *prescription* as well. Not only did women spend most of their adult energies raising a family rather than pursuing paid employment; this pattern was thought to be congruent with, and supportive of, a set of intrinsically female skills and preferences.

Of course, women have always been part of the paid labor force. Poor women and women of color have rarely had the luxury of being able to devote their energies to full-time family care, whatever the cultural expectations. Equally significant, large numbers of women (at least in this century) have made paid labor an adjunct to their primary role of wife and mother; they have worked before the first child is born and again after the last child is in school or has left the home. This has been called the "M-shaped" pattern: when graphed against age, women's employment peaks in the years before active childbearing starts, declines during the middle years of active family life, and increases again as children become older.[8]

This pattern, however, makes visually clear the fact that until recently, employment in a paying job was very much an adjunct to what was seen as women's primary (i.e., family) role. In fact, the structure of the labor market and the kinds of jobs in which women worked served to strengthen that traditional division of expectations about appropriate gender roles. It is generally conceded that the labor market in America is "sex segregated": women work in women's jobs and men work in men's jobs, and there is relatively little movement between the two. For example, Edward Gross, using an index originally developed to measure racial segregation, found that two-thirds of all women would have to change jobs in order to establish a sexually integrated work force. Contrary to popular expectation, he found that this index of segregation remained relatively stable between 1900 and 1960 and that most movement was accounted for by men going into what had traditionally been women's work (e.g., nursing). Abbot Ferriss, using a slight variation in technique, found virtually identical results.[9]

The segregation of jobs according to gender (into a "segmented" or "dual" labor market) is a product and to some extent a cause of traditional conceptions of women's roles. The majority of women work in certain well-defined (and largely female) sectors of the labor market.* The jobs women hold, when examined in detail, tend to have similar features in common. On the whole, they are easy to enter, and long years of preparation are not required to gain the necessary skills. For example, it is possible to become a "diploma" nurse within two years after high school (by receiving an A.A. degree, instead of the B.A. and R.N. degrees) whereas physicians need at least eight and sometimes twelve post–high school years to attain their skills. By the same token, these jobs are easy to reenter. The skills needed to be a nuclear physicist deteriorate dramatically over time, but the skills needed to be an elementary school teacher do not. Thus, women who plan to (and are expected to) spend a good part of their adult lives raising children find the easy entry and reentry of women's jobs congruent with their life patterns. Because they are congruent with raising a family, they are seen as "good jobs for a woman"; women have been encouraged to prepare for them and discouraged from preparing for and entering the kinds of "men's jobs" that are less congruent with a family life.

However, the same features that make women's jobs attractive to people for whom paid employment is secondary to family life also

* Victor Fuchs writes: "When sex differentials across occupations are examined, one of the striking findings is how few occupations employ large numbers of both sexes. Most men work in occupations which employ few women, and a significant fraction of women work in occupations which employ very few men" ("Differentials in Hourly Earnings Between Men and Women," pp. 10–14).

make them unattractive to people who would choose to make a career out of them. Entry into these jobs is easy because relatively little preparation is called for, and the kinds of skills needed are relatively diffused throughout the population. But precisely because entry is so easy, the pay in these jobs is relatively low.[10] Similarly, although reentry is easy because there is little build-up of skills over time (or stated conversely, people who leave the job for a number of years do not get hopelessly "rusty"), those who stay on the job do not find themselves with a significant build-up of skills which then increases their worth and thus their pay. A schoolteacher (or a nurse, or a clerical worker) who has been on the job for ten years does not as a rule receive the relative increase in income that a doctor or a lawyer receives over that time. Put another way, by the age of thirty-five the average woman is earning as much as she ever will whereas the average man's income increases throughout his fifties.[11] Similarly, "women's jobs" tend not to have much in the way of seniority, and what there is is often system-specific: if a woman changes jobs, she must often start again at the bottom. Women making life decisions in the 1950s and 1960s were therefore faced with the prospect of low-paid, lower-status, and low-prospect jobs, which were acceptable as interim roles but were less gratifying as a primary role. Conversely, those few women who wanted to enter careers in law, medicine, or science were often warned that they would have to give up the prospects of marriage and a family. The structure of the segregated labor market met the needs of women who accepted the traditional role of wife and mother, and it worked to sustain that role.

The 1960s and 1970s brought dramatic changes in this traditional pattern.[12] First, more women went to work. In 1950 women made up 29.6 percent of the paid workforce, but in 1960, they made up 33.4 percent and in 1970, 38.1 percent. (By 1981 the figure had risen to 43 percent.) Even these figures understate the amount of change. Differences in age distribution tend to dilute the very real changes in women's work patterns. For example, in 1970, 43.3 percent of all women over sixteen years of age were in the paid workforce, and between the peak working ages of twenty-five and forty-four, women's participation had become increasingly close to that of men. By 1979, 64 percent of all women in that age group worked, compared with 77 percent of all men.[13] Moreover, women in this period began increasingly to combine motherhood and careers. The birth of the first child, which traditionally had signaled a woman's withdrawal from the workforce, did so no longer. Women with children under six, who were traditionally *least* likely to work, showed the greatest gains.[14]

At least three other changes in this traditional intermeshing occurred during the 1960s and 1970s. First, the period after 1960 saw a dramatic decline in the marriage rate. When standardized for age, women aged twenty to twenty-four were 3 percent less likely to be married in 1965 than they were in 1960. And the trend accelerated in the 1970s: by 1975, women twenty to twenty-four were 12 percent less likely to be married than similar women were in 1960.[15] This may in part have been due to the process already examined: the expansion of women's jobs could lead individual women to take more time before deciding to marry. But the combination of an increase in women's jobs and a growing number of women who were not married at the "traditional" time forced at least some women to be increasingly skeptical about the chances of the "right man" coming along. Second, the steady increase in divorce during this period meant that there were increasing numbers of women who had to work to support themselves and their children.[16] (Various studies suggest that alimony and child support payments are seldom sufficient to support a woman and her children and that few men continue to make such payments consistently anyway.)[17]

Finally, as family sizes began to decline, women were increasingly faced with long periods of time after the period of active childrearing had ended. As the American family moved toward the norm of two children, spaced two years apart, women found themselves engaged in full-time parenting for only a maximum of eight years from the birth of the first child until the time when both children could be expected to spend much of the day in school. As life expectancies increased, an average, healthy American woman who had her first child in her early twenties could expect to face a half-century in which her role as a wife and mother was far from a full-time activity.[18]

As a result, many women with jobs had both personal and structural reasons to question the traditional assumption that paid work was something women did only as an adjunct to the "real work" of having a family. And public opinion followed. In 1960 there was widespread popular condemnation of the working woman and, in particular, the working mother; by 1975 there was a great deal of public acceptance.[19] (One might speculate that the ability of the labor market to draw married women with children into it was a critical factor in changing public opinion. Single and divorced women could be thought of as working because they had to, and they could be pitied for having failed at the task of making a family. Their employment did not fundamentally challenge cultural assumptions about women's roles in the ways that working married women and working mothers did.)

When at least certain sectors of the female working population began to accept and enjoy the expectation that work would be a central part of their adult lives, it is not surprising that they found much to disturb them. As noted, the features that made "women's work" attractive when viewed as an adjunct to wifehood and motherhood made it quite unattractive when viewed as a core part of life. Suddenly the segregation, low pay, lack of job security, inability to advance on the job, and general low status of women's jobs came to seem profoundly unjust. This feeling must have been especially keen for college-educated women. In 1950 men were awarded three "first-level" degrees (a bachelor's degree or five-year first professional degree) for every one awarded to women; by 1960, this figure had dropped to 1.8 degrees awarded to men for every one awarded to women.[20] As a result, some groups of women in the labor market had "human capital" skills approaching those of their male counterparts.

Consequently, during the 1960s more and more women found themselves in a position to question the meaning of work in their lives. At least some of them had skills and training equal to those of their male colleagues and were thus in a position to challenge the idea that men's jobs deserved better pay and were more attractive because men were more qualified. For those who were considering the prospect of working for most of their lives, this meant a revolution in the way they thought about work. This was particularly true of the women activists we interviewed. All but two of the twenty-one reform activists and all but one of the eight repeal activists were full-time workers for considerable portions of their lives and as a group valued their work experiences highly.

Given the analysis made so far, it is not surprising that abortion was a major focus, if not the single most important one, around which these women became militant. As the traditional intermeshing of women's paid employment and family activities began to break down, women found themselves segregated in what were now seen as relatively unattractive jobs or denied opportunities for rewards or advancement *be-*

cause they were mothers or potential mothers. When they began to compare themselves with men who had roughly similar "human capital" advantages, they found they were paying a very high price for being women.

The mobilization of significant numbers of women around the issue of abortion laws can therefore be seen as an attack on a symbolic linchpin that held together a complicated set of assumptions about who women were, what their roles in life should be, what kinds of jobs they should take in the paid labor force, and how those jobs should be rewarded. "Equal pay for equal work" was already a revolutionary demand in this context, but until women could get equal work, even this demand was irrelevant. And women could not get equal work until they could challenge the assumption that their work activities were, or ought to be, or might be subordinated to family plans. Since significant numbers of women were *already* combining work and family, the idea that they should pay a large economic penalty for being women with family obligations came to seem fundamentally unfair.

A Theory of Abortion Mobilization

It is in this context that we can understand what women activists meant when they claimed that they had a *right* to their own bodies. As they came to expect to work much or most of their adult lives, just as men did, an unplanned pregnancy came to be seen as a tragedy. And for men, or the state, or physicians to have control over whether pregnancy would take place—and for women to suffer alone the consequences that decision would have for their careers, or education, or social status—came to seem eminently wrong and cruelly oppressive.

When women accepted the definition that a woman's primary role was as wife and mother, control of one's own body meant little. When the biological workings of one's body and one's social status (or intended social status) are congruent, who needs control? In everyday terms, if one's role in life is to be a mother, it is not such a problem that one's biology often seems singlemindedly bent on producing children. But when some groups of women began to think of themselves as having a different primary role in life, the brute facts of biology came to seem at odds with how they saw themselves. Once they had choices about life roles, they came to feel that they had *a right to use abortion in order to control their own lives*.

Thus one activist said:

> If I hadn't had that abortion early in my life, my life would have been a disaster. I never would have gotten to medical school. I was married at that point to a very ill man, and it would have just been terrible to have a baby. So many times I've heard similar stories from people. I mean, people who need abortions are frequently in some sort of turmoil, and it's really a life-saving thing for many people. . . . Women are manipulated to have babies or not have babies by the needs of the state, and I have a lot of pent-up emotion about that.

Another woman, a reformer (who still subscribes to the remnants of physician control over abortion), articulated the same theme:

> For women to achieve any kind of equality in the employment market requires acceptance by society that they are in control of their reproductive lives. . . . Legalized abortion, the right of every woman to have an abortion, given a reason that her doctor concurs with, is certainly a factor in freeing women from the blanket accusation that they're going to be divided in their loyalty to their career because they're going to have children. I think they're free to have children anyway, but I think the attitude is different to some extent.

One of the earliest activists in favor of repeal made the point most directly:

> I started in 1963. I was interested in doing a book for young women, perhaps sophomores in high school. I wanted to explain to them what I could see, and what everyone else our age can see—that they would not live the ideal dream life of getting married and having the house with the fence around it and the two or three children and the man who would take care of them forever. I wanted to [urge them to] finish their education and prepare themselves to take care of themselves, by work or whatever. . . . I know that most young women will have to work sometime during their lives, and I felt that a little book slanted toward them at this time in their lives might be more effective in making them understand [this]. . . . Anyhow, when I researched this business of how we could prepare young women—in other words, even get a scholarship for young women—we were being blocked at every turn. . . . They would say, "Oh, she's only going to get married and have babies."

A happily married Catholic woman with a small child, who joined the movement in 1970, is typical of how the message of rights was heard by the wider public after 1967. Unlike earlier activists, she never had any direct experience with abortion (although she did distress her conservative Catholic family by using birth control), but as a working woman the message of the movement made sense to her. (Note incidentally the point at which she unconsciously switches from using the term "they" to "we" when speaking of women.)

> I went to this meeting where women spoke about having children. I had a lot of thoughts about the role of having children, about how having children should be your choice. I was trying to figure out how women got into the position they were in, and what were some of the main points that kept women in what I think was a very bad situation—by themselves, isolated, in these little houses with their children, with no educational opportunities, no jobs. And a lot of it seemed to me to focus around the having children aspect of it—having children at times when they weren't prepared to have them, in the middle of going to school, whatever. And maybe abortion was just one more aspect of that. [I was] beginning to think that if we actually decided ourselves when and where we were going to have children, that would be a big step toward taking some kind of charge. . . .

Thus the "framework of understanding" that SHA proposed was well suited to the changing social situations of significant numbers of American women. As one early activist put it: "I was alone at first, but every time I gave a speech I was no longer alone because people came from everywhere saying, 'You've said what I felt, but I didn't know how to say it.' "

If this group had simply wanted access to abortion, that is, if their needs had been simply pragmatic, it is unlikely that they would have continued to agitate for abortion repeal. On the contrary, in California, within a year or two of the passage of the Beilenson bill, 99 percent of the "demand" for abortions was being satisfied. The fact that this constituency continued to organize against any legal restrictions on abortion, in the face of a law that in practice permitted "abortion on demand," indicates that abortion laws had assumed a position of great symbolic importance in the new political and social landscape created by the expanded activities of women in the labor market.

The demand for repeal of all abortion laws was an attack on both the segregated labor market and the cultural expectations about women's roles. It allowed women to argue (and symbolically demonstrate) that although childbearing was important, it was not the single most important thing in a woman's life. And by asserting the right of women to control fertility, it vitiated the arguments of employers that only certain jobs were "good for a woman." Once women obtained control of their fertility, it would become clear that the labor market discriminated against them simply because they were women. In a society that had recently experienced a nationwide upheaval over civil rights, such discrimination would be difficult to justify.[21] With the control over fertility in their own hands, even this ground would be disqualified.

Many women, therefore, believed that simply reforming abortion laws was no solution. From their point of view, the only difference between men and women who worked over a lifetime was that women got pregnant and paid very high "opportunity costs" for their pregnancies. Since the structure of the situation meant that men did not generally have to share such costs, the interests of men and women became polarized; many women became skeptical about the ability of mostly male physicians on therapeutic abortion boards to fully appreciate what having a child could mean to a woman. More to the point, the structural necessity of having someone else make the decision about abortion meant that both symbolically and practically, traditional women's roles could be upheld. Symbolically, reform laws supported the idea that childbearing was of such great social importance that the state and the father of the embryo were entitled to have a voice in abortion. In practical terms, women could be denied opportunities that were open to men simply on the ground that they might become pregnant. However remote such chances actually were—with the pill (and later the IUD) and a reform law that granted 99 percent of all requests—the mere fact that pregnancy *might* occur served to make such discrimination legitimate.

The Radicalization of the Reformers

This social, political, and symbolic situation helps explain why most of the women who had originally supported *reform* were recruited in a remarkably short time to the "abortion-on-demand" position. Their conversion is most dramatically illustrated by a set of events that occurred almost immediately after the passage of the 1967 Beilenson bill, even before it began to be implemented as law.

As we noted in Chapter Four, when the bill (modeled on the American Law Institute's Model Penal Code) was sent to Governor Reagan, he threatened to veto it unless the clause permitting abortion for fetal indications was dropped. That clause was objectionable to what was later to become the pro-life constituency because it would have written into law one of the contested meanings of the embryo—that it is a "fetus" whose existence can be ended for its own good. The pro-life forces, who believed that the embryo is a person (or virtually a person), were nevertheless willing to accept a law that permitted the embryo's life to be ended when necessary to preserve the life or even the health of the mother. The bill's sponsor dropped the clause, and Governor Reagan signed the bill in a pragmatic compromise: the reform movement, now representing a broad segment of public opinion, would get its liberalized law, but that law would not employ a definition of the embryo that was basically offensive to another segment of society.

Our interviews indicate that physicians, for their part, felt they could live with this compromise. Having been given legal permission to perform abortions to protect the mental health of the woman, many of them believed they could safely perform abortions for fetal indications on the grounds of maternal mental health rather than "eugenic" considerations relating to the embryo. The reform women we interviewed were also prepared to accept the law as the best they could get at the moment.

But unlike the physicians, the women reformers were not willing to stop there. The logic of the argument made by the women in SHA, that women had a right to abortion, had by this time become persuasive to them as well. Their consciousness, as it were, had been raised. The fact that Governor Reagan had been willing to "water down" the bill in order to appease anti-abortion groups suggested that they could not rely on a largely male medical establishment to do what was necessary. Thus, even before they had a chance to see how the new law would work in practice, these reform women—a professional elite who had worked closely with their male physician peers—embraced a tactic that would have been unthinkable a few years earlier. They took up civil disobedience. With money left over from a grant given to the original reform group (CCTA), they borrowed SHA's list of trustworthy illegal abortionists and began to set up a referral system.

The actual design of this referral system was important. Letters were sent out to members of the clergy inviting them to become active in a new organization, which would talk to women who wanted abortions, helping them to decide whether abortion was the right decision for them, and in appropriate cases advising them of the best and safest way to obtain an illegal abortion. Significantly, this new organization did almost all of what was now called "problem pregnancy counseling" inside churches.

It is important to understand the full meaning of this new turn of events. First, it meant that reform women were now more conscious of being *women* than of being *reformers*. When they were confronted with a legal compromise that maintained certain limits on women's rights to abortion, they clearly understood that the new law would not work in the way they had intended it to. Next, the strategy of including the clergy as allies suggests that reform women had accepted SHA's argument that abortion was a *moral* right, the right of a woman to own her own body. Thus, liberal clergy—who had already been active in the civil rights movement, the "war on poverty," and anti-war activities—now gave their stamp of approval to the pursuit of abortion rights as a moral enterprise. Interviews and documentary evidence show that well over a hundred clergymen (and women) of various denominations throughout the state were willing to be publicly identified with the abortion counseling group. Furthermore, many churches passed resolutions in support of women's right to abortion. The Episcopalians, the United Church of Christ, the United Methodist church, and the United Presbyterian church, among others, voted to take a public stand in favor of the right of a woman to have an abortion.[22] Thus, the moral right of a woman to have an abortion was officially sanctioned in some denominations.

For many women, the original decision to support reform rather than repeal had been made on tactical rather than ideological grounds. They agreed in principle with the argument for repeal, but perhaps because they had become professionals in the "man's world" of the professions of the 1940s and 1950s, they were pessimistic about how far the state legislature would go. Many of the male abortion reformers supported in principle a mediated decision that took women's interests into account along with a number of other interests; the women reformers wanted no laws at all on abortion but believed that total repeal was politically unlikely. Also, their gender experiences had been filtered through their social status: their similarities with the professionals who would make up the proposed therapeutic abortion boards predisposed them to believe that the boards would work in acceptable ways. They were willing to settle for half a loaf and were often surprised that the movement for repeal took off as fast as it did:

> Well, I would have liked something . . . more along the lines of what finally happened, which was the legalization of abortion. But I didn't think it was politically feasible. I thought this was all that was possible, and in fact I was really quite delighted when the Beilenson bill was passed because it opened up the whole situation for the very first time in a whole century, and it proved to be right. What astonished me was the rapidity with which the educational effort snowballed through the country and how wide the sections of the public [were] that took up this issue. . . . I was frankly astonished when four states repealed their laws.

Significantly, most of the male abortion law reformers (who were physicians) were either unaware of the activities of the repeal faction (most notably SHA) or actively condemned it as a "lunatic fringe." The women reformers, in contrast, not only supported SHA but thought its role was an important one:

> Nothing [that SHA did] was really in poor taste, nothing was done that was against the law or against the rights of citizens to petition their government for change, but it . . . was a more activist group in some ways than our group. We felt we were probably more constructive, but we didn't condemn them. Some people thought they hurt the movement, but I don't think so.

> No, they weren't troublemakers. I think [the founder] was an initiator, not a troublemaker. Sure, troublemaking goes with it, but I'm grateful. We have to have an extreme in order for moderation to make historical changes. I respect them. Politically, and also in other things.

It is in a broad sociological and historical context, then, that one must understand the recent claims that women have made for the right to control their own bodies. From time immemorial, children had been central to the society at large and to the kinship networks in which children played a vital role. Until the modern era, a child usually represented a concrete investment in the future—as a potential "marker" in marital alliances that could extend the resources available to the larger kinship network and as an active producer within the nuclear family at an early age. Where no centralized state existed, a large number of healthy sons had assumed important police functions, and both sons and daughters played important roles in supporting their parents in old age.[23]

It was only toward the end of the last century that the economic and social value of children—and hence their numbers—declined. As children became increasingly excluded from the labor force and simultaneously expected to spend large parts of their childhood in school, the economic value of children declined and their emotional value increased. Parents in virtually all urban, industrialized countries chose to have fewer children and to invest more resources—both economic and emotional—in each individual child. These events were the background against which the American birth rate, with the help of abortion, declined from an average of more than seven children per couple in 1800 to just over three in 1900. And these factors undoubtedly account for the very visible presence of abortion in the nineteenth century.[24]

The mobilization of certain women against abortion laws in the 1960s can be seen as the next step in this historical process. In the twentieth century the value of children as economic producers in the family continued to be low, and the forces that made children economically "costly"—their exclusion from the labor market and the extension of compulsory schooling—continued to expand. If the first abortion controversy was a reaction to the declining economic value of large families to nineteenth-century Americans, then the second abortion controversy can be seen as a reaction to the increasing economic cost of children to *women* in the twentieth century. When women wanted control of their own bodies, they wanted control over the number and, more important, the timing of their births because an untimely or unintended birth (or even the threat of one) could have dramatic consequences for their lives.

The control these women sought through abortion was a meaningful one given the changing context of their lives. Their concerns, when combined with the desire of physicians to perform the kinds of abortions they had traditionally done, free of "religious" or "outside" interference, grew into a compelling social movement. It was so compelling, in fact, that the U.S. Supreme Court agreed to hear arguments about the legality of nineteenth-century abortion laws in general. After hearing arguments for both sides, the Court found all abortion laws unconstitutionally vague. Although the Supreme Court's decision was a stunning judicial victory for the physicians who supported liberalized abortion and for the women we have described in this chapter, it gave birth to a new opposition, an opposition dedicated to making abortion as illegal as the first reformers had always assumed it was.

6

The Emergence of the Right-to-Life Movement

THE HEADLINES on Tuesday, January 22, 1973, were momentous. On the previous day former President Lyndon Baines Johnson had died of a heart attack in his Texas home. Peace negotiations in Paris were beginning to make the end of the war in Vietnam look almost possible. And in Washington, two landmark opinions delivered by the U.S. Supreme Court—*Roe* v. *Wade* and *Doe* v. *Bolton*—struck down all state abortion laws, not only the remaining nineteenth-century laws but also the new, liberal "reform" laws such as California's.*

For many of the anti-abortion people we interviewed, the 1973 Supreme Court decision came, as one of them put it, "like a bolt out of the blue." It seemed to them that the Court had suddenly and irrationally decided to undermine something basic in American life, and they were shocked and horrified. As one of them said: "I thought the American public would stand up and scream bloody murder, and they didn't. Even the Catholic bishops in this country didn't scream bloody murder—which is what abortion is."

* Both cases dealt with the constitutionality of abortion laws: the law challenged in *Roe* was a nineteenth-century Texas law of the kind described in Chapter Two; the law challenged in *Doe* was a 1968 Georgia law modeled, like California's 1967 law, on the American Law Institute's Model Penal Code. These two separate cases, handed down the same day, addressed different facets of the abortion issue and are thus usually referred to in the singular, as the Court's abortion decision.

Historically, of course, the Supreme Court decision on abortion was in no way sudden or unprecedented. It was the result of over a decade of political activity, during which sixteen states, including California, had passed greatly liberalized abortion laws. Still, there was a grain of truth in the pro-life perception that the abortion issue came to life for the first time on that Thursday morning in January of 1973. Although pro-choice activists had been struggling for just such a decision since at least 1961 and "abortion on demand" had for all practical purposes existed in California since 1971, the Supreme Court decision really did usher in a new era. Abortion was no longer a technical, medical matter controlled by professionals; it was now emphatically a public and *moral* issue of nationwide concern.

When the California Committee on Therapeutic Abortion (CCTA) and the Society for Humane Abortion (SHA) began to mobilize support for a liberalized abortion law in California, they attracted the attention of those who opposed abortion in principle. But the early activities of abortion opponents, who came to call themselves the right-to-life movement, were marked by failure. Despite their opposition, the Beilenson bill became law in California in 1967, and the law's passage was rapidly followed by dramatic changes in the frequency of legal abortions. On the federal level, opponents of abortion were unable to persuade the Supreme Court to uphold traditional abortion laws or even to put limits on the new "reform" laws. When we examine the early pro-life activists in California—who they were, where they were located socially, and how they understood the issue—the reasons for this almost unbroken string of failures prior to 1973 will become clearer.

Pre-1973 Recruits

Early activists, 1959 to 1967

In the course of our interviewing for this book, we spoke with eleven activists throughout the state who began their public opposition to abortion before the passage of the 1967 Beilenson bill.* Of these

* The pool of people likely to have become early anti-abortion activists was small to begin with. The early group we interviewed remember the core group as having been "a dozen or so." As might be imagined from a group of people who were middle-aged in 1967, the original group has dwindled owing to death. I am reasonably sure there are very few early pro-life activists in California who were not interviewed for this book.

eleven, nine were Catholic male professionals and one was a housewife active in conjunction with her husband, himself a Catholic male professional. Since those who favored abortion reform in these early years made much of the fact that their opponents were predominantly Catholic, it is important to clarify what we mean by "Catholic male professionals" and to explain why so many of them were recruited into this early group of activists. With a few minor exceptions, they had the following characteristics in common: they were physicians, lawyers, or other professionals; they were raised in the Catholic religion and remained active in their faith; they were members of Catholic voluntary associations such as the Catholic Physicians' Guild or the St. Thomas More Society; they had graduated from elite Catholic universities such as Notre Dame and Georgetown; and they tended to be affiliated in their work lives with institutions such as Catholic hospitals, law schools, and colleges. Moreover, they were all professionally successful, having been officers in their professional organizations, notably bar associations and county medical societies. In short, all were what might be thought of as "pillars" of their communities.

In this group of eleven activists, there were four lawyers, four physicians, one college professor, one scientist, and a housewife originally trained as a social worker. Only one of the eleven was not Catholic, and only one was a woman. Eight of them became involved in anti-abortion activity in a professional setting; typically, they were members of a bar association or county medical association that had been asked to support the Beilenson bill.

To these early activists, such a request for support was both unexpected and unsettling. From their point of view, an attempt to *broaden* the reasons for undertaking an abortion was simply baffling for several reasons. First, with the exception of the only non-Catholic in the group, all of them had grown up with the belief that an embryo is a child from conception onward and that abortion therefore ends the life of an innocent child. This belief was not an explicit or salient part of their upbringing; it was simply something they had always taken for granted. And because they took it for granted, they assumed that all decent and respectable people shared their point of view. In particular, they interpreted the relative social invisibility of abortion prior to the 1960s as proof that their opinion was the common one. And in a way, their assumption was plausible. If people didn't talk about abortion very much (or talked about it only in hushed tones in back rooms), wasn't that because most people believed it was the taking of an innocent life, hence morally repugnant? What these early pro-life activists did not understand was that for many people abortion was "unspeakable" not because it represented the death of a child but because it represented "getting caught" in the consequences of sexuality. Sex, not abortion, was what people didn't talk about.

When pro-choice activists began to press for a more "rational" treatment of abortion, that pressure was inexplicable to those with pro-life sympathies. They had made the mistake of assuming that other people's unwillingness to discuss abortion had been based on fundamental values that approximated their own, values that were part of the ordinary fabric of social life. Moreover, their very limited experience with abortion tended to confirm their views: other people seemed to *behave* as if they assumed that abortions were wrong. The one woman activist recalled that when she first heard of the Beilenson bill, her husband assured her that it would find no support in the medical profession: "I read in the newspaper that the legislation was being introduced, and I thought, My God. My husband is a physician, he's a family doctor and did a lot of obstetrics at that time. . . . He said, 'Oh, that will never go, doctors will never do that . . . in medical school, in our embryology class, we were shown why it was so brutally unethical.' "

Another early activist, a physician, made much the same point and called attention to the fact that in practice, at least in his own experience, opposition to abortion was not limited to physicians of his own religion:

> I think abortion is a horrible thing, it's killing your unborn child. When I went to medical school, that was the accepted view within the profession. . . . The respectable, acceptable view was that abortion was not something you did unless you really had a problem. . . . When I trained at the county hospital, the number of abortions per live births, I think was one in 10,000 or something like that; it was pretty rare. And what's more, the Seventh-Day Adventists were there, [and they] competed with the university service, which had a lot of Catholic obstetricians, to see who could do the fewest abortions. That was the challenge, to bring a woman through without needing to resort to this drastic thing.

These early pro-life activists reported very low levels of exposure to abortion. Most of them had no awareness of it until it became a political issue. The rest were aware of it only through rumors (a certain less-than-reputable physician was said to be the town abortionist). Even the physicians in this group knew little about the prevailing vagaries in medical interpretation of the abortion law, vagaries so graphically chronicled by Packer and Gampell in their 1959 *Stanford Law Review* article, which had started the whole debate. Partly this was due to their location in the social world: they were family doctors or obstetricians trained in either county or religious hospitals where they had not been exposed to alternate definitions of "justifiable" abortion. Further, as physicians raised in the Catholic faith and as active members of Catholic organizations, they were unlikely to enter those realms of practice in which abortion was common. (And as one of them said, abortion *was* acceptable "if you really had a problem." In other words, as long as abortion opponents believed there were some medical grounds for abortion, they were unwilling to challenge abortions undertaken by their colleagues "in good faith.")

These social factors created a situation in which the early activists were caught off guard. Their own values about the meaning of embryonic life, their own previous experience with the "immorality" of abortion, their own lack of exposure to the ambiguities that had motivated the pro-choice people to seek a more formal and explicit clarification of the law—all these combined to make them unprepared to cope with the movement to liberalize abortion.

Perhaps the most important reason why pro-life activists were not well prepared to resist abortion reform was that they simply couldn't believe such a movement would get very far. They tacitly assumed that the unsavory connotation of abortion rested on a deep belief in the sacredness of embryonic life, and they found it hard to understand how such a belief could be changed so quickly. They counted on public opinion to be outraged and were stunned when most of the public was either unaware or unconcerned.

This same tacit assumption made it difficult for them to rally those that shared their values. If "everyone knew" that abortion was the death of a baby, who could take the Beilenson bill seriously? At most, it would allow only a minor revision of the rules about when a physician could induce an abortion to save the mother's life. In principle, of course, pro-life people were opposed to any change from what they thought was absolute legal protection of the embryo (a protection only occasionally overlooked in order to save a woman's life). But, in practice, they felt they could live with minor adjustments that would give physicians a little more latitude in weighing one life against another. What was in fact the case—that one group of physicians saw themselves as weighing a "real" life against a "potential" life—was not yet part of their understanding.

Their belief that everyone accepted a common definition of the meaning and moral nature of abortion left these pro-life people with few arguments to use against the abortion reformers. They tried to appeal to what they thought was the commonly shared value, but when it turned out to be not so common after all, they were literally at a loss for words. One activist, a lawyer who resigned from the bar association when it awarded a prize to an essay in favor of abortion reform, noted: "Well, I don't exactly recall how I stated it, but the views that I communicated were that abortion took an innocent life, and that it was considered, and that I considered it wrong. I think I had a quotation from a papal encyclical in connection with it, and that's about all I remember about it." Once the abortion reformers had pointed out how broadly the actual letter of the law was being interpreted and once it proved difficult to rally public opinion, the early pro-life activists were stymied. The diverse and in some respects nonpartisan groups whose aid the pro-abortion forces were able to muster—including the Young Republicans and the Junior Chamber of Commerce—showed that there was real support for at least some reform of the existing law. The depth and breadth of that support must have been discouraging.

Thus far we have focused on the typical members of this early group of pro-life activists—the Catholic male professionals. It will now be worthwhile to examine the two atypical people as well: the one woman and the one male non-Catholic. Each represents a theme that would become far more salient in the next phase of the pro-life movement. Whereas the elite pro-life activists had focused their attention on fellow professionals and the state legislature—because, after all, that was where the issue was being contested—these two people had experiences that suggested a new direction for the movement, new "interested publics" ready for its message.[1]

The woman had joined the movement with her husband, a physician. Like the other early activists, she was a Catholic and had always assumed that abortion was wrong because it meant the taking of an innocent life. But, unlike the others, she had direct and personal reasons for finding the issue a troubling one:

> I had recently had a baby, at age forty I think, and you know they were talking an awful lot about [abortions]; a lot of the arguments were not only about rape and incest but [about] women, older women, and Down's syndrome babies, and this and that and the other thing, so it was very real to me, because my little guy was very much there [in utero], and all of these things together made me jump in with both feet.

The sole non-Catholic man was not a part of the social world of these other activists. Although he was not a Catholic, he later married a woman who was, and he did not meet the other early activists until he sought them out because of his feelings on the issue. Rather, because he found the idea of abortion so upsetting, he flew to Sacramento when the Beilenson bill was under discussion and handed out his own statement in opposition. Unlike the others in this group, until he became active in this issue he had been surrounded chiefly by people who favored abortion, and his larger social circle of family and friends supported liberalized abortion laws. Nonetheless, he found abortion profoundly disturbing for personal reasons:

> It was the late 1940s. I was nine, ten years old. Roughly it was the time of the war for the Israeli independence, and I was feeling very nationalistic, chauvinistic, whatever you want to call it. And the school I went to, they had a six- or seven-volume history of ancient Israel there. And I opened it up, and toward the beginning there was a discussion of the Canaanite culture, and here was this picture. I don't remember exactly, [but] I think what it was was a cross-section of a clay jar that they'd found in an excavation, and inside was a little kid with his skull cracked. And the caption saying that the Canaanites had practiced the sacrifice of the first-born male child. I'm a first-born male child. And I was aware, although the ramifications of course didn't sink into me then . . . that there was a ceremony when I was a month old, where my parents [symbolically] buy me back from . . . a Cohen, who's a representative of the ancient priesthood. Anyway, it was something that hit a nerve. At that time I didn't know what abortion was or anything. The only time I'd ever come across the word before that I can remember is in descriptions in the Hearst newspaper, the *Journal American* in New York, of the things Russian troops were doing in what's now East Germany. And I didn't know [the word] and I asked my folks to tell me, and they wouldn't tell me. . . . A few years later, apparently, when I first came across the concept of abortion, it was just this immediate, personal identification. [I thought] that's like what happened to the little boy in the jar, and that's what could have happened to me if things had worked out

differently historically or something like that. And so, just from the first time I became aware of what the concept meant, I was just violently opposed to it.

These quotations suggest that one's own experiences—either as a mother or as someone who could have been the victim of abortion "if things had worked out differently"—might be shared by "interested publics" much broader than professional elites. In the long run, appeals to these personal experiences would prove far more compelling than references to papal encyclicals.

The beginnings of organization, 1967 to 1972

The passage of the Beilenson bill was a dispiriting loss for the pro-life activists, but given their original definition of the issue, it was not a crushing one. As we have noted, because the clause permitting abortion for fetal indications was removed from the bill (after Governor Reagan's threatened veto), the new law did not explicitly violate the belief that the embryo was a person. It broadened the grounds upon which one life could be sacrificed for another, but without necessarily calling into question the absolute value of embryonic life. Many early activists decided, therefore, that it might be possible to prevent further liberalization by continuing to persuade people that abortion was wrong *in principle* because it took a life. The one woman activist among our eleven recalled the genesis of the first formal pro-life organization in the state in this way:

So in 1967 the legislation passed, and it was very depressing because we had done a very good job in Southern California . . . but Northern California lost it [for us]. . . . And Ronald Reagan signed it and that was that, everyone went home sad, but strangely enough . . . the debate continued. . . . The handful [of volunteers who remained active] decided by golly we were going to form an educational organization because there was a lot of interest in it. And the founding president, he was elected president [even though] he wasn't there, that's how excited we all were about the organization at the beginning. At any rate, [he] said . . . the reason we need this organization is that even if abortion is legal and even if what happens—and of course all the things he predicted happened, regarding the welfare and everything—it's still the decision of an individual, we're still in a free country and nobody's really making you submit to an abortion, so we said that, [if] we can educate people about the reality, the reality of life before birth, the humanity of the unborn child, we'll do a lot of good.

The actual situation regarding abortion changed rapidly after passage of the Beilenson bill. Both pro-life and pro-choice forces had underestimated the willingness of doctors to perform abortions and the eagerness of women to seek them. Consequently, by 1971, almost everyone who applied for an abortion was granted one. As abortion came to be offered, for all practical purposes, "on demand," it became integrated into everyday life. Blue Cross began to cover therapeutic abortions as a routine part of medical care, and Kaiser-Permanente, the state's largest health maintenance organization, did likewise. By the end of the 1960s abortion was officially covered as a routine medical procedure under Medi-Cal, the state of California's program of medical services for those on welfare.

This state of affairs gave new impetus to the movement to formalize the new status quo. For example, in its 1969 decision in *People* v. *Belous*, the California Supreme Court used language that raised doubts as to whether the state was willing to exercise *any* control over abortions so long as they were performed by licensed physicians. In rejecting as unconstitutionally vague the old California law (which in any case had been made moot by the passage of the Beilenson bill), the California court anticipated a number of arguments that the U.S. Supreme Court would make four years later. It held that the right to seek an abortion was covered by the right to privacy and that in deciding whether an abortion was "medically necessary" physicians could weigh the statistical risks of abortion against the statistical risks of childbirth.[2] Because statistically, early abortion carries fewer risks for the woman than childbirth, this decision was widely seen as signaling the unwillingness of the court to entertain complaints that individual physicians had overstepped the intended boundaries of the Beilenson Act.[3] With no consensus inside the medical profession about when abortions should be performed and the state's highest court apparently unwilling to try to regulate those decisions, the last remnants of the physicians' historical role as arbiters between the competing rights of women and embryos came quietly to an end. More truly than ever before, abortion became an individually negotiated decision between a woman and her physician.

Throughout the state during this period, several factors—the increasing number of abortions, their relatively uncomplicated acceptance into daily life, and the *Belous* decision formalizing what was in practice a very liberal abortion situation—served to bring new people into the pro-life cause. But although these factors enhanced the likelihood that a person with pro-life sympathies would encounter something distressing enough to cause him or her to become active, abortion was not yet a public issue for most people. Most of those mobilized between 1967 and the eve of the Supreme Court decision were still those who were *strategically placed* in the social world to notice the new abortion situation.

The backgrounds of the activists mobilized in this period, between the passage of the Beilenson bill of 1967 and the Supreme Court decision of 1973, make that clear. Like the earliest activists, many of them were people who worked in situations where they were likely to encounter some aspect of the abortion debate; they were physicians, social workers, or people who counseled unmarried pregnant women. The remainder were people who might be described as having accidentally "bumped into" the abortion debate. Let us consider what some of them had to say about their activities.

One of them was a college professor whose interest in population made him aware of the emerging debate:

> Well, I had been a little taken aback, actually dismayed [in 1967] when California passed the law that would allow abortion for a woman's mental health. And like most people, I didn't do much about it in terms of protesting. But in 1970, Senator Beilenson tried to pass a law in California which would knock down all the restrictions to abortion. So I began to get concerned *that this was more than just a minor movement that was trying to relax a few laws.* And so I phoned around to see if there was any organization which was trying to stop Senator Beilenson and I found there wasn't any at all; that the previous defeat pro-life people had had at the hands of the pro-abortionists in 1968, it really kind of shattered them. So, finding none, I contacted a friend of mine who is a Lutheran minister in Pacific City, and another who happens to be an attorney. And we got together and called a meeting of some attorneys and college professors and a few students. I put it to them that there's nothing being done but we should certainly do something [emphasis added].

In another part of the state a Catholic nun and social worker who had worked with unmarried pregnant women was asked by her local bishop to "look into" the developing abortion situation. She was joined by two others—a Catholic woman who had taught natural childbirth classes in a local hospital and a non-Catholic social worker whose agency also dealt with unmarried pregnant women. Thus all three were in a position to be aware of the increasing impact of abortion. The non-Catholic woman had also previously volunteered to work in a family planning clinic that made referrals for abortion; it was there that she realized that her own values (on population control and sexuality in particular) were very much at odds with those who were advocating abortions:

> So I found out that their statistics [those of abortion advocates] were pretty well distorted, and I found out that their point of view was tied in with another cause, which is the population explosion cause. So you had a messianic message: as you deal with the individual, you see that this country is overpopulated. . . . So you would discourage the poor from having children. You were doing a good thing for the client. But even if the client were not poor . . . you'd find another rationale for why the abortion would be necessary. . . . I began to question the people first, and I began to become uneasy about abortion; I began to see that I had bought a lot of stuff that wasn't accurate. I also saw the tie-in . . . there was a promotion of freer sexuality; an acceptance of freer sexuality is different than promotion. So there was a promotion of freer sexuality.

These three women drove to another city to visit a pro-life group. Equipped with new ideas and movement literature, they began to work with a group called Support Life, whose members were concerned about the increasingly widespread public acceptance of abortion. One of the Support Life members gave this report:

> I suppose I got interested in the [Support Life] hot-line because I was working for welfare at the time. I saw girls coming to apply for assistance for Medi-Cal to pay for their abortion. I saw them coming in uninformed, uneducated. You'd ask them, "Do you want to see a social worker?" because eligibility workers do not get into counseling—I never have on a work basis. But you'd ask them if they wanted to see a social worker and assess the, you know, consider the other solutions, and they would say, "No, my mind's made up," and I'd say, "O.K., who'd you see?" and they'd say, "Oh, well, my doctor said he would do it on such-and-such a day." But obviously nothing had ever been discussed—whether it would be good for them, much less whether it was right or wrong.

The period between 1967 and 1973 was one of slow but steady growth for the pro-life movement as a pool of activists was gradually drawn from the larger segment of the population that was becoming aware of legalized abortion activities in California. This process might have continued indefinitely had it not been for one dramatic event of national significance.

Post-1973 Recruits

The "bolt from the blue"

On January 22, 1973, the U.S. Supreme Court decided the case of *Roe* v. *Wade*. More of the people we interviewed joined the pro-life movement in 1973 than in any other year, before or since; and almost without exception, they reported that they became mobilized to the cause on the very day the decision was handed down. For many of them, the memories of that day are extraordinarily vivid. A woman who felt herself to be the product of an unwanted pregnancy—and who, like the man we have quoted, felt that if things had been different she would have been aborted—had this to say:

> [It was my oldest son's] third birthday and I was making his cake . . . and we were at this table, this same table, and I was decorating, it was right over here, and there was a bunch of junk piled, like normal, on this table. This time it was toys—birthday toys. My husband came in with a newspaper. It said there would be peace in Vietnam, and of course that overshadowed the Supreme Court decision. So he was going through the paper and he saw this [article] about legalizing abortion. After I'd felt so good about those states voting it down in the referendums . . . the people voting it down. I wasn't in any organizations or anything, and I had only written one letter several years before. I had read [newspaper] articles because the issue had struck me as something I felt from the heart. . . . And so, all of a sudden he walked into the kitchen and he showed me, he said, "Hey, did you see this, Maria?" I says . . . you know I was too busy doing the cake but he says, "Lookit here," he says, "read this." And I read that and it very much upset me. I've got that paper to this day. It wasn't saved because of the peace in Vietnam. It was saved because inside in the pages is that article. . . . It had a photograph of the justices, and it mentions how [abortion] was to be legal and all of that. And it was Jamie's birthday. And I sat down, I was very upset. . . . I wanted to cry in a way. . . . All of these things in my per-

> sonal life—things that were no concern of mine, so to speak, you say "that's somebody else's business"—all came together in one. And being Jamie's birthday, my very first son . . . that kind of made it a personal thing . . . almost like seeing Providence. God was saying, "Lookit, sister, you better see what's going on there." Because . . . I'm religious even though my background isn't.

Why was the Supreme Court decision so vivid and upsetting as to make people like this woman political activists overnight? The answer can be sought in two areas: the social characteristics of the post-1973 activists and the features of the Court decision that had particular significance for them.

The new group of people brought into active participation in the anti-abortion movement by the Supreme Court decision were predominantly women with high school educations (and occasionally some college) who were married, had children, and were not employed outside the home. They were, as the earlier pro-life activists called them, "the housewives."* None of them had ever had an abortion, and only a few of them had ever had a friend who had had an abortion; the closest most of them came to actual experience in the matter was having heard rumors in high school about someone who had "gotten in trouble" and "done something" about it. Their values and life circumstances made it unlikely that they themselves would need abortions, and they were surrounded by people who shared these values. Moreover, since they were known to be devout, traditional women who valued motherhood highly, they were not likely to be on the receiving end of confidences from women who did not share these values. As one of them said, "Look, I'm a devout Catholic and people know how I stand on these kinds of things. I'm not the kind of person you would confide in if you were having an abortion."

These characteristics explain, at least in part, why these new recruits could say that they were largely unaware of the abortion situation in California prior to the Supreme Court decision. Unlike both the pro-life and pro-choice activists who were involved before the Supreme Court decision, they had never been actively concerned with political

* This finding might be questioned because the sampling method used in this study was not strictly random; it is remotely possible, for example, that for some reason housewives were disproportionately available for interviews (almost a decade later). But statistical data and comments by the activists themselves support this finding. For details, see Appendix One.

issues. They were not members of the League of Women Voters, they had no ties with professional associations or labor unions, they were not active in local party politics, and many of them had not even voted in previous elections. Perhaps more unexpectedly, they were not active in PTA, church groups, scouting, or other political and social activities traditionally thought of as being compatible with the role of wife and homemaker.

Partly this was because these new members had large families to contend with. Half of the people interviewed for this study who joined the pro-life movement during 1973 had four or more children. Actually, their family sizes were not substantially different from those of the people who had already joined the movement: the median number of children was 3.5 for those who joined before 1967 and 4.25 for those who joined between 1967 and 1973. But on the average, the 1973 recruits were a full decade younger than their predecessors and were thus more likely to have *small* children to care for.

It seems apparent that because of who these women were, abortion was simply not part of their social lives. One out of every three pregnancies in California might end in an induced abortion by 1971—but these did not include their pregnancies or those of their friends. And their relative social isolation—their lack of participation in community activities—further removed them from opportunities to interact with others who might at least have held different views.

We may now ask why the Supreme Court decision of 1973 provoked such a massive response from people who had tolerated (or at least lived with) what were in effect very liberal abortion laws for years. It will be recalled that reform physicians in California originally claimed that the Beilenson bill would do little more than "clarify" the legal grounds for the sort of abortions they were doing anyway and that the deletion from the bill (under threat of a veto by Governor Reagan) of a clause permitting abortion for "fetal indications" removed any explicit challenge to the belief that the embryo is a full human life. Pro-life people could believe, therefore, that the *principle* they cherished was still safe, that only the decision rules about how to weigh one life against another had been modified. Equally important, the new California law said that the abortion decision had to be made not by the woman involved, nor even by the woman and her doctor, but by a panel of three doctors—in effect, by representatives of the medical community. Thus, from the pro-life point of view, abortion was still medical, still the taking of a human life, and still wrong, except in extraordinary circumstances.

The Supreme Court decision changed all that. It demonstrated that an unwillingness to discuss abortion in public did not necessarily imply a commitment to the sacredness of embryonic life. Moreover, the Court not only discussed abortion but finally addressed the issue of personhood in an explicit way. As the Court itself put it in *Roe* v. *Wade*:

> All this . . . persuades us that the word "person" as used in the Fourteenth Amendment does not include the unborn. . . . We need not resolve the difficult question of when life begins. When those trained in the respective disciplines of medicine, philosophy, and theology are unable to arrive at any consensus, the judiciary, at this point in the development of man's knowledge, is not in a position to speculate as to the answer.[4]

From the pro-life point of view, this took what "everyone knew" to be *fact* and threw it into the realm of *opinion*. To be sure, the differences of opinion about the moral nature of the embryo go back to the ancient Greeks. But in America, there had been little plain-spoken public debate about the moral status of the embryo since the middle of the nineteenth century, and many mistook a century of silence for a millennium of consensus.

For those with pro-life sympathies, therefore, the Supreme Court decision contained a number of deeply disturbing symbolic messages. First, the Court had listened respectfully to and therefore legitimized an opinion that pro-life people found anathema: that the embryo is not a person but only a potential person. Second, by noting that "reasonable people" do not agree on whether the embryo is a person, the Court had in effect given both sides equal respectability. And, finally, by eliminating the right of the state to regulate what happens to the embryo, the Court had declared in effect that the embryo no longer deserves institutional protection, that its value and meaning had become sufficiently unimportant to be entrusted to the individual discretion of a woman and her doctor.

Accustomed as they were to thinking that theirs was the majority opinion, the pro-life people we interviewed saw in the Supreme Court decision a way of thinking that seemed bizarre and unreal. Something they believed to be both fundamental and obvious—that the embryo was a human life as valuable as any (and perhaps more valuable than some because it was innocent, fragile, and unable to act on its own behalf)—was now defined as simply one opinion among several. What was worse, it was defined as an opinion belonging to the *private* sphere, more like a religious preference than a deeply held social belief, such as belief in the right to free speech. It was as if the Supreme Court had suddenly ruled that a belief in free speech was only one legitimate opinion among many, which could not therefore be given special protection by any state or federal agency.

From this perspective, we can see why the Court decision struck many pro-life people as a "bolt from the blue," a frighteningly radical departure from traditional views. It alerted a whole new group of people to the fact that abortion reform was a powerful movement across the nation; it validated that movement by giving it equal standing with the pro-life view; and it called into question not only beliefs about the embryo but also beliefs about society in general. Here is how three women answered the question, "How did you react to the Supreme Court decision?"

> Well, I think just about like everyone else in the [Support Life] league, we felt as though the bottom had been pulled out from under us. It was an incredible thing, I couldn't believe it. In fact, I didn't. For a couple of months I kept thinking, "It can't be right, I'm not hearing what I'm hearing."

> I'm a political scientist, and that's my background. I speak not only from the tragic feeling of what is happening to women who have abortions, or [what they] are doing to themselves psychologically, physically. . . . I'm terribly concerned that the Supreme Court would have presumed to have taken upon itself the right to give life to any special group of citizens. Who gave the Supreme Court the right to give life? You know it took this power by itself; now when a government [claims] the power to give life, to me this is a fascist-dominated philosophy of life.

> I think we all sort of took a lot of things for granted and one of them was that our government would follow itself, wouldn't start deviating from its original purpose, and this was such a strong deviation that it was kind of appalling to me. And it was sort of the beginning of a lot of deviations in various areas.

Why the Court chose to hear the *Roe* and *Doe* cases and why they made the decisions that they did must of course remain speculative.

Only the Court itself knows its reasoning, and it is notoriously unwilling to open the logic of its collective decision-making to public view. Nonetheless, the circumstances surrounding these cases suggest important structural factors that explain some of the Court's actions.

On the simplest level, the Court ruled on abortion cases because abortion reform advocates had cared enough about the issue to press it to the top of the judicial system. Theoretically, it was possible that the Court could have refused to hear the cases or that it could hear them but rule only on procedural or narrowly substantive grounds. But several features of the situation made these outcomes unlikely.

First, these cases were products of a nationwide social movement: Roe (a Texas woman) and Doe (a Georgian) were supported by a number of national organizations. Reflecting the fact that the abortion reform movement was still in large part dominated by elite physicians, amicus briefs were submitted by the American College of Obstetricians and Gynecologists, the American Medical Association, the American Women's Medical Association, the New York Academy of Medicine, "a group of 178 doctors as amicae," the American Psychiatric Association, "medical school deans and professors," the American Public Health Association, and the American Association of Planned Parenthood Physicians. This elite support was augmented by the efforts of several nonprofessional groups, who saw fit to list their membership numbers in their amicus briefs: CCTA from California (see Chapter Five) claimed 5,000 members and offered 300,000 signatures, a single California chapter of NOW noted that it had 20,000 members, and Zero Population Growth claimed 300,000 members nationwide.

Thus, from the official data presented to the Court, abortion reform appeared to be a national movement that commanded widespread public support. If this movement did not get satisfaction with the *Roe* and *Doe* cases, it was doubtless prepared to argue others. More important, perhaps, the abortion reform advocates appeared to be in large part "disinterested"; they belonged to organizations that could not be called "single-issue" groups. Conversely, the justices could conclude from the amicus briefs presented to them that the pro-life movement was perilously close to what its detractors claimed it was: a small, isolated group, ideologically suspect because of the predominantly religious nature of its beliefs. Whereas the pro-abortion forces had mustered the support of over twenty "disinterested" organizations, the pro-life forces were able to deliver amicus briefs from only four groups—Americans United for Life, "Certain Physicians and Fellows of the American College of Obstetricians and Gynecologists," National Right to Life, and LIFE (League for Infants, Fetuses, and the Elderly)—and all four were clearly "single-issue" organizations, concerned exclusively with the abortion issue. The organizer of LIFE claimed that his nationwide group had "over a thousand" members, which hardly compared with the 20,000 members of *one* California women's group, or the 300,000 members claimed nationwide by Zero Population Growth.[5]

Another incentive for the Court to rule on these cases was the fact that over a dozen states already had liberalized abortion laws with different and often conflicting provisions in them. Colorado's liberalized law explicitly required residency for women seeking abortions whereas the laws in New York and California did not. California, at least on paper, did not permit abortions for fetal indications, but these were legal grounds for abortion in both New York and Colorado. Washington state bypassed the legislature entirely, passing a public referendum that in effect set only medical, rather than legal, limits on abortions.[6] The actions of state legislatures (and lower courts) had therefore served to complicate rather than clarify the issues. What one state (or court) deemed legal was often declared illegal by another state (or a higher court). Until it offered a ruling, the Supreme Court would have to deal with a growing patchwork of conflicting state laws, each of which represented an idiosyncratic attempt to forge a new compromise from the array of competing demands.*

It may also have been true that the Court simultaneously perceived the political pressures *against* ruling as weak. The anti-abortion movement was still largely elite, male, and predominantly Catholic and not as broadly based or as visible as the abortion reform movement. Individual pro-life activists had testified before state legislatures and taken stands in professional meetings, but the pro-life forces had so far been largely unable to present demonstrations of massive support of the kind that characterized the pro-choice movement. Perhaps more important, many of the same anti-abortion arguments, presented by the

* To give one clear example, residency requirements ranged from none (ten of the sixteen states with ALI-type laws) to thirty days (Alaska), to four months (North Carolina), to ninety days (South Carolina), to 120 days (Virginia) (Duffy, "Effects of Changes in the State Abortion Laws").

same sort of spokespersons, had been considered by the Court in its 1964 decision in *Griswold* v. *Connecticut*, which abolished the last remnants of state Comstock laws prohibiting the dispensing of contraceptives or information about them.[7] Despite sectarian arguments that legalizing contraception would legalize sin and promote a great social outcry, by 1964 contraceptive use was an accepted fact of life for the American public, and the *Griswold* decision aroused very little controversy.[8] The Supreme Court may very well have thought that the same thing would happen with the abortion cases. After all, by 1973 public opinion polls showed considerable support for liberalized abortion, and the opposition to it seemed small and sectarian.

What neither the Court nor anyone else anticipated was that the *Roe* decision would mobilize a new and much stronger opposition to abortion reform. The Supreme Court, asked to adjudicate between two views of the embryo, could not. In *Roe* v. *Wade* it recognized the fact that abortion in the United States was no longer a question of boundaries—when may an embryo's rights be compromised? It was now a question of principle—is an embryo a person or something not yet a person? Once the question of personhood was squarely addressed, new groups of people were mobilized into the movement because they saw this issue as one that would have important and far-reaching consequences.

Growth and Expansion: 1973 to the Present

From the point of view of pro-life organizations, the period since the Supreme Court decision has been one of satisfying expansion in both membership and financial resources. Before 1973 most major cities in California had only one pro-life organization (or one political group and one service and education group), but most major cities now have several, and most suburban areas have their own. But this growth is not without its price: it has brought new strains into the movement, most notably considerable friction between the "old" activists (those involved before the Supreme Court decision) and "new" activists (those involved after the decision). Some of the old activists, members of the pre-1973 movement, have drifted out of active participation. Though fatigue and organizational "burnout" were doubtless factors in some cases, the comments of early activists themselves suggest a more general explanation. A founder of the pro-life hot-line in her area had this to say:

> I don't take a very active part in the Lifeline, and . . . I'm not always happy with the ways things have gone. . . . I guess I'm pro-life in a very large sense of the word, and I found that a lot of people involved in the Support Life League are very narrow in their anti-abortion. I'm anti-abortion, but I guess I have more of an understanding of why some people do what they do, and people that are accusing other people of murder and all, those kinds of things really go against me. . . . The league people will issue a list of candidates who are pro-life, and [you're supposed to vote for them]. Well, I'm not [going to vote] just because someone is pro-life, if he's not a good candidate for the office. . . . I'm not that kind of pro-life. I'm pro-life in that I'm interested in things like world hunger, and I'm against capital punishment, and I'm against war, and a lot of things that are broad areas of being pro-life.

This tension is explicable in terms of the social differences between old and new activists. The new activists were predominantly women homemakers without previous experience in political activities. Equally important, they were people who feared what they saw as symbolic messages in the Supreme Court decision: if babies could have personhood so quickly wrenched away from them, who might be next? These two factors explain why the movement became increasingly emotional and passionate after the Supreme Court decision. Unlike the predominantly male professionals who had preceded them, the new activists were people who had direct experiences with pregnancy. Moreover, they were people whose values made pregnancy central to their lives. Now they were faced with a Supreme Court decision that seemed to devalue not only the status of the embryo but pregnancy itself. Because of their previous social isolation, the argument to which the Supreme Court had given approval—that the embryo is not a person—was distinctly new and shocking to them. The Court's decision, by extension, seemed to threaten the personal worth of the women who bore them and anyone else who was weak and helpless.

The social status of those people recruited into the pro-life movement after the 1973 decision also meant that they felt fewer constraints about expressing their concerns in vivid, public, and emotional ways. Early members of the movement, by virtue of being members of an elite, faced what social scientists call "cross-pressures." Although they were pro-life, they were also physicians, lawyers, or other professionals; they were active in their professional communities and were highly visible members of their communities at large. They faced a number of pressures not to appear "fanatic" on the pro-life issue but to be "dignified" and "professional" in pursuit of pro-life goals.

Those recruited after January 1973, in contrast, faced very few of these cross-pressures. Because they had relatively few social or political ties to a larger social or professional community, they could be fearlessly "single-issue" activists. For example, virtually all of the early pro-life activists had some friends who disagreed with them on abortion. Most of the new recruits, in contrast, do not have such friends, and many spontaneously said during the interviews that they would simply end a friendship with a person who did not share their views on abortion.

Getting Involved in the Pro-Life Cause

Their differences notwithstanding, all pro-life people have certain experiences in common with respect to their abortion activism. In all periods of the movement's history, for example, the recruits had grown up taking for granted the idea that the embryo is a baby. Similarly, almost all were self-recruits—in contrast to their pro-choice peers, who were typically recruited through "consciousness-raising" activities. Finally, a very large number of them made their own commitment to get involved after a personal experience that "brought the issue home" to them.

The embryo as person

Only four of the pro-life activists we interviewed had ever considered holding any other attitude on abortion than the one they hold now. For the rest, abortion was something they had known was wrong since earliest childhood. Over and over again, activists mentioned the same themes:

> Well, as a kid you learned about it in school—you know, the various good things and bad things in life. But it was, you know, something you read about, it just wasn't done at the time, or it was surreptitious. So I think I knew of it in that sense. . . . I went to Catholic school in the seventh and eighth grades and in the catechism classes . . . things like this were brought up. Other than that, you know, it was just like you knew there was war and murder and various other things.

> I don't know, maybe it was our background. Our religious belief does not [permit abortion], you know, it's murder and that's that.

> I knew my background would lead me to be pro-life, because of my mother mainly, and probably in a very small sense [because of] my faith. I'm from a faith that holds a pro-life view. However, I had never heard any discussion in my faith on this issue; I just knew it was something they believed in.

> Well, of course I'm a Catholic [physician] so let's say when you're in school, we were taught about what things are wrong. [Abortion] wasn't really a big issue, although I suppose I wouldn't even have known abortions were being performed.

As these quotes suggest, very few of these activists remember a "big issue" being made about abortion when they were growing up either at home, in church, or at school. There was some teaching about abortion, but it was usually buried in rather abstract and theoretical terms. Those few who could remember explicit discussions about it during childhood could recall remarkably few details. For the overwhelming majority, learning about the moral status of abortion was like learning about patriotism, honesty, or love. They simply grew up with it, absorbed it in passing, and never thought about it very much. It never crossed their minds that anyone held a different opinion on it.

Although they had differing amounts of exposure to the abortion situation (the early activists tended to have more), few of them had what might be called firsthand experience with abortion itself. When confronted with evidence that abortion was widely accepted, they were first baffled and then mobilized.

Self-recruitment: the converts mobilize

Another feature that many pro-life activists had in common, whenever they joined the movement, is that they recruited themselves into active membership. Two-thirds of the pro-life activists we interviewed were what might be described as self-recruits to the anti-abortion cause. That is, they encountered on their own information about the abortion situation that distressed them, and then they actively sought out an organized political group that shared their values. Another 20 percent were recruited by friends who knew of their sympathies and took them to a meeting of a pro-life group. Less than 10 percent were recruited in the way the typical pro-choice activist was, by being exposed to a formal presentation of arguments.[9] In fact, even this 10 percent figure probably exaggerated the effectiveness of formal presentations because it includes people who chose to attend a pro-life meeting after hearing it announced in church and people who were already eager to respond to any opportunity for active involvement.[10]

Once they encountered some aspect of the abortion situation that offended them, the self-recruits showed remarkable determination in finding ways to "connect" with a formal pro-life group. Shortly after the Supreme Court decision, for example, one woman, who did not own a car, heard on television about a pro-life demonstration planned at a local hospital and talked a friend into giving her a ride to it so she could join up. Several others availed themselves of pro-life "hot-lines," twenty-four-hour counseling services for women considering abortions:

> I've always been against abortion. I'd written letters and things like that, but the final straw was this class I had at Cal State. . . . Abortion came up, and the teacher was saying that it didn't matter, that the child wouldn't ever know the difference. And I tried to say a few things, but I really didn't know what to say. And it just made me angry that he didn't know the facts at all. And I tried to say something, but it just didn't work. So I came home that night and it was about nine o'clock and I just said, I told my mom, "Mom, I just have to do something." I didn't know that much about the groups, but I looked up Pro-Life in the phone book, and I thought, "Oh, they won't be open at nine o'clock at night." But I just called anyway, and it was the twenty-four-hour hot-line. So I got one of the hot-line listeners and I just said I wanted to do something. They were starting a training for the hot-line just the next month, so they told me where the meeting was and I went.

> While I was pregnant, somebody said something about abortions [being performed] at five months, and I was about four and a half months pregnant at the time, and I thought, "*Five months*! I can feel this baby kicking and moving inside of me and I just heard the heart begin to beat, what do you mean they're giving abortions at five months!" I mean, I thought what everybody else thought, that nobody had abortions after two or three months; I thought the Supreme Court said you couldn't do that. . . . One night I was sitting talking with my niece who is now at the university and we were talking about abortion. She told me that they have a clinic at the university called "Eve, a Sensitive Solution." I said,

"Excuse me, but that's a bunch of bull-blank, there's no sensitive solution to murder." And two o'clock in the morning, I got on the phone. . . . I didn't know who to call, and I said to the operator, "I don't know what I want, but there's got to be something, Support Life, For Life, Lifeline, Anti-Abortion, something. I don't care, any number," and this poor operator said, "Well, there's a Support Life hot-line." So I said, "Give it to me." I thought, you know, like they'd have a suicide hot-line where people sit in a office-type thing, you know that movie where they have the suicide hot-line. . . . So I thought this was what I had called. I had no idea I was calling this girl out of bed at two o'clock in the morning, and she gets on the phone thinking that I'm a hysterical woman who's about to have an abortion. I said, "No, I'm not hysterical, I'm not about to have an abortion, what do I do?" So we talked till about four o'clock in the morning, and this darling girl, she told me all about it, about the movement on abortion.

Among the 20 percent of activists who were recruited by friends, several things are notable. The friends were almost always close friends of long standing: co-workers or old classmates, neighbors, people who had children in the same school. Interestingly, many of the people who were recruited this way reported that their friends never had a formal discussion with them about abortion but simply assumed that their anti-abortion values were shared.

The following comment illustrates how attitudes and events often came together to make pro-life people active in the movement:

I've always felt very strongly about children and family, and I have a large family. . . . And I was a nurse, an R.N. I trained at St. Mary's, which had a very strong ethical code so far as medical moral ethics were concerned. And I felt very strongly and agreed with this [anti-abortion] philosophy and then when I was working at Mercy Hospital before I married, I worked in the obstetrical nursery for a period of time taking care of premature babies. Working very hard to keep them alive and then when the abortion issue came up, we were killing babies at the same stages as the babies that we were fighting to keep alive. And there was a period when abortion was becoming legal, they were fighting for the legality of abortion in California starting in 1967. Where I kept thinking, "This can't be happening, it can't be true. Why isn't someone doing something about it?" And I kept waiting for someone to get in there and fight it. At this period I had many small children and had not been one to join at all . . . I felt I belonged at home with my family. . . . I felt very strongly about being home with my children, and so I sat back and it kept happening and happening and I guess it finally hit me that something's got to be done, and sometimes that somebody that's got to get involved is you. So I guess I really didn't get involved until 1972–1973, and then I guess the biggest thing, the two things which would have been the impetus at the moment was the Supreme Court decision which just kind of hit many of us, like, well, we couldn't believe it would go that far. And then the other was a friendship with a local woman I knew through school, her children were in the same school and so forth . . . and she kind of pushed me to actually get into it. And she was doing some speaking at the time, and she got me to go along and speak, and I met people in the movement. I made the mistake of saying to someone, "Well, if there's anything I can do to help. . . ." So from then on, from about the time of the Supreme Court decision, it's been very much a part of my life, in spite of still having a family.

To summarize, we may say that at least 80 percent of these activists were not "recruited by" the movement. Rather, they (or their friends) independently learned something sufficiently upsetting about the abortion situation to make them seek out a group that was trying to do something about it. A highly visible public presence of the pro-life movement, therefore, helped them find what they were already looking for; but it did not create the desire to search for it in the first place. Circumstances, not the movement, did that.

Many pro-life activists would disagree with this assessment. They believe that the presentations their groups make are important recruiting tactics, and many referred to their slide show as "our most effective weapon." The slide show, which consists of intrauterine photographs taken during pregnancy, is a standard feature of the talks that pro-life groups give to church groups, women's groups, young mothers' groups, and high school and college groups.But when activists speak of the emotional impact the slide show had on them, they overlook a fundamental point: they were already "primed" to hear the message that the slide show conveys. Our interviews show that with rare exceptions, these presentations, including the slide shows, were persuasive only to people who had sought them out because they were already troubled or concerned about abortion.*

Sometimes, it is true, the presentations did play a subtle role in recruitment: they served to deepen already existing pro-life commit-

* It is worth repeating that this is a study of *activists*. It is quite possible that pro-life activities that fail to mobilize people into becoming activists can affect behavior in other ways, as in voting.

ments or to forestall potential objections. One woman, for example, saw a pro-abortion program on television that caused her to question her own anti-abortion beliefs. In her search to clarify her opinions, she first paid careful attention to a physician who spoke against abortion at mass and then decided to attend the slide show:

> Really, I was looking for answers because I knew I was against abortion but I really didn't know why. My church was against it, and I was against it because of that. But . . . when I thought of those young girls [unmarried and pregnant] who had so many problems, I had no solutions to those. You know it was . . . kind of an opportunity for me. If I hadn't seen that [pro-abortion] program on TV I probably wouldn't have given it much thought. But I was looking for answers myself because I realized how much knowledge I lacked on the subject. And then I saw the slides and I knew that all right, these are people that perhaps I can get answers from, and I knew I had to do something to stop it.

Similarly, another woman said:

> I always believed that abortion was wrong. I read [a pro-life ad] in the paper that said they were showing some slides and having a workshop, and I just went to it, at St. Mary's Hospital, two years ago. And I saw how terrible abortion really is, and more, determined that it was wrong and cruel. I had always thought it was wrong, but I hadn't thought it was cruel.

Mobilizing people who already care about an issue is no trivial achievement for any political movement. Nor is the ability to bring in those who care but might hesitate to become more active because of doubts about the wisdom of the movement's stands. On this dimension, the movement's recruiting activities have certainly been successful: it has elicited commitments of heroic proportions in the defense of its views.

Bringing the issue home

A significant proportion of those who made the decision to become active in the pro-life cause did so because of an experience that convinced them that abortion was not simply an abstract, theoretical issue but something that was both personal and relevant. For an astounding one-third of the pro-life people we interviewed, the event that "brought the issue home" was a problem of parenthood: an inability to conceive, a miscarriage, a newborn child lost to congenital disease or defect, or an older child lost to childhood illness. Since the pro-life group is so diverse, it is hard to tell whether this is a higher than average rate of parental loss, but it is dramatically higher than the level reported by pro-choice activists.[11] Here are excerpts from what three people said when asked what was going on in their lives when they decided to become active in the pro-life cause:

> Well . . . it very well could have been that the previous year we lost a baby, yes, we had a third child, Amy, and she was premature by Caesarian section because of the RH factor and she lived for thirty-seven hours after the C-section. Strangely enough, it wasn't the incompatibility of blood that killed her, it was the staph infection that did it. That made me very much aware of the fragility of life in general and in particular the life of a very young child, and when my child died at an age of development when a child could be carved out of its mother's womb and butchered, by the California law, that's very strong . . . now you're scratching below the surface at this point, you don't take very long to get down to past the b.s., do you? . . . it came down home, you see, literally, it came to home, that what was going on out there someplace was very much a reality, and that it wasn't an academic question like whether or not we should admit Red China to the U.N.

> I lost a baby, my first one, when I was just into the sixth month, and it was at the point where the baby had to be buried [according to] the church. We went to the mortuary and I grieved for that baby for a long, long time. I lost another baby very early within the next year, but it wasn't as real to me because it was in the first few weeks. But then it was seven years before I had my first living child. . . . I don't know if that made me feel more strongly [about abortion] . . . because, I mean, you're at a certain level, you can't really go beyond it. But I know that that baby was very precious to me. I wanted it so badly. I grieved for years, you know, for that baby. I still think of him and how old he would be now. So every baby's life is a valuable thing to me. I wonder what it would've been like. I think women who have abortions must go through that, too.

> Our first son was natural born and then we couldn't have any more children so we went to adopt, and when we were at our interview, the man mentioned that because of abortion there weren't very many babies available. . . . And I remember saying, "You mean they would have abortions when they knew people were waiting to adopt their children?" If they didn't want them, you know, someone else does. I don't remem-

ber what he said, but anyway it kind of stuck with me, and in a way it becomes like [all] abortions were my children . . . all children should be all of our children. It kind of became more personal.

It would be unfair, however, to conclude that the connection between the loss of a child and later pro-life activism is usually simple and direct. For example, one woman (who had given an earlier, out-of-wedlock, child up for adoption) angrily rejected a friend's suggestion that her pro-life activity was related to the recent death of her infant daughter and noted the complexity of her decision to become more involved:

> I remember my mother was very upset when the Supreme Court legalized abortion in 1973, and I thought, well, it doesn't mean everyone's going to run out and have an abortion. . . . I thought that [abortion] is not the way to handle [unwanted pregnancy], but I still didn't have this activist streak in me. . . . I've had some bitter fights with some people I'm close to about this activism. [They say that] because my first baby had to be given up for adoption and my second baby [died of] hyaline membrane disease, it's like I'm a frustrated mother, but I'm not. . . . I think this is what started my activism, so it is a result of Michelle, sort of, but it's not that she's dead and I'm mad and other mothers are having their babies and I could get pregnant again in a minute, I'm sure. I don't want to right now, I'm just not healed and maybe I'll have another baby, probably I won't, maybe I will. But I'm not resenting anyone with babies, [I'm not thinking] "you stupid people don't know how lucky you are. . . ." I don't know when it really just hit me [that I should become active in the movement]. But I think what snapped was the idea that my baby's life, in a lot of people's eyes, wouldn't have been very meaningful [because of the lung disease]. Okay, she only lived twenty-seven days, and that's not a very long time, but whether we live ninety-nine years or two hours or twenty-seven days, being human is being human, and what it involves, we really don't understand.

It is important to recall that these people, like virtually everyone else in the movement, had always believed that the embryo is an unborn child; but it is also clear from our interviews that even those who were aware of the spreading practice of abortion did not always see it as a social problem; as one said, "not everyone's going to run out and get an abortion." More typically, they were simply unaware of the extent of legal abortion; and if they were aware of it, they saw it as the result of ignorance or the stretching of the one permissible ground for abortion—to save the life of the mother. They did not become pro-life activists because they had lost a child. They were pro-life already, and their loss helped make them active in the movement. They were made aware, in a tragically personal way, how precious a child can be. Their perception of the disparity between the loss of a deeply wished-for child and the seemingly casual ending of pregnancies in abortion was very painful to them. Some were deeply distressed to learn that, from their point of view, more than a million children in America are lost to abortion every year because of what they considered human caprice.

Also, as one of the women we have just quoted suggests, some people hear pro-abortion arguments as saying that "damaged" babies (as well as parents who are incapable of producing "perfect" babies) are less valuable and that the death of these babies is a blessing in disguise. This again highlights the fundamental conflict of values between the pro-life and pro-choice viewpoints. For people who consider the embryo only a potential person, death at the stage of potential (or very early) personhood is preferable to a life as an actual person with "diminished capacities." But for people who believe that the embryo is an actual person, this opinion, though often expressed with the intent of comforting a newly bereaved parent, trivializes a great human loss. More to the point, it seems to make invidious distinctions between the perfect and the not-so-perfect.

The personal effect of this contrast between "perfect" and "less-than-perfect" individuals was suggested even more directly by another group of pro-life activists, who believed that if some people (the not-yet-born) can have their lives ended by the relatively unchecked personal choice of others (pregnant women), then anyone's life is potentially in danger. To be sure, this is a standard pro-life argument, and many of the people we interviewed mentioned the idea that abortion fosters a general "disrespect for life." But it took something more than this belief to make activists of them. They had to perceive a connection between the embryo and some other vulnerable group with which they identified. Here is how two activists, a man and a Mexican-American woman, made such a connection:

> I've been active in the movement since 1972, and I guess probably two things had the most effect on me in getting me involved. [The first] was this discussion I had with a guy at work. . . . He has some pretty way out political beliefs. He thinks Hitler is okay, and he was saying how most of the stuff we heard about Hitler were lies, and then he got onto abortion [and] I could just kind of see the link between what he was

> saying about the Nazis and his ideas on abortion. . . . As far as he's concerned he doesn't care whether [the embryo is] a human or not . . . Another thing that happened back [in 1972] that really had a big influence was the issue in Northern Ireland. . . . The argument they've always used for not unifying the two countries is because of economic reasons. Now the [Irish] Republic is the poorest nation in Western Europe, and the part controlled by the British is the second wealthiest in Western Europe. . . . You listen to every single argument for abortion, and it will have the same central theme, that we should be killing babies because from an economic standpoint it's to our advantage to do so. And I just kind of see a link between the two issues because to me, Ireland just proves that a just society with a lower economic standard of living is better than an unjust society with a high economic standard of living. So these two issues to me are the same.

> As I said, [I'm] working with the low-income and the non-English-speaking people of the [agricultural] area. I guess I'm considered a Chicana activist. I grew up in the area picking fruit, "migrant workers" I guess we were called in those days. . . . It's been a long hard battle in obtaining any type of rights or recognition, or just normal human rights, you know having come from a family that just grew up picking fruit, and realizing that you would never get anywhere. And so that is what is in the forefront of Chicano activism, the fact that we've had to fight so hard for every little right we've had. The only right that the system is so willing to give freely, no questions asked, are free abortions. And so right away we start getting suspicious, it's a natural conclusion for us. . . . We see that the thrust of the [environmental] movement is to get rid of the poor. . . . We have the environmental groups who are saying that the only way to deal with the immigrant problem—in this case, they are referring to the undocumented aliens from Mexico—is either to catch them before birth or after birth. [They are] in favor of funding abortions for low-income people . . . [in other words] kill them off before they even get a chance to multiply.

For people who are not pro-life supporters, the logic that links abortion to the genocidal policies of the Third Reich, to the treatment of the Irish by the British, and to the treatment of minorities or handicapped people in this country may seem baffling. But to pro-life people, who have grown up taking it for granted that the embryo is a child, abortion *in principle* defines all embryos as "nonpersons" or persons who lack equal rights.

In fact, supporters of abortion do believe that any rights embryos may have are weaker than the rights of actual persons. Pregnant women, by virtue of being full rather than potential persons, are entitled to end their own pregnancies because their rights "outrank" the weaker rights of the embryo.

It is precisely this logic that deeply offends all pro-life activists. Because they were not on the whole exposed during childhood and youth to the idea that embryos belong to a different moral category than persons already born, the abortion reform movement strikes them as a sudden and capricious rejection of centuries of "respect for unborn life." At times in the abortion debate, this argument is used in a tactical way, to justify a continuing rejection of abortion: if opposition to abortion has such a long social pedigree, only very weighty causes can justify changing abortion laws. But this argument has even deeper emotional and social roots. For people who really do believe that embryos have *always* been treated with respect—and our data suggest that almost all pro-life people believe this—the wide acceptance of abortion in American society is truly frightening because it seems to represent a willingness of society to strip the rights of personhood from "persons" who have always enjoyed them. If the rights of personhood can be so easily taken away from babies (embryos), who among us will be next?

The presumed stripping of personhood from embryos has other frightening and horrifying dimensions for pro-life people. It is probably safe to say that in our society (as in most), the relationship between mother and child is assumed to be the most intimate, most sacred, and most self-sacrificing relationship of all. To people who assume that the embryo is a child, the logic is clear: if even this most sacred, least "worldly," least "useful" relationship can be disrupted, no relationship is safe. As one mother said: "If a baby can't be safe in his mother's womb, where *can* he be safe?"

Given this assumption, not only the death of an embryo but the *rationale* of its death is offensive to pro-life people. For them, pro-choice logic would permit the development of a totalitarian society like Orwell's *Animal Farm* where "some are more equal than others." Abortion seems to place the "convenience" of some over the very lives of others, and these others can be defined as having "lesser lives" *by another social group*. Embryos can be defined as less valuable because other people—the women carrying those embryos, politicians who want to cut welfare rolls, eugenicists who want only the "best" babies born—have selfish reasons for doing so. Embryos, like newborns, infants, and in some cases the elderly, epitomize those stages in the life cycle when all humans are basically helpless and in some social sense "useless." For pro-life people, to accept the principle of abortion means to accept the notion that a person's life may be dependent upon his or her *social worth*, which may in turn be defined by others whose motives may not be trustworthy.

It is not surprising, therefore, that embryos represent a nonnegotiable boundary for pro-life people. By definition embryos cannot "pull their own weight" socially; they are at the most dependent and least "productive" stage of the life cycle. Nor is it surprising that people who belong to socially vulnerable groups, or identify with them, find the plight of the embryo so distressing: it is innocent, it is human (at least at the genetic level), and all of its social worth is yet to come. To argue that embryos are entitled to all the rights of personhood, despite their "condition of dependency," because they possess the entry card of forty-six human chromosomes is to emphatically assert that *personhood is a "natural," inborn, and inherited right, rather than a social, contingent, and assigned right.*

7

World Views of the Activists

As previous chapters have suggested, when pro-life and pro-choice activists think about abortion, abortion itself is merely "the tip of the iceberg." Different beliefs about the roles of the sexes, about the meaning of parenthood, and about human nature are all called into play when the issue is abortion. Abortion, therefore, gives us a rare opportunity to examine closely a set of values that are almost never directly discussed. Because these values apply to spheres of life that are very private (sex) or very diffuse (morality), most people never look at the patterns they form. For this reason the abortion debate has become something that illuminates our deepest, and sometimes our dearest, beliefs.

At the same time, precisely because these values are so rarely discussed overtly, when they are called into question, as they are by the abortion debate, individuals feel that an entire *world view* is under assault. An interesting characteristic of a world view, however, is that the values located within it are so deep and so dear to us that we find it hard to imagine that we even have a "world view"—to us it is just reality—or that anyone else could not share it. By definition, those areas covered by a "world view" are those parts of life we take for granted, never imagine questioning, and cannot envision decent, moral people not sharing.

When an event such as the abortion controversy occurs, which makes it clear that one's world view is not the only one, it is immediately apparent why surprise, outrage, and vindictiveness are the order of the day. Individuals are surprised because for most of them this is the first time their deepest values have been brought to explicit consciousness, much less challenged. They are outraged because these values are so taken for granted that people have no vocabulary with which to discuss the fact that what is at odds is a fundamental view of reality. And they are vindictive because denying that one's opponents are decent, honorable people is one way of distancing oneself from the unsettling thought that there could be legitimate differences of opinion on one's most cherished beliefs.

In the course of our interviews, it became apparent that each side of the abortion debate has an internally coherent and mutually shared view of the world that is tacit, never fully articulated, and, most importantly, completely at odds with the world view held by their opponents. This chapter will examine in turn the world views of first the pro-life activists, then the pro-choice activists to demonstrate the truth of what many of the activists we interviewed asserted: that abortion is just "the tip of the iceberg." To be sure, not every single one of those interrelated values that I have called a "world view" characterized each and every pro-life or pro-choice person interviewed. It is well within the realm of possibility that an activist might find some individual areas where he or she would feel more akin to the values expressed by their opponents than by those on their own side. But taken as a whole, there was enough consistency in the way people on each side talked about the world to warrant the conclusion that each side has its own particular "world view," that these world views tend to be isolated from competing world views, and that forced to choose, most activists would find far more in common with the world view of their side than that of their opponents.

Pro-Life Views of the World

To begin with, pro-life activists believe that men and women are intrinsically different, and this is both a cause and a product of the fact that they have different roles in life. Here are some representative comments from the interviews:

> The question is, what is natural for human life and what will make people happy? Now I deplore the oppression of any people, and so I would ipso facto deplore the oppression of women but a lot of things are being interpreted as oppression simply [out of] restless agitation against a nat-

ural order that should really be allowed to prevail. The feminist movement has wanted to, as it were, really turn women into men or to kind of de-sex them, and they [feminists] pretend that there are no important differences between men and women. Now when it comes to a woman doing a job, a woman being paid the same rate that a man gets for the same job, I'm very much in favor of all that. [What] I find so disturbing [about] the whole abortion mentality is the idea that family duties—rearing children, managing a home, loving and caring for a husband—are somehow degrading to women. And that's an idea which is very current in our society—that women are not going to find fulfillment until they get out there and start competing for a livelihood with men and talking like men, cursing and whatever, although not all men curse. I don't mean that to sound . . . maybe that's beginning to have an emotional overtone that I didn't want it to have.

The women's lib thing comes in, too. They've got a lot of good ideas, but their whole thing ran off so far on it. How can they not see that men and women are different? I don't know, they're different, period, that's truth.

[Men and women] were created differently and we're meant to complement each other, and when you get away from our [proper] roles as such, you start obscuring them. That's another part of the confusion that's going on now, people don't know where they stand, they don't know how to act, they don't know where they're coming from, so your psychiatrists' couches are filled with lost souls, with lost people that for a long time now have been gradually led into confusion and don't even know it.

I believe that there's a natural mother's instinct. And I'm kind of chauvinist this way, but I don't believe men and women are equal. I believe men and women are very different, and beautifully different, and that they're complementary in their nature to one another.

Pro-life activists agree that men and women, as a result of these intrinsic differences, have different roles to play: men are best suited to the public world of work, and women are best suited to rear children, manage homes, and love and care for husbands. Most pro-life activists believe that motherhood—the raising of children and families—is the most fulfilling role that women can have. To be sure, they live in a country where over half of all women work, and they do acknowledge that some women are employed. But when they say (as almost all of them do) that women who work should get equal pay for equal work, they do not mean that women *should* work. On the contrary, they subscribe quite strongly to the traditional belief that women should be wives and mothers *first*. Mothering, in their view, is so demanding that it is a full-time job, and any woman who cannot commit herself fully to it should avoid it entirely.

> Well, if that's what you've decided in life, I don't feel that there's anything wrong with not being a wife or mother. If someone wants a career, that's fine. But if you are a mother I think you have an important job to do. I think you're responsible for your home, and I think you're responsible for the children you bring into the world, and you're responsible, as far as you possibly can be, for educating and teaching them; obviously you have to teach them what you believe is right—moral values and responsibilities and rights. . . . It's a huge job, and you never know how well you're doing until it's too late.

Because pro-life activists see having a family as an emotionally demanding, labor-intensive project, they find it hard to imagine that a woman could put forty hours a week into an outside job and still have time for her husband and children. Equally important, they feel that different kinds of emotional "sets" are called for in the work world and in the home.

> Right, it's a pride or an egotism that hits women. . . . When a challenge is met and faced by a woman in the man's world, it's a gratifying situation, but it creates a need to feed on that, too. . . . But when you start . . . competing in the marketplace for what you can do and how you can get one-up or whatever, then I think we get into problems. It's harder to come down off that plane [of activity] and come home to a life where everything is quite mundane, and the children are way beneath you. It's hard to change from such a height to such a depth in a short time, and it becomes more and more difficult, I would think, as time goes on, to relate to [both] planes.

For a woman to shift gears from her emotional role in the home to a competitive role in the office is not only difficult, they argue, but damaging to both men and women, and to their children.

These views on the different nature of men and women and the roles appropriate to each combine to make abortion look wrong three times over. First, it is intrinsically wrong because it takes a human life and what makes women special is their ability to nourish life. Second, it is wrong because *by giving women control over their fertility*, it breaks up an intricate set of social relationships between men and women that has traditionally surrounded (and in the ideal case protected) women and children. Third and finally, abortion is wrong because it fosters and supports a world view that deemphasizes (and therefore *downgrades*) the traditional roles of men and women. Because these roles have been satisfying ones for pro-life people and because they believe this emotional and social division of labor is both "appropriate and natural," the act of abortion is wrong because it plays havoc with this arrangement of the world. For example, because abortion formally diminishes male decision-making power, it also diminishes male responsibility. Thus, far from liberating women, pro-life people argue, abortion oppresses them.

> One of the problems [of abortion], I think, is the further degradation of women in society. I know that feminists would disagree with me on this, and I consider myself a feminist, so it's difficult for me to relate to other feminists on this issue. I think having abortion as an alternative—as a way out, I guess—makes it easier for men to exploit women than ever before. I think they are less inclined probably to take responsibility for their actions or to anticipate the consequences of their actions as long as abortion is available. And I think it makes it harder for women who do not choose to engage in premarital sex to say no, or to be accepted in society, because there's always this consideration that there's something wrong with them.

> [Women] are losing when they have abortions; the men play with them and they [have to] get their abortions. Like the Supreme Court decision was backed by lots of money from *Playboy*, and *Playboy* isn't really interested in the women's movement except what they can get out of women. This is where a lot of women are hurting. They have abortions and they do this or that and their lives . . . don't have any meaning and their families fall apart.

> I think I like men enough to know that men still want women to be a little bit feminine and all the rest of it, and I think [pro-choice people] have helped destroy that, I think they've made women into something like the same as men, and we're not. I think we're totally different. I don't think that means that we can't do some jobs they do, but I think we're totally different. I think that they've helped destroy the family because they want to make it so free for the woman to go to work, like with the childcare centers and all the rest of it. You know, now, evidently they're

> thinking up Social Security for the woman who works in the home and all the rest of it, and I just think that's ridiculous.

Because pro-life people see the world as inherently divided both emotionally and socially into a male sphere and a female sphere, they see the loss of the female sphere as a very deep one indeed. They see tenderness, morality, caring, emotionality, and self-sacrifice as the exclusive province of women; and if women cease to be traditional women, who will do the caring, who will offer the tenderness? A pro-life doctor argued that although women may have suffered from the softening influence they provided for men and for the society as a whole, they had much to gain as well.

> I think women's lib is on the wrong track. I think they've got every [possible] gripe and they've always been that way. The women have been the superior people. They're more civilized, they're more unselfish by nature, but now they want to compete with men at being selfish. And so there's nobody to give an example, and what happens is that men become *more* selfish. See, the women used to be an example and they had to take it on the chin for that . . . but they also benefited from it because we don't want to go back to the cavemen, where you drag the woman around and treat her like nothing. Women were to be protected, respected, and treated like something important.

In this view, everyone loses when traditional roles are lost. Men lose the nurturing that women offer, the nurturing that gently encourages them to give up their potentially destructive and aggressive urges. Women lose the protection and cherishing that men offer. And children lose full-time loving by at least one parent, as well as clear models for their own futures.

These different views about the intrinsic nature of men and women also shape pro-life views about sex. The nineteenth century introduced new terms to describe the two faces of sexual activity, distinguishing between "procreative love," whose goal is reproduction, and "amative love," whose goal is sensual pleasure and mutual enjoyment. (Although these two aspects of sexuality have undoubtedly existed for millennia, the Victorian era in the West democratized amative love so that it was no longer restricted to an elite who enjoyed the pleasures of lovers and courtesans.)[1]

For the pro-life people we talked with, the relative worth of procreative sex and amative sex was clear. In part this is because many of them, being Catholic, accept a natural law doctrine of sex, which holds that a body part is destined to be used for its physiological function. As one man put it: "You're not just given arms and legs for no purpose. . . . There must be some cause [for sex] and you begin to think, well, it must be for procreation ultimately, and certainly procreation in addition to fostering a loving relationship with your spouse."

In terms of this view, the meaning of sexual experiences is distorted whenever procreation is not intended. Contraception, premarital sex, and infidelity are wrong not only because of their social consequences but also because they strip sexual experience of its meaning. The man just quoted continued to spell out the implications of this position:

> Most pro-lifers think that people, regardless of their station in life, ought to be chaste—this means chaste also for married people. . . . I think this is because [pro-lifers], much more than pro-abortion people, are in reverence of sexuality and believe it literally to be a sacred thing. I really think pro-abortion people have a hard time arguing that they think that. [But] if you do think this way, [sex is] something very special, it's the means by which two people can express their union with one another, spiritual and physical. Then you see that it must be protected somehow, by certain forms and conventions, including marriage. . . . I think it's logical to say that someone who's pro-life on the abortion issue would be against artificial contraception, would be in favor of chastity in and outside of marriage. On the other hand, those who are pro-abortion, very few of them would be against contraception—I've never heard of any that are—and they will consider that the chastity question is not really a moral question, but up to the parties involved. . . . So I think you will have close to a unanimous opinion on each side on these questions.

(It is worth noting that this man uses the word *chastity* in its original sense of meaning morally acceptable sexuality. Thus a married couple who are sexually active and faithful to one another are "chaste.") One woman, a Catholic social worker, reiterated this connection between sex, procreation, and the sacred:

> At my father's funeral my aunt was telling me that she was the younger sister in a large family, and so as the older girls were having babies she would go from home to home and stay with them and help them out when the baby was born, and eventually there were enough sisters having babies that she had a little circuit. And she was telling me that my father never treated her with anything but respect—I guess she was

> about a fifteen-year-old at the time. I realized then that my father was a very literal Catholic, like he would never miss mass on Sunday, but he never really understood much about his religion. I think maybe his genuine respect for sex is the only thing that kind of filtered down [to me].

Because many pro-life people see sex as literally sacred, they are disturbed by values that seem to secularize and profane it. The whole constellation of values that supports amative (or "recreational") sex is seen by them as doing just that. Values that define sexuality as a wholesome physical activity, as healthy as volleyball but somewhat more fun, call into question everything that pro-life people believe in. Sex is sacred because in their world view it has the capacity to be something transcendent—to bring into existence another human life. To routinely eradicate that capacity through premarital sex (in which very few people seek to bring a new life into existence) or through contraception or abortion is to turn the world upside down.

As implied by our discussion so far, the attitudes of pro-life people toward contraception are rooted in their views about the inherent differences between men and women and about the nature and purpose of sexuality. Although the activists we interviewed often pointed out that the pro-life movement is officially neutral on the topic of contraception, this statement does not fully capture the complexity of their views and feelings. Virtually all of them felt very strongly that the pill and the IUD are abortifacients (they may cause the death of a very young embryo) and that passage of a human life law against abortion would also ban the pill and the IUD. Most of them, furthermore, refused to use traditional contraceptives on moral grounds. As a pro-life doctor said:

> I think it's quite clear that the IUD is abortifacient 100 percent of the time and the pill is sometimes an abortifacient—it's hard to know just when, so I think we need to treat it as an abortifacient. It's not really that much of an issue with me, [but] I think there's a respect for germinal life that is equivalent to a respect for individual life, and if one doesn't respect one's [own] generative capacity, I think one will not respect one's own life or the progeny that one has. So I think there's a spectrum there that begins with one's self and one's generative capacity.

Their stance toward other people's use of contraception is therefore ambivalent. They disapprove of "artificial" contraception, by which they mean use of the condom, the diaphragm, and vaginal spermicides. Many of them feel that the only acceptable "natural" method of birth control is natural family planning (NFP), the modern version of the rhythm method. As one woman said:

> I know that some Catholics are split on the contraceptive issue, but I feel contraception is a stopping of the consequences of a natural act, so therefore I don't believe in it. And I have a certain faith [that] if the Lord has sent this problem, He'll send a solution, and so [here is] this natural family planning thing which is beginning to be perfected—well, it's just like I was telling a priest who was beginning to believe in contraceptives, I said there's going to be an answer through natural law.

Developed in large part by Drs. John and Evelyn Billings of Australia, NFP improves upon the older rhythm method by teaching couples to recognize changes in the woman's body that signal the onset of ovulation.[2] NFP is morally acceptable to Catholics because, at least in the original formulation of the method, individuals abstain from sex right before, during, and right after ovulation.[3] Pro-life people who practice NFP argue that it has secular benefits as well. Here is what one woman and one man, respectively, had to say:

> It's really a whole new way of life for a married couple because it demands very close communication, to have to communicate with one another every day about their fertility. I think that's so beautiful. They both learn about one another's bodies, and it creates a tremendous closeness, and I think it demands a very mature love. Because, you know, a husband sees that he can't just demand love from his wife if she is not feeling good, if she is sick. So the same thing applies if she's fertile and they just can't afford to have another child right then. They have to postpone . . . making love in that fashion during those few days of the cycle. . . . It creates a completely new closeness and respect for one another, and devotion, and they live very much closer and happier, with much more love in their lives.

> Well, you know, the natural family planning books make a big thing out of how affection should be shown during the period of abstaining, and how this can bring you closer together than you might otherwise be—because . . . it would be easy to fall into a mechanical view of the spouse if you were to use mechanical means [of contraception]. . . . You have a better buttress against [a mechanical view] if you use a natural means. And I think that's got to be good for the marriage. Because if you work through an eight- or nine-day period of abstaining every month and showing affection in other ways—buying flowers and so on, holding hands like you did in courtship—that's what helps build a mar-

riage. Whereas in a situation where the only way you can show affection is conjugal, your marriage is very deficient. . . . And I think if you're sort of forced to do prudent things each month, it builds up a marriage.

Again, several factors interact to reinforce the belief that "artificial" contraception is wrong. To begin with, if the goal of sex is procreation, then contraceptives are by nature wrong, and this is the starting point for many pro-life people. But it is important to remember that this is a personal choice for them, not a matter of unquestioning obedience to doctrine. Many will say that they do not use contraception because their church does not approve; but, in fact, Catholics are increasingly using contraception in patterns similar to those of non-Catholics, and their families (and family ideals) are becoming increasingly hard to distinguish from those of the population at large.[4] Moreover, some data suggest that the most direct representative of the church, the parish priest, is also likely to be tacitly in favor of birth control.[5] Most pro-life people are therefore part of an institution that proclaims a value that most of its members and some of its officials ignore.

When pro-life people use NFP as a form of fertility control, they have not only a different moral rationale but also a different goal than pro-choice people have when they use contraception. They are using it *to time the arrival of children, not to foreclose entirely the possibility of having them*. For them, the risk of pregnancy while using NFP is not only *not* a drawback, it is a positive force that can enhance the marriage. As one man said:

I'll tell you, when you're using a so-called natural method . . . you can be incredibly perceptive as to when the fertile period is. But you're not going to be so perceptive that you're going to shut off every pregnancy. You know, there are a lot of things that people just simply do not understand because they've had no experience with them. It's like people who eat in restaurants all the time and have never been on the farm and had a natural meal—you know, where the food comes from the freshly killed animals the same day, from the fields. They don't have any concept of what a natural meal is like, and I think the same thing is true in the sexual area. I think that when you take the step of cutting off all possibility of conception indefinitely, it puts emotional and physical restraints on a relationship that remove some of its most beautiful values. . . . The frame of mind in which you know there might be a conception in the midst of a sex act is quite different from that in which you know there could not be a conception. . . . I don't think that people who are con-

> stantly using physical, chemical means of contraception really ever experience the sex act in all of its beauty.

Thus the one thing we commonly assume that everyone wants from a contraceptive—that it be 100 percent reliable and effective—is precisely what pro-life people do *not* want from their method of fertility control.

Pro-life values on the issue of abortion—and by extension on motherhood—are intimately tied to the values we have just illustrated. But they also draw more directly on notions of motherhood (and fatherhood) that are not shared by pro-choice people. This might seem obvious from the fact that pro-life people often account for their own activism by referring to the notion that babies are being murdered in their mothers' wombs. But pro-life feelings about the nature of parenthood draw on other more subtle beliefs as well.

Pro-life people believe that one becomes a parent by *being* a parent; parenthood is for them a "natural" rather than a social role. One is a parent by virtue of having a child, and the values implied by the in-vogue term *parenting* (as in *parenting classes*) are alien to them. The financial and educational preparations for parenthood that pro-choice people see as necessary are seen by pro-life people as a serious distortion of values. Pro-life people fear that when one focuses on job achievement, home owning, and getting money in the bank *before* one has children, children will be seen as barriers to these things. As one pro-life woman put it:

> There has been a very strong attitude that the child represents an obstacle to achievement. Not just that the child is something desirable that you add further down the line . . . but that the child is an obstacle to a lifestyle that will include the yacht and weekend skiing. . . . A great many couples are opting not to have any children at all because of the portrayal of the child as an obstacle, especially to a woman's career and a two-salary family.

It is worth noting, in this context, that several pro-life women said that few people actually *enjoy* the state of being pregnant.* Here are the comments of three of them:

> I think it's a normal thing [not to enjoy pregnancy]. I think it's also kind of built into the system because everything changes in your body and

* I know of no survey data that would demonstrate whether women on the average like being pregnant or not. It seems likely, however, that the way in which women *define*

very often you're sick and . . . you kind of hate the thought that things are changing, but after you start feeling a little better, you start looking forward to the baby. [But] a lot of the abortions are already done by that time.

I never wanted to have a baby, I never planned to have five children, I never felt the total joy that comes from being pregnant. I mean I was *sick* for nine months. I mean my general attitude was, "Hell, I'm pregnant again." But I thought pregnancy was a natural part of marriage, and I believed so much in the word *natural*, and so I loved the babies when they were born. I realized that a lot of women have abortions in that first trimester out of the . . . physical and psychological fear that they experience, and the depression. . . . A lot of them will regret having that abortion later on. They work too fast, the doctors advise them too fast. They can outgrow that feeling of fear if they give themselves a chance.

Another of the doctors I know said that you see a lot of unwanted pregnancies, but you almost never find an unwanted baby. . . . Many people, even married people, are very ambivalent about a pregnancy in the very early stages, and yet these abortion decisions have to be made at that [time]. And really, if you just stayed with it a little longer, you might welcome that trial very much.

Clearly, pro-life activists are concerned about the fact that women may seek abortions before they have had a chance to accommodate themselves to the admittedly unpleasant reality of being pregnant.

Pro-life people tacitly assume that the way to upgrade motherhood is to make it an *inclusive* category, that all married people should be (or be willing to be) parents. In particular, women who choose to be in the public world of work should eschew the role of wife and mother, or, if they marry, should be prepared to put the public world of work second to their role as wife and mother. If a man or woman is to be sexually active, they feel, he or she should be married. And if married, one should be prepared to welcome a child whenever it arrives, however inopportune it may seem at the time. In their view, to try to balance a

---

pregnancy depends on the kinds of resources and social supports they have for facing it. The reason that pro-life women might assume that women in general do not like pregnancy is that, for them, pregnancy is a taken-for-granted part of marital life rather than something one plans for, waits for until one can afford it, and then tries eagerly to achieve. Pregnancy is not a scarce resource in their lives. For a different logic about why some women may assume that pregnancy is hard to get used to, see Lillian Rubin, *Worlds of Pain* (New York: Basic Books, 1978).

number of competing commitments—especially when parenthood gets shuffled into second or fourth place—is both morally wrong and personally threatening.

Pro-life people also feel very strongly that there is an anti-child sentiment abroad in our society and that this is expressed in the strong cultural norm that families should have only two children.

> Well, I think there's always been a problem with kids. But it doesn't seem to me that they're looked on as positively as they used to be. People look down on someone who wants to have more than two kids. Kids are looked on as a burden, [as] work. And they are. [People aren't] looking at the fun side of it and the nice side of it.

> Every place you go it's just for two children, or for families with two children. Children's furniture, they make only to last for two kids, and you go to restaurants and there's only enough [room] for two kids, and games, they are only for two people and maybe four, [including] the parents. When you look at all these things, it's amazing.

Since one out of every five pro-life activists in this study had six or more children, it is easy to see how these values can seem threatening. In the course of our interviews, a surprising number of activists said they did not feel discriminated against because of their pro-life activities, including their opposition to abortion, but that they did feel socially stigmatized because they had large families. As one woman with several children said: "[My husband,] being a scientist, gets a lot [of questions]. You know, having a large family, it's just for the poor uneducated person, but if you have a doctor's degree and you have a large family, what's wrong with you?" The pro-choice argument that parents must plan their families in order to give their children the best emotional and financial resources therefore sounds like an attack on people with large families. "[People think] children can't possibly make it and be successful if they come from a large family . . . because you can't give them all the time and energy that they need. Well, first of all, I'm here [at home], I'm not out working, which adds to the amount of time that I can give."

Pro-life values on children therefore represent an intersection of several values we have already discussed. Because pro-life people believe that the purpose of sexuality is to have children, they also believe that one should not plan the exact number and timing of children too carefully, for it is both wrong and foolish to make detailed life plans that depend upon exact control of fertility. Because children will influence life plans more than life plans will influence the number of children, it is also wrong to value one's planned accomplishments—primarily the acquisition of the things money can buy—over the intangible benefits that children can bring. Thus, reasoning backwards, pro-life people object to every step of the pro-choice logic. If one values material things too highly, one will be tempted to try to make detailed plans for acquiring them. If one tries to plan too thoroughly, one will be tempted to use highly effective contraception, which removes the potential of childbearing from a marriage. Once the potential for children is eliminated, the sexual act is distorted (and for religious people, morally wrong), and husbands and wives lose an important bond between them. Finally, when marriage partners who have accepted the logic of these previous steps find that contraception has failed, they are ready and willing to resort to abortion in order to achieve their goals.

This is not to say that pro-life people do not approve of planning. They do. But because of their world view (and their religious faith) they see human planning as having very concrete limits. To them it is a matter of priorities: if individuals want fame, money, and worldly success, then they have every right to pursue them. But if they are sexually active (and married, as they should be if they are sexually active), they have an obligation to subordinate other parts of life to the responsibilities they have taken on by virtue of that activity.

These views about the nature of parenthood and the purpose of sexuality also come together to shape attitudes about premarital sex, particularly among teenagers.* Not surprisingly, people who feel that sex should be procreative find premarital sex disturbing. Since the purpose of sex is procreation (or at least "being open to the gift of a new life"), people who are sexually active before marriage are by definition not actively seeking procreation; and in the case of teenagers, they are seldom financially and emotionally prepared to become parents. So for pro-life people, premarital sex is both morally and socially wrong. As one man put it:

> One of my pet peeves is the words *sexually active young person* because I don't equate being sexually active with having sex—that's not my

* People in this study used the terms *teen-aged* and *premarital* sex interchangeably, although they are two separate categories: older people are just as capable of having premarital (or nonmarital) sex as are teens. But teen-aged premarital sex represents the

> value system. "Sexually active" [sounds like what] any nice Christian teen-aged girl and guy ought to be. I trust that my sexuality is broader than the act of sex. . . . I want young people to be reinforced so they don't think of themselves as some kind of neuter because [they are not having sex]. And that's what we're doing with sex.

Although they agree that there is a very real problem with teen-aged pregnancy in the United States today, pro-life people believe that the availability of contraception is what encourages teens to have sex in the first place, so they feel that sex education and contraception simply add fuel to the fire.

> I don't think that we would have as many sexually active teenagers, first of all, if contraception weren't readily available and acceptable. And when they use the term *responsible sex*, they don't mean the same thing I do, or that many of us do. *Responsible sex* to people who are in the contraceptive world means use contraception so you don't get pregnant [or catch a] venereal disease, which I've been reading is a false security they've been given. . . . So there's possibly more of a temptation to participate in sex than we had when we were young, aside from morality, because you just knew that if you were sexually active you might well get pregnant.

> Planned parenthood . . . it seems so logical—we've got all of these problems here, and if we just do sex education and contraceptives and everything, we'll solve all of them. It's kind of like two people coming to a fire. One says, "Let's put out this fire by throwing water on it." The other says, "Oh no, we always did it that way. I've got something better, it's called gasoline . . . [and] it's *cooler* than water." Well, there's a term in the equation that's being overlooked, and that term . . . is responsibility—caring, real honest-to-God caring for other people.

For most pro-life people, the answer to the problems of teen-aged sexuality is *moral* rather than practical: teenagers should be taught that sex before marriage is wrong. For example: "There is really only going to be one way to avoid the tremendous increase in teen-age pregnancies, abortion, unwed mothers, and venereal disease. And that is to try very hard to promote and go back to an ethic that makes a strong standard of abstinence for the unwed—I guess I can't just say teens."

---

worst of both worlds to most pro-life people. Sexually active teenagers are from their point of view people who on two different grounds should not be having sex: they are unmarried and they are too young even to contemplate marriage seriously.

Providing contraception (and abortion) services for teenagers represents a clear threat to pro-life views. A series of legal and policy decisions in the United States as a whole have put teenagers in a rather peculiar situation. A person under the age of eighteen, as a minor, cannot have medical treatment without parental consent, but there are three exceptions to this doctrine. Teenagers may seek contraceptive services, may have an abortion, and may seek treatment for venereal disease without parental consent. As a matter of public policy, the social benefits to these treatments are considered to outweigh the social benefits of requiring parental consent.

Pro-life people believe that this policy acts to cut off parental support and resources precisely when children need them most. They feel that children underestimate how accepting and supportive parents will be and therefore make hasty (and irrevocable) decisions alone. They also think the policy serves to loosen the ties between parent and child. They argue that families have enough pressures on them anyway and that this policy in effect gives children permission to engage in activities whose consequences they cannot fully appreciate—and more to the point, activities their parents disapprove of.

Equally important, pro-life people see public policy in this realm as intruding the state into areas where it does not belong, namely, within the family. From their point of view, the family is both beleaguered and sacred, and any policy that seeks to address the members of a family as separate entities, rather than as an organic whole, is a priori harmful.* As one woman put it:

> Even this . . . family planning is sexual education. It's planned downtown with Planned Parenthood, it's not planned with the parents. So [under] the laws which exist now, the children get contraceptives without parental consent. What it's doing is [creating] a gap in family rela-

* This explains the frequent opposition of pro-life people to policies one would think they would support as the intended beneficiaries are children. Programs such as free school lunches, day care centers, extra nutrition for pregnant women, and anti-child-abuse programs have been known to run into vociferous opposition by pro-life groups, not because they are necessarily opposed to the *content* of such programs, but because they resist the idea of letting the state into the sacrosanct territory of the home. The seeming inconsistency between pro-life support of unborn children and resistance to programs aimed at helping children already born is what engenders the bitter pro-choice quip that pro-life people believe "life begins at conception and ends at birth."

> tionships. And the home and the family . . . should be the primary source of moral values. Well, if some parents don't take responsibility, then I think it's the responsibility of education *to encourage parents to do it, rather than take it away from them*—which is what has happened [emphasis added].

This pro-life opposition to sex education, however, springs from feelings that are even deeper than a concern about the state intruding itself between members of a family. Their opposition draws on certain strongly felt but rarely articulated beliefs about the nature of morality. Pro-life people as a group subscribe to explicit and well-articulated moral codes. (After all, many of them are veterans of childhood ethics and religion classes.) Morality, for them, is a straightforward and unambiguous set of rules that specify what is moral behavior. Since they believe that these rules originate in a Divine Plan, they see them as transcendent principles, eternally valid regardless of time, cultural setting, and individual belief. "Thou shalt not kill," they argue, is as valid now as it was 2,000 years ago, and the cases to which it applies are still the same. They tend to locate their morality in traditional, ancient codes such as the Ten Commandments and the "Judeo-Christian" law, which have stood the test of time and exist as external standards against which behavior should be judged.

Thus, abortion offends the deepest moral convictions of pro-life people in several ways. To begin with, it breaks a divine law. The Commandment says "Thou shalt not kill." The embryo is human (it is not a member of another species) and alive (it is not dead). Thus, according to the reasoning by syllogism they learned in childhood religion classes, the embryo is a "human life," and taking it clearly breaks one of the Commandments.

Moreover, the logic used by pro-choice advocates (and the Supreme Court) to justify abortion affronts the moral reasoning of pro-life people. For them, either the embryo is a human life or it is not; the concept of an intermediate category—a *potential* human life—seems simply inadmissible. Further, the argument that individuals should arrive at a *personal* decision about the moral status of this intermediate category is as strange to most of them as arguing that individual soldiers in wartime should act according to their own judgment of the wisdom of the army's battle plan.

A professed unwillingness to deviate from a strict moral code naturally has its repercussions in private life. Pro-life people, their rhetoric notwithstanding, do have abortions. Among pro-choice people who were associated with organizations that arrange abortions, it was something of a cliché that pro-life people were believers only until they found themselves with an unwanted pregnancy, which made them more than willing to seek an abortion. When pressed for proof, however, these pro-choice activists retreated behind medical ethics, claiming they could not invade a patient's privacy by actually naming names. Later in the study, however, more persuasive evidence was offered by pro-life people active in Life Centers. These centers, staffed and funded by the pro-life movement, are located in hospitals or other medical settings and offer free pregnancy tests and pregnancy counseling should the pregnancy test prove positive. Although counselors in Life Centers actively encourage women to continue their pregnancies, they do not openly advertise their pro-life stand; they explain only that they provide free pregnancy tests and counseling. But since most places that offer free tests and counseling are also abortion referral centers, many women come to Life Centers in order to get such a referral. Life Center counselors estimate that as many as a third of the women they see go on to have an abortion, even after having had pro-life counseling. Since Life Centers are by definition pro-life, when people who work in them say that pro-life members (and in particular the children of pro-life members) have come into their centers seeking abortions, we can probably believe them. After all, they have nothing to gain by admitting that their own members (and their own children), like the rest of us, sometimes have trouble living up to their ideals.

Thus, pro-life people, like the pro-choice people we will examine shortly, have a consistent, coherent view of the world, notwithstanding the fact that like anyone else, they cannot always bring their behavior in line with their highest ideals. The very coherence of their world view, however, makes clear that abortion, and all it represents, is profoundly unsettling to them. By the same token, the values that pro-life people bring to bear on the abortion issue are deeply threatening to those people active in the pro-choice movement.

Pro-Choice Views of the World

On almost all the dimensions just considered, the values and beliefs of pro-choice diametrically oppose those of pro-life people, as does the logic whereby they arrive at their values. For example, whereas pro-life people believe that men and women are inherently different and therefore have different "natural" roles in life, pro-choice people believe that men and women are substantially equal, by which they mean substantially similar. As a result, they see women's reproductive and family roles not as a "natural" niche but as potential barriers to full equality. The organization of society, they argue, means that motherhood, so long as it is involuntary, is potentially always a low-status, unrewarding role to which women can be banished at any time. Thus, from their point of view, *control* over reproduction is essential for women to be able to live up to their full human potential. Here is how one woman put it:

> I just feel that one of the main reasons women have been in a secondary position culturally is because of the natural way things happen. Women would bear children because they had no way to prevent it, except by having no sexual involvement. And that was not practical down through the years, so without knowing what to do to prevent it, women would continually have children. And then if they were the ones bearing the child, nursing the child, it just made sense [for them to be] the ones to rear the child. I think that was the natural order. When we advanced and found that we could control our reproduction, we could choose the size of our families or whether we wanted families. But that changed the whole role of women in our society. Or it opened it up to change the role. It allowed us to be more than just the bearers of children, the homemakers. That's not to say that we shouldn't continue in that role. It's a good role, but it's not the *only* role for women.

Pro-choice people agree that women (and men) find children and families a satisfying part of life, but they also think it is foolhardy for women to believe that this is the only life role they will ever have. They argue, in essence, that pro-life women who do not work outside the home are only "one man away from disaster." A death, a divorce, a desertion, or a disability can push a woman with no career skills or experience perilously close to the edge of penury—as shown by the ever-increasing numbers of "displaced homemakers"—widows and divorcées left with virtually no financial or employment resources.

At the same time, pro-choice people value what I have called "amative" sex, that is, sex whose primary purpose is not reproduction. The idea that sexual activity is valuable and indeed sacred because of its inherent reproductive capacity strikes many pro-choice people as absurd. From their point of view, if the purpose of sex were limited to reproduction, no rational Creator would have arranged things so that an individual can have hundreds or even thousands of acts of intercourse in a lifetime, with millions of sex cells—egg and sperm—always at the ready. More to the point, they argue that belief in the basically procreative nature of sex leads to an oppressive degree of *social regulation of sexual behavior, particularly the behavior of women*, who must be protected (in their viewpoint, repressed) because free expression of sexual wishes will get them "in trouble" and lead the species into overpopulation. In the pro-choice value system, both the "double standard" and "purdah"—the ancient custom of veiling women and keeping them entirely out of the public eye, lest they be too sexually arousing to men—are logical outcomes of a preoccupation with protecting and controlling women's reproductive capacities.

Significantly, many of the pro-choice activists described themselves as having grown up in families with traditional, "sex-negative" values that focused on the dangers of uncontrolled sexual feelings. They now see themselves as seeking a set of "sex-positive" values, for themselves and for the society as a whole, that emphasize the pleasure, beauty, and joy of sex rather than the dangers. When pro-choice people speak of being raised under "sex-negative" values, they mean that sex was not openly talked about, that it was certainly not portrayed as something to be enjoyed for its own sake, and that budding childish sexuality—masturbation and adolescent flirting—was often treated harshly. Premarital sexuality leading to pregnancy was a "fate worse than death." The following anecdote, though more vivid and unusual than some that pro-choice people recounted, indicates the kind of thing they had in mind when they spoke about "sex-negative" attitudes:

> The custom in my youth was that if a woman became pregnant and she was unmarried . . . the penalty was in effect to be excommunicated. Not literally, because she was still somewhat in touch, but she was removed from the roll of [church] members and became a "listener" as they said, an auditor. She could attend [church] but she would not be a member. And [she was] ostracized in that little community. . . . I'm thinking of one woman in particular, Kitty. Before she was known to be pregnant, people would talk to her after the evening service was over, when everybody was outside socializing; but once this happened they wouldn't talk to her. None of the [church] elders would, except one—my father. . . . He was the one who eventually made the motion that she should be readmitted to membership.

Such harsh treatment makes sense if it is presumed that sexuality inevitably finds genital expression and that pregnancy is a thing that can (and indeed *should*) occur as a result. But for people who plan anyway to have small families, who have no moral opposition to contraceptives, who value rational planning in all realms including pregnancy, and whose other values focus on the present and other people rather than on the future and God, putting a taboo on sexual expression seems irrelevant at best and potentially damaging at worst.

Pro-choice people believe that sexual activity is good as an end in itself. For much of a lifetime at least, its main purpose is not to produce children (or to remind them of that possibility) but to afford pleasure, human contact, and, perhaps most important, intimacy. Whereas for pro-life people sex is *inherently* transcendent—because a new life may be created at any time—for pro-choice people, it is *potentially* transcendent, and its spiritual meaning is a goal to be pursued rather than a fact to be faced. Despite the claims of some pro-life people, pro-choice people *do* believe that sex can be sacred, but it is a different kind of sacredness that they have in mind. For them, sex is sacred when it is mystical, when it dissolves the boundaries between self and other, when it brings one closer to one's partner, and when it gives one a sense of the infinite. Transcendent sex, for them, grows out of feelings experienced in the present rather than beliefs about what may happen in the future. It can be achieved only when people feel secure, when they feel trusting, and when they feel love for themselves and for the other. And because mobilizing such delicate social and emotional resources as trust, caring, and intimacy requires *practice*, pro-choice people do not denigrate sexual experiences that fall short of achieving transcendence. They judge individual cases of premarital sex, contraception, and infidelity according to the ways in which they enhance or detract from conditions of trust and caring. In their value scheme, something that gives people opportunities for intimacy simply cannot be seen as wrong.

These general attitudes about the nature and meaning of sex influence pro-choice views on contraception. To be sure, the significance of contraception in itself is not a very salient issue for most pro-choice people. They see using contraceptives as something like taking good care of one's teeth—a matter of sensible routine, a good health habit. (Indeed, they find pro-life objections to contraception mysterious and dismiss them as "medieval" or "religious.") They do have some pragmatic concerns about contraceptive methods—how unpleasant or how safe they are—but contraception in the abstract has no moral connotations for them. Since the primary moral value they see in sexuality is its potential for creating intimacy with the self and another, a good contraceptive (and a moral one, to stretch the term) is one that is safe, undistracting, and not unpleasant to use. And since they *do* use contraception to postpone childbearing for long periods of time, their ideal contraceptive is easy to use, *highly effective*, and not a risk to their health.

The few pro-choice people who have heard of Natural Family Planning, which so many pro-life people advocate so enthusiastically, tend to dismiss it as irrelevant or irresponsible. NFP can require abstinence for as many as ten or twelve days a month, and some studies suggest that one-fourth of the couples who use it may get pregnant.[6] Since pro-choice people place a high value on the intimacy offered by sexual activity, abstaining from it for ten or twelve days a month is a high price to pay, and NFP's high pregnancy rate (and what they see as a corresponding need for abortions) is an unacceptable cost. Thus, pro-choice people reject NFP for precisely the reasons that pro-life people find it attractive: it calls for abstinence and keeps pregnancy a lively possibility.

Pro-choice people do have one clearly moral concern about sexuality, however: most of them oppose the use of abortion, instead of traditional methods of contraception, as a routine method of birth control. In part, their opposition is pragmatic; repeated abortions have their own set of health risks.* But physical risks are not the whole story. Here is what a pro-choice minister said:

> Last time at my class in human sexuality, a young woman brought this up [the morality of abortion as birth control], and I was grateful to her because I seldom bring it up myself because it's a spiritual issue. There's a spiritual force within a woman when she's pregnant, and people of great spiritual sensitivity have to deal with the reality of that potential life. A lot of people don't think there's this kind of subtlety, and

* It is not clear whether repeated abortions have a cumulative effect, that is, whether the risk of a second abortion is greater than the risk of the first. But even if the risks are simply additional, each subsequent abortion puts the woman at new risks. The actual health risk of one (or several) abortions is still a matter of some controversy since women who have abortions may also do other things (such as smoke cigarettes) that carry their own sets of risks. For a review of the risks of abortion, see Christopher Tietze, *Induced Abortion: A Factbook* (New York: Population Council, 1981).

> when they do I'm very supportive of them. Yes, there's a spiritual issue involved. I take the idea of ending the life of the fetus very, very gravely. . . . [That] doesn't in any way diminish my conviction that a woman has the right to do it, but I become distressed when people regard pregnancy lightly and ignore the spiritual significance of a pregnancy.

As this comment suggests, opposition to abortion as a routine form of birth control is based on a complex and subtle moral reasoning. For most pro-choice people, the personhood of the embryo does not exist at conception, but it does develop at some later time. The pro-choice view of personhood is thus a *gradualist* one. An embryo may not be a full person until it is viable (capable of sustaining its own life if born prematurely), but it has the rights of a potential person at all times, and those rights increase in moral weight as the pregnancy continues. (Wearing an IUD is morally acceptable to pro-choice people because they consider very early embryos to be little more than fertilized eggs.) Pro-choice people accept that sometimes the potential rights of the embryo have to be sacrificed to the actual rights of the mother. But a woman who arbitrarily or capriciously brings an embryo into existence, *when she had an alternative*, is seen as usurping even the potential rights of the embryo by trivializing them, and this offends the moral sense of pro-choice activists.

This explains an otherwise baffling feature of pro-choice morality. A great many pro-choice activists in this study, particularly those active in helping women have abortions, find multiple abortions morally troubling. Some of them even volunteered the fact that they felt like personal failures when a woman came back to them for a second, third, or higher-order abortion. At first glance, this would appear to be illogical: if it is morally acceptable for a woman to end one pregnancy with an abortion, why is it wrong for her to end subsequent pregnancies by abortion? For pro-choice people, the answer is simple and draws on both the gradualist and contextualist moral reasoning outlined above. The first abortion presumably represents the lesser of several evils, where the abortion of an embryo is seen as less morally wrong than bringing a child one cannot effectively parent into the world.* But

* Keeping in mind the pro-choice distinction between an embryo and a baby, the values expressed here account for why having a baby and giving it up for adoption, as pro-life people advocate, is not seen by most pro-choice people as a moral solution to the abortion problem. To transform an embryo into a baby and then send that baby out into a world where the parents can have no assurance that it will be well loved and cared for is, for pro-choice people, the height of moral irresponsibility.

since most women are given contraceptive services after an abortion, every abortion after the first represents a case where a woman had the option of avoiding pregnancy and did not. Except in extraordinary cases, pro-choice people see this bringing of an embryo into existence when it could have been avoided as morally wrong.

It is in the context of the relative rights of babies and embryos that pro-choice values about parenting—about the kind of life the baby-to-be might be reasonably expected to have—play such an important role. Pro-choice people have very clear standards about what parenting entails: it means giving a child the best set of emotional, psychological, social, and financial resources that one can arrange as a preparation for future life. Pro-choice people believe that it is the duty of a parent to prepare the child for the future, and good parents are seen as arranging life (and childbearing) so that this can be done most effectively.

These values about what constitutes a good parent therefore support and shape pro-choice attitudes toward children and the timing of their arrival. Since children demand financial sacrifices, for example, couples should not have them until they have acquired the financial position to give their children the best. Otherwise, under pressure, parents will come to resent a child, and this will limit their ability to be caring, attentive, and nurturing to their children. As a corollary, pro-choice people want children who feel loved, who have self-esteem, and who "feel good about themselves"; they believe that parents should postpone childbearing until they have the proper emotional resources needed to do the intense one-to-one psychological caring that good parenting requires. (It is these two factors that they have in mind when they make the statement, which pro-life people find unfathomable, that they are not "ready" for childbearing.)

Because pro-choice people see the optional raising of children as requiring financial resources, interpersonal and social skills, and emotional maturity, they often worry about how easy it is to have children. In their view, too many people stumble into parenthood without really appreciating what it takes.

> I would say that the tip of the iceberg is purposeful parenthood. I think life is too cheap, I think we're too easy-going. We assume that everybody will be a mother—that's Garrett Hardin's "compulsory motherhood" concept. Hell, it's a privilege, it's not special enough. The contraceptive age affords us the opportunity to make motherhood really special. And I think we have a moral obligation, in Emerson's sense: new occasions teach new duties. . . . Motherhood used to be an act of

> omission, I mean you just didn't have any choices, philosophically speaking, you did it because there wasn't anything else to do. And now we have to change the question. We used to say, why not have a baby? and now we say why? So that things have changed just plain philosophically about parenthood, and that's just one part of it.

Since pro-choice activists think that in the long run abortion will enhance the quality of parenting by making it optional, they see themselves as being on the side of children when they advocate abortion. In contrast to pro-life people, who believe that parenthood will be enhanced by making it *inclusive*, that is, making it a mandatory part of the package of being a sexually active person, pro-choice people feel that the way to improve the quality of parenthood is to make it more *exclusive*. Here is what a minister had to say:

> [My attitude on abortion] stems out of, I think, the same basic concern about the right [of children] to share the good life and all these things; children, once born, have rights that we consistently deny them. I remember giving a talk [in which I said] that I thought one of my roles was to be an advocate for the fetus, and for the fetus's right not to be born. I think the right-to-lifers thought I was great until that point. . . . I think if I had my druthers I'd probably advocate the need for licensing pregnancies.

In part, this attitude stems from the value placed on planning. A planned child is a wanted child, and a child who is wanted starts out on a much better basis than one who is not. But the pro-choice activists did not necessarily accept a narrow view of "being wanted."

> I think that raising a child is a contract of twenty years at least, and I've still found it going on after thirty. . . . So if you're not in a life situation where you can [make] the commitment to raising a child, you should have the option of not doing so at that time. Of course many people don't want the child when they find out that they're pregnant, but they resolve negative feelings and by the time the child is born, they do want it. . . . But if they don't want it enough to seek an abortion, [when they can't offer it the best], then probably they shouldn't have it. And I'm as much concerned with the [rights of the] child as the rights of the woman.

Connected to this value is an acceptance of teen-aged sex. Pro-choice people are concerned about teen-aged *parenthood* because young people and the unwed are in no position to become good parents, but they have no basic objection to sexual activity among young people *if they are "responsible*," that is, if they do not take the risk of becoming parents. Because pro-choice people view the goal of sex as being the creation of intimacy, caring, and trust, they also believe that people need to practice those skills before making a long-term commitment to someone. They may practice them with a number of people or with the person they intend to marry. In either case, premarital sex is not only likely to occur but desirable. Because pro-choice people see premarital sex as reasonable and because their values give them no intrinsic reason to be against it, any concerns they may have about premarital and teen-aged sex are almost exclusively pragmatic. In some respects, pro-choice people agree with the pro-life conclusion: teenagers are not ready to be parents. But whereas pro-life people see the answer as chastity, pro-choice people are skeptical. In part because of the experiences of their own lives, they do not believe that individuals choose not to have sex merely because someone tells them that they shouldn't. Taboos, from their point of view, merely inhibit planning for sex, not sex itself. This point was made by a pro-choice woman who has spent much of her professional life counseling teenagers. She said it is unreasonable to tell young people they aren't supposed to have sex at all and then ask them to be responsible about it:

> If driving were fraught with all the moral and ethical dilemmas [posed by sexual experience], would you stand up in the motor vehicle department, hold your head up high and say, "Look world, I'm being responsible, I'm taking out a license"? Hell no, you'd do it the way all of us did it—we took the car out before we were licensed, just a little bit at a time. And that's what we're doing with sex.

Naturally enough, the values that pro-choice people attach to sex, contraception, and abortion are rooted in certain basic convictions about the nature of morality, and to some extent their opponents recognize this. Several pro-life activists spoke disparagingly of pro-choice morality as "situation ethics," and a few of the more sophisticated mentioned Joseph Fletcher by name.[7] Although this is hardly sympathetic, it does imply that pro-life people are aware that pro-choice people use a different basis for their moral reasoning. In fact, pro-choice people *do* believe in what might be called "situation ethics." Partly because they are pluralists, they seriously doubt whether a single moral code can serve everyone. Partly because they are secularists, they do not accept the traditional Judeo-Christian codes as absolute moral standards; they see them as ethical guidelines that emerged in one historical period and may or may not be relevant to the present. Perhaps most centrally, they see morality not as obedience to a set of inflexible rules, such as the Ten Commandments, but rather as the application of a few general ethical principles to a vast array of cases. All of these factors, combined with a staunch belief in the rights of the individual, lead them to believe that only individuals, not governments or churches, can ultimately make ethical decisions—which makes it tempting to describe their moral position as quintessentially protestant, in a secular rather than a religious sense. Hence pro-choice people emphasize that abortion is an *individual, private* choice. As one activist said:

> Well, of course you can't deny that abortion is ending something that's alive, but we take the position that the decision to bear a child, to raise a child, is a private decision—an ethical private decision—and the state has no [legitimate] interest in regulating it. Now if this is a matter of conscience, and if your beliefs are contrary to abortion, then of course you can decide not to have an abortion, even if it means some other sacrifice.

This comment illustrates three key features of pro-choice moral logic. First, there is a distinction between an embryo and a child, which all pro-choice people take for granted. Second, there is the idea that the embryo, though not a baby or a full human being, is nonetheless "alive" and therefore has some implicit moral rights. Finally, there is a pluralist bias: if a person has a different moral view of abortion, she should follow her own conscience, "even if it means some other sacrifice." Morality thus consists of weighing a number of competing situations and rights and trying to reconcile them under general moral principles rather than specific moral rules. This view is not confined to laypeople in the pro-choice movement; it is embraced by men and women of the clergy as well. One minister said: "Throughout [an earlier] period, my theological thinking [was still] an amorphous thing, but I felt okay. The bottom line on it was that if there be a God, then God could hardly object to people asking questions. And I looked at life, as I guess I still do to some extent, as a kind of laboratory where you test things and what's okay [you keep] and what isn't you junk it."

To use another religious metaphor, pro-choice activists seem to have a New Testament approach to morality. Although relatively few of them mention either the New Testament or Joseph Fletcher's ethics by name, they do call on the moral principles associated with these two sources. That is, when trying to decide what is the moral thing to do, pro-choice people ask what is the *loving* thing to do. The choice of the word *loving* emphasizes the fact that moral judgment relies upon a subjectively reasoned application of moral principles rather than upon an externally existing moral code.

As a result, pro-choice activists often find themselves debating moral dilemmas with themselves. Because they do not see certain activities as intrinsically right or wrong, they find that they must decide how individual moral conflicts are to be resolved in the light of moral principles. (To be sure, pro-choice people, like pro-life people, do find certain behaviors intrinsically wrong and justify their rejection of such behaviors in terms not far afield from those of the pro-life people.)* However, because they believe in and can afford a moral world that has many shades of gray, they often, as in the case of the embryo, find themselves drawing fine distinctions that their opponents dismiss as "hair-splitting." The moral conflict about abortion for pro-choice people is in some way the mirror image of the pro-life conflict. If pro-life people have trouble accommodating complex real-life situations, such as their own need for an abortion, with a strict moral code, then pro-choice people face the dilemmas inherent in having a code so flexible that what is right and wrong is not immediately apparent but is discovered only as the product of immense amounts of intellectual effort. Because the morality of the pro-choice people rests on a delicate balancing of a range of competing rights, they are always slightly insecure as to whether they have covered all of the relevant data. Moreover, they are aware that the average person in the street is not as morally nuanced

* For example, pro-choice people would oppose necrophilia. Given their explicit values, however, this does not make sense. After all, necrophilia does not "harm" the participants in any direct physical way, and at least one of the participants is beyond the reach of physical (and moral) harm by definition. Moreover, one participant is presumably a consenting adult, and the other's consent (and age) is irrelevant. But the rejection of necrophilia as an accepted sexual lifestyle by pro-choice people demonstrates that pushed far enough, even pluralists have their boundaries. When pushed, pro-choice people say they find necrophilia wrong because it diminishes the dignity of someone who was once a person, is "sick" behavior, damaging to the person who does it, and demeans the humanness of us all. This sense of damage to an abstract notion of what it is to be human is exactly the grounds upon which pro-life people reject abortion. At the extremes, then, both sides call for the protection of diffuse human values that cannot be easily operationalized.

as they are, and they worry that what is for them the product of careful moral thought will just be taken for granted. Given these two very different methods of moral assessment, therefore, it might fairly be said that the demon of pro-life people is guilt, and the demon of pro-choice people is anxiety.

World Views

All these different issues that divide pro-life and pro-choice activists from one another—their views on men and women, sexuality, contraception, and morality—in turn reflect the fact that the two sides have two very different orientations to the world and that these orientations in turn revolve around two very different moral centers. The pro-life world view, notwithstanding the occasional atheist or agnostic attracted to it, is at the core one that centers around God: pro-life activists are on the whole deeply committed to their religious faith and deeply involved with it. A number of important consequences follow.

Because most pro-life people have a deep faith in God, they also believe in the rightness of His plan for the world. They are therefore skeptical about the ability of individual humans to understand, much less control, events that unfold according to a divine, rather than human, blueprint. From their point of view, human attempts at control are simply arrogance, an unwillingness to admit that larger forces than human will determine human fate. One woman made the point clearly: "God is the Creator of life, and I think all sexual activity should be open to that [creation]. That does not mean that you have to have a certain number of children or anything, but it should be open to Him and His will. The contraceptive mentality denies his will, 'It's my will, not your will.' And here again, the selfishness comes in."

This comment grew out of a discussion on contraception, but it also reveals values about human efficacy and its role in a larger world. While individuals can and should control their lives, pro-life people believe they should do so with a humility that understands that a force greater than themselves exists and, furthermore, that unpredicted things can be valuable. A woman who lost two children early in life to a rare genetic defect makes the point: "I didn't plan my son, my third child, and only because I was rather frightened that I might have a problem with another child. But I was certainly delighted when I became pregnant and had him. That's what I mean, I guess I feel that you can't plan everything in life. Some of the nicest things that have happened to me have certainly been the unplanned." Another woman went further: "I think people are foolish to worry about things in the future. The future takes care of itself."

Consequently, from the pro-life point of view, the contemporary movement away from the religious stand, what they see as the "secularization" of society, is at least one part of the troubles of contemporary society. By this they mean at least two things. First, there is the decline in religious commitment, which they feel keenly. But, second, they are also talking about a decline of a common community, a collective sense of what is right and wrong. From their viewpoint, once morality is no longer codified in some central set of rules that all accept and that finds its ultimate justification in the belief in a Supreme Being, then morality becomes a variation of "do your own thing."

For pro-life people, once the belief in a Supreme Being (and by definition a common sense of culture) is lost, a set of consequences emerge that not only creates abortion per se but creates a climate where phenomena such as abortion can flourish. For example, once one no longer believes in an afterlife, then one becomes more this-worldly. As a consequence, one becomes more interested in material goods and develops a world view that evaluates things (and, more importantly, people) in terms of what Marxists would call their "use value." Further, people come to live in the "here-and-now" rather than thinking of this life—and in particular the pain and disappointments of this life—as spiritual training for the next life. When the belief in God (and in an afterlife) are lost, pro-life people feel that human life becomes selfish, unbearably painful, and meaningless.

> I think basically a secular nature of our society, that we basically lost our notion of God as being important in our lives . . . it's hard at times to see that suffering can make you a better person, so people don't want any part of it.

> I think there's a decline in our civilization. Bracken, Dr. Julius Bracken, said that the problem used to be why does God allow suffering or pain or things like that, and now the problem is man's own existence, you know, man believes that he's in a circle of nothingness and therefore there is no such thing as a moral or immoral act.

One of the harshest criticisms pro-life people make about pro-choice people, therefore, which encapsulates their feeling that pro-choice people are too focused on a short-term pragmatic view of the present world rather than on the long-term view of a transcendent world, is that pro-choice people are "utilitarian."

In part, pro-life people are right: the pro-choice world view is not centered around a Divine Being, but rather around a belief in the highest abilities of human beings. For them, reason—the human capacity to use intelligence, rather than faith, to understand and alter the environment—is at the core of their world; for many of them, therefore, religious or spiritual beliefs are restricted only to those areas over which humans have not yet established either knowledge or control: the origin of the universe, the meaning of life, etc. As one pro-choice activist, speaking of her own spiritual beliefs, noted: "What should I call it? Destiny? A Supreme Being? I don't know. I don't worship anything, I don't go anyplace and do anything about it, it's just an awareness that there's a whole area that might be arranging something for me, that I am not arranging myself—though every day I do more about arranging things myself."

Whatever religious values pro-choice people have are subordinated to a belief that individuals live in the here and now and must therefore make decisions in the present about the present. Few pro-choice people expressed clear beliefs in an afterlife so that their time frame includes only the worldly dimension of life. Thus, the entire articulation of their world view focuses them once again on human—rather than divine—capacities and, in particular, on the capacity for reason.

There are important implications to the fact that reason is the centerpiece of the pro-choice universe. First, they are, as their opponents claim, "utilitarian." Without explicitly claiming the heritage of the Scottish moralists, utilitarianism is consonant with many of the pro-choice side's vaguely Protestant beliefs and, more to the point, with their value of rationality and its extensions: control, planning, and fairness. Second, as this heritage implies, they are interventionists. From their point of view, the fact of being the only animal gifted with intellect means that humans should use that intellect to solve the problems of human existence. What the pro-life people see as a humility in the face of a God whose ways are unknowable to mere humans, pro-choice people see as a fatalistic reliance upon a Creator whom humans wishfully endow with magical powers. These same values lead pro-choice people to be skeptical of the claim that certain areas are, or should be, sacrosanct, beyond the reach of human intervention. *Sacred* to them is too close to *sacred cow*, and religion can merge imperceptibly into dogma, where the church could persecute Galileo because science was too threatening both to an old way of thinking of things and an established power structure. Truth, for pro-choice people, must always take precedence over faith.

Because of their faith in the human ability to discover truth, pro-choice people are on the whole optimistic about "human nature." While in their more despairing moments they can agree with the pro-life diagnosis of malaise in contemporary American life—that "things fall apart and the center does not hold" in Yeats' terms—they emphatically disagree upon the solution. Rather than advocate what they see as a retreat from the present, an attempt to re-create idealized images of the past, they would argue that "the Lord helps those who help themselves" and that people should rally to the task of applying human ingenuity to the problems that surround us.

In consequence, pro-choice people do not see suffering as either ennobling or as spiritual discipline. In fact, they see it as stupid, as a waste, and as a failure, particularly when technology exists to eliminate it. While some problems are not at present amenable to human control, pro-choice people will admit, they are sure to fall to the march of human progress. Thus, not only can humans "play God," it is, in an ironic sort of way, what they owe their Creator, if they have one: given the ability to alter Nature, it is immoral not to do so, especially when those activities will diminish human pain.

All of these values come home for pro-choice people when they talk about the *quality of life*. By this term they mean a number of things. In part they use this phrase as a short-hand way of indicating that they think of *life* as consisting of social as well as biological dimensions. The embryo, for example, is only a potential person to them in large part because it has not yet begun to have a social dimension to its life, only a physical one. In corollary, a pregnant woman's rights, being both social and physical, transcend those of the embryo. This view is rooted in their values about reason: biological life is physical and of the body. Humans share physical life with all other living beings, but reason is the gift of humans alone. Thus social life, which exists only by virtue of the human capacity for reason, is the more valuable dimension of life for pro-choice people. (This viewpoint explains in part why many pro-choice people find unfathomable the question of "when does life begin?" For them it is obvious: physical life began only once, most probably when the "cosmic soup" yielded its first complex amino acids, the forerunners of DNA; social life begins at "viability" when the embryo can live—and begin to form social relationships—outside of the womb.)

But for pro-life people, this line of reasoning is ominous. If social life is more important than physical life, it then follows that people may be ranked by the value of their social contributions, thus making invidious distinctions among individuals. In contrast, if physical life is valued because it is a gift from the Creator, then no mere human can make claim to evaluate among the gifts with which various individuals are born. A view that the physical or genetic dimension of life is paramount—that all who are born genetically human are, a priori, persons—means that at some level all are equal. A hopelessly damaged newborn is, on this level, as equally deserving of social resources as anyone else. What pro-life people fear is that if the pro-choice view of the world is adopted, then those who are less socially *productive* may be deemed less socially *valuable*. For pro-life people, many of whom have situational reasons to fear how pro-choice people would assign them a social price tag, such a prospect is a nightmare.

The phrase *quality of life* evokes for pro-choice people a pleasing vista of the human intellect directed to resolving the complicated problems of life—the urge for knowledge used to tame sickness, poverty, inequality, and other ills of humankind. To pro-life people, in contrast, precisely because it is focused on the here and now and actively rejects the sacred and the transcendent, it evokes the image of Nazi Germany where the "devalued" weak are sacrificed to enlarge the comfort of the powerful.

Thus, in similar ways, both pro-life and pro-choice world views founder on the same rock, that of assuming that others do (or must or should) share the same values. Pro-life people assume that all good people should follow God's teachings, and moreover they assume that most good-minded people would agree in the main as to what God's teachings actually are. (This conveniently overlooks such things as wars of religion, which are usually caused by differences of opinion on just such matters.) Pro-choice people, in their turn, because they value reason, assume that most reasonable people will come to similar solutions when confronted with similar problems. The paradox of utilitarianism, that one person's good may be another person's evil, as in the case of the pro-life belief that a too-effective contraceptive is a bad thing, is not something they can easily envisage, much less confront.[8]

What neither of these points of view fully appreciates is that neither religion nor reason is static, self-evident, or "out there." Reasonable people who are located in very different parts of the social world find themselves differentially exposed to diverse realities, and this differential exposure leads each of them to come up with different—but often equally reasonable—constructions of the world. Similarly, even deeply devout religious people, because they too are located in different parts of the social world and, furthermore, come from different religious and cultural traditions, can disagree about what God's will is in any particular situation. When combined with the fact that attitudes toward abortion rest on these deep, rarely examined notions about the world, it is unambiguously clear why the abortion debate is so heated and why the chances for rational discussion, reasoned arguments, and mutual accommodation are so slim.

8

Motherhood and Morality in America

ACCORDING TO interested observers at the time, abortion in America was as frequent in the last century as it is in our own. And the last century, as we have seen, had its own "right-to-life" movement, composed primarily of physicians who pursued the issue in the service of their own professional goals. When abortion re-emerged as an issue in the late 1950s, it still remained in large part a restricted debate among interested professionals. But abortion as we now know it has little in common with these earlier rounds of the debate. Instead of the civility and colleagueship that characterized the earlier phases of the debate, the present round of the abortion debate is marked by rancor and intransigence. Instead of the elite male professionals who commanded the issue until recently, ordinary people—and more to the point, ordinary women—have come to predominate in the ranks of those concerned. From a quiet, restricted technical debate among concerned professionals, abortion has become a debate that seems at times capable of tearing the fabric of American life apart. How did this happen? What accounts for the remarkable transformation of the abortion debate?

The history of the debate, as examined in previous chapters in this book, provides some preliminary answers. Technological advances in obstetrics led to a decline in those abortions undertaken strictly to preserve the life of the woman, using the narrowly biological sense of the word *life*. These technological advances, in turn, permitted (and indeed forced) physicians over time to make more and more nuanced decisions about abortion and eventually brought to the fore the underlying philosophical issue that had been obscured by a century of medical control over abortion: is the embryo a person or only a potential person? As Chapter Seven has illustrated, once this question is confronted directly, a unified world view—a set of assumptions about how the world is and ought to be organized—is called into play. As that chapter made clear, world views are usually the product of values so deeply held and dearly cherished that an assault upon them is a deeply disturbing assault indeed. Thus to summarize the argument of this book up to this point, the abortion debate has been transformed because it has "gone public" and in so doing has called into question individuals' most sacrosanct beliefs.

But this is only part of the story. This chapter will argue that all the previous rounds of the abortion debate in America were merely echoes of the issue as the nineteenth century defined it: a debate about the medical profession's right to make life-and-death decisions. In contrast, the most recent round of the debate is about something new. By bringing the issue of the moral status of the embryo to the fore, the new round focuses on the relative rights of women and embryos. Consequently, the abortion debate has become a debate about women's contrasting obligations to themselves and others. New technologies and the changing nature of work have opened up possibilities for women outside of the home undreamed of in the nineteenth century; together, these changes give women—for the first time in history—the option of deciding exactly how and when their family roles will fit into the larger context of their lives. In essence, therefore, this round of the abortion debate is so passionate and hard-fought *because it is a referendum on the place and meaning of motherhood*.

Motherhood is at issue because two opposing visions of motherhood are at war. Championed by "feminists" and "housewives," these two different views of motherhood represent in turn two very different kinds of social worlds. The abortion debate has become a debate among women, women with different values in the social world, different experiences of it, and different resources with which to cope with it. How the issue is framed, how people think about it, and, most importantly, where the passions come from are all related to the fact that the battlelines are increasingly drawn (and defended) by women.

While on the surface it is the embryo's fate that seems to be at stake, the abortion debate is actually about the meanings of *women's* lives.

To be sure, both the pro-life and the pro-choice movements had earlier phases in which they were dominated by male professionals. Some of these men are still active in the debate, and it is certainly the case that some men continue to join the debate on both sides of the issue. But the data in this study suggest that by 1974 over 80 percent of the activists in both the pro-choice and the pro-life movements in California were women, and a national survey of abortion activists found similar results.[1]

Moreover, in our interviews we routinely asked both male and female activists on both sides of the issue to supply information on several "social background variables," such as where they were born, the extent of their education, their income level, the number of children they had, and their occupations. When male activists on the two sides are compared on these variables, they are virtually indistinguishable from one another. But when female activists are compared, it is dramatically clear that for the women who have come to dominate the ranks of the movement, the abortion debate is a conflict between two different social worlds and the hopes and beliefs those worlds support.

Who Are the Activists?

On almost every social background variable we examined, pro-life and pro-choice women differed dramatically. For example, in terms of income, almost half of all pro-life women (44 percent) in this study reported an income of less than $20,000 a year, but only one-fourth of the pro-choice women reported an income that low, and a considerable portion of those were young women just starting their careers. On the upper end of the income scale, one-third of the pro-choice women reported an income of $50,000 a year or more compared with only one pro-life woman in every seven.

These simple figures on income, however, conceal a very complex social reality, and that social reality is in turn tied to feelings about abortion. The higher incomes of pro-choice women, for example, result from a number of intersecting factors. Almost without exception pro-choice women work in the paid labor force, they earn good salaries when they work, and if they are married, they are likely to be married to men who also have good incomes. An astounding 94 percent of all pro-choice women work, and over half of them have incomes in the top 10 percent of all working women in this country. Moreover, one pro-choice woman in ten has an annual *personal* income (as opposed to a family income) of $30,000 or more, thus putting her in the rarified ranks of the top 2 percent of all employed women in America. Pro-life women, by contrast, are far less likely to work: 63 percent of them do not work in the paid labor force, and almost all of those who do are unmarried. Among pro-life married women, for example, only 14 percent report any personal income at all, and for most of them, this is earned not in a formal job but through activities such as selling cosmetics to groups of friends. Not surprisingly, the personal income of pro-life women who work outside the home, whether in a formal job or in one of these less-structured activities, is low. Half of all pro-life women who do work earn less than $5,000 a year, and half earn between $5,000 and $10,000. Only two pro-life women we contacted reported a personal income of more than $20,000. Thus pro-life women are less likely to work in the first place, they earn less money when they do work, and they are more likely to be married to a skilled worker or small businessman who earns only a moderate income.

These differences in income are in turn related to the different educational and occupational choices these women have made along the way. Among pro-choice women, almost four out of ten (37 percent) had undertaken some graduate work beyond the B.A. degree, and 18 percent had an M.D., a law degree, a Ph.D., or a similar postgraduate degree. Pro-life women, by comparison, had far less education: 10 percent of them had only a high school education or less; and another 30 percent never finished college (in contrast with only 8 percent of the pro-choice women). Only 6 percent of all pro-life women had a law degree, a Ph.D., or a medical degree.

These educational differences were in turn related to occupational differences among the women in this study. Because of their higher levels of education, pro-choice women tended to be employed in the major professions, as administrators, owners of small businesses, or executives in large businesses. The pro-life women tended to be housewives or, of the few who worked, to be in the traditional female jobs of teaching, social work, and nursing. (The choice of home life over public life held true for even the 6 percent of pro-life women with an advanced degree: of the married women who had such degrees, at the time of our interviews only one of them had not retired from her profession after marriage.)

These economic and social differences were also tied to choices that women on each side had made about marriage and family life. For example, 23 percent of pro-choice women had never married, compared with only 16 percent of pro-life women; 14 percent of pro-choice women had been divorced, compared with 5 percent of pro-life women. The size of the families these women had was also different. The average pro-choice family had between one and two children and was more likely to have one; pro-life families averaged between two and three children and were more likely to have three. (Among the pro-life women, 23 percent had five or more children; 16 percent had seven or more children.) Pro-life women also tended to marry at a slightly younger age and to have had their first child earlier.

Finally, the women on each side differed dramatically in their religious affiliation and in the role that religion played in their lives. Almost 80 percent of the women active in the pro-life movement at the present time are Catholics. The remainder are Protestants (9 percent), persons who claim no religion (5 percent), and Jews (1 percent). In sharp contrast, 63 percent of pro-choice women say that they have no religion, 22 percent think of themselves as vaguely Protestant, 3 percent are Jewish, and 9 percent have what they call a "personal" religion. We found no one in our sample of pro-choice activists who claimed to be a Catholic at the time of the interviews.

When we asked activists what religion they were raised in as a child, however, a different picture emerged. For example, 20 percent of the pro-choice activists were raised as Catholics, 42 percent were raised as Protestants, and 15 percent were raised in the Jewish faith. In this group that describes itself as predominantly without religious affiliation, therefore, only 14 percent say they were not brought up in any formal religious faith. By the same token, although almost 80 percent of present pro-life activists are Catholic, only 58 percent were raised in that religion (15 percent were raised as Protestants and 3 percent as Jews). Thus, almost 20 percent of the pro-life activists in this study are converts to Catholicism, people who have actively chosen to follow a given religious faith, in striking contrast to pro-choice people, who have actively chosen not to follow any.

Perhaps the single most dramatic difference between the two

groups, however, is in the role that religion plays in their lives. Almost three-quarters of the pro-choice people interviewed said that formal religion was either unimportant or completely irrelevant to them, and their attitudes are correlated with behavior: only 25 percent of the pro-choice women said they *ever* attend church, and most of these said they do so only occasionally. Among pro-life people, by contrast, 69 percent said religion was important in their lives, and an additional 22 percent said that it was very important. For pro-life women, too, these attitudes are correlated with behavior: half of those pro-life women interviewed said they attend church regularly once a week, and another 13 percent said they do so even more often. Whereas 80 percent of pro-choice people never attend church, only 2 percent of pro-life advocates never do so.

Keeping in mind that the statistical use of averages has inherent difficulties, we ask, who are the "average" pro-choice and pro-life advocates? When the social background data are looked at carefully, two profiles emerge. The average pro-choice activist is a forty-four-year-old married woman who grew up in a large metropolitan area and whose father was a college graduate. She was married at age twenty-two, has one or two children, and has had some graduate or professional training beyond the B.A. degree. She is married to a professional man, is herself employed in a regular job, and her family income is more than $50,000 a year. She is not religiously active, feels that religion is not important to her, and attends church very rarely if at all.

The average pro-life woman is also a forty-four-year-old married woman who grew up in a large metropolitan area. She married at age seventeen and has three children or more. Her father was a high school graduate, and she has some college education or may have a B.A. degree. She is not employed in the paid labor force and is married to a small businessman or a lower-level white-collar worker; her family income is $30,000 a year. She is Catholic (and may have converted), and her religion is one of the most important aspects of her life: she attends church at least once a week and occasionally more often.

Interests and Passions

To the social scientist (and perhaps to most of us) these social background characteristics connote lifestyles as well. We intuitively clothe these bare statistics with assumptions about beliefs and values.

When we do so, the pro-choice women emerge as educated, affluent, liberal professionals, whose lack of religious affiliation suggests a secular, "modern," or (as pro-life people would have it) "utilitarian" outlook on life. Similarly, the income, education, marital patterns, and religious devotion of pro-life women suggest that they are traditional, hard-working people ("polyester types" to their opponents), who hold conservative views on life. We may be entitled to assume that individuals' social backgrounds act to shape and mold their social attitudes, but it is important to realize that the relationship between social worlds and social values is a very complex one.

Perhaps one example will serve to illustrate the point. A number of pro-life women in this study emphatically rejected an expression that pro-choice women tend to use almost unthinkingly—the expression *unwanted pregnancy*. Pro-life women argued forcefully that a better term would be a *surprise* pregnancy, asserting that although a pregnancy may be momentarily unwanted, the child that results from the pregnancy almost never is. Even such a simple thing—what to call an unanticipated pregnancy—calls into play an individual's values and resources. Keeping in mind our profile of the average pro-life person, it is obvious that a woman who does not work in the paid labor force, who does not have a college degree, whose religion is important to her, and who has already committed herself wholeheartedly to marriage and a large family is well equipped to believe that an unanticipated pregnancy usually becomes a beloved child. Her life is arranged so that for her, this belief is true.This view is consistent not only with her values, which she has held from earliest childhood, but with her social resources as well. It should not be surprising, therefore, that her world view leads her to believe that everyone else can "make room for one more" as easily as she can and that therefore it supports her in her conviction that abortion is cruel, wicked, and self-indulgent.*

* As might be imagined, it is not an easy task to ask people who are anti-abortion activists about their own experiences with a certain kind of unanticipated pregnancy, namely, a premarital pregnancy. Most pro-choice people were quite open about having had such pregnancies; as we noted in Chapter Four, their pregnancies—and subsequent abortions—were central to their feelings about abortion. Pro-life women, by contrast, were deeply reluctant to discuss the topic. Several of them, after acknowledging premarital pregnancies, said that they did not want people to think that their attitudes on abortion were merely a product of their personal experiences. Thus we have no comparative figures about the extent to which the values represented here are the product of different experiences or just different opinions. We know only that unanticipated pregnancy was common among pro-choice women, and the interviews suggest that it was not

It is almost certainly the case that an unplanned pregnancy is never an easy thing for anyone. Keeping in mind the profile of the average pro-choice woman, however, it is evident that a woman who is employed full time, who has an affluent lifestyle that depends in part on her contribution to the family income, and who expects to give a child as good a life as she herself has had with respect to educational, social, and economic advantages will draw on a different reality when she finds herself being skeptical about the ability of the average person to transform unwanted pregnancies into well-loved (and well-cared-for) children.

The relationship between passions and interests is thus more dynamic than it might appear at first. It is true that at one level, pro-choice and pro-life attitudes on abortion are self-serving: activists on each side have different views of the morality of abortion because their chosen lifestyles leave them with different needs for abortion; and both sides have values that provide a moral basis for their abortion needs in particular and their lifestyles in general. But this is only half the story. The values that lead pro-life and pro-choice women into different attitudes toward abortion are the same values that led them at an earlier time to adopt different lifestyles that supported a given view of abortion.

For example, pro-life women have *always* valued family roles very highly and have arranged their lives accordingly. They did not acquire high-level educational and occupational skills, for example, because they married, and they married because their values suggested that this would be the most satisfying life open to them. Similarly, pro-choice women postponed (or avoided) marriage and family roles because they chose to acquire the skills they needed to be successful in the larger world, having concluded that the role of wife and mother was too limited for them. Thus, activists on both sides of the issue are women who have a given set of values about what are the most satisfying and appropriate roles for women, and they have made *life commitments that now limit their ability to change their minds*. Women who have many children and little education, for example, are seriously handicapped in attempting to become doctors or lawyers; women who have reached

---

uncommon among pro-life women. The difference in experience is, of course, that those in the first group sought abortions and those in the second group, with only a few exceptions, legitimized their pregnancies with a marriage.

their late forties with few children or none are limited in their ability to build (or rebuild) a family. For most of these activists, therefore, their position on abortion is the "tip of the iceberg," a shorthand way of supporting and proclaiming not only a complex set of values but a given set of social resources as well.

To put the matter differently, we might say that for pro-life women the traditional division of life into separate male roles and female roles still works, but for pro-choice women it does not. Having made a commitment to the traditional female roles of wife, mother, and homemaker, pro-life women are limited in those kinds of resources—education, class status, recent occupational experiences—they would need to compete in what has traditionally been the male sphere, namely, the paid labor force. The average pro-choice woman, in contrast, is comparatively well endowed with exactly those resources: she is highly educated, she already has a job, and she has recent (and continuous) experience in the job market.

In consequence, anything that supports a traditional division of labor into male and female worlds is, broadly speaking, in the interests of pro-life women because that is where their resources lie. Conversely, such a traditional division of labor, when strictly enforced, is against the interests of pro-choice women because it limits their abilities to use the valuable "male" resources that they have in relative abundance. It is therefore apparent that attitudes toward abortion, even though rooted in childhood experiences, are also intimately related to present-day interests. Women who oppose abortion and seek to make it officially unavailable are declaring, both practically and symbolically, that women's reproductive roles should be given social primacy. Once an embryo is defined as a child and an abortion as the death of a person, almost everything else in a woman's life must "go on hold" during the course of her pregnancy: any attempt to gain "male" resources such as a job, an education, or other skills must be subordinated to her uniquely female responsibility of serving the needs of this newly conceived person. Thus, when personhood is bestowed on the embryo, women's nonreproductive roles are made secondary to their reproductive roles. The act of conception therefore creates a pregnant woman rather than a woman who is pregnant; it creates a woman whose life, in cases where roles or values clash, is defined by the fact that she is—or may become—pregnant.

It is obvious that this view is supportive of women who have already decided that their familial and reproductive roles are the major ones in their lives. By the same token, the costs of defining women's reproductive roles as primary do not seem high to them because they have already chosen to make those roles primary anyway. For example, employers might choose to discriminate against women because they might require maternity leave and thus be unavailable at critical times, but women who have chosen not to work in the paid labor force in the first place can see such discrimination as irrelevant to them.

It is equally obvious that supporting abortion (and believing that the embryo is not a person) is in the vested interests of pro-choice women. Being so well equipped to compete in the male sphere, they perceive any situation that both practically and symbolically affirms the primacy of women's reproductive roles as a real loss to them. Practically, it devalues their social resources. If women are only secondarily in the labor market and must subordinate working to pregnancy, should it occur, then their education, occupation, income, and work become potentially temporary and hence discounted. Working becomes, as it traditionally was perceived to be, a pastime or hobby pursued for "pin money" rather than a central part of their lives. Similarly, if the embryo is defined as a person and the ability to become pregnant is the central one for women, a woman must be prepared to sacrifice some of her own interests to the interests of this newly conceived person.

In short, in a world where men and women have traditionally had different roles to play and where male roles have traditionally been the more socially prestigious and financially rewarded, abortion has become a symbolic marker between those who wish to maintain this division of labor and those who wish to challenge it. Thus, on an intimate level, the pro-life movement is women's version of what was true of peasants in the Vendée, the part of France that remained Royalist during the French Revolution. Charles Tilly has argued that in the Vendée, traditional relationships between nobles and peasants were still mutually satisfying so that the "brave new world" of the French Revolution represented more loss than gain, and the peasants therefore resisted the changes the Revolution heralded.[2] By the same logic, traditional relationships between men and women are still satisfying, rewarding, and meaningful for pro-life women, and they therefore resist the lure of "liberation." For pro-choice women, however, with their access to male resources, a division of labor into the public world of work and the private world of home and hearth seems to promise only restriction to "second-class" citizenship.

Thus, the sides are fundamentally opposed to each other not only on the issue of abortion but also on what abortion *means*. Women who have many "human capital" resources of the traditionally male variety want to see motherhood recognized as a private, discretionary choice. Women who have few of these resources and limited opportunities in the job market want to see motherhood recognized as the most important thing a woman can do. In order for pro-choice women to achieve their goals, therefore, they *must* argue that motherhood is not a primary, inevitable, or "natural" role for all women; for pro-life women to achieve their goals, they *must* argue that it is. In short, the debate rests on the question of whether women's fertility is to be socially recognized as a resource or as a handicap.

To the extent that women who have chosen the larger public world of work have been successful, both legally and in terms of public opinion and, furthermore, are rapidly becoming the numerical majority, pro-life women are put on the defensive. Several pro-life women offered poignant examples of how the world deals with housewives who do not have an official payroll title. Here is what one of them said:

> I was at a party, about two years ago—it still sticks in my mind, you see, because I'm a housewife and I don't work—and I met this girl from England and we got involved in a deep discussion about the English and the Americans and their philosophies and how one has influenced the other, and at the end of the conversation—she was a working gal herself, I forget what she did—and she says, "Where do you work?" and I said, "I don't." And she looked at me and said, "You don't work?" I said "No." She said, "You're just a housewife . . . and you can still think like that?" She couldn't believe it, and she sort of gave me a funny look and that was the end of the conversation for the evening. And I've met other people who've had similar experiences. [People seem to think that if] you're at home and you're involved with children all day, your intelligence quotient must be down with them on the floor someplace, and [that] you really don't do much thinking or get yourself involved.

Moreover, there are subtle indications that even the pro-life activists we interviewed had internalized their loss of status as housewives. Only a handful of married pro-life activists also worked at regular jobs outside the home; but fully half of those who were now full-time homemakers, some for as long as thirty years, referred to themselves in terms of the work they had given up when they married or had their first child: "I'm a political scientist," "I'm a social worker," "I'm an accountant." It is noteworthy that no one used the past tense as in "I used to be a social worker": every nonemployed married woman who used her former professional identification used it in the present tense. Since this pattern was not noticed during the interviewing, what the woman themselves had in mind must remain speculative. But it does not seem unreasonable to imagine that this identification is an unconscious bow to the fact that "just plain" individuals, and in particular "just plain housewives," lack the status and credibility of professionals. Ironically, by calling on earlier identifications these women may have been expressing a pervasive cultural value that they oppose as a matter of ideology. They seemed to believe that when it comes to making public statements—or at least public statements to an interviewer who has come to ask you about your activities in the abortion debate—*what* you are counts more than *who* you are.

Because of their commitment to their own view of motherhood as a primary social role, pro-life women believe that other women are "casual" about abortions and have them "for convenience." There are no reliable data to confirm whether or not women are "casual" about abortions, but many pro-life people believe this to be the case and relate their activism to their perception of other people's casualness.[3] For example:

> Every time I saw some article [on abortion] I read about it, and I had another friend who had her second abortion in 1977 . . . and both of her abortions were a matter of convenience, it was inconvenient for her to be pregnant at that time. When I talked to her I said, "O.K., you're married now, your husband has a good job, you want to have children eventually, but if you became pregnant now, you'd have an abortion. Why?" "Because it's inconvenient, this is not when I want to have my child." And that bothered me a lot because she is also very intelligent, graduated magna cum laude, and knew nothing about fetal development.

The assertion that women are "casual" about abortion, one could argue, expresses in a short-hand way a set of beliefs about women and their roles. First, the more people value the personhood of the embryo, the more important must be the reasons for taking its life. Some pro-life people, for example, would accept an abortion when continuation of the pregnancy would cause the death of the mother; they believe that when two lives are in direct conflict, the embryo's life can be considered the more expendable. But not all pro-life people agree, and many say they would not accept abortion even to save the mother's life. (Still others say they accept the idea in principle but would not make that choice in their own lives if faced with it.) For people who accept the personhood of the embryo, any reason besides trading a "life for a life" (and sometimes even that) seems trivial, merely a matter of "convenience."

Second, people who accept the personhood of the embryo see the reasons that pro-abortion people give for ending a pregnancy as simultaneously downgrading the value of the embryo and upgrading everything else but pregnancy. The argument that women need abortion to "control" their fertility means that they intend to subordinate pregnancy, with its inherent unpredictability, to something else. As the pro-choice activists in Chapters Four and Five have told us, that something else is participation in the paid labor force. Abortion permits women to engage in paid work on an equal basis with men. With abortion, they may schedule pregnancy in order to take advantage of the kinds of benefits that come with a paid position in the labor force: a paycheck, a title, and a social identity. The pro-life women in this study were often careful to point out that they did not object to "career women." But what they meant by "career women" were women whose *only* responsibilities were in the labor force. Once a woman became a wife and a mother, in their view her primary responsibility was to her home and family.

Third, the pro-life activists we interviewed, the overwhelming majority of whom are full-time homemakers, also felt that women who worked *and* had families could often do so only because women like themselves picked up the slack. Given their place in the social structure, it is not surprising that many of the pro-life women thought that married women who worked outside the home were "selfish"—that they got all the benefits while the homemakers carried the load for them in Boy and Girl Scouts, PTA, and after school, for which their reward was to be treated by the workers as less competent and less interesting persons.*

* In fact, pro-life women, especially those recruited after 1972, were *less* likely to be engaged in formal activities such as Scouts, church activities, and PTA than their

Abortion therefore strips the veil of sanctity from motherhood. When pregnancy is discretionary—when people are allowed to put anything else they value in front of it—then motherhood has been demoted from a sacred calling to a job.* In effect, the legalization of abortion serves to make men and women more "unisex" by deemphasizing what makes them different—the ability of women to visibly and directly carry the next generation. Thus, pro-choice women are emphatic about their right to compete equally with men without the burden of an unplanned pregnancy, and pro-life women are equally emphatic about their belief that men and women have different roles in life and that pregnancy is a gift instead of a burden.

The pro-life activists we interviewed do not want equality with men in the sense of having exactly the same rights and responsibilities as men do, although they do want equality of status. In fact, to the extent that *all* women have been touched by the women's movement and have become aware of the fact that society often treats women as a class as less capable than men, quite a few said they appreciated the Equal Rights Amendment (ERA), except for its implied stand on abortion. The ERA, in their view, reminded them that women are as valuable *in their own sphere* as men are in theirs. However, to the extent that the ERA was seen as downplaying the differences between men and women, to devalue the female sphere of the home in the face of the male sphere of paid work, others saw it as both demeaning and oppressive to women like themselves. As one of the few married employed pro-life women argued:

> I oppose it [the ERA]. Because I've gotten where I am without it. I don't think I need it. I think a woman should be hired on her merits, not on her sex or race. I don't think we should be hiring on sex or on race. I think we should be taking the competent people that are capable of doing the job. . . . I don't think women should be taking jobs from the breadwinner, you know. I still think that our society should be male . . . the male should be the primary breadwinner. For example, my own husband cannot hope for promotion because he is white and Anglo, you know, I mean white male. He's not going to get a promotion. If he could get the promotion that others of different minorities have gotten over him, I

---

pro-choice peers. Quite possibly they have in mind more informal kinds of activities, premised on the fact that since they do not work, they are home most of the time.

* The same might be said of all sacred callings—stripped of its layer of the sacred, for example, the job of the clergy is demanding, low status, and underpaid.

probably wouldn't have to work at all. So from my own point of view, purely selfishly, I think we've got to consider it. On the other hand, if I'm doing the same job [as a man], I expect to get the same pay. But I've always gotten it. So I really don't think that's an issue. I see the ERA as causing us more problems than it's going to [solve]. . . . As I see it, we were on a pedestal, why should we go down to being equal? That's my feeling on the subject.

It is stating the obvious to point out that the more limited the educational credentials a woman has, the more limited the job opportunities are for her, and the more limited the job opportunities, the more attractive motherhood is as a full-time occupation. In motherhood, one can control the content and pace of one's own work, and the job is *intrinsically meaningful*. Compared with a job clerking in a supermarket (a realistic alternative for women with limited educational credentials) where the work is poorly compensated and often demeaning, motherhood can have compensations that far transcend the monetary ones. As one woman described mothering: "You have this little, rough uncut diamond, and you're the artist shaping and cutting that diamond, and bringing out the lights . . . that's a great challenge."

All the circumstances of her existence will therefore encourage a pro-life woman to highlight the kinds of values and experiences that support childbearing and childrearing and to discount the attraction (such as it is) of paid employment. Her circumstances encourage her to resent the pro-choice view that women's most meaningful and prestigious activities are in the "man's world."

Abortion also has a symbolic dimension that separates the needs and interests of homemakers and workers in the paid labor force. Insofar as abortion allows a woman to get a job, to get training for a job, or to advance in a job, it does more than provide social support for working women over homemakers; it also seems to support the value of economic considerations over moral ones. Many pro-life people interviewed said that although their commitment to traditional family roles meant very real material deprivations to themselves and their families, the moral benefits of such a choice more than made up for it.

My girls babysit and the boys garden and have paper routes and things like that. I say that if we had a lot of money that would still be my philosophy, though I don't know because we haven't been in that position. But it's a sacrifice to have a larger family. So when I hear these figures that it takes $65,000 from birth to [raise a child], I think that's ridicu-

> lous. That's a new bike every year. That's private colleges. That's a complete new outfit when school opens. Well, we've got seven daughters who wear hand-me-downs, and we hope that sometime in their eighteen years at home each one has a new bike somewhere along the line, but otherwise it's hand-me-downs. Those figures are inflated to give those children everything, and I think that's not good for them.

For pro-life people, a world view that puts the economic before the noneconomic hopelessly confuses two different kinds of worlds. For them, the private world of family as traditionally experienced is the one place in human society where none of us has a price tag. Home, as Robert Frost pointed out, is where they have to take you in, whatever your social worth. Whether one is a surgeon or a rag picker, the family is, at least ideally, the place where love is unconditional.

Pro-life people and pro-life women in particular have very real reasons to fear such a state of affairs. Not only do they see an achievement-based world as harsh, superficial, and ultimately ruthless; they are relatively less well-equipped to operate in that world. A considerable amount of social science research has suggested, at least in the realm of medical treatment, that there is an increasing tendency to judge people by their official (achieved) worth.[4] Pro-life people have relatively fewer official achievements in part because they have been doing what they see as a moral task, namely, raising children and making a home; and they see themselves as becoming handicapped in a world that discounts not only their social contributions but their personal lives as well.

It is relevant in this context to recall the grounds on which pro-life people argue that the embryo is a baby: that it is genetically human. To insist that the embryo is a baby because it is genetically human is to make a claim that it is both wrong and impossible to make distinctions between humans at all. Protecting the life of the embryo, which is by definition an entity whose social worth is all yet to come, means protecting others who feel that they may be defined as having low social worth; more broadly, it means protecting a legal view of personhood that emphatically rejects social worth criteria.

For the majority of pro-life people we interviewed, the abortions they found most offensive were those of "damaged" embryos. This is because this category so clearly highlights the aforementioned concerns about social worth. To defend a genetically or congenitally damaged embryo from abortion is, in their minds, defending the weakest of the weak, and most pro-life people we interviewed were least prepared to compromise on this category of abortion.

The genetic basis of the embryo's claim to personhood has another, more subtle implication for those on the pro-life side. If genetic humanness equals personhood, then biological facts of life must take precedence over social facts of life. One's destiny is therefore inborn and hence immutable. To give any ground on the embryo's biologically determined babyness, therefore, would by extension call into question the "innate," "natural," and biological basis of women's traditional roles as well.

Pro-choice people, of course, hold a very different view of the matter. For them, social considerations outweigh biological ones: the embryo becomes a baby when it is "viable," that is, capable of achieving a certain degree of social integration with others. This is a world view premised on achievement, but not in the way pro-life people experience the word. Pro-choice people, believing as they do in choice, planning, and human efficacy, believe that biology is simply a minor given to be transcended by human experience. Sex, like race and age, is not an appropriate criterion for sorting people into different rights and responsibilities. Pro-choice people downplay these "natural" ascriptive characteristics, believing that true equality means achievement based on talent, not being restricted to a "women's world," a "black world," or an "old people's world." Such a view, as the profile of pro-choice people has made clear, is entirely consistent with their own lives and achievements.

These differences in social circumstances that separate pro-life from pro-choice women on the core issue of abortion also lead them to have different values on topics that surround abortion, such as sexuality and the use of contraception. With respect to sexuality, for example, the two sides have diametrically opposed values; these values arise from a fundamentally different premise, which is, in turn, tied to the different realities of their social worlds. If pro-choice women have a vested interest in subordinating their reproductive capacities, and pro-life women have a vested interest in highlighting them, we should not be surprised to find that pro-life women believe that the purpose of sex is reproduction whereas pro-choice women believe that its purpose is to promote intimacy and mutual pleasure.

These two views about sex express the same value differences that lead the two sides to have such different views on abortion. If women plan to find their primary role in marriage and the family, then they face a need to create a "moral cartel" when it comes to sex. If sex is freely available outside of marriage, then why should men, as the old saw puts it, buy the cow when the milk is free? If many women are willing to sleep with men outside of marriage, then the regular sexual activity that comes with marriage is much less valuable an incentive to marry. And because pro-life women are traditional women, their primary resource for marriage is the promise of a stable home, with everything it implies: children, regular sex, a "haven in a heartless world."

But pro-life women, like all women, are facing a devaluation of these resources. As American society increasingly becomes a service economy, men can buy the services that a wife traditionally offers. Cooking, cleaning, decorating, and the like can easily be purchased on the open market in a cash transaction. And as sex becomes more open, more casual, and more "amative," it removes one more resource that could previously be obtained only through marriage.

Pro-life women, as we have seen, have both value orientations and social characteristics that make marriage very important. Their alternatives in the public world of work are, on the whole, less attractive. Furthermore, women who stay home full-time and keep house are becoming a financial luxury. Only very wealthy families *or families whose values allow them to place the nontangible benefits of a full-time wife over the tangible benefits of a working wife* can afford to keep one of its earners off the labor market. To pro-life people, the nontangible benefit of having children—and therefore the value of procreative sex—is very important. Thus, a social ethic that promotes more freely available sex undercuts pro-life women two ways: it limits their abilities to get into a marriage in the first place, and it undermines the social value placed on their presence once within a marriage.

For pro-choice women, the situation is reversed. Because they have access to "male" resources such as education and income, they have far less reason to believe that the basic reason for sexuality is to produce children. They plan to have small families anyway, and they and their husbands come from and have married into a social class in which small families are the norm. For a number of overlapping reasons, therefore, pro-choice women believe that the value of sex is not primarily procreative: pro-choice women value the ability of sex to promote human intimacy more (or at least more frequently) than they value the ability of sex to produce babies. But they hold this view because they can afford to. When they bargain for marriage, they use the same resources that they use in the labor market: upper-class status, an education very similar to a man's, side-by-side participation in the man's world, and, not least, a salary that substantially increases a family's standard of living.

It is true, therefore, that pro-life people are "anti-sex." They value sex, of course, but they value it for its traditional benefits (babies) rather than for the benefits that pro-choice people associate with it (intimacy). Pro-life people really do want to see "less" sexuality—or at least less open and socially unregulated sexuality—because they think it is morally wrong, they think it distorts the meaning of sex, and they feel that it *threatens the basis on which their own marital bargains are built*.

These differences in social background also explain why the majority of pro-life people we interviewed were opposed to "artificial" contraception, and had chosen to use natural family planning (NFP), the modern-day version of the "rhythm method." To be sure, since NFP is a "morally licit" form of fertility control for Catholics, and many pro-life activists are very orthodox Catholics, NFP is attractive on those grounds alone. But as a group, Catholics are increasingly using contraception in patterns very similar to those of their non-Catholic peers.[5] Furthermore, many non-Catholic pro-life activists told us they used NFP. Opposition to contraception, therefore, and its corollary, the use of NFP, needs to be explained as something other than simple obedience to church dogma.

Given their status as traditional women who do not work outside of the home, the choice of NFP as the preferred method of fertility control is a rational one because NFP enhances their power and status as women. The NFP users we talked with almost uniformly stated that men respect women more when they are using NFP and that the marriage relationship becomes more like a honeymoon. Certain social factors in the lives of pro-life women suggest why this may be so. Because NFP requires abstinence during the fertile period, one effect of using it is that *sex becomes a relatively scarce resource*. Rather than something that is simply there—and taken for granted—sex becomes something that disappears from the relationship for regular periods of time. Therefore, NFP creates incentives for husbands to be close and intimate with their wives. The more insecure a woman and the less support she feels from her husband, the more reasonable it is for her to want to lengthen the period of abstinence to be on the safe side.* The increase in power and status that NFP affords a woman in a traditional marriage was clearly recognized by the activists who use NFP, as these two quotations suggest:

> The rhythm [method] is the most freeing thing a woman can have, if you want me to tell you the honest-to-God truth. Because if she's married to someone that she loves, and she ought to be, then you know [when she abstains] she's got a romance time, she's got a time when she doesn't have to say she has a headache. He's just got to know, hey, either we're going to have another baby and you're going to pay for it or we're going to read our books tonight. And once in a while we're going to get to read our books, that's the way I look at it. I think it's wonderful, I really do, it might not sound too romantic to people, but it is, this is super romantic.

> You know, if you have filet mignon every day, it becomes kind of disinteresting. But if you have to plan around this, you do some things. You study, and you do other things during the fertile part of the cycle. And the husband and wife find out how much they can do in the line of expressing love for one another in other ways, other than genital. And some people can really express a lot of love and do a lot of touching and be very relaxed. Maybe others would find that they can only do a very little touching because they might be stimulated. And so they would have to find out where their level was. But they can have a beautiful relationship.

NFP also creates an opportunity for both husbands and wives to talk about the wife's fertility so that once again, something that is normally taken for granted can be focused on and valued. Folk wisdom has it that men and women use sexuality in different ways to express their feelings of caring and intimacy: men give love in order to get sex and women give sex in order to get love. If there is some truth to this stereo-

* One NFP counselor described a case to me in which a woman found herself unavailable for sex an average of twenty-five days a month in what seemed a deliberate attempt to use sex to control a spouse's behavior. But the interpretation of oneself as fertile (and hence sexually unavailable unless the spouse wishes to risk the arrival of another child) need not be either calculating or conscious. The more insecure a woman is in her marriage the more insecure she may be about interpreting her fertility signs, both because the insecurity in her marriage translates into a more general insecurity and because she may wish to err "on the safe side" if she is worried about the effects of a pregnancy on a shaky relationship.

type (and both popular magazines and that rich source of sociological data, the Dear Abby column, suggest that there is), then it means that men and women often face confusion in their intimate dialogues with one another. Men wonder if their wives really want to have sex with them or are only giving it begrudgingly, out of a sense of "duty." Wives wonder if husbands really love them or merely want them for sexual relief. Natural Family Planning, by making sex periodically unavailable, puts some of these fears to rest. Some women said their husbands actually bring them flowers during the period of abstinence. Though husbands were much less forthcoming on this topic, it would seem reasonable that a woman who has been visibly reassured of her husband's caring for her might approach the renewal of sexual activity with the enthusiasm of someone who knows she is cared for as a whole person, to the husband's benefit and pleasure.

Furthermore, a few mutually discreet conversations during our interviews suggest that during abstinence at least some couples find ways of giving each other sexual pleasure that do not involve actual intercourse and hence the risk of pregnancy. Given traditional patterns of female socialization into sexuality and the fact that pro-life women are both traditional and devout women, these periods of mutual caressing may be as satisfying as intercourse for some women and even more satisfying than intercourse for others.*

The different life circumstances and experiences of pro-life and pro-choice people therefore intimately affect the ways they look at the moral and social dilemmas of contraception. The settings of their lives, for example, suggest that the psychological side benefits of NFP, which do so much to support pro-life values during the practice of contraception, are sought in other ways by pro-choice people. Pro-choice people are slightly older when they marry, and the interviews strongly suggest that they have a considerably more varied sexual experience than pro-life people on average; the use of NFP to discover other facets

* In short, these interviews were describing both "petting" and oral sex. Feminist literature has called to our attention the fact that traditional notions about sexuality are "male-centered": it is assumed that there will be insertion and that there will be a male ejaculation. Ironically, NFP—the birth control method preferred by the devout, traditional women we interviewed—may come very close to achieving the feminist ideal. Under NFP, the "rules" of "regular" sex are suspended, and each couple must discover for themselves what feels good. For a generation of women who were raised when long periods of "necking" and "petting" occurred before—and often instead of—intercourse, NFP may provide a welcome change from genitally centered, male-oriented sexual behavior to more diffuse, body-focused "female" forms of sexual expression.

of sexual expression is therefore largely unnecessary for them. Moreover, what little we know about sexual practices in the United States (from the Kinsey Report) suggests that given the different average levels of education and religious devoutness in the two groups, such sexual activities as "petting" and oral-genital stimulation may be more frequently encountered among pro-choice people to begin with.*

The life circumstances of the two sides suggest another reason why NFP is popular among pro-life people but not seriously considered by pro-choice people. Pro-choice men and women act on their belief that men and women are equal not only because they have (or should have) equal rights but also because they have substantially similar life experiences. The pro-choice women we met have approximately the same kinds of education as their husbands do, and many of them have the same kinds of jobs—they are lawyers, physicians, college professors, and the like. Even those who do not work in traditionally male occupations have jobs in the paid labor market and thus share common experiences. They and their husbands share many social resources in common: they both have some status outside the home, they both have a paycheck, and they both have a set of peers and friends located in the work world rather than in the family world. In terms of the traditional studies of family power, pro-choice husbands and wives use the same bargaining chips and have roughly equal amounts of them.[6]

Pro-choice women, therefore, value (and can afford) an approach to sexuality that, by sidelining reproduction, diminishes the differences between men and women; they can do this *because they have other resources on which to build a marriage*. Since their value is intimacy and since the daily lives of men and women on the pro-choice side are substantially similar, intimacy in the bedroom is merely an extension of the intimacy of their larger world.

Pro-life women and men, by contrast, tend to live in "separate spheres." Because their lives are based on a social and emotional divi-

* Kinsey's data suggest that for males the willingness to engage in oral-genital or manual-genital forms of sexual expression is related to education: the more educated an individual, the more likely he is to have "petted" or engaged in oral sex (Alfred Kinsey, *Sexual Behavior in the Human Male*, pp. 337–81, 535–37). For females, the patterns are more complicated. Educational differences among women disappear when age at marriage is taken into account. But as Kinsey notes: "Among the females in the sample, the chief restraint on petting . . . seems to have been the religious tradition against it." The more devout a woman, the less likely she is to have ever petted (Kinsey, *Sexual Behavior in the Human Female*, pp. 247–48).

sion of labor where each sex has its appropriate work, to accept contraception or abortion would devalue the one secure resource left to these women: the private world of home and hearth. This would be disastrous not only in terms of status but also in terms of meaning: if values about fertility and family are not essential to a marriage, what supports does a traditional marriage have in times of stress? To accept highly effective contraception, which actually and symbolically subordinates the role of children in the family to other needs and goals, would be to cut the ground of meaning out from under at least one (and perhaps both) partners' lives. Therefore, contraception, which sidelines the reproductive capacities of men and women, is both useless and threatening to pro-life people.

The Core of the Debate

In summary, women come to be pro-life and pro-choice activists as the end result of lives that center around different definitions of motherhood. They grow up with a belief about the nature of the embryo, so events in their lives lead them to believe that the embryo is a unique person, or a fetus; that people are intimately tied to their biological roles, or that these roles are but a minor part of life; that motherhood is the most important and satisfying role open to a woman, or that motherhood is only one of several roles, a burden when defined as the only role. These beliefs and values are rooted in the concrete circumstances of women's lives—their educations, incomes, occupations, and the different marital and family choices they have made along the way—and they work simultaneously to shape those circumstances in turn. Values about the relative place of reason and faith, about the role of actively planning for life versus learning to accept gracefully life's unknowns, of the relative satisfactions inherent in work and family—all of these factors place activists in a specific relationship to the larger world and give them a specific set of resources with which to confront that world.

The simultaneous and on-going modification of both their lives and their values by each other finds these activists located in a specific place in the social world. They are financially successful, or they are not. They become highly educated, or they do not. They become married and have a large family, or they have a small one. And at each step of the way, both their values and their lives have undergone either ratification or revision.

Pro-choice and pro-life activists live in different worlds, and the scope of their lives, as both adults and children, fortifies them in their belief that their own views on abortion are the more correct, more moral, and more reasonable. When added to this is the fact that should "the other side" win, one group of women will see the very real devaluation of their lives and life resources, it is not surprising that the abortion debate has generated so much heat and so little light.

9

The Future of the Debate

The Paradox of Success

In the years since the 1973 Supreme Court decision, the political successes of the pro-life movement have been dramatic. In 1976, for example, the Republican party platform supported a constitutional amendment banning abortions. In the same year, Congress passed the Hyde amendment, which prohibited the use of public funds to pay for the abortions of poor women, and in 1978 the Supreme Court held that amendment to be constitutional. Congress has taken action to cut off federal funding of the abortions of government employees, Peace Corps volunteers, and members of the military and their dependents. In the 1980s, the Senate Judiciary Committee has held hearings on a Human Life statute that would outlaw virtually all abortions by declaring that human life begins at conception, and several anti-abortion bills, including the Hatch amendment, are presently under congressional discussion.[1]

But the social background against which these successes have been achieved suggests a paradox. Not only is the American public generally sympathetic to abortion; it is apparently becoming more sympathetic all the time. In 1962, the first Gallup poll on abortion asked people if they approved of abortion under certain specified circumstances (when pregnancy threatened the life or health of the mother, when it was the result of rape, incest, and so on). At that time, 10 percent of those surveyed supported abortion under any circumstances, that is, "on demand."[2] In contrast, the 1980 Gallup poll, which used a somewhat different wording, found that 25 percent of those surveyed supported abortion "on demand" and that another 53 percent supported abortion in a very broad range of circumstances. The series of polls on abortion conducted by the National Opinion Research Center between 1965 and 1980 show similar increases in public support, as do a variety of other polls.[3]

To be sure, relying on poll data as the only gauge of public opinion has its perils; all public opinion polls, and particularly those on abortion, reflect certain philosophical problems that cast doubt on what they actually mean. Nonetheless, the present state of the abortion controversy poses an irresistible question. Why is it that the opponents of abortion are becoming more effective politically at a time when public support and acceptance of abortion seem to be increasing?

There are both political and pragmatic reasons for the recent successes of the pro-life movement. Politically, the women who make up the grass-roots membership of the movement, in California and other states, are women who are on the defensive; they are fighting to support a way of life that is increasingly under assault.[4] As more women combine jobs and careers with motherhood and as the public comes to assume that the ordinary woman can readily do this, women who choose to be exclusively housewives and mothers find their values, their status, and their way of life devalued. They see these assaults symbolically represented in an ultimate devaluation—the capricious taking of life from the embryo, whom they have always seen as human, helpless, and innocent. It is therefore not surprising that they are vigorous in opposing abortion. Indeed, in light of the analysis we have offered, it is surprising that the abortion debate has not been even more emotional and violent than it has.*

Given this, the recent successes of the pro-life movement may be attributed to a combination of three factors: the intensity of commitment its members bring to their cause, the use of new technologies to translate that commitment into new political resources, and the willingness of pro-life supporters to make their position on abortion the

* Two incidents of violence are cited in the beginning of Chapter One. During our interviews, several pro-life activists said that although they personally rejected the use of violence, they could understand how it could occur. More disturbingly, some of them advanced a moral basis for it. Even if lives were lost in violence directed at an abortion center, they argued, that loss would be outweighed, and justified, by the greater net saving of unborn lives.

sole determinant of their political behavior and, specifically, their voting behavior.

Intensity of commitment

In terms of commitment, in order to qualify for interviewing according to our research plan, pro-life activists had to be working at least ten hours a week on the abortion issue. (For an explanation of our research method, see Appendix One.) Though ten hours a week is not in itself a trivial commitment, almost all of the pro-life activists made the cut-off point easily; in fact, most worked between thirty and forty hours a week on this issue. This is especially remarkable when contrasted with pro-choice levels of activity. Although pro-choice activists reported working similar hours in the 1960s when they were the group seeking to overturn the status quo, by the time of the present study, we had to define the minimum involvement as five hours a week in order to find a sample of pro-choice activists. For most of the current activists, five hours a week represented the maximum, and this group included people who were full-time employees of family planning agencies with responsibility for outreach, education, and lobbying on the abortion issue.*

This passionate level of commitment to the pro-life cause is important because it is a truism of American political life that small groups with strong opinions (e.g., the National Rifle Association) can have a disproportionately large impact, especially when the issue they are concerned with is not one of particular importance to a wider political public. And although activists on both sides would prefer to believe otherwise, the abortion issue is not a matter of great concern to the average American. For example, in 1976, after abortion had already become an issue about which presidential candidates debated, concern about abortion ranked nineteenth in a list of twenty "issues important to voters"; it was outranked by such diverse issues as inflation, government spending, bussing, and national health care. Of the twenty issues, only the pardon of former President Nixon was ranked as less important than abortion.[5] Thus, the pro-life movement has been politically successful despite growing public support for abortion in part

* This may no longer be as true as it once was. As the pro-life movement became more visibly successful during the course of this study, pro-choice activists became correspondingly more committed. By 1982, a real resurgence of pro-choice interest and activity was noted in our interviews.

because it has been intensely committed to the goal of outlawing abortion during a period when the general public has been only weakly committed to supporting it.

New technology and political activism

Only a few years ago it was conventionally assumed that political activity depended upon having access to certain kinds of social resources—time, information, convenient transportation, money for "appropriate" clothing. The political process, at the local level, was imagined as a series of meetings among concerned citizens who wanted social and political change. The relative uninvolvement of certain groups of people—lower-class people, for example, or housewives—was consequently seen as a result of their limited access to these resources (in particular, time and money).[6]

At the beginning of this study, we asked pro-life activists during interviews how many meetings a month they attended. On average, they reported attending fewer than four meetings a *year*, but they also reported working more than ten (and often forty) hours a *week* for the pro-life cause. This remarkable discrepancy can only be accounted for by some changes in the nature of political activity as conventionally understood.

It will be recalled that after 1973, the average right-to-life activist was a woman who did not hold a paying job, did not have a college degree, and had not been politically active before, even in community activities such as PTA. Therefore, she belonged to each of the three categories—housewives, the less educated, and those without previous experience in local politics—that were traditionally thought to be outside the political process.[7]

The primary factor in this reversal of traditional patterns, at least in this study, is the emergence of a new technology of telecommunications, which has enabled political activism *to occur in the home*. Virtually every pro-life person we interviewed reported using at least one of several new technologies. First, many small pro-life groups subscribe to a telephone answering service with a "roll-over" feature, which can electronically forward a phone call to another number. Thus, a single phone number for the organization can be printed in telephone books, pamphlets, and campaign literature. Individual activists need only commit themselves to be "on call" and to keep their own telephones free for a regularly scheduled block of time (e.g., from nine to noon every Wednesday). The schedule is then given to the answering service, and when a phone call comes in to the service (whose number is usually the one printed for the organization), the phone call is automatically forwarded to the home of the person who is "on call" at that particular time. In this way an individual can do political work on her own time, without ever leaving the house.

Most of the pro-life groups we identified also used another telecommunications method, the "telephone tree," which enables them to capitalize on one of their major resources—the passionate commitment of housewives who spend a great deal of time at home. In theory, telephone trees are very effective: if person *A* calls five people, and each of those five in turn calls five more people, and so on two more times, some political action can be requested from 781 people, with no member having had to make more than five telephone calls. In practice, however, the effectiveness of a telephone tree declines dramatically with a decrease in the probability that the person called will be in. Pro-life women, because they are seldom employed outside the home, are likely to be near their home phones much of the day. In contrast, pro-choice women are rarely home and often are not reachable even at their offices; they must be contacted through messages left with secretaries, co-workers, family members, or telephone answering machines. (Interestingly enough, answering machines do not seem to be part of the new political technology. Two humans who alternate talking to each other's machines appear to be far less effective than two humans talking to one another; the loss of information in each exchange between answering machines is usually quite high.)

In California, where much of our study was conducted, a number of pro-life groups had used yet another new technology and put their mailing lists into small home computers. Such lists provide a cheap and efficient way to get information to members. Once the list of member names is put into the memory bank of a small home computer, getting mailings to the group is simply a matter of printing or copying material and having the computer print a set of mailing labels. The computer can also sort these labels by zip code, thus entitling the group to lower mailing rates.* For years our own research office was on the

* These lower mailing rates are of particular value to the more frankly political organizations. An "educational" group (defined by the IRS as a 501c–3 organization) is a nonprofit organization and as such is permitted (as of 1982) to use low cost mailings (less

mailing list of several pro-life and pro-choice organizations. It became clear to us that the pro-life organizations with computerized mailing lists could alert their members to a critical event, such as a vote on a bill in Congress, within twenty-four hours. They could get literally thousands of letters sent to senators or representatives at crucial moments, a fact that could not help but shape the perception of public opinion within congressional offices.

Finally, a few pro-life organizations have begun to use electronic banking. With the capacity to handle "automatic debits" through electronic funds transfer (EFT), a pro-life organization can offer its members the opportunity to sign an automatic deduction form that authorizes their bank to take money electronically from their checking or savings accounts each month and transfer it to the pro-life organization's account. These automatic deposits continue until an individual signs a second form that cancels the first. The advantages of this system are obvious. Member inertia serves the organization because an active decision is needed to stop the flow of donations. Furthermore, the monthly donations suggested are relatively small—five, ten, and fifteen dollars. Individuals who would balk at being asked to give $60, $120, or $180 a year may find it easy to sign up for the small monthly amounts. They may not like to think they are committed to the organization to the tune of $60 a year, but only the poorest and most ambivalent among them would be willing to say that the organization is not worth five dollars a month.

The point here is not that the pro-life movement exists because of technology—to which, in any case, the more affluent pro-choice people should have greater access.* It is rather that a sophisticated use of technology has allowed the pro-life movement to convert the spare

---

than six cents per item); but it cannot engage in political activity—it cannot lobby, it can only inform. Partly for this reason, the pro-life and the pro-choice movements have tended to set up two organizational structures, one nonprofit and nonpolitical and one that is more openly political. The political groups must pay the bulk rate for their mailings, about eleven cents an item. But if these items are sorted by zip code and meet other requirements from the post office (they must be bundled, with a minimum number of items per bundle), they receive a discount of almost 25 percent. On a mailing of 5,000 items, which is not uncommon, the savings are considerable.

* As noted in Chapter Six, almost half of all the pro-choice people studied earned more than $50,000 a year; only a third of all the pro-life people earned that much. One-fifth of the pro-choice people earned less than $20,000, but one-third of the pro-life people earned less than that.

time of a largely housewife membership, a relatively far-flung grassroots organization, and small but regular donations into effective and reliable political resources. This fact is particularly important because it means that the pro-life movement, at least at the state level, has been able to compensate for its relative lack of a primary traditional resource—money, "the mother's milk of politics."

To suggest that the pro-life movement is not a wealthy one goes so strongly against public belief (particularly among pro-choice people) that a few caveats are in order. In the course of this study, a number of pro-life activists who had official financial and executive status within the movement were interviewed, a number of financial disclosure statements filed in connection with political campaigns were examined, rough "intake-outgo" estimates of expenditures based on careful attendance at group meetings of selected organizations were calculated, and all of the pro-choice documents that claim that the pro-life movement is heavily funded by outside sources such as the Catholic church and the New Right were scrutinized.[8] This procedure, of course, has its weak points, which could encourage skepticism about our findings. Even with new laws on campaign financing, it is easy not to report money, especially if the campaign is small and the organization is neither a nonprofit organization nor an official campaign-based organization. Officially available records of campaign contributions by several pro-life organizations in California, although all had been politically active to some degree, were woefully inadequate. It is also probably wise to be suspicious about the willingness of any activist (on either side of the issue) to tell a researcher the whole truth about the financial worth of his or her organization. Moreover, our research focused on the organization of the movement at the state and local level, and it is clear that the national pro-life organizations have a very different financial structure and are also much more affluent than the state and local organizations. In 1980, for example, the national Life Amendment Political Action Committee (LAPAC) was one of the ten wealthiest political action committees reported to the Federal Election Commission.

Despite these caveats, there is considerable circumstantial evidence to suggest that the pro-life movement, *at least at the state and local level*, is not a wealthy one. In most of the organizations we studied, the single largest event was the yearly pro-life dinner, which nets about $1,000. Other groups hold bake sales and raffles, hardly the hallmarks of well-funded and well-organized groups. Some groups do quite well in collecting "tithes" and dues from members, but the average donation is quite small. In general, the kinds of activities undertaken by most of the groups we studied were not consistent with large budgets; most groups confined themselves to xeroxing, mailing, and telephoning members.

Finally, many pro-choice people have vigorously investigated pro-life finances, often with an eye to discrediting the movement or disallowing nonprofit status to pro-life groups that have it. These investigations have not exposed any major sources of income, either internal or external, that flow to local organizations. The National Abortion Rights Action League (NARAL), for example, has published a list of contributions by the Catholic church to one national pro-life organization, but even in this list, individual contributions are on average quite small—three to ten thousand dollars.* Although even a small amount of money can have considerable political effect when judiciously placed, the overall impact of the Catholic church (or the New Right) on state and local organizations seems to be small.

Single-issue politics

Thus commitment, not money, is the well-spring of the pro-life movement. And this commitment translates into voting. Pro-life activists are active voters. This in itself should not be remarkable in a country that prides itself on the breadth and extensiveness of its franchise, but the fact remains that fewer than half of all Americans vote regularly, and the proportion of those who do has been shrinking in recent years. In the 1980 presidential election, for example (presidential elections draw higher turnouts than others), only 59 percent of all eligible voters actually voted.[9]

In this context, the willingness of pro-life people to vote becomes important. Because they are part of a very small proportion of citizens who vote regularly, their opinions are weighted more heavily than the

* See "Who Finances the Anti-Abortion Movement?", a flyer issued by the National Abortion Rights Action League. In fact, the real power of the church may lie in its ability to bring together in one place a group of people who have grown up believing that the embryo is a baby and who are disproportionately likely to be women who have made personal investments in certain lifestyles. A pro-life activist who wishes to recruit need only leaflet cars parked outside a Catholic church during mass; pro-choice people cannot so easily find sympathizers who meet regularly in one place.

opinions of nonvoters. And because they also vote during primaries, where turnout is usually at its lowest, their votes can often eliminate candidates who do not have pro-life views. To illustrate how few votes it actually takes to make political history in an era when very few people vote, in 1980 the Right-to-Life party of New York state officially qualified for a place on the 1982 ballot by gaining less than 3 percent of the votes cast.[10]

At least until very recently, pro-life voters have also been single-issue (or "bullet") voters, willing to vote for or against a candidate solely on the basis of that candidate's stand on abortion. Whether or not single-issue voting is a good thing for the American political system (and the pro-life movement is far from the first group to have engaged in it), it is clear that it is effective, particularly when combined with the general willingness of pro-life voters to go to the polls in the first place.[11]

In summary, the pro-life movement has been successful in recent years for three reasons: its rank-and-file members are largely women who care deeply about the issue; it has been able to use new communications technology to make effective political use of the time they have to spend at home; and it has been able to translate the depth of their concern into a willingness to vote exclusively in terms of the abortion issue. Given the fact that the abortion issue is not of major concern to the general public (and pro-choice supporters may have become complacent, thinking the battle has been won), the political successes of the pro-life movement are not surprising.

The Paradox of Public Opinion

But do these political successes mean that the pro-life movement is changing public opinion? Are pro-life activists, as they claim, actually reaching their cherished goal of "educating the public to the humanity of the unborn child"? As we begin to seek an answer, we should recall that motherhood is a topic about which people have very complicated feelings, and because abortion has become the battleground for different definitions of motherhood, neither the pro-life nor the pro-choice movement has ever been "representative" of how most Americans feel about abortion. More to the point, all our data suggest that *neither of these groups will ever be able to be representative*.

Historically, the two political groups that joined forces in California in the early 1960s in order to press for changes in the state's century-old abortion laws were much more liberal in their support of abortion than most Americans. At that time large numbers of Americans still rejected abortion even when the woman's health was "seriously endangered," when the pregnancy was the result of rape or incest, or when there was a "strong chance of a serious defect in the baby." And so-called "discretionary" abortions—when the woman was not married, did not want a child, or could not afford to care for one—were resoundingly rejected by most Americans.[12]

What is remarkable about public opinion on abortion prior to the U.S. Supreme Court decision, however, is how quickly it changed. Within a decade of the first pro-choice calls for abortion reform, most Americans had come to accept the logic of the pro-choice position. In 1965 only 73 percent of those polled in the National Opinion Research Center (NORC) study approved of abortion when there was a threat to the woman's health; by 1972 that figure had grown to 87 percent. Even more dramatic were the increases in support for abortion in the cases of rape and fetal deformity. In 1965 only 59 percent and 57 percent of those polled had supported abortion in these two circumstances; by 1972, approval rates had risen to 79 percent in both categories, and other polls show similar results.[13]

The increase in public support for "discretionary" abortions was more dramatic. Whereas only 22 percent of those polled in the 1965 NORC survey approved of abortion on grounds of low family income, 49 percent had come to approve of it on these grounds by 1972. Similarly, approval of abortion for unmarried women increased from 18 percent in 1965 to 43 percent in 1972; approval of abortion for couples who already had all the children they wanted climbed from a mere 16 percent in 1965 to 40 percent in 1972. Again the Gallup polls show a similar trend: only 26 percent of those surveyed in 1962 approved of abortion for economic reasons, but by 1968 approval for this reason had increased to 32 percent.[14]

Thus, although poll data should be used cautiously, the overall trend is clear: the pro-choice activists started out being considerably more liberal than many Americans, but within a very short period of time American public opinion had moved much closer to the pro-choice position. It is tempting to argue that the pro-choice people simply "persuaded" a great many fellow Americans to accept their point of view. To some extent, they probably did; certainly the mere fact that they made the abortion issue a subject for public debate allowed many more people to become familiar with it and to form personal opinions about the merits of their case. It seems likely, however, that American public opinion was shaped more significantly by the large-scale social changes going on at the same time—changes in the status of women, changes in traditional sexual morality, and an increasing concern with poverty.

Two critical facts should be kept in mind, however: these changes in public opinion occurred *before* the 1973 Supreme Court decision on abortion, and the Court's decision did not "legislate morality." Public opinion on the issue had already been shaped during the previous decade of debate, and the Court's decision did very little to change patterns of opinion.[15]

The NORC data show that general support for abortion declined slightly between 1974 and 1978, after which public opinion stabilized at high levels of approval of abortion. The Gallup polls also seem to show an inability on the part of the pro-life movement to sway public opinion: support for the most liberal position—approval of abortion "on demand"—has slowly *increased*, from 21 percent in 1975 to 25 percent in 1980; and in the same years, support for the most conservative position—disapproval of abortion for any reason—has *declined* by the same amount, from 22 percent in 1975 to 18 percent in 1980.[16]

One could argue, therefore, that the situation now facing the pro-life movement is quite different from the one that faced the pro-choice movement in the early 1960s. The pro-life movement feels it is now confronted with the task of trying to change public opinion in the face of a well-known Supreme Court decision that has encouraged public attitudes in favor of abortion. But the history of the two movements—and their relationship to public opinion—suggests that although the Supreme Court decision had major effects on the *practice* of abortion, it did very little to change public attitudes. The real test of the ability of the pro-life movement to change public attitudes is yet to come. It will come, if it does, during public debate over passage of a national anti-abortion law. Before that happens, the pro-life movement must surmount several critical barriers.

The Dilemma of Winning Public Support

Many social scientists have argued that the relationship between attitudes as expressed in opinion polls and future behavior is at best a problematic one, and the topic of abortion presents some special problems in this respect. There has been a tendency to use the Gallup and NORC questions verbatim over the last years, in part because public opinion on abortion, more so than on most issues, varies according to the wording used. When the exact same wording of questions is used, one can be relatively confident that the questions are measuring approximately the same things every time. (In social science terms, such questions are "reliable.") The instability of the response that occurs when different wordings are used suggests a common sense explanation: people have very complicated feelings about abortion, which simple "yes-no" questions on a public opinion poll cannot capture. The Gallup questions may measure some broad tendencies relatively well, but it is unclear whether they capture any of the nuances or details of what people actually think.

However, if we treat poll data as a skeleton to be clothed with some modest inferences, several interesting things seem to be true. First, depending on the poll, the year it was taken, and the wording used, somewhere between 20 and 40 percent of the American public are deeply committed to either the pro-life or the pro-choice position; they believe either that the embryo has an obvious "right to life" or that abortion is a woman's choice. However, keeping in mind these same variables—the poll, the year taken, and the wording—somewhere between 50 and 80 percent of the American public, although in general approving of abortion, do not subscribe to either of these opposing views. Despite what the activists on either side of the debate would like to think, the overwhelming majority of Americans hold what might be thought of as middle-of-the-road opinions on the topic of abortion. A careful reading of the polls suggests that a fair rendering of this middle ground would be as follows: a majority of Americans approve of abortions in general, but this does not necessarily indicate an unqualified acceptance of a woman's "right" to her own body; they simultaneously approve of "necessary" abortions and disapprove of "casual" abortions.

Judith Blake has argued that public opinion polls actually reflect two sets of attitudes on abortion. From the first national polls onward, she says, a substantial number of Americans have supported abortion for "hard" reasons: when pregnancy would represent a risk to the woman's life, when the pregnancy was the product of rape or incest, and when there was substantial likelihood that the embryo would be born with a defect. But these same polls show a public opinion decidedly less supportive of abortions undertaken for "soft" or discretionary reasons. American public opinion accepts abortions when continuation of the pregnancy would cause hardship, but there is a deep division about just what kinds of hardships are severe enough to merit an abortion.[17]

Given this situation, the future of the debate will belong to the side that most effectively captures the middle ground of opinion. To win a clear victory on abortion, the pro-choice side will have to persuade many middle-of-the-road people that legal abortion is a good thing and must be protected; or the pro-life side will have to convince the same people that abortion is a bad thing that must be outlawed. Even if one side chooses to concentrate on persuading legislators rather than citizens and succeeds in passing laws that serve its cause, this middle group of citizens will still have to be persuaded to accept those laws without undue protest. But the peculiar structure of public attitudes on abortion creates dilemmas that both pro-life and pro-choice activists will have to face. Because Americans approve of some but not all abortions, each group will face political, pragmatic, and ideological problems in "selling" its position to those in the middle.

Public opinion and the Pro-Life Movement

The first problem facing pro-life activists is political. Their activism is premised on the deeply held belief that every embryo is a baby. And for the overlapping ideological, social, and emotional reasons we have already explored, they cannot be expected to compromise on their belief that every abortion takes a baby's life. Yet in order to capture the middle ground, this is exactly what they will have to do. All the available poll data suggest that American support for certain categories of abortion is deeply ingrained and that any unswerving application of pro-life principles that ignores that support will create massive obstacles to capturing the middle ground.

The polls suggest that pro-life people are right in their perception that many Americans feel a deep uneasiness about abortion. Abortions performed on women without the knowledge and consent of their husbands, abortions performed on "promiscuous" teenagers, abortions performed on women who "couldn't be bothered" to use contraception—all offend, to some degree, certain deeply held American values. To the extent that abortion as now practiced in America gives women unilateral control over their fertility, and thereby undoes traditional relationships surrounding that fertility—controls by husbands, parents, and "society"—many "middle-of-the-road" Americans probably feel disturbed by it.

In trying to make effective use of this uneasiness about abortion, however, the pro-life activists will face a delicate task indeed. They must persuade the average American that their political goal—a law banning *all* abortions—will eliminate only the abortions people find disturbing and will somehow respond to the need for the abortions most Americans support. If they are to seem at once "reasonable," sympathetic to the plight of women with unwanted pregnancies, and politically respectable, they must contend with the fact that all but a tiny minority of Americans support abortion under three conditions: when the woman's life is endangered, when the pregnancy is the result of rape or incest, and when there is a good chance that the child will be born with substantial handicaps.[18] Yet each of these conditions poses a number of problems for the right-to-life movement.

On the face of it, approving abortion in cases where the life of the woman is threatened would not seem to pose serious political problems. After all, almost all Americans favor abortions in such cases, and so do many pro-life people. (In our interviews about three-quarters of the pro-life activists indicated that they found abortion in these cases at least tolerable.) Presumably the case where a pregnancy threatens the life of a woman presents the simplest moral dilemma, inasmuch as the woman and the embryo claim the same right (a right to continued life) instead of different ones (a right to life and a right to control one's body) that would have to be given different weights.

But even this category presents a complex set of dilemmas to pro-life people, both as individuals and as members of the movement. On the ideological level, one cannot accept abortion in this case without assuming that an embryo that threatens the life of its mother somehow belongs in a different moral category from anyone else who threatens the life of another, however inadvertently. To agree that embryos *are* in fact different because they depend upon the physical body of the woman in a way that no other person ever depends on anyone else would be to accept the very basis of the pro-choice argument that abortion is morally tolerable because the embryo is not really a "baby" or a "person" but a "fetus," whose different physical status confers upon it different (and weaker) rights. Thus the dilemma: if all embryos really are "babies" and by definition "innocent" and physically dependent, on what moral grounds can the lives of some of them be ended? For example, it is not hard to imagine that the activities of a healthy, active three-year-old could threaten the life of an overburdened, anemic mother with active cardiac disease. But even the most active abortion supporter would recoil from the suggestion that this three-year-old should have its life ended in order to save the life of its mother. In part this is common sense: three-year-olds can be cared for by others, but embryos, at least for now, cannot. But if pro-life groups concede that the physical dependence of embryos makes them different in this critical way from already-born children, then they have seriously called into question their own argument that there is no moral difference between an embryo of three days and a child of three years.

Thus, to accept abortion *even when it is undertaken to save the life of the mother* would be a potentially devastating concession for pro-life groups. It would imply acceptance of one of two premises: that embryos belong to a different moral order from people who have already been born or (more perniciously, from the pro-life point of view) that embryos are persons, but some persons (women) have more rights than others (embryos). To tolerate any abortions at all, even abortions to "save the life of the mother," would be the first step on a "slippery slope," the beginning of a long slide away from the logic of their moral position. The pro-life movement has therefore attempted to accommodate itself to the need for abortion in life-threatening cases in two ways.

The first is to argue, as the movement and individual activists have, that there are virtually no cases in modern obstetrical science where the life of the mother need be pitted against the life of the embryo. This is true, as far as it goes: medical advances in obstetrics over the last fifty years have indeed virtually eliminated most conditions—such as cardiac disease, tuberculosis, and renal failure—that once made pregnancy a very real threat to maternal life. But it also misses the point: people are concerned not for statistical but for moral reasons because a pregnancy that threatens the life of a woman poses a moral challenge about how to balance the rights of the two parties involved. In a sense, it is a garden variety version of the sort of problem put to students in ethics classes. When one is asked to decide whether it is morally right to steal an expensive medicine from a hard-hearted pharmacist in order to save the life of a dying spouse, it is irrelevant to argue that the example is improbable. It is true that pharmacists are rarely that hard-hearted, that alternative resolutions (such as negotiation or buying on credit) almost always exist, and that it is unlikely that a pharmacist would be the only person in possession of the life-saving medicine. But the dilemma as posed asks individuals to come up with a *moral principle* that ranks the relative merits of private property and human life. So it is with the case of abortion when the life of the woman is at stake: no matter how unlikely it is that this dilemma will occur, most persons will want a moral principle that helps them determine the relative rights of embryos and mothers in such a case, where the rights of one must preclude the rights of the other. The pro-life movement may argue vigorously that the issue is moot in a practical sense. But even if only one case occurs every ten years, we can be sure that it will be brought to public attention and that pro-life people will be put under great pressure to come up with a moral stand on it.

Given this reality, which at least some pro-life activists recognize on the intuitive level, a second strategy of accommodation has been proposed: to develop or adapt a moral rationale that would permit abortion when the life of the woman is at stake without conceding too much ideological ground, that is, without bringing into question either the babyhood of the embryo or its right to life. Two doctrines that attempt to do this were mentioned during the course of our interviews. The origins of both can be traced to pro-life persuasive literature and more distantly to Catholic moral theology. The first is the doctrine of "indirect effect"; the second is the doctrine of the "unjust aggressor."

The doctrine of "indirect effect," first articulated by Thomas Bouscaren in 1928 with respect to ectopic pregnancies, holds that although it is never morally right to "directly" perform a forbidden act (such as taking the life of the embryo), it is morally permissible to undertake another act that may have the forbidden action as an unintended consequence.[19] In the case of ectopic pregnancies, where an embryo begins growing in the Fallopian tube rather than in the uterus, Bouscaren argued that although it would be wrong to surgically remove the embryo, thus causing its death, it would be acceptable to remove the diseased tube, thus causing the death of the embryo indirectly. In this reasoning, "direct" abortion, intended to terminate the life of the embryo, is always wrong, but other activities that "indirectly" cause the death of the embryo may be acceptable. The classic example given in textbooks, and often repeated verbatim by the people we interviewed, is the X-ray treatment of a pregnant cancerous uterus, which indirectly causes the death of the embryo. For some of the pro-life people we interviewed, an abortion undertaken primarily to save the life of the woman (rather than primarily to end the life of the embryo) was morally acceptable under the doctrine of "indirect effect."

The doctrine of the "unjust aggressor" holds that although it is never right to take another person's life, when an unjust aggressor (such as an armed intruder in your home) threatens your life, it is permissible to protect yourself even at the cost of the intruder's life. Under this doctrine, embryos that threaten the lives of those who carry them may be considered inadvertent "unjust aggressors" whose lives may be ended. In this line of argument, individuals have an affirmative responsibility not to take the life of an embryo arbitrarily, but the discharge of this responsibility does not require the sacrifice of one's own life in order to do so.

These two doctrines have been sketched out as they appear in pro-life literature and on our interview tapes, rather than in their more elegant expression in moral theology, because the problem will in fact be the subject of political debate between individuals, not a topic for refined academic discussion. Moreover, it is likely that there will be a flurry of new thinking and writing around these two doctrines as time goes on, because to be successful, the pro-life movement *must* come up with some way of justifying abortions intended to preserve the life of the mother, and it must be a way that does not also cut the ground out from under its moral position vis-à-vis abortion in other circumstances.

It is unlikely that either of these doctrines will be very persuasive to the general public. Their appeal is probably limited to persons raised in and familiar with the tradition of Catholic moral theology. Furthermore, except in the unusual case of a treatment (such as radiation therapy) designed to treat a condition clearly not related to pregnancy, the doctrine of "indirect effect" relies unduly upon the *intent* of the physician; and the problems of policing an abortion policy based on measuring and judging *intent* are probably insurmountable. More to the point politically, the application of both doctrines would depend upon the subjective judgments of a host of individual physicians, and these judgments could seem capricious, arbitrary, and even "Jesuitical" to the general public.

The doctrine of the "unjust aggressor" fares marginally better. On pragmatic grounds, it has its virtues. If any embryo that threatens maternal life is by definition an unjust aggressor, then the problems inherent in having a physician define the intent of an abortion are sidestepped. It also has the advantage of being neatly bounded in an ideological situation where boundaries are critical: it preserves the premise that all embryos are babies and that all babies have a right to life and argues only that the right to life is compromised when (and only when, as the philosophers would say) the embryo has become despite itself an "unjust aggressor" to its mother. For these reasons, it may be the only argument the movement can use to remain ideologically pure while accepting a category of abortion that is morally acceptable to the overwhelming majority of the general public.

As pro-choice activists have noted, this doctrine has its weaknesses. Will the public accept the notion that embryos can be "aggressors"? And if it does, won't that undercut one of the latent goals of the pro-life movement, namely, to create public support and sympathy for children and childbearing? As we have noted in earlier chapters, people oppose abortion for a number of reasons, but one thing that unites them is the perception of an innocent, defenseless embryo whose life is ended arbitrarily and capriciously. Won't the doctrine of the "unjust aggressor" introduce the notion into the public mind that embryos are not inherently innocent? And if physical circumstances can turn the embryo into the moral equivalent of an armed intruder into a woman's life, why can't it be admitted that social and emotional circumstances may threaten a woman in similar ways? Finally, if the pro-life movement were to accept a law that prohibits all abortions except those necessary "to save the life of the mother," they would have accepted a situation that includes serious problems of monitoring. Pro-choice people are probably right when they argue that such a law would be interpreted within a wide range of discretion, that at least some women would seek illegal abortions anyway, and that rich women would be more likely than poor women to find that their pregnancies are "life-endangering." We described in Chapter Three how a similar law was interpreted in California in the 1950s and 1960s: there were widely varying interpretations of what constituted a woman's "life" and whether or not an abortion was necessary to "save" it.

These pragmatic objections should not comfort the pro-choice movement, however, because they also miss the point. Pro-life advocates are seeking a *moral* victory as well as a political one. They would prefer that there be no abortions in the United States (or anywhere), but their political goal is based on a moral belief (buttressed by social and practical circumstances) that abortion is morally wrong. They want a human life amendment to the Constitution (or a federal law) primarily in order to make a *moral* statement about abortion and only secondarily in order to prevent all abortions in practice. In other words, although pro-life activists would prefer a law that is both symbolic and effective, they might settle for a symbolic victory. Their desire to see a moral affirmation of the wrongness of abortion outweighs their concern about the problems of implementing a human life law. As they have argued, laws against murder are difficult to enforce, but that is no reason to legalize murder.

Similar political and ideological problems confront pro-life people when they try to deal with the two other kinds of abortion that have a great deal of generalized public support: abortion when the pregnancy is a result of rape or incest and abortion when the pregnancy is likely to result in a child born with a physical or mental handicap. Pro-life people often argue that cases of pregnancy caused by rape are so rare as to be irrelevant.[20] But, again, this is not a satisfactory response: just as in the case of the pregnancy that threatens the life of the woman, people want a moral principle, not a statement of statistical probability. Furthermore, rape-engendered pregnancy raises questions that go beyond the question of whether the mother's life is threatened. The thought of a woman being forced to bear her rapist's child is deeply disturbing to most Americans. Yet if the pro-life movement were to accept a law that permitted abortion in cases of rape (and incest), it would be conceding a great deal of ideological ground: if a pregnancy can be ended because it is the product of rape, then the assumption must be that some embryos (those whose fathers are rapists) are less valuable than others. And pro-life people recognize this. Several of them asked us, rhetorically, if one would put a five-year-old to death simply because its father was a rapist, and the answer was always no. To approve of abortion in cases of rape would be to start down the "slippery slope" toward believing that not all embryos are innocent persons of equal worth. Equally troubling, ideologically, is the presumption that a rape-engendered pregnancy can be ended because of the circumstances under which it came about. If a pregnancy can be ended simply because intercourse was forced on a woman, how can the pro-life movement argue that it is wrong for women to end pregnancies that occurred as a result of some lesser degree of coercion? When neither partner took contraceptive measures, how can we distinguish between coercion and seduction? A great deal of ideological elaboration would be necessary to make abortion in the cases of rape and incest plausible in the light of pro-life beliefs and commitments.

Finally, the case of abortions for rape and incest victims presents a complicated problem that the pro-life movement has yet to deal with. Most of the pro-life people we interviewed said that women who are raped simply don't become pregnant very often, and many of them said they thought this was because something biological happens to rape victims that precludes the possibility of pregnancy. In fact, they are half-right: among *women who promptly report the rape*, pregnancy is uncommon. But there is nothing mysterious about this. Women who report a rape are generally given prophylactic treatment for venereal disease and pregnancy, and in the state of California, the treatment for pregnancy is generally large doses of diethylstilbesterol (DES, better known as the "morning-after" pill) or a vacuum curettage of the uterus.* Thus few reported rape victims become what one might call "officially pregnant" because although conception may have occurred, the pregnancy is eliminated in its earliest stage.

Needless to say, the only reason this has not become a pressing ideological question for the pro-life movement is that few people know how rape victims are treated. Although the matter has been discussed in congressional hearings, our interviews suggest that it is not yet a matter of public knowledge.[21] But when it does become more public, it is certain to pose another unpleasant problem. To maintain ideological purity, the pro-life movement will have to call for an end to the prophylactic treatment of rape victims, or it will have to tolerate what amounts to very early abortion in these cases, or it will have to declare that very early embryos are not actually babies. (In the congressional hearings, some pro-life proponents suggested that the protection of the law be extended only to embryos past the point of implantation, an event that occurs approximately five to seven days after fertilization.)[22] In any event, the more successful the pro-life movement is in attaining its goals and the more public all aspects of the debate become, the more

* We conducted telephone interviews with major hospitals throughout the state of California. All agreed that they offered women who had been raped the option of either a curettage or the morning-after pill. Several volunteered the fact that they follow a protocol developed by a statewide rape-crisis task force.

the issue of pregnancy in cases of rape and incest (and especially the treatment of rape victims right after the event) will become.

The pro-life movement will also eventually have to come to terms—one way or another—with abortion intended to prevent the birth of a deformed child. According to public opinion polls, such abortions are acceptable to more than four-fifths of the American public.[23] However, compared with the other two cases, this one is the *least* ideologically tolerable for pro-life people. Many of the pro-life activists we interviewed were ambivalent about abortions to save the life of the mother, and a few were ambivalent in the cases of rape or incest, but there was no ambivalence at all about the case of "fetal indications."

On the surface, this appears strange: opinion polls seem to suggest that the general public accepts abortion in this case as "necessary" rather than "discretionary." But abortions for fetal deformity cut to the deepest level of pro-life feelings about "selective" abortion. Because the logic of abortion in this case depends upon a judgment that the embryo is "damaged" in one respect or another, it suggests to pro-life people an acceptance of the idea that humans can be ranked along some scale of perfection and that people who fall below a certain arbitrary standard can be excluded. For all the reasons detailed in earlier chapters, therefore, the pro-life movement will probably continue to be most intransigent against negotiation in the case of "fetal deformity." Already, for example, the movement is vigorously opposing amniocentesis, a diagnostic test performed on pregnant women to see if the embryo has any of a number of physical or mental handicaps. The present surgeon-general of the United States, Everett Koop, an active pro-life supporter, has called amniocentesis exams "search-and-destroy missions," and the movement itself has labeled amniocentesis "selective genocide against the disabled."[24]

In summary, then, the pro-life movement has a complex set of policy decisions ahead of it. It is a small (though disproportionately effective) group of people that can apparently win broad support only by accommodating somehow to public attitudes that are at odds with its ideological position.

Public opinion and the Pro-Choice Movement

In part because of the history of the abortion debate, the pro-choice movement now faces a different set of dilemmas than the pro-life movement does. Rather than capturing a share of middle-of-the-road support, as the pro-life movement must do in order to succeed, it must find ways to *hold on* to the middle. At first glance, this would appear to be an easier task. But given the structure of public attitudes toward abortion, it may not be for at least two different sets of reasons.

First, there is no evidence that the pro-choice movement, any more than the pro-life movement, understands that Americans have mixed feelings about abortion. Despite widespread support for abortion in general, there continues to be a disjuncture between public support of abortion for the "hard reasons" (preserving the life of the woman, preventing birth in cases of rape, incest, or fetal deformity) and public support for the "soft reasons" (the woman or the couple don't want a child or can't afford one). It is important to remember that it was public attitudes toward abortions for the "soft" reasons that changed the most between 1962 and 1972 partly because support of abortion for the "hard" reasons was already fairly extensive.

If polls on American attitudes toward "abortion" are accurate in indicating feelings about two kinds of abortions—those that women *need* in contrast to those that women *want*—then the pro-choice movement would be making a strategic mistake to assume that support for one is identical to support for the other. It is quite possible tht the average American feels not unlike some of the more moderate pro-choice activists we interviewed. He or she believes that although abortion is preferable to some alternatives (the death of the woman, bearing a rapist's child, the birth of a deformed or an "unwanted" baby), it is less preferable than others (planning for sex "responsibly" and using contraception). When women are perceived as using abortion not to avoid one of these calamities but because they are "irresponsible," public opinion may be much "softer" than generally appreciated.[25] Our interviews with pro-choice activists (primarily at the state and local levels) suggest that most of them do not appreciate the fact that most Americans support abortion somewhat reluctantly, as the least of several evils. But that fact suggests two scenarios for the future.

The first scenario, admittedly speculative but worth considering, is that the pro-life movement will succeed in creating an ideological "package" that persuades Americans that the abortions women *need* (with the possible exception of those connected with fetal deformity) will continue to exist even under an anti-abortion law. Should this happen, the pro-choice movement would be very vulnerable. It was originally successful in part because it convinced people that the abortions women *needed* were not in fact being provided under the old law. Therefore, an anti-abortion law that explicitly protected these kinds of abortions might be acceptable to many Americans who have previously supported the pro-choice position. Furthermore, the traditional rhetoric used by the pro-choice movement in its heyday would lose much of its effectiveness and might very well boomerang nastily. The claim that women have a right to their own bodies can seem powerful when it is taken to mean that women should not have to lay down their lives for an embryo or bear the child of a rapist. But if the pro-life movement succeeds in effectively removing these cases from the debate, the claim that women have a right to their own bodies may be heard as selfish and petulant, a confirmation of the public's fears that abortion may be too powerful an event to leave under the control of women.

It is also possible that some sectors of the American public might become even less sympathetic to what is seen as female "selfishness" and hence less supportive of abortion. Despite the fact that the relationship between men, women, and the economy is complex, it is not hard to imagine a set of circumstances in which the continued presence of women in the labor market might be interpreted by some as both "uppity" and "threatening." For this to happen, parenthetically, it would not even be necessary for women to be objectively threatening; it is an article of faith among many Americans that white males cannot find jobs because of the competition from women and minorities. Although there is considerable evidence that white males still fare better than others in the employment market, the overall tightening of the economy in recent years may drive some people to seek scapegoats, even implausible ones.[26] In particular, people with (or without) jobs in depressed sectors of the economy may feel a diffuse hostility toward women, who seem at times to have been given unfair advantage. And if the pro-life movement should succeed in passing a law that would take care of "necessary" abortions, this hostility could focus more sharply on "discretionary" abortions, which could be seen as just one more example of women's "selfishness."

This scenario would not unfold in a smooth and predictable way, nor would it pit all women against all men. After all, many families make ends meet (and many more live according to their desires) because both husband and wife work; and many men love and are married to women who are deeply committed to their work. We are not suggesting a mechanical model whereby an increase of so many points in the inflation rate or the unemployment rate leads directly to an equivalent decline in public support for abortion. But if there is one thing that the history of the abortion debate shows clearly, it is that the social meaning of abortion is not static but is continually being redefined, by individuals and by the society as a whole.

If the pro-life movement were able to "sell" the American public an anti-abortion law that protected abortions for the "hard" reasons, it is possible that under certain social conditions much of the present support for abortion could evaporate. If the pro-life movement were successful in labeling abortions for the "soft" reasons "irresponsible" and "selfish," under certain conditions even working women might find themselves giving up some of their support for abortion. Many women would undoubtedly believe that any abortion they themselves might need would by definition be a "necessary" one and likely to be covered by the law.

More subtly, people may feel more isolated and disconnected because of some of the social changes that have occurred during the last decade such as fewer marriages, more childlessness, and less commitment to traditional community-supported ideals.[27] If social and demographic pressures *do* increase in the future, people may begin to fear loneliness and alienation more than they fear unintended pregnancies. The latent message that the pro-life movement offers—that it is possible to "swing the pendulum back" to more traditional lifestyles—may seem increasingly appealing to them. If working women find themselves facing bleaker economic prospects, more job discrimination in the market, and a public temper increasingly unsupportive of such things as affirmative action, they may reconsider their own mix of traditional roles. Beyond a certain point, discrimination in the job market (both social and economic) may make being only a wife and mother seem more attractive.

Speculation aside, there is a second scenario—a much likelier one—that could threaten the political goals of the pro-choice movement. The pro-life movement could achieve at least some of its major political goals without ever winning widespread public support simply by persuading Congress—which has been notoriously susceptible to small, dedicated pressure groups—to pass an anti-abortion law. More difficult, but still possible, it could persuade Congress to pass something like the Hatch amendment, which would give individual states the right to outlaw abortions once again. This latter strategy would make use of the grass-roots nature of pro-life resources quite effectively because in most states the pro-life movement would have little trouble mounting letter-writing campaigns directed at Congress and the state legislature. In both cases, however, the pro-life movement need only persuade legislators, not the public, that an anti-abortion law is needed and wanted.

Thus, we have two scenarios: the pro-life movement persuades the public to accept a law that separates "good" (necessary) abortions from "bad" (discretionary) ones; or it takes an end-run around public opinion and secures an anti-abortion law by going directly to the Congress and state legislatures. Should either event occur, the pro-choice movement will face two intertwined tasks, one ideological and one political.

Ideologically, the pro-choice movement will have to convince the public (and perhaps lawmakers) that although abortions may be divided into two categories in the public mind, successfully dividing them into two categories in public policy is quite a different matter. They must successfully argue that no public policy in a country as diverse and large as the United States can be "fine-tuned" well enough to discriminate in practice between the two kinds of abortions. Put another way, they will have to convince both the general public and legislators that tolerating some "unacceptable" abortions is simply the cost that must be paid if "acceptable" abortions are to remain available. To do this will call for stressing all of the problems inherent in defining which kinds of abortions "protect the life of the woman" and how heavily those problems of definition will weigh upon the discretion of individual doctors. But this argument will not be very persuasive if it is presented only in pragmatic terms. It must also make a *moral* claim: that outlawing certain "unacceptable" abortions will make all abortions harder to obtain—including those that are accepted as moral by the overwhelming majority of Americans.

But this may be hard for the pro-choice movement to do because of internal ideological obstacles to accommodating to public opinion. Pro-choice people who are also firmly dedicated to women's rights, for example, may find it impossible to accommodate to a public opinion that holds that women's rights to their own bodies are relative, not absolute, and should be shared with husbands, fathers of embryos, parents (in the case of teen-aged women), and "society." In this respect, they are more like the pro-life activists than they would like to admit: they are likely to be torn between what they firmly believe is right and moral and what they may have to do in order to win a larger share of middle-of-the-road support.

The pro-choice movement will also face a number of strategic political problems in staving off either of the two hypothesized pro-life scenarios. First, it faces the difficult task of rallying its members into full-fledged political activity. As we have shown, for all practical purposes there was a nominal pro-life movement before the Supreme Court decision, and there is a nominal pro-choice movement now. The price of its stunning successes up to 1973 has been complacency: many pro-choice supporters assume that the battle was won years ago. And as their pro-life opponents discovered in the days after the Supreme Court decision, it is much easier to rally the indignant than to arouse the complacent. Also, it is easier to generate enthusiasm for a bold offensive than for a dogged resistance; easier to attack in pursuit of a goal than to dig in and prepare for a siege. In addition, when political activists are on the offensive, as the pro-choice people were before 1973 and the pro-life people are today, it is easy to portray what the problem is to potential recruits; as noted in Chapter Five, activists need only to tell recruits to "look around them" or to "wake up" to a reality whose meaning they have not fully appreciated. In trying to preserve the fruits of a political victory, however, activists have a more difficult task: they must paint a vivid and frightening picture of what the future will be like if the opposition is successful.

However, this strategy has an unanticipated cost. Because it is difficult to rouse sympathizers with the argument that weak and unsophisticated opponents must be "nipped in the bud," an ironic situation arises: both the pro-life and the pro-choice movements have a vested interest in portraying the pro-life movement as more powerful and successful than it really is. It is obvious, of course, why the pro-life movement would want to do this. Paradoxically, the pro-choice movement must also do it in order to convince its own members that the pro-life movement is a serious threat, against which all available resources must be mobilized quickly. When both sides seem to agree that the pro-life movement is a veritable political juggernaut, neutral bystanders, such as legislators, can easily be confused or misled about its real nature. They may not see it for what it is—a relatively small, dedicated group of people who use a peculiar set of political resources extraordinarily well in a setting that rewards small, dedicated groups. They may think its alleged strength signifies a profound change in public attitudes that is sweeping the nation.

Although the pro-life movement often compares itself to the Abolition movement, it may more aptly be compared to the Temperance movement that produced Prohibition, and the probable effects of a national anti-abortion law may be suggested by the effects of Prohibition. Passed in 1919 to implement the Eighteenth Amendment, the Volstead Act was never effective in capturing the moral sentiments of the American public or in eliminating the consumption of alcoholic beverages.[28] Wholehearted support for the moral principles of Temperance was limited to a very few, and although the Volstead Act changed the *patterns* of American drinking, it did not eliminate drinking. Because the public at large did not support its moral goals and felt little compunction about breaking a law they found morally irrelevant, the Volstead Act created a number of political and moral costs of its own. The American police, once generally thought to be as "clean" as the English, emerged from the Prohibition experience tainted with corruption. The effects on the public of living with a law that was constantly (and often flagrantly) ignored were probably not healthy.[29] And the creation of a black market in alcohol is thought by many to be a key factor in the emergence of a sophisticated and financially powerful system of organized crime in America.

Barring major changes in the larger social context or in the structure of American public opinion on abortion, the best the pro-life movement can hope for, should one of the current anti-abortion bills pass, is a modern form of the Prohibition experience. This assertion is based on three central facts: public opinion on certain kinds of abortion is close to unanimous; this opinion *preceded and was not produced by* the Supreme Court decision of 1973; and people who have come of sexual age since that decision take it for granted that fertility decisions are to be made only by the individuals involved.

In a Prohibition-type situation, abortions would be nominally illegal, but those with the right combination of money and information would be able to get them. (And the combination would be important: a rich person in the heartland of Iowa would probably have a harder time than a middle-income person in New York with feminist connections.) Well-to-do people in general would get better abortions, and the poor would get worse ones. Every physician would have to interpret the law individually, and great variation would result. States like California would almost surely be liberal in interpreting the new law, and states like Mississippi almost surely would not. Occasionally, some hapless woman and her partner at the wrong place at the wrong time would be caught, tried, and given the maximum allowable sentence as a way of maintaining boundaries.[30] Such cases would make the national headlines. After several years of this, public opposition to the law would increase to massive proportions, and the law would be repealed.

More speculatively, several other things might happen before repeal. Organized crime might take over the illegal abortion business; a black market in abortion might emerge, complete with high profits and a corrupt police and judiciary.* On the other hand, "civil disobedience" rings of morally committed abortionists might appear, charging little or no money for their services and operating rather openly. (The chances of this happening are increased by the fact that most abortions, folklore notwithstanding, are relatively easy to perform.)†

But given the current configuration of public opinion and the inability of the pro-life movement to change it so far, the most the movement is likely to produce (in the absence of the kinds of political, social, and economic changes outlined above) is a Prohibition-like situation in which abortions become harder and more expensive to get but still continue to exist in almost the same numbers as before. Demographers remind us that this is approximately what happened in both Rumania and the Soviet Union when official concerns about population decline led to restrictions on previously liberal abortion policies.[31]

Pro-choice people, however, can take little comfort from this prospect. Prohibition, after all, was the law of the land for many years, and it took considerable political resources to overturn it. A Prohibition-style ban on abortions might last throughout the reproductive years of every woman now active in the pro-choice movement, and it would almost surely have its greatest effect on poor and socially vulnerable women.

* There is some anecdotal evidence from our interviews that the Mafia considered entering the illegal abortion market when it had become more open in the late 1960s.

† Pauline Bart has written of just such a feminist collective, which was active prior to the Supreme Court decision. Staffed by nonphysicians, it performed 11,000 illegal abortions in four years for women who needed them—with no reported mortality; see Bart, "Seizing the Means of Reproduction," in Helen Roberts, ed., *Women, Health, and Reproduction* (Boston: Routledge and Kegan Paul, 1981).

The Future of Abortion

All of these considerations suggest that the future of abortion in America remains unpredictable. It is possible that the pro-life movement may succeed in getting abortion defined—at least at the legal level—as something that is morally wrong, to be used only in extraordinary cases. On the other hand, it is just as likely that the pro-choice movement will be able to maintain the definition of abortion as a complicated moral dilemma whose dimensions must be defined by the woman herself. Abortion may therefore stay legal, or it may be outlawed in all but a few cases. If it is outlawed, it is possible (almost certain, according to pro-life people) that the IUD, the birth control pill, and treatment after rape could also disappear from the American scene.

Keeping in mind how volatile public opinion can be and how complex and potentially changeable American attitudes on abortion are, what does the future hold? In large part, the future of this issue is unknowable. How people think about abortion is intimately tied to their thoughts about women, children, and the family; and their feelings on these topics will undoubtedly be affected by large-scale social and economic changes now in progress.

The history of women over the last two centuries, however, suggests that notwithstanding the ebbs and flows, women have entered the paid labor force to stay. Although it is safe to predict that women's roles will continue to change, in all probability the long-term trend is that women will continue to combine work and motherhood in increasing numbers. It is also probably safe to predict that technological forces, which have historically triggered new debates about abortion, will continue to confront us with new social, political, and ethical dilemmas. We must soon consider the implications of a new technology in abortions so that they can be accomplished at home, the ability to transplant one woman's fertilized egg to another woman's womb, and even artificial uteruses that can support an embryo outside the woman's body from the earliest days of pregnancy. These developments are all closer to reality than to science fiction.

Thus, a few cautious predictions are in order. For all of the reasons explored in this book, the abortion debate will not become noted for civility, calm, or reasoned discourse. Barring massive social changes, however, it is also quite probable that the debate itself will gradually become less important to the American public. (Indeed, the sound and fury of these last few years may have been the tail-end of the storm.) As more and more women work and the economy shows no signs of returning to the good old days, the struggle between the supporters of exclusive motherhood and the supporters of working mothers may very well become moot for all but a tiny minority of women. But given the history of abortion in America, none of us should be too surprised if, by the turn of the century, technological changes were once again to make abortion a battleground for competing social, ethical, and symbolic values.

Appendix 1: Methodology

Any book that makes claims about social life—in this case about the origin and meaning of the abortion debate—entitles readers to ask questions about the methodological legitimacy of the research that led the author to her or his conclusions. What were the data on which this book was built? How were they selected? Are there reasons to believe that the author might have come up with different conclusions had a different set of data been chosen? How generalizable are the data from this study to some larger arena of social life?

No author, no matter how conscientious, can fully answer these questions. The same social and psychological "blind spots" that lead to errors of omission (and sometimes commission) preclude us except in unusual cases from even noticing that we have anything other than 20/20 vision. Fish, as the aphorism goes, never notice that they swim in water. On the other hand, authors can give an account of some of the research decisions and strategies that were decided upon at various points in the research process so that readers can begin to evaluate whether those decisions and the data that resulted from them are flawed.

This book is based on two different kinds of data: written records that were not created for the purposes of this research and intensive, verbatim interviews that were. (A third source of data, almost a year's worth of notes from participant observation of meetings of both pro-life and pro-choice groups, almost certainly contributed to a sense of what was going on in the abortion debate but is not formally represented in this book.)

The written records for this study consisted of the following items. First, there is a content analysis of the *San Francisco Chronicle*, the *Los Angeles Times*, and the *San Diego Union* on the topic of abortion. These three papers were selected from *Ayers' Directory* to be both widely read and geographically distributed and were analyzed from the earliest issues to the present by a team of research assistants. After indexing of these papers began (in approximately the early 1970s), indexes were used, but prior to that date, researchers simply scanned microfilms of back issues, copying relevant articles. After the 1970s, indexes were checked by a sampling process to ensure that indexers had not overlooked important stories.

Three other newspapers, the *San Jose Mercury*, the *San Diego Tribune*, and the *Sacramento Bee*, were also examined, but only for the period 1960 to the present. The content analysis of these papers (including letters to the editor) gave us a picture of the social perception of abortion in California from the nineteenth century, through the tumultuous days of abortion reform in the 1960s, and up to the present day. Not incidentally, the analysis also yielded us a list of names of people involved in or identified with one side or the other of the abortion debate.

The second body of written data included the persuasive literature of both sides. In the course of the study, we subscribed to, were sent, or analyzed in libraries and private homes the contents of newsletters, pamphlets, hand-outs, flyers, and other items designed to sway public opinion. We have representative literature from such groups as the California Abortion Rights Action League (CARAL), the National Abortion Rights Action League (NARAL), Planned Parenthood, the National Organization for Women (NOW), the Feminist Women's Health Collectives, Abortion Rights Mobilization (ARM), National Women's Political Caucus, the American Association of University Women, the Religious Coalition for Abortion Rights (RCAR), National Women's Health Network, the Coalition for the Medical Rights of Women, as well as a host of organizations created in the 1960s to press for abortion repeal and reform.

On the other side, we analyzed material produced by groups that included the Human Life Center, the Pro-Family Forum, Catholics United for Life, Shield of Roses, Christian Action Council, Americans for Life, American Citizens Concerned for Life, Alliance for Life, Crusade for Life, the Pro-life Council, the Pro-life League, the Right-to-Life League, Concerned Citizens for Human Life, Mobilization for the Unnamed, Life Amendment Political Action Committee (LA-PAC), U.S. Coalition for Life, the Save-a-Baby League, and Birthright.

A third source of written records came from a number of organizations, especially those active before the 1973 Supreme Court decision, who made their archival material available to us. Minutes of meetings, constitutions and by-laws, lists of funders and donations were all opened to us to review. Examining those documents enabled us to cross-check with documentary evidence some of the assertions made in interviews about the early history of pro-life and pro-choice organizations and, in particular, the social composition of the early movements. (The argument in the text, for example, that the abortion reform movement started out with a hefty proportion of physician support is clearly buttressed by the very large number of doctors among the list of early donors to the cause.)

The other source of data for this study, created in the course of the study itself, were long, semistructured interviews with 212 people who had been identified as activists in the abortion debate.[1] These activists were approached by means of a letter from the research office in the university, telling them that we had been given their names as people who had "thought a great deal about this issue." The letter promised them confidentiality and anonymity and alerted them that the interview would take approximately an hour and a half. (This turned out to be optimistic. Some interviews took five or more hours, and a number of people kindly consented to be reinterviewed several times in order to clarify some questions that had come up during the interviews with themselves or others.) They were also informed that the interview would be tape-recorded (unless they objected) and that they would be sent transcripts in order to check for acccuracy. (In practice no one in this study objected to the accuracy of the interview, although a few people upon receipt of the transcript did avail themselves of an open invitation to call us; they wanted to share with us additional thoughts that had occurred to them upon reading it.)

An important research decision was to limit the interviews in this book to *activists*, that is, those people most heavily involved in the movement. I have argued in Chapter Five that activists are critical because it is they who do the work. They are the ones who call up others to write letters, who circulate petitions, who write the voters' guides that tell interested people who the movement's "friends and enemies" are. Activists, then, are those who shape and define the movement.

I chose activists as the focus of this study on the following logic. I am not particularly interested in why people have a given set of *attitudes* on the topic of abortion. There are a number of good studies that discuss at length both the distribution of public opinion on the topic of abortion and the social antecedents (or at least correlates) of such opinions.[2] This study was designed to look at something else: at those people for whom the issue was so salient that they felt they had to take *action* on it. And the definition of action was quite rigorous in this study. Voting for a pro-choice or a pro-life candidate, sending money to an organization, or even adding one's name to a mailing list or a petition are, to be sure, higher levels of activity than the simply uninvolved. But are these people "involved" in the issue? Of course to some extent they are, and movements can and do use the absolute numbers of these people both to assess their own strength and to make political demands based on that strength.

But interviews and other research[3] suggest that there are clear divisions between those whom I have called activists and the rank and file. Rather than a continuum of activity that moves in gentle steps from the fully involved to the marginally involved, interviews with people on both sides of this issue suggest that they tend to be involved in it either as a consuming passion or to be people who are only on the mailing list, who send in a check once a year, and perhaps write a letter or two to a congressperson every year.

Thus, activists are not only the ones who shape the movement; they are the ones for whom the issue is the most salient. If one wants to study what the pro-choice and pro-life movements *mean* to those involved in it, I propose that studying those most heavily involved is the way to get the "purest" cases.

In practice, who were these activists and how were they chosen? In order to be defined as an activist in this study, an individual had to spend ten hours or more a week in activity on the issue if pro-life and five hours a week or more if pro-choice. These two different levels were chosen for the following set of interrelated reasons. First, the two sides are in different historical phases. The pro-choice movement was most active and visible before the Supreme Court decision of 1973, and inasmuch as that decision represented a substantial victory for them, the movement's members have since experienced the relaxation and retirement to private life that follows a successful campaign. The pro-life movement, on the other hand, barely existed prior to the Supreme Court decision; it is now a movement on the upswing, still growing in the face of what it sees as a very real threat.

Thus, it is not surprising to find that the pro-life movement qua movement is more highly mobilized than the pro-choice movement since it is easier to galvanize members to oppose something than to hold on to something that is presumably settled. Had we used the cutoff point of ten hours for pro-choice people, in the early years of this study (1977–1980), there simply would not have been any pro-choice activists to study. Even those people who worked in "public affairs" in family planning agencies, a job that has as part of its responsibility surveillance and education on the topic of abortion, admitted that they were "holding the line" with only a small portion of their time allocated to the issue. (That this is a product of the historical phases of the two movements is indicated by the fact that all of the pro-choice activists who joined the movement prior to the Supreme Court decision described work schedules on behalf of legal abortion that equaled and in some cases surpassed the levels of activity of pro-life activists.)

As the pro-life movement became more successful, however, their very successes served to reactivate the pro-choice movement. Over the five years of this study, there was a statistically significant increase in the number of hours that pro-choice people put into the movement. Most dramatically, the election of an anti-abortion president in 1980, Ronald Reagan, upset pro-choice people to the extent that it was for the first time possible to find pro-choice activists who worked ten hours a week or more on the issue. However, to keep symmetry with earlier phases of the movement, the five-hour-a-week cutoff was still kept.

Activists on either side of the issue came into the study via a snowball sample. A number of names of people active in the pro-life and pro-choice movements were culled from newspapers and letterhead stationery, and these were supplemented by a list of names of elected leaders on file with the state attorney general's office in connection with election campaign statements. Once a key activist was identified, he or she was asked to list all of the important activists involved in the area on their side of the issue. (Sometimes these activists told us about "the enemy"—their opposite numbers on the other side—and these names were kept in a file to be compared with intramovement nominations. In fact, the correlation was very high—activists are agreed about who does the work, both on their own side and among the opposition.) Every activist had to be nominated by two, and in most cases three, other activists in order to be included. Finally, after the interview was concluded, activists were asked to fill out a background information sheet, and unless their answer to an open-ended question about how many hours a week they spent on this issue met the criteria, their interview was dropped from the analysis. With the exception of one category to be discussed in a moment, virtually everyone who was nominated as an activist did in fact meet the criteria. (Indeed, pro-life people met the criteria easily; most of them spent thirty hours a week or more on the issue.)

The one category of people whom all activists agree are activists but who do not meet the criteria of activity used in this study are those people whom I call "stars." A "star" is a person who by virtue of his or her social characteristics is immensely valuable to the movement simply by willing to be publicly affiliated with it. This phenomenon was encountered almost exclusively on the pro-life side, but there is reason to believe that the pro-choice movement in its heyday had its own "stars." In the late 1960s for example, the pro-choice movement tried to incorporate Sherri Finkbine, the woman whose abortion for Thalidomide had been a cause célèbre in the early part of the decade. At the same time, pro-choice activists called on famous physicians and jurists to lend their prestige to the cause. Its present lack of "stars," therefore, may be more a product of its organizational phase than of something intrinsic to the movement itself.

Pro-life "stars" in this study included a Hassidic rabbi, a prestigious Mormon official, a former movie star, some radio and television personalities, and a woman who had previously been the director of one of the largest abortion centers in the state. While all of these people had sentiments that put them well in the center of pro-life beliefs, none of them actually did very much concrete day-to-day political work to further the cause. In part this is because their presence is work enough. To a movement that is concerned about charges that it is sectarian, having a rabbi and a Mormon willing to make public appearances once a year at a march that commemorates the 1973 Supreme Court decision is highly effective. Radio and television personalities lend legitimacy and perhaps glamour to the cause, and a woman who used to be an active purveyor of abortions is a symbol that speaks for itself.

Because these people are used so publicly, it is not surprising that true activists think of them as being activists. The same social dynamics that create "stars" in the first place, that is, something about them which makes their public visibility very valuable to the movement, also creates vested interests for activists to *think* of them as deeply involved. After all, one's own activity on behalf of a cause is enhanced by people whose presence demonstrates for all to see how glamorous, important, and varied the movement really is. But when looked at carefully, very few of these "stars" do anything more substantial than appear in public. Interesting as they are, therefore, interviews with "stars" are not included in this study.

Whenever a study is based on a group of people who have been selected in any other way than by a strict random sample, there is always the question as to how representative that selection is. Has there been a true cross-section of the category under consideration (in this case activists) or have some been inadvertently under- or overselected? Unless the sample is random, this question must remain unanswered. A random sample would have been impossible in the present study because there is no "sampling frame" from which to randomly draw people. Mailing lists are sometimes suggested as alternatives to sampling frames in cases like this, but mailing lists are usually jealously guarded by their owners[4] and indiscriminant. They mix together activists, rank-and-file members, interested by-standers, people whose friends signed them up because of presumed interest, and—in all the organizations in the present study—at least one research sociologist (namely the author), and perhaps more.

The following procedures were used to make sure that the net was cast as far as possible and to guard against the possibility that only "safe" or acceptable activists were nominated. First, different paths into the pool of activists were used. As noted, names were gathered from newspapers, from letterhead stationery, and from lists of elected leaders named in documents in the state attorney general's office. The list of elected leaders was subsequently enlarged by identifying at least one central organization on each side that is de facto an "umbrella" organization over the others. Each of these "umbrella" organizations gave us a list of groups associated with their side of the issue and the names of the elected officials in these groups.

Armed with these three lists (newspapers, letterhead, and elected leaders), we began interviewing. Once interviewed, individual activists were asked to name all other activists they knew in their town. New names were thus added to the list, earmarked by who had nominated them. These names were all compared with one another and with the names generated from other sources. (We were aided in this tracking process by a computer "search-and-find" listing system, as well as the traditional index cards.) As a result, we came to create simultaneously a pool of elected leaders ("positional" leaders) and "reputational" leaders throughout the state. It seems unlikely that there were activists of any significance who escaped the net, with the possible exception of isolated activists located in small, rural towns far from metropolitan areas.

How representative was the group of activists that emerged out of this many-faceted approach? I have reason to believe that it was quite representative and approached exhaustive at times. Although both movements are diffuse and grass-roots at the present time, the core of people who are currently active is small. I asked positional leaders their estimate of how many people they could reliably count upon to do the work of the organization, and while it is true that the higher in the statewide organizations we interviewed, the larger the numbers, even those at the top of such organizational hierarchy as exists cannot name more than about two dozen people. Local grass-roots activists, in contrast, can name an average of eight to ten people who can be reliably counted on to do the work of the organization. (Of course, the pool of people who can be called on to do a single, specific task is far larger, but I would argue that these eight—or twenty-four—people are the core of the movement.) Thus the total pool of dedicated activists is small.

Finally, I took a rather unorthodox step. Content analysis of the interviews made quite clear that in each area there were "key activists." These people, often founding mothers or fathers of the movement, were the kinds of people whose names would come up if activists were asked: "Who are the half dozen people in this area—on your side of the issue or the other side—who are the key people?" (Newspaper accounts, by the way, confirm that these key people are in fact key. Although it's hard to tell whether being a key person leads to being a spokesperson, or whether being a spokesperson leads to being perceived as a key person, these key activists are the ones who are called on by the media to make comments when important events take place.) I then called these key activists in the final phase of the study and read them the following question: "This is a list of people whose names have come up as being actively involved in the (pro-life) (pro-choice) movement. As I read each name, will you tell me: (a) if this person is currently actively involved, (b) if this person used to be but is no longer actively involved, or (c) if you have never heard of this person." As a check, I inserted a number of fictitious names into the list. Subsequently, I asked these activists if there were other people actively involved in the issue whose names were not on the list.

The results of these phone calls were reassuring. While not every single activist in a given geographic area had heard of every single name on our list, all the real names on the list were recognized by a substantial majority of key activists. None of the fictitious names, on the other hand, was ever recognized by anyone. While each of the key activists offered us new names, in all except two cases these were the names of truly new activists, that is, people who had gotten involved after the interviewing period had been completed. Consequently, I am confident that the pool of true activists on this issue is relatively small, that within a community and often within the state activists know who they are, that they usually know who their opposite numbers are, and that this study interviewed all or virtually all of them.

Perhaps the final methodological question is the most difficult: how generalizable are these data? The very nature of the research design used in this book, a case study of events in one state, raises questions about whether or not these findings are true in any other settings. This is particularly the case since California is often regarded, to be blunt, as atypical. Only preliminary answers are possible, but so far none of the cross-checks built into the research suggests that these findings are limited to California alone. A number of historical accounts of state abortion reform movements describe processes very much like the ones recounted here.[5] Although the players in Hawaii, Arizona, Georgia, and North Carolina differed, and there are very real differences depending upon the era when the issue was contested, the same general pattern that marks California is true in these states.

In all cases, there was a mobilization of elites, in particular physicians, who became concerned about the emerging use of what I have called in the text a "strict constructionist" view of abortion. These elites pushed for abortion reform laws, in order to write explicitly into law long-standing patterns of practice that were technically illegal if a "strict construction" were to be invoked. In all these states, opposition, as in California, was organized at least in part by the Catholic church, with varying degrees of success. Thus, the process by which abortion became an "issue" was the result of national social forces, which were responded to in different ways in different states.

With respect to the second half of this book, the meanings of the abortion debate to those involved, the logic recounted here will almost certainly be as familiar to activists in other states as it is to those in California. In the course of this research, comparative interviews in six other states—Georgia, Minnesota, Wisconsin, Virginia, Arizona, and Massachusetts—were undertaken. Raters could not distinguish these interviews from the California interviews. In other words, activists in these other states account for their involvement in this issue in substantially the same terms (and tones) as California activists. To be sure, there are undoubtedly some regional differences. The only one that has emerged so far, based on the participant observation part of the study in California, is that pro-life activity (and perhaps pro-choice activity as well) may be organized differently in those parts of the country where, in contrast to California, there are well-defined ethnic and religious communities. These differences in organization do not affect the content of interviews, however, so that *how* people are involved does not seem to affect *why* they see themselves as involved.

In short, this is a study that is technically only a study of very deeply committed activists in the abortion debate in one state. But the foregoing lead me to believe that it is probably a reasonably accurate picture of how abortion activists think and feel throughout the United States, as well as a picture of the background that made them feel the way they do. As to the ultimate question—whether this book is an adequate study of why abortion touches and moves us the way it does—the reader will have to be the ultimate judge.

Appendix 2: Tables

Table 1 *Ratio of Therapeutic Abortions to Total Deliveries, Selected U.S. Hospitals, 1926–1960*

Year	*Location*	*Total Therapeutic Abortions*	*Ratio*	*Source*
1926–1930	University of Iowa	12	1:124	Moore and Randall
1931–1935	University of Iowa	27	1:161	Moore and Randall
1931–1935	Los Angeles County	133	1:106	Russell
1931–1939	Chicago Lying-In	134	1:195	Loth and Hesseltine
1932–1943	New York Lying-In	280	1:167	Kuder and Finn
1936–1940	Los Angeles County	108	1:166	Russell
1936–1940	University of Iowa	42	1:188	Moore and Randall
1941–1945	Los Angeles County	42	1:357	Russell
1942–1948	University of California	58	1:88	Overstreet
1935–1945	Bellevue	199	1:76	Perlmutter

Table 1 *Continued*

Year	*Location*	*Total Therapeutic Abortions*	*Ratio*	*Source*
1943–1947	NYC Dept. of Health (fetal death certificates)	3,592	1:196	Gold et al.
1946–1950	Los Angeles County	12	1:2,864	Russell
1946–1950	University of Iowa	26	1:204	Moore and Randall
1941–1950	Hospital survey	2,717	1:420	Heffernan and Lynch
1951–1953	NYC Dept. of Health (fetal death certificates)	1,698	1:286	Gold
1952	Ohio State University	4	1:646	Copeland et al.
1953	Ohio State University	6	1:497	Copeland et al.
1953	University of Pennsylvania	12	1:213	Boulas et al.
1950–1955	Sloane Hospital for Women	n/a	1:69	Hall
1954–1956	NYC Dept. of Health (fetal death certificates)	1,096	1:146	Gold
1956	Ohio State University	1	1:3,780	Copeland et al.
1956	University of Pennsylvania	8	1:339	Boulas et al.
1959	Ohio State University	1	1:3,839	Copeland et al.
1959	University of Pennsylvania	11	1:216	Boulas et al.
1963	Ohio State University	4	1:820	Copeland et al.

Table 1 *Continued*

Year	*Location*	*Total Therapeutic Abortions*	*Ratio*	*Source*
1963	Professional activities survey of 200 + hospitals	390	1:788	Tietze
1964	Ohio State University	9	1:363	Copeland et al.
1964	Professional activities survey	823	1:424	Tietze

SOURCES: J. G. Moore and W. H. Randall, "Trends in Therapeutic Abortion: A Review of 137 Cases," *Am. J. Ob. Gyn.* 63(1) (Jan. 1952):28–40; Keith Russell, "Changing Indications for Therapeutic Abortion," *JAMA* 151 (Jan. 10, 1953):108–11; Myrna Loth and H. Close Hesseltine, "Therapeutic Abortion at the Chicago Lying-In Hospital," *Am. J. Ob. Gyn.* 72(2) (Aug. 1956):304–11; Katherine Kuder and William Finn, "Therapeutic Interruption of Pregnancy," *Am. J. Ob. Gyn.* 49 (Jan. 1945):762–73; E. W. Overstreet, *Medical Staff Conferences: University of California Hospital* 1 (1948):167; Irving K. Perlmutter, "Analysis of Therapeutic Abortions, Bellevue Hospital, 1935–1945," *Am. J. Ob. Gyn.* 53 (1947):1008–18; Edwin Gold et al., "Therapeutic Abortions in New York City: A Twenty-Year Review," *AJPH* 55(7) (July 1965):964–72; Roy Heffernan and William Lynch, "What Is the Status of Therapeutic Abortion in Modern Obstetrics?" *Am. J. Ob. Gyn.* 66 (Aug. 1953):335–44; William Copeland et al., "Therapeutic Abortion," *JAMA* 207(4) (Jan. 1962):713–15; Stanley H. Boulas et al., "Therapeutic Abortion," *Ob. Gyn.* 19(2) (Feb. 1962):222–27; R. E. Hall, "Therapeutic Abortion, Sterilization, and Contraception," *Am. J. Ob. Gyn.* 91 (1965):518–32; Christopher Tietze, "Therapuetic Abortions in the United States," *Am. J. Ob. Gyn.* 101(6) (July 13, 1968):784–87.

Table 2 *Percentage of Abortions Performed for Psychiatric Indications*

Year	*Location*	*Percentage*	*Source**
1938	University of California	0.0	Overstreet and Traut
1939	University of California	6.0	Overstreet and Traut
1940	University of California	5.0	Overstreet and Traut
1940	Chicago Lying-In	3.0	Loth and Hesseltine
1941–1943	University of California	0.0	Overstreet and Traut
1935–1945	Bellevue	1.9	Perlmutter
1943	NYC Dept. of Health (fetal death certificates)	8.2	Erhardt
1944	NYC Dept. of Health (fetal death certificates)	10.7	Erhardt
1944	University of California	6.6	Overstreet and Traut
1945	NYC Dept. of Health (fetal death certificates)	11.4	Erhardt
1941–1945	University of Virginia	25.0	Thornton
1946	NYC Dept. of Health (fetal death certificates)	15.3	Erhardt
1946	University of California	36.0	Overstreet and Traut
1947	NYC Dept. of Health (fetal death certificates)	19.1	Erhardt
1947	University of California	14.0	Overstreet and Traut

*In some of the cited sources, "neurologic and psychiatric" indications are conflated. Since "neurological" indications include such things as myasthenia gravis and epilepsy, which are more properly considered medical conditions, I have used data from the original articles to recalculate some of the figures in Table 2 so that they reflect *psychiatric* indications only.

Table 2 *Continued*

Year	*Location*	*Percentage*	*Source**
1949	NYC Dept. of Health (fetal death certificates)	26.9	Erhardt
1949	"Largest obstetrical hospital in Portland, Oregon"	33.0	Scherman
1944–1949	Private hospital in California	14.0	Russell
1950	Portland, Ore.	50.0	Scherman
1946–1950	University of Virginia	30.0	Thornton
1951	Portland, Ore.	10.0	Scherman
1951	NYC Dept. of Health (fetal death certificates)	34.4	Erhardt
1952	NYC Dept. of Health (fetal death certificates)	40.0	Erhardt
1952	Portland, Ore.	26.0	Scherman
1953	NYC Dept. of Health (fetal death certificates)	40.0	Erhardt
1953	Portland, Ore.	19.0	Scherman
1954	Portland, Ore.	50.0	Scherman
1955	Portland, Ore.	39.0	Scherman
1951–1955	Sloane Hospital for Women	14.0 (ward) 55.0 (private)	Hall
1956–1966	Sloane Hospital for Women	33.0 (ward) 49.0 (private)	Hall
1952–1954	Roosevelt Hospital	80.0	Laidlaw
1953–1955	Mt. Sinai	39.0	Rovinsky and Gusberg
1956–1958	Mt. Sinai	34.0	Rovinsky and Gusberg
1959–1961	Mt. Sinai	60.0	Rovinsky and Gusberg
1962–1964	Mt. Sinai	57.0	Rovinsky and Gusberg

Table 2 Continued

SOURCES: Edmund Overstreet and Herbert Traut, "Indications for Therapeutic Abortion," *Postgrad. Med.*, 1951, p. 19; Myrna Loth and H. Close Hesseltine, "Therapeutic Abortion at the Chicago Lying-In Hospital," *Am. J. Ob. Gyn.* 72(2) (Aug. 1956):304–11; Irving K. Perlmutter, "Analysis of Therapeutic Abortions, Bellevue Hospital, 1935–1945," *Am. J. Ob. Gyn.* 53 (1947):1008–18; C. Erhardt, "Therapeutic Abortion in the United States," in *Abortion in the United States*, ed., Mary Calderone (New York: Hoeber & Harper, 1958), p. 84; W. N. Thornton, "Therapeutic Abortion," *Ob. Gyn.* 2 (1953):473; Quinten Scherman, "Therapeutic Abortion," *Ob. Gyn.* 11 (1958):323–35; Keith Russell, "Therapeutic Abortion in a General Hospital," *Am. J. Ob. Gyn.* 62 (1951):434–38; R. E. Hall, "Therapeutic Abortion, Sterilization, and Contraception," *Am. J. Ob. Gyn.* 91 (1965):518–32; R. Laidlaw, "Therapeutic Abortion in the United States," in Calderone, ed., *Abortion in the United States*, p. 106; J. J. Rovinsky and S. B. Gusberg, "Current Trends in the Therapeutic Termination of Pregnancy," *Am. J. Ob. Gyn.* 98 (1967):11–17.

Notes

Chapter 1

1. Cf. *New York Times*, Sept. 9, 1977, p. 77; ibid., Mar. 12, 1979, p. 13.

2. See "Abortion Clinic Zoning." (Readers should consult the bibliography for full references to works cited in abbreviated form in the notes.)

3. *New York Times*, July 20, 1981, p. 14; ibid., Feb. 20, 1978, p. 12; ibid., Feb. 21, 1978, p. 1; ibid., Feb. 16, 1979, p. 1.

4. *Newsweek*, Aug. 30, 1982, pp. 29–30.

5. John Noonan, *Contraception*, pp. 88–106; and Roger Huser, *The Crime of Abortion in Canon Law*, pp. 28–35.

6. Germain Grisez, *Abortion*, pp. 361–73.

7. It is estimated that American crude birth rates were on the order of fifty per 1,000 (U.S. Bureau of the Census, *Historical Statistics of the United States*). The French demographer Louis Henry has argued that crude birth rates of sixty per 1,000 are close to the human maximum. As a point of comparison, in the years 1974–1978, the crude birth rates for Chile, Morocco, and India were 23.9, 46.8, and 34.0, respectively. Only a few African countries had crude birth rates (CBR) that are similar to those estimated for the United States. In this same period, e.g., Niger had a CBR of 50.8, and Botswana had a CBR of 50.7. See United Nations, *Demographic Yearbook* (New York: United Nations, 1979), Table 9: "Live Births and Crude Live Birth Rates: 1974–1978," pp. 237–41.

8. Christopher Tietze, *Induced Abortion: 1979*, pp. 84–86.

9. Pro-choice people sometimes accuse pro-life people of not being consistent, in that the pro-life movement has not been noted for its opposition either to the death penalty or to the nuclear arms race. What this argument overlooks is that pro-life people object to what they see as the *arbitrary* taking of life since both criminals and soldiers lose their lives only after a careful

decision-making process, which is, at least in principle, replete with a great deal of due process.

10. Victor Fuchs, *Who Shall Live?*

11. See, e.g., Diana Crane, *The Sanctity of Social Life*.

Chapter 2

1. *Encyclopedia of Religion and Ethics*, ed. James Hastings (New York: Scribner's, 1961), Vol. 6, pp. 54–56. See also Ludwig Edelstein, "The Hippocratic Oath," pp. 16–18.

2. The major authors in this tradition are as follows: John Connery, *Abortion*; Grisez, *Abortion*; Huser, *Crime of Abortion*; John Noonan, ed., *The Morality of Abortion*; Noonan, *Contraception*; and Eugene Quay, "Justifiable Abortion." For specific time periods, see E. Nardi, *Procurato Aborto Nel Mundo Graeco-Roman*; James C. Mohr, *Abortion in America*; R. Hahnel, "Der künstliche Abortus im Altertum"; F. J. Dolger, "Das Lebensrecht"; and M. Moïssidés, "Contribution à l'étude de l'avortement dans l'antiquité grecque."

3. Juvenal, Sixth Satire, p. 149; Seneca, "Consolation to Helvia," p. 473; Ovid (P. Ovidus Naso), *Heroides and Amores*, ed. Grant Showerman (Cambridge, Mass.: Loeb Classical Library, 1914), II, xiii–xiv, p. 425; and Pliny (the Elder), *Natural History*, ed. H. Rackham (Cambridge, Mass.: Loeb Classical Library, 1947), pp. 142–43. On Roman law, see Theodore Mommsen, *Le droit pénal romain*, pp. 350–55; and Theodore Mommsen, ed., *Digest: Corpus Juris Civilis* (Berlin: Weidman, 1892), 47.11.4. See also Huser, *Crime of Abortion*, p. 11.

4. See Noonan, *Contraception*, pp. 88–106.

5. For the ruling in the Didache, see the Didache itself, II, 1–2, in *The Apostolic Fathers*, p. 312. For commentaries on the Didache, see Grisez, *Abortion*, p. 138; and Noonan, *Contraception*, p. 97. For Tertullian, see *Apology*, ix, 8, p. 49; and see Noonan, ed., *Morality of Abortion*, p. 12. For Clement of Alexandria, see Simon Wood, ed., *Clement of Alexandria* (Washington, D.C.: Catholic University Press, 1974), p. 174. And see Grisez, *Abortion*, p. 139; and Huser, *Crime of Abortion*, p. 10. The Council of Elvira explicitly held that abortion penalties were to be assessed against women whose husbands were absent and who conceived "per adulterium" (Huser, *Crime of Abortion*, p. 17). While Huser notes that "adulterium" is not limited to the modern notion of adultery, the specific reference to absent husbands seems to make the case that in fact adultery is what is meant. By the same token, the Council of Ancyra specified penalties for abortion only for women who prostituted themselves and used abortion on the "children thus begotten" (ibid., p. 19). For the rulings on abortion in the collections of laws (the Hadriana, the

Hispana, the Dionysian, etc.), the capitulas, and the penitentials, which gave guidelines to clerical confessors, see ibid., pp. 28–35; and Grisez, *Abortion*, p. 151.

6. On Ivo of Chartres, see Huser, *Crime of Abortion*, pp. 38–39. On Gratian, see ibid., p. 41; Noonan, ed., *Morality of Abortion*, p. 20; and Grisez, *Abortion*, p. 152.

7. Huser notes: "In cases of doubt regarding the sex of the fetus, the norm of eighty days was accepted" (*Crime of Abortion*, p. 65). For information about the visual appearance of embryos, see John Money and Anke Ehrhardt, *Man and Woman, Boy and Girl*, pp. 7, 36–45.

8. For the place of canon law in Western history, see R. C. Mortimer, *Western Canon Law*.

9. Noonan, ed., *Morality of Abortion*, p. 1.

10. For the fact that abortion before quickening was not a crime at common law, see Henry de Bracton, *De Legibus et Consuetudinibus Angliae*, 3.2.4; Edward Coke, *The Third Part of the Institutes of the Laws of England*, sec. 50; and *Commonwealth* v. *Wood*, 11 Gray (Mass.), 85; *Hatfield* v. *Gano*, 15 (Iowa), 177; and *Smith* v. *State*, 33 Me. 48, 54 Am. Dec. 607. On the question whether abortion after quickening was punished as homicide at common law, see William Blackstone, *Commentaries on the Laws of England*, pp. 129–30; Matthew Hale, *The History of the Pleas of the Crown*; and *State* v. *Cooper*, 22 N.J.L. 52 51 Am. Dec. 248. This latter, an 1849 New Jersey case, held that there was "no precedent, no authority, not even a dictum [prior to the English statute of 1803, Lord Ellenborough's Act] which recognizes the mere procuring of an abortion as crime known to the law."

11. *Commonwealth* v. *Bangs*, 9 Mass. (Tyng) 387, 388 (1812): "There can be no sentence upon this verdict . . . if an abortion had been alleged and proved to have ensued, the averment that the woman was quick with child at the time is a necessary part of the indictment." Similarly, abortion with a woman's consent was not punishable at common law unless the pregnancy was quick: *Commonwealth* v. *Parker*, 50 Mass. (9 Met.) 263, 43 Am. (1845). See Quay, "Justifiable Abortion," p. 481. For cases which upheld *Bangs*, see *State* v. *Cooper* (New Jersey, 1849); *Smith* v. *State* (Maine, 1851); *Abrams* v. *Foshee* (Iowa, 1856); *Smith* v. *Gafford* (Alabama, 1857); and *Mitchell* v. *Commonwealth* (Kentucky, 1879).

12. For the dates of these laws, their provisions, and the penalties they specify for induced abortion, see Appendix One in Quay, "Justifiable Abortion," pp. 447–520. For the loss of the woman's common law protection, see Mohr, *Abortion in America*, pp. 43, 143.

13. On the decline of American birth rates in the nineteenth century, see Ansley Coale and Melvin Zelnick, *A New Estimate of Fertility*, Table 2, p. 36. See also Colin Forster and G. S. L. Tucker, *Economic Opportunity and White*

American Fertility Ratios, 1800–1860; and Yasukichi Yasuba, *Birth Rates of the White Population in the United States, 1800–1860*. On immigration, see David Ward, *Cities and Immigrants: A Geography of Change in Nineteenth-Century America*. On the first wave of feminism, see William O'Neill, *Everyone Was Brave*, and Eleanor Flexner, *Century of Struggle*. Declining birth rates among native-born whites were a constant source of concern to those active in the anti-abortion movement. For an intellectual history of where these concerns led, see Mark Haller, *Eugenics*. For examples of concern about declining birth rates in the writings of anti-abortion physicians, see the following: Horatio Storer, *Why Not?* pp. 63–64, 85; Horatio Storer, "On the Decrease of the Rate of Increase of Population Now Obtaining in Europe and America"; Andrew Nebinger, *Criminal Abortion*, pp. 7–8; J. Winslow Ayer, *The Great Crime of the Nineteenth Century and Perils to Child Life, Physical and Moral*, p. 20; Edwin Hale, *The Great Crime of the Nineteenth Century*, p. 4. Perhaps because the nonphysician authors (who tended to write in the later part of this period) did not have a legitimate claim to biological information, they tended to stress the "race suicide" aspect even more heavily. See Brevard Sinclair, *The Crowning Sin of the Age*, pp. 55–69; and Abbot Kinney, *The Conquest of Death*, pp. v–ix. A number of modern authors (in particular, Linda Gordon, *Woman's Body, Woman's Right*) have suggested that public attitudes toward abortion also reflected conflicts between men and women. My reading of nineteenth-century material, however, suggests that while women may have had the *responsibility* for actually seeking abortions, in most cases they are reported to have done so with the knowledge and support of their husbands.

14. On the status of colonial American doctors, see Richard Shryock, *Medicine and Society in America, 1660–1860*, pp. 2–9, 15; William Norwood, *Medical Education in the United States Before the Civil War*; and Rosemary Stevens, *American Medicine and the Public Interest*, p. 13.

15. Robert Derbyshire, *Medical Licensure and Discipline in the United States*, pp. 2–3; Shryock, *Medicine and Society*, pp. 31–34.

16. See Richard Shryock, *Medical Licensing in America, 1650–1965*; also Henry Shafer, *The American Medical Profession, 1783–1850*, pp. 208–14; Richard Shryock, *The Development of Modern Medicine*, pp. 248–72; William Rothstein, *American Physicians in the Nineteenth Century*, pp. 177–90.

17. The term *regular* was limited to those who were both formally trained and who subscribed to an allopathic medical model. This ancient model, based on the principles of opposites, came to be in ideological contrast to such models as homeopathy, Galvanism, eclecticism, and the like. See Joseph Kett, *The Formation of the American Medical Profession*, pp. 100–65; Rothstein, *American Physicians*, pp. 125–73; and Shryock, *Medical Licensing in America*, pp. 28–32.

18. This estimate on the number of schools is from Abraham Flexner, *Medical Education in the United States and Canada*, p. 6.

19. "No applicant for instruction who could pay his fees or sign his notes was turned down" (ibid., p. 7). For confirmation from a less self-serving source (Flexner wanted to reduce the number of medical schools and was harsh about their shortcomings), see Henry Sigerist, *History of Medicine* (New York: Oxford University Press, 1951), p. 133.

20. Charles Rosenberg, "The Therapeutic Revolution," pp. 485–506; see also Rothstein, *American Physicians*, pp. 42–43.

21. See, e.g., William Buchan, *Domestic Medicine*, pp. 357–59. (Buchan was the "Dr. Spock" of his era.) The following widely reprinted gynecology textbooks, the standard texts of the era, contain virtually the same information: William Dewees, *A Treatise on the Diseases of Females*, pp. 100–02; Samuel Bard, *A Compendium on . . . Midwifery*, p. 73; and Charles Meigs, *Woman: Her Diseases and Remedies*, p. 453.

22. Until the invention of the first accurate pregnancy test in 1928, most could agree with T. Gaillard Thomas, one of the deans of nineteenth-century obstetrics, when he asserted that "the diagnosis of pregnancy is often one of the most difficult that the physician is called upon to make" (*Abortion and Its Treatment*, p. 97). On the invention of the first pregnancy test, see S. Ascheim, "Early Diagnosis of Pregnancy," *Am. J. Ob. Gyn.* 19 (1930):118.

23. Sinclair, *Crowning Sin*, p. 51.

24. *San Francisco Chronicle*, Jan. 5, 1873, p. 3.

25. Shryock, *Development of Modern Medicine*, p. 250.

26. For the Ohio medical investigation, see Arthur Calhoun, *The Social History of the American Family*, 3:243. The one-to-four ratio is suggested in Horatio Storer and Franklin Heard, *Criminal Abortion*. Storer and Heard conflated criminal and spontaneous abortions, but the authors assert that the vast majority of these abortions are induced (pp. 28–34). For the Michigan survey (1882), see Edward Cox et al., "Report of the Special Committee on Criminal Abortion," pp. 164–88. For the AMA committee report, see *Transactions of the AMA* 22 (1871):250–51.

27. Center for Disease Control, Division of Family Planning Evaluation, *Abortion Surveillance Report* (1974).

28. Calhoun, *Social History*, 3:245.

29. See, e.g., F. Gaillardet, *L'aristocratie en Amérique* (1883); Zincke, *Last Winter in the United States* (1868); and Thomas Nichols, *Forty Years of American Life* (1864).

30. In the *New York Times Index*, which dates back to 1851, there are no stories on abortion until the mid-1860s, and only a few stories until the early 1870s. From 1871 onward, however, there is increasing coverage of the prob-

lem of "criminal abortion." This process reached a high point in the year 1878 when there was a total of sixty-nine stories devoted to abortion in that year alone. This increase in coverage in part reflects the new phenomenon of running "follow-up" stories on succeeding days, but James Mohr sees in this increased coverage a self-conscious campaign on the part of the *Times* to uncover criminal abortion (*Abortion in America*, pp. 177–82).

31. *Transactions of the AMA* 12 (1859):75; ibid. 13 (1860):55–58; "Report of the Section on Practical Medicine and Obstetrics," ibid. 16 (1867):91. Perhaps the best-documented case of physicians lobbying state legislatures against abortion comes from New York; see Cyril Means, "The Law of New York Concerning Abortion."

32. See Calhoun, *Social History*, 3:243; J. Bradley, "A Contribution to the Jurisprudence of Abortion," p. 489; E. W. Burdett, "Medical Jurisprudence," pp. 200–14; and P. S. Haskell, "Criminal Abortion," 465–73.

33. Mohr, *Abortion in America*, pp. 147–70.

34. Nebinger, *Criminal Abortion*, pp. 15–16; see also p. 10.

35. Hugh Hodge, *Foeticide, or Criminal Abortion*, pp. 32–33.

36. Ely Van de Warker, *The Detection of Criminal Abortion*, p. 43.

37. For the assertion that women who practiced abortion were of the "better classes," see Hodge, *Foeticide*, p. 32; Nebinger, *Criminal Abortion*, p. 13; Ayer, *Great Crime*, p. 45; and Isaac Quimby, "Introduction to Medical Jurisprudence," p. 164.

38. Ayer, *Great Crime*, p. 52.

39. Thomas Ewell, *Letters to Ladies*, pp. 112–14.

40. Richard Reece, *The Ladies' Medical Guide*, p. ii.

41. Guenther Risse et al., eds., *Medicine Without Doctors*; and Shryock, *Medicine and Society*, p. 119.

42. Buchan, *Domestic Medicine*, p. 535. Interestingly enough, this phrase did not occur in the original London edition and may have been appended by an American editor. It is found in the 1797 American edition, and from then on. Buchan's book went through at least twenty-eight editions in the United States alone, making it one of the most popular of home reference works. For background information on its popularity, see Robert Austin, *Early American Medical Imprints*.

43. On Pander, see James Ricci, *One Hundred Years of Gynecology*, p. 10. For a woodcut of a relatively detailed early embryo in utero, see Bard, *Compendium on . . . Midwifery*, p. 58.

44. E.g., the discovery of the mechanism of human fertilization is conventionally attributed to Oscar Hertwig in 1875, a full eighteen years after the AMA had passed its first anti-abortion resolution; see Ricci, *One Hundred Years of Gynecology*, p. 10.

45. Ewell, *Letters to Ladies*, p. 126.

46. William Dewees, *A Compendious System of Midwifery*, p. 477; Gunning Bedford, *Principles and Practice of Obstetrics*, p. 679; and Meigs, *Woman: Her Diseases and Remedies*, p. 552.

47. Mohr, *Abortion in America*, pp. 147–70; that most physicians active in the "right-to-life" movement were "regulars," see pp. 33–34.

48. See Barbara Ehrenreich and Deidre English, *For Her Own Good*.

49. "The nation's regular doctors, probably more so than any other identifiable group in the late nineteenth century, including the clergy, defended the value of human life per se as an absolute" (Mohr, *Abortion in America*, p. 36).

50. Carl Degler, *At Odds*, p. 247.

51. For exemplars of this viewpoint, see Morris Fishbein, *History of the American Medical Association*; and Sigerist, *History of Medicine*.

52. Rosenberg, "The Therapeutic Revolution," p. 487. For exemplars of this point of view, see Magali Larson, *The Rise of Professionalism*; Kett, *Formation of the American Medical Profession*; and Rothstein, *American Physicians*.

53. Shryock, *Medicine and Society*, pp. 18, 124–26. As Larson has noted: "Because American colleges—and *a fortiori* European universities—were accessible only to the wealthy, this recognition indirectly sanctioned the preeminence of rank and social class" (*Rise of Professionalism*, p. 109). This quotation refers, strictly speaking, to the colonial period, but the observation was still largely true in the middle of the nineteenth century.

54. "By 1850 it was easy for a man of no particular training to attend lectures for one winter and emerge a full-fledged doctor" (Shryock, *Development of Modern Medicine*, p. 258). Even as late as 1873, only one medical school had a course of lectures longer than two years (*JAMA* 37 [Sept. 21, 1901]: 778), and even then students did not attend courses religiously (Rothstein, *American Physicians*, p. 97). On proprietary schools, see ibid., p. 85. For the background in the second quarter of the nineteenth century, see Norwood, *Medical Education*.

55. See Shryock, *Development of Modern Medicine*, pp. 248–72. See also Rosenberg, "Therapeutic Revolution"; and Rothstein, *American Physicians*, pp. 177–90.

56. On "chlorosis" see Buchan, *Domestic Medicine*, p. 398. After Sänger proposed suturing the uterus in 1882, maternal mortality following Caesarian section dropped to between 5 and 24 percent, as opposed to mortality rates of 50 to 100 percent earlier in the century (Palmer Findley, *Priests of Lucina*, pp. 380–81). For mortality in miscellaneous gynecological surgery, see Theodore Cianfrani, *A Short History of Obstetrics and Gynecology*, pp. 341–58.

57. Singer and Underwood, *A Short History of Medicine*. Shryock dates the "turning point" in American medicine as 1875 (*Medicine and Society*, p. 148).

58. It may be the case that physician-patient interactions are what Oliver Williamson has called "idiosyncratic transactions"—exchanges that cannot be assessed by normal market mechanisms. The competence of a physician might be measured by the *aggregate* well-being of her (or his) patients as a group, but it is very difficult (and perhaps impossible) for one individual to make such discriminations on the basis of his or her own state of health; see Williamson, "Transaction-Cost Economics."

59. On the invention of the stethoscope and the thermometer, see Stanley Joel Reiser, *Medicine and the Reign of Technology*. Reiser also demonstrates that the most "up-to-date" physicians might also have had access to laryngoscopes and opthalmoscopes, but even those instruments could be purchased without an M.D. For the history of forceps and in particular their use in America, see Richard Wertz and Dorothy Wertz, *Lying-In*, pp. 34–50.

60. For the relative absence of physicians in these other medico-moral issues, see Joseph Gusfield, *Symbolic Crusade* (on the Temperance movement); David Pivar, *Purity Crusade* (on the crusade against prostitution and venereal disease); Troy Duster, *The Legislation of Morality*; and David Musto, *The American Disease* (on drug addiction).

61. Jakobovits, *Jewish Medical Ethics*, p. 184.

62. Francis Kenrick, *Theologiae Moralis*, pp. 110–13.

63. Hodge, *Foeticide*, p. 23.

64. For the exact text of these laws, see Quay, "Justifiable Abortion," pp. 447–520.

65. Hugh Hodge, *The Principles and Practice of Obstetrics*, p. 301.

66. Thomas, *Abortion and Its Treatment*, p. 99. For other indications in this same tradition, see anonymous report entitled "Excessive Vomiting of Pregnancy—Artificial Abortion—Recovery," *American Journal of Obstetrics* 14 (1881):470–71; L. Woodruff, "Case of Pregnancy Necessitating Abortion," pp. 470–71; M. H. Jordan, "A Case of Artificial Abortion," p. 275. These cases all deal with vomiting during pregnancy, which Thomas notes is often "faked" (*Abortion and Its Treatment*, p. 98). Another range of indications is noted by an indignant physician, rhetorically rejecting a woman's request for abortion, who says that she wants it, "not because of some malformation of maternal passages which would injure your life at full term," "not because your health and strength are not adequate to the proper performance of your duty," but because of "fashion"; see "On Producing Abortion: A Physician's Reply to the Solicitations of a Married Woman to Produce a Miscarriage for Her," *Nashville Journal of Medicine and Surgery* 17 (1876):200.

67. Storer, *Why Not?* p. 25.

68. For a claim that a "female culture" on abortion existed, see Van de Warker, *Detection of Criminal Abortion*, p. 7; and Carl Degler, *At Odds*, pp. 210–48.

69. For the herbs that women actually took, see Van de Warker, *Detection of Criminal Abortion*, pp. 57–88. See also Alfred Hall, *Mother's Own Book*; and Theodoric Beck and John Beck, *Elements of Medical Jurisprudence*, pp. 479–88. For the effectiveness of such herbs, see Norman Farnsworth et al., "Potential Value of Plants as Sources of New Anti-Fertility Agents." See also H. de Laszlo and P. S. Henshaw, *Science* 119 (1954):626.

70. See Rosenberg, "Therapeutic Revolution," for evidence that physicians became more willing to enter the body surgically. See also Thomas, *Abortion and Its Treatment*, pp. 104–12, for a list of surgical methods of abortion; and also Thomas Emmett, *The Principles and Practice of Gynecology*. When compared with Buchan (*Domestic Medicine*) or even Dewees (*Diseases of Females*), the willingness of later physicians to do surgery is dramatic.

71. On the invention of Hegar dilators (in 1879), see Harold Speert, *Obstetric and Gynecological Milestones*, p. 225. On the invention of the curette, see Cianfrani, *A Short History of Obstetrics*, p. 357. To be sure, both dilators *and* curettes existed in some form at least as early as the first or second century B.C.; see Harold Speert, *Iconographia Gyniatrica*. Instruments fall into and out of repute, but the nineteenth-century dates cited here represent clear evidence that these tools were being used by nineteenth-century physicians.

72. Wertz and Wertz, *Lying-In*, pp. 119–27.

Chapter 3

1. See, e.g., Howard Taylor, ed., *The Abortion Problem*; Harold Rosen, ed., *Therapeutic Abortion*; Mary Calderone, ed., *Abortion in the United States*; and Frederick Taussig, *Abortion*.

2. For illustrative (but hardly comprehensive) examples of the scholarly debates physicians held among themselves, see H. A. Patterson, "Abortion," *Illinois Med. J.* 11 (1907):652–58; T. W. Hurley, "The Prevention of Conception—Abortions, Justifiable and Criminal," *Transactions of the Arkansas Med. Soc.* 28 (1903):262–74; C. B. Reed, "Therapeutic and Criminal Abortion," *Illinois Med. J.* 7 (March 1905); P. J. O'Callaghan, "The Religious and Moral Objections to Inducing Abortion," *Illinois Med. J.* 7 (1905); Frederick J. Taussig, "The Ethics and Laws Regarding the Interruption of Pregnancy," *Interstate Med. J.* 13 (1906); George Kain, "Is Induced Abortion Justifiable? If So, When? From the Legal View," *Pennsylvania Med. J.* 13 (1909–1910); C. Johnson, "Artificial Abortion, Criminal and Therapeutic: Its Relation to Ethics and Sociology," *Am. J. Clinical Medicine* 17 (1910); William Nicholson, "When, Under the Present Code of Medical Ethics, Is It Justifiable to Terminate Pregnancy Before the Third Month?" *Am. J. Ob. and Diseases of Women and Children* 69 (1914):1004–13; C. Culbertson, "Therapeutic Abortion and Sterilization," *Surgical Clinics of Chicago* 1 (1917):605–20; Clar-

ence Cheney, "Indications for Therapeutic Abortion," *JAMA* 103 (1934): 1914–19; Joe Kopecky, "Modern Indications for Therapeutic Abortion in Nephritic Complications," *Texas State J. Medicine* (1935); Thomas V. Moore, "Moral Aspects of Therapeutic Abortion," *Am. J. Ob. Gyn.* (1940); P. Buchler, "Mental Indications for Therapeutic Abortion"; H. C. Hesseltine et al., "Limitation of Human Reproduction–Therapeutic Abortion"; S. A. Cosgrove and Patricia Carter, "A Consideration of Therapeutic Abortion"; Katherine Kuder and William Finn, "Therapeutic Interruption of Pregnancy"; Franklin Ebaugh and Keith Huser, "Psychiatric Aspects of Therapeutic Abortion"; Samuel Harvey, "Indications for Therapeutic Abortion from the Point of View of the Surgeon," *JAMA* 137(4) (1948).

3. Colorado passed an abortion reform bill that took effect Apr. 25, 1967. North Carolina passed a reform bill on May 9, 1967, and California passed its bill on Nov. 8, 1967. Twelve states passed laws based on the American Law Institute's (ALI) Model Penal Code; Washington citizens repealed their abortion law by a referendum; and Alaska and Hawaii wrote new and more liberalized laws. The twelve states that had passed ALI-type laws by 1970 were the following: Georgia (1968), South Carolina (1970), North Carolina (1967), Virginia (1970), Maryland (1968), Delaware (1969), Colorado (1967), New Mexico (1969), Oregon (1969), California (1967), Arkansas (1969), Kansas (1969). See Edward Duffy, "The Effects of Changes in the State Abortion Laws."

4. E.g., women in the peak childbearing years (15–44) during the Depression were those women born between 1886 and 1925. The mean number of children per mother dropped from 3.75 in the 1886–1890 birth cohort to 2.99 in the 1916–1920 cohort. It is only with the 1916–1920 birth cohort (whose peak fertile years would have come in large part after the Depression) that the average number of children per mother increased again. Along with smaller average family sizes, the percentage of childlessness (no children at all) among women who had been married also increased steadily during the Depression: from 15.2 percent among women born between 1886 and 1890, to 16.2 percent of women born between 1891 and 1900, to 20.4 percent of those born between 1901 and 1905; see U.S. Census of Population, 1940, *Differential Fertility, 1910–1940* (Washington, D.C.: U.S. Government Printing Office, 1940), Tables 1–16; 1950 Census, *Fertility* (Washington, D.C.: U.S Government Printing Office, 1950); 1960 Census, *Women by Children Ever Born* (Washington, D.C.: U.S. Government Printing Office, 1960).

Note also that the Kinsey studies found that induced abortions among the women they studied peaked during the Great Depression. "The maximum proportion [of abortions] within each birth decade occurs in the age period coinciding with the depth of the depression" (Paul Gebhard et al., *Pregnancy, Birth, and Abortion*, p. 113).

5. Hodge, *Foeticide*, p. 20.

6. Warren Sanderson, "Quantitative Aspects of Marriage, Fertility, and Family Limitation in Nineteenth-Century America," pp. 352–57.

7. See Eliot Freidson, *The Profession of Medicine*; and Charles Bosk, *Forgive and Remember*.

8. See, e.g., Taussig, *Abortion*, p. 185.

9. For elaboration of this point, please see Table 1: "Ratio of Therapeutic Abortions to Total Deliveries in Selected U.S. Hospitals, 1926–1960," in Appendix Two.

10. For illustrative purposes, see Quinten Scherman, "Therapeutic Abortion," p. 332; Rovinsky and Gusberg, "Current Trends in the Therapeutic Termination of Pregnancy," pp. 11–17; Robert Kretzschmer and Albert Norris, "Psychiatric Implications of Therapeutic Abortion," p. 369; Keith Russell, "Therapeutic Abortion in a General Hospital," *Am. J. Ob. Gyn.* 62 (1951):436; Roy Heffernan and William Lynch, "What Is the Status of Therapeutic Abortion in Modern Obstetrics?" p. 342; Stanley Boulas et al., "Therapeutic Abortion," p. 224; Lewis Savel and Irving Perlmutter, "Therapeutic Abortion and Sterilization Committee," p. 1194; and Christopher Tietze, "Therapeutic Abortions in the United States," p. 785.

11. W. J. Dannreuther, "Therapeutic Abortion in the General Hospital," p. 54.

12. Taussig, *Abortion*, p. 281.

13. Modern public opinion polls as we know them date from the 1936 presidential election when George Gallup, Elmo Roper, and Archibald Crossley successfully predicted the outcome of the election on the basis of sample surveys. See W. Phillips Davison, "Public Opinion," *International Encyclopedia of the Social Sciences* 13 (1968):189. For the background of the first scholarly uses of public opinion polls, see Paul F. Lazarsfeld et al., *The People's Choice: How the Voter Makes Up His Mind in a Presidential Campaign* (New York: Columbia University Press, 1968).

14. E.g., in the thirty-eight years between 1890 and 1928, there are no American articles listed on abortion in the *Readers' Guide to Periodical Literature*. For 1929–1932, there are five articles; for 1932–1935, three articles; for 1935–1937, nine articles; for 1937–1939, five articles; for 1939–1941, one article; for 1941–1943, four articles; for 1943–1945, three articles; for 1945–1947, three articles; and for 1947–1949, five articles. The content analysis revealed that these articles were in large part either a response to the legalization of abortion in the Soviet Union and Eastern Europe or to the phenomenon of criminal abortion.

15. See Gebhard et al., *Pregnancy, Birth, and Abortion*, pp. 93–94, 54.

16. Calculated from Taussig, *Abortion*. Like many medical writers of the era, Taussig combined spontaneous and induced abortions, indicating inciden-

tally the low level of concern with induced abortion. The figures presented in this chapter, therefore, have been recalculated for induced abortions only. For birth control clients in New York, see Marie Kopp, *Birth Control in Practice*, p. 124. For poor Jewish women in Chicago, see Harry Lurie, "Sex Hygiene of Family Life," p. 66. For upper-income women, see Katharine Davis, *Factors in the Sex Lives of 2,200 Women*, p. 20. For the New York clinic, see Endre Brunner and Louis Newton, "Abortions in Relation to Viable Births in 10,609 Pregnancies," p. 85; for the New York City study, see Regina Stix, "A Study of Pregnancy Wastage"; for Cincinnati, see Regina Stix and Dorothy Wiehl, "Abortion and the Public Health," p. 621; for Baltimore, see Bessie Moses, *Contraception as a Therapeutic Measure* (Table 3); for Minnesota, see Milton Abrahamson, "A Study of 2,113 Cases Given Contraception at the Minnesota Birth Control League Clinic"; for Newark, see Hannah Stone and Henriette Hart, *Maternal Health and Contraception*; and for Philadelphia, see Stix and Wiehl, "Abortion and the Public Health," p. 621. It is important to recall that none of these groups is a "representative" group of American women because each represents distinct ethnic, religious, or income groups. Moreover, in many of these groups, the women came into the sample because they were clients at a contraceptive clinic. As such they may have been seeking to replace abortion with a method of contraception; and they may have been more fertile women to begin with. Both of these factors would make it hazardous to generalize from them to a larger population.

17. U.S. Dept. of Labor, Children's Bureau, *Maternal Mortality in Fifteen States*, p. 105. See also Henry Sangmeister, "A Survey of Abortion Deaths in Philadelphia from 1931 to 1940 Inclusive."

18. On the rise and spread of medical insurance, see Shryock, *Development of Modern Medicine*, pp. 409–30. See also Harry Moore, ed., *Medical Care for the American People*.

19. The Flexner report of 1910 signaled the end of open competition among American healers. Increasingly after 1910, the closing of the proprietary medical schools, the spread of state licensure laws, and the vigor of local medical societies affiliated with the AMA meant that healing was restricted to a smaller number of licensed M.D.'s who had graduated from "approved" medical schools. See Derbyshire, *Medical Licensure*; and Shryock, *Medical Licensure in America*.

20. See Center for Disease Control, *Abortion Surveillance Report*, annual summaries: 1977 and 1979. For a state in which one of every three pregnancies ends in abortion, see California State Department of Health, Bureau of Maternal and Child Health, *A Report to the State Legislature on the Implementation of the 1967 Therapeutic Abortion Act*.

21. See Calhoun, *Social History of the American Family*, 3:243; *Transactions of the AMA* 22 (1871):250–51.

22. Van de Warker, *Detection of Criminal Abortion*, pp. 40–73; G. R. Davis, "Abortifacient Drugs Simulating Frequently Observed Diseases," pp. 337–39; "Abortifacient Pastes: Report of the Bureau of Investigation," p. 2155; "Abortion and Leunbach's Paste," p. 535; "Poisoning with Chichester's Pills"; Konstantine Lowenberg, "Cerebral Damage in a Case of Fatal Poisoning Due to Compound of Ergot and Apiol," pp. 573–75; "Two Abortifacients Barred"; James McDonough, "Vaginal Bleeding from Potassium Permanganate as an Abortifacient," pp. 189–90; A. T. Licciardello and J. B. Stanbury, "Acute Hemolytic Anemia from Quinine Used as an Abortifacient," pp. 120–21; Walter Jetter and Francis Hunter, "Death from Attempted Abortion with a Potassium Permanganate Douche," pp. 794–98; and F. D. Wanamaker, "The Lay Use of Potassium Permanganate as an Abortifacient," pp. 259–64.

23. Sinclair, *Crowning Sin of the Age*, p. 10.

24. Philippe Ariès, *Histoire des populations françaises*.

25. Taussig, *Abortion*, p. 49.

26. Pascal Whelpton, untitled article in Taylor, ed., *Abortion Problem*, p. 16.

27. Carolyn Robinson, *Seventy Birth Control Clinics*, p. 182.

28. Taussig, *Abortion*, p. 441; T. E. Harris, "A Functional Study of Existing Abortion Laws," *Columbia Law Review*, Jan. 1935, p. 91.

29. Jerome Bates and Edward Zawadzki, *Criminal Abortion*, p. 202.

30. For more details, please see Table 2: "Percentage of Abortions Performed for Psychiatric Indications," in Appendix Two.

31. For a discussion of the breakthrough in hyperemesis gravidarum by the development of intravenous feeding, see Paul Titus, "Hyperemesis Gravidarum: Treatment by Intravenous Injections of Glucose and Carbohydrate Feedings," *JAMA* 85 (1925):488–93. See also John Moyer et al., "Observations on an Effective Anti-Emetic: Chlorpromazine," *Archives of Internal Medicine* 94 (1954):497.

32. See Myre Sim, "Abortion and the Psychiatrist"; Allan J. Rosenberg and Emmanuel Silver, "Suicide, Psychiatrists, and Therapeutic Abortion," *California Medicine* 102 (1965):410; and Calderone, ed., *Abortion in the United States*, pp. 140–41.

33. Rovinsky and Gusberg, "Current Trends," pp. 11–17; C. Ford et al., "Is Abortion a Therapeutic Procedure in Psychiatry?"; and T. N. A. Jeffcoate, "Indications for Therapeutic Abortion."

34. David Wilson, "Psychiatric Implications in Abortions," pp. 448–51. Although this may have been the most dramatic example of the effect of therapeutic abortion boards on the granting of abortions, the effect is well documented in a number of sources. E.g., Hall noted that in his setting, abortion ratios per delivery went from 1:141 (ward) and 1:37 (private) prior to the insti-

tution of a therapeutic abortion board to 1:429 (ward) and 1:111 (private). See R. E. Hall, "Therapeutic Abortion, Sterilization, and Contraception," pp. 518–32. See also Alan Guttmacher, "Therapeutic Abortions: The Doctor's Dilemma"; and David C. Wilson, "Abortion Problem in the General Hospital," in Rosen, ed., *Therapeutic Abortion*, pp. 189–97.

35. See Hall, "Therapeutic Abortion, Sterilization, and Contraception," pp. 518–32; and James Ingram, "Interruption of Pregnancy for Psychiatric Indications: A Suggested Method of Control." Alan Guttmacher, "The Legal Status of Therapeutic Abortions," in Rosen, ed., *Therapeutic Abortion*, asserts that sterilization is frequent after abortion and suggests that it is motivated by a desire to show "high-mindedness"—a physician who sterilizes a woman will never again have her as a private obstetrical patient (p. 182).

36. Guido Calabresi and Phillip Bobbit, *Tragic Choices*.

37. Alan Guttmacher, in Calderone, ed., *Abortion in the United States*, p. 94.

38. See, e.g., Edwin Gold et al., "Therapeutic Abortions in New York City," p. 968; Rovinsky and Gusberg, "Current Trends," pp. 11–17; R. E. Hall, "Therapeutic Abortion, Sterilization, and Contraception," p. 518; Savel and Perlmutter, "Therapeutic Abortion and Sterilization Committee," p. 1194.

39. Donnell Pappenfort, *Journey to Labor*; and AMA Council on Medical Education and Hospitals, *Hospital Service in the United States* (Chicago, 1936), pp. ix–xv.

40. Taussig, *Abortion*, p. 24.

41. For the fact that abortion teachings are relatively vague for non-Catholics, see Frank J. Curran, "Religious Implications," in Rosen, ed., *Therapeutic Abortion*, pp. 153–65. Though many of the Protestant ministers surveyed by Curran said they thought abortion was probably not acceptable to their churches, this is a typical comment: "The Methodist church, nor any other Protestant church of which I have any knowledge, has never taken any official action on therapeutic abortion on the grounds that this is a scientific, medical matter on which only competent medical opinion has any value" (ibid., p. 156). Similarly, Grisez notes: "I have found no study of the topic of abortion in Reformation moral teachings, and contemporary Protestants discussing abortion seldom refer to their tradition" (*Abortion*, p. 156). For other religious traditions, see ibid., pp. 117–84. The vagueness of Jewish and Protestant teachings on abortion is, as the text notes, in marked contrast to the Catholic tradition.

42. Kenrick, *Theologiae Moralis*, pp. 110–13.

43. Huser, *Crime of Abortion*, pp. 103–05.

44. See Grisez, *Abortion*, pp. 179–84.

45. See Noonan, *Contraception*, pp. 491–504; Joan Anzia, *Marital Inti-*

macy; and Thomas Hart, *Living Happily Ever After*. See also Karol Wojitla (Pope John Paul II), *Fruitful and Responsible Love*.

46. 73rd Cong., 2nd sess., *Hearings on H.R. 5978 Before the House Committee on the Judiciary*, Jan. 18–19, 1934.

47. For an overview of the Thalidomide debate, see *New York Times*, Aug. 2, 1962, p. 1. See also R. A. Fine, *The Great Drug Deception* (New York: Stein & Day, 1972); and Henning Sjostrom and Robert Nilsson, *Thalidomide and the Power of the Drug Companies* (Harmondsworth: Penguin, 1972).

Chapter 4

1. Comparative interviews and research in six other states suggest that many of the same forces and beliefs were operating elsewhere. For comparative purposes with other states, see Patricia Steinhoff and Milton Diamond, *Abortion Politics*; Daniel O'Neil, *Church Lobbying in a Western State*; Sagar Jain and Laurel Gooch, *Georgia Abortion Act, 1968*; and Sagar Jain and Steven Sinding, *North Carolina Abortion Law, 1967*. It is worth noting that Jain also wrote an account of the legislative in-fighting that led to the passage of the 1967 Beilenson bill. Although its focus is quite different (it is a study of a legislative process), it is in substantial accord with the arguments made in this book. See Sagar Jain and Steven Hughes, *California Abortion Act, 1967*.

2. For the history of California's nineteenth-century law, see Quay, "Justifiable Abortion," p. 451. For case law, see *People* v. *Long*, 15 Cal. 2d 590, 103 p.2d, 969 (1940) (burden on state to prove abortion not necessary) and *People* v. *Ballard*, 167 Cal. App. 2d 803, 335, p.2d 204 (1959) (threat to life need not be imminent).

3. Based on a content analysis of the *Los Angeles Times*, the *San Francisco Chronicle*, and the *San Diego Union*. See Appendix One. These papers were selected from circulation figures published in *Ayers' Directory of Publications*.

4. Herbert Packer and Ralph Gampell, "Therapeutic Abortion: A Problem in Law and Medicine."

5. An earlier review by Russell had found in 1950 that only 11 percent of a sample of sixty-one hospitals were using therapeutic abortion committees. See Keith Russell, "Therapeutic Abortions in California in 1950." In contrast, Packer and Gampell found that fifteen of the twenty-nine hospitals in their survey had such committees and that six of them had instituted the committee within the last five years; Packer and Gampell, "Therapeutic Abortion," p. 428.

6. For examples, see K. A. Kerr, ed., *The Politics of Moral Behavior*; and Gilbert Geis, *Not the Law's Business*. The classic statement is probably Edwin Schur's *Crimes Without Victims*.

7. See the American Law Institute, *Model Penal Code* (1959). The American Law Institute is a nonprofit organization composed of judges, lawyers, and law professors whose goal since its founding in 1933 has been to "modernize" American law in almost all of its aspects. The Model Penal Code was just one venture of many; others include model laws on land codes, securities, international law, the jurisdiction of federal courts, and torts. For illustrative purposes, see David P. Currie, "The Federal Courts and the ALI," *University of Chicago Law Review* 36(1) (Fall 1968–Winter 1969); and John Wade, "The Second Restatement of Torts Completed," *New York State Bar Journal* 52 (Fall 1980).

8. See Moore, "Moral Aspects of Therapeutic Abortion"; Buchler, "Mental Indications for Therapeutic Abortion"; Hesseltine et al., "Limitation of Human Reproduction–Therapeutic Abortion"; S. A. Cosgrove and Patricia Carter, "A Consideration of Therapeutic Abortion"; Kuder and Finn, "Therapeutic Interruption of Pregnancy"; Ebaugh and Huser, "Psychiatric Aspects of Therapeutic Abortion"; Heffernan and Lynch, "What Is the Status of Therapeutic Abortion in Modern Obstetrics?"

9. Zad Leavy, "Criminal Abortions: Facing the Facts," pp. 335–83.

10. Gene Bardach, *The Skill Factor in Politics*.

11. For studies that list accounts of abortions done for fetal indications (usually rubella), see Scherman, "Therapeutic Abortion," p. 332 (10 percent of the abortions in that series done for fetal indications); Rovinsky and Gusberg, "Current Trends," pp. 11–17 (25 percent of the abortions in this series done for fetal indications); Kretzschmer and Norris, "Psychiatric Implications of Therapeutic Abortion," p. 369 (28 percent done for fetal indications); Edmund Overstreet and Herbert Traut, "Indications for Therapeutic Abortion," pp. 16–25 (3 percent done for fetal indications); Heffernan and Lynch, "What Is the Status of Therapeutic Abortion in Modern Obstetrics?" p. 339; and Myrna Loth and H. Close Hesseltine, "Therapeutic Abortion at the Chicago Lying-In Hospital," p. 307 (7 percent done for fetal indications). Data for abortions for rape are less easy to come by since interview data suggest that they were often located within the broader category of psychiatric indications. For studies that do list abortions done specifically for the indication of rape, see Kretzschmer and Norris, "Psychiatric Indications," p. 369; Russell, "Therapeutic Abortion in a General Hospital," p. 436; Keith Russell, "Changing Indications for Therapeutic Abortion," p. 110; and Heffernan and Lynch, "What Is the Status of Therapeutic Abortion in Modern Obstetrics?" p. 342. The numbers of abortions reported for rape are small, but the point is clear: abortions were done for this indication, and doctors were willing to note this fact for the public record.

12. State of California, State Assembly Interim Committee on Criminal Procedure, *Abortion Hearing AB 2614* (Dec. 17–18, 1962); testimony of

Theodore Montgomery, M.D., State Department of Public Health, ibid., pp. 72–74.

13. U.S. Center for Health Statistics, *Vital Statistics of the United States* (Washington, D.C., 1960), vol. 2, pt. A, Table 1–Y: "Maternal Mortality Rates by Color: Birth Registration States or United States," and pp. 1–49.

14. In 1960, death rates from maternal mortality were 1.7 per 1,000 females; the rate from motor vehicle accidents was 11.0 per 1,000 females (*Vital Statistics of the United States*, vol. 2, pt. A, Table 1–M: "Death Rates from 59 Selected Causes by Age, Color and Sex, United States, 1960"). However, because the age range of females who die from traffic accidents is larger than that of maternal mortality, the figure in the text represents *age-specific* rates for these two causes. (Females from birth to puberty and after menopause are still likely to die from automobile accidents but unlikely to die from pregnancy-related causes.) When age-specific rates for females aged fifteen to forty-four from both causes are examined, 105 women aged fifteen to forty-four died in the state of California in 1960 from *all* maternal mortality causes (640–689 inclusive in the International Listing of Causes of Death), and 470 women aged fifteen to forty-four died in that same year from motor vehicle accidents (*Vital Statistics of the United States*, vol. 2, Table 9–6: "Deaths from 59 Selected Causes, Age, Color and Sex, Each State, 1960," and pp. 9–149).

15. See Jerome Skolnick, *Justice Without Trial*; and S. Kadish, "Legal Norms and Discretion in the Police and Sentencing Process," *Harvard Law Review* 75 (1961):904–31.

16. Based on a content analysis of California newspapers. On the high end of the scale, the *San Francisco Chronicle* ran twenty-one articles on the case; on the low end, the *Los Angeles Times* ran four articles.

17. See Nicholson Eastman and Louis Hellman, eds., *Williams' Obstetrics*, 12th ed. (New York: Appleton-Century-Crofts, 1961). The authors hold that if rubella is unambiguously diagnosed, then therapeutic abortion is warranted if "the parents do not wish to assume the obvious risks involved" (p. 786). *Williams' Obstetrics* is one of the classic obstetrical textbooks, as evidenced by its frequent reprintings.

18. This is probably a conservative estimate. Boulas et al., "Therapeutic Abortion," p. 224, report 5 percent of all abortions for this indication in 1953–1957 and 38 percent for 1956–1959. Similarly, Savel and Perlmutter, "Therapeutic Abortion and Sterilization Committee," p. 1194, report 14.3 percent of the abortions in their series were done for rubella. Finally, Tietze in a nationwide survey of hospitals reporting to the Professional Activities Survey found 22 percent of the abortions performed between 1960–1963 in the hospitals surveyed were for this indication (Tietze, "Therapeutic Abortion in the United States," p. 785). Note that all of these sources report abortions done for rubella *before* the full onset of the 1964–1965 rubella epidemic.

19. State of California, State Assembly Interim Committee on Criminal Procedure (1964), p. 36.

20. George Gallup, *The Gallup Poll*, vol. 1, pt. 3 (1959–1971), p. 1784.

21. State of California, State Assembly . . . Criminal Procedure (1964), p. 50.

22. Ibid., pp. ii–iii.

Chapter 5

1. To be sure, some form of feminism has existed in the United States since at least the Seneca Falls convention of 1848. But dating the "second wave" of the women's movement has its problems, since there are always forerunners, interest groups, and individuals who can be shown (after the fact) to have had a tremendous impact on the nascent movement. Judith Hole and Ellen Levine (*Rebirth of Feminism*) argue that the women's movement became a *nationally recognized* movement on Sept. 9, 1968, when women protesters picketed the Miss America Contest (pp. 123–27). On the other hand, Betty Friedan published *The Feminine Mystique* in 1963, and the National Organization for Women (NOW) was founded in 1966. However, Jo Freeman (*Politics of Women's Liberation*) tells of her unsuccessful attempts to join NOW, in large part because it was so low-profile. She also makes a subtle distinction between "the movement" and preexisting networks that were responsive to (and vital to the success of) the women's movement (pp. 44–62). By the same token, William Chafe (*The American Woman: Her Changing Social, Economic, and Political Roles, 1920–1970*) distinguishes between how quiet and low-key women's issues were in 1962 and how high-profile they had become a mere eight years later.

2. State of California, State Assembly . . . Criminal Procedure (1964), p. 78.

3. California State Department of Health, Bureau of Maternal and Child Health, *A Report . . . on the Implementation of the 1967 Therapeutic Abortion Act*.

4. See, e.g., Doris Haire, *The Cultural Warping of Childbirth*; Suzanne Arms, *Immaculate Deception*; Nancy Shaw, *Forced Labor*; and Sheryl Ruzek, *The Women's Health Movement*.

5. U.S. Bureau of the Census, "Fertility Indicators: 1970," *Current Population Reports*, series P-23, no. 36, Table 32, p. 53.

6. Mariano Requena, "Abortion in Latin America," in Robert Hall, ed., *Abortion in a Changing World*, pp. 338–52.

7. On the climate that makes a society "receptive" to social movements, see William Gamson, *The Strategy of Social Protest*.

8. The M-shaped pattern of women's work has been elegantly analyzed

and interpreted by Valerie Oppenheimer, *The Female Labor Force in the United States*.

9. Edward Gross, "Plus ça change . . . the Sexual Structure of Occupations over Time," pp. 198–208; Abbott Ferriss, *Indicators of Trends in the Status of American Women*.

10. Women on average earn less than two-thirds of men's pay, and the gap is widening. Women's pay was 63.9 percent of men's pay in 1955, 60 percent in 1965, and 58.8 percent in 1975 (U.S. Dept. of Labor, Bureau of Labor Statistics, *Perspectives on Working Women*, Table 52: "Median Earnings of Men and Women" [Washington, D.C.: U.S. Government Printing Office, 1980]). Although this is partly a function of the occupations that women choose to enter (see Victor Fuchs, "Differentials in Hourly Earnings Between Men and Women"), it is also a function of sex discrimination: within occupations, men are always paid better than women. See U.S Dept. of Labor, Bureau of Labor Statistics, *Area Wage Surveys*; and U.S. Dept. of Labor, *1975 Handbook on Women Workers* (Washington, D.C.: U.S. Government Printing Office, 1978), pp. 131–32.

11. U.S. Dept. of Labor, Women's Bureau, *The Earnings Gap Between Men and Women*, pp. 4–5.

12. There is controversy among economists about what explains this dramatic shift in female expectations vis-à-vis the job market. A compelling model is presented by Oppenheimer, *Female Labor Force*. But see also Jacob Mincer, Glen Cain, W. G. Bower, T. A. Finegan, and J. A. Sweet for alternative models. For an overview, see Hilda Kahne and Andrew Kohen, "Economic Perspectives on the Roles of Women in the American Economy," as well as "Women in the Workplace," *Monthly Labor Review* 97 (1974), Special Section, n.p.

13. Calculated from U.S. Dept. of Labor, Bureau of Labor Statistics, *Employment and Earnings*, vol. 25 (Washington, D.C.: U.S. Government Printing Office, Jan. 1978); and U.S. Dept. of Labor, Bureau of Labor Statistics, *Perspectives on Working Women: A Data Book*, Bulletin 2080, Tables 3–5 (Washington, D.C.: U.S. Government Printing Office, 1980).

14. U.S. Dept. of Labor, Bureau of Labor Statistics, *Perspectives on Working Women*, p. 27; see also U.S. Dept. of Labor, Women's Bureau, *Working Mothers and Their Children* (Washington, D.C.: U.S. Government Printing Office, 1977).

15. Between 1960 and 1979 there were dramatic declines in the numbers of first marriages of single women in those ages when women traditionally marry for the first time, namely, twenty to twenty-four. While there were 263.9 marriages per 1,000 single women in that age group in 1960, the number declined to 237.3 in 1965, 220.1 in 1970, 159.5 in 1974, 143.8 in 1975, 133.4 in 1976, and 123.0 in 1978. Nor was this simply a product of women postpon-

ing marriage for a year or two; statistics for women aged twenty-four and above show the same kinds of declines: in 1960 there were 87.5 first marriages per 1,000 single women aged twenty-four and above; in 1965, 84.4; in 1970, 82.9; in 1974, 74.8; in 1977, 62.7; in 1978, 62.7 (U.S. Center for Health Statistics, *Vital Statistics of the United States*, "Marriages per One Thousand Single Women Fourteen Years of Age and Over" (Washington, D.C.: U.S. Government Printing Office, 1980).

16. Divorce rates were indeed rising: a marriage contracted in 1983 has a 50 percent chance of ending in divorce if present trends continue. But the divorce rate is often artificially inflated because divorces granted in a given year are compared with the number of marriages celebrated in that year. A moment's thought makes clear that people getting divorced represent many different years of marriage; hence a better figure is the rate of divorces per 1,000 married people, which has increased, but not as much as is commonly assumed. Divorces per 1,000 married women increased from 7.5 divorces per 1,000 marriages in 1930 to 10.3 divorces per 1,000 marriages in 1950 to 14.9 per 1,000 in 1970 (U.S. Bureau of the Census, *Historical Statistics of the United States: Colonial Times to 1970*, Part One [Washington, D.C.: U.S. Government Printing Office, 1975], p. b214).

17. A 1978 study, undertaken by the U.S. Bureau of the Census, found that of women with children under the age of twenty-one, who were separated from their husbands, only 59 percent were awarded any child support whatsoever, and only 48.9 percent of women awarded child support actually received full payment. The average amount of child support reported by women in this study was $150 a month. The same study showed that only 14 percent of these same women received alimony, and of these 14 percent, less than half (41 percent) received the full amount. In terms of property settlement, less than one-half of the 12 million women divorced as of spring 1979 had received any form of property settlement, and of those who did, the median value was $4,650 ("Child Support and Alimony," *Current Population Reports*, Series P-23, no. 112, Sept. 1978).

18. American *completed* family sizes declined in the 1960s, but this reflects the fact that a great many families begun during the Depression (and completed during the 1960s) were unusually small. More relevant is the number of children young women aged eighteen to twenty-four *expected* to have during this period, and this figure declined significantly from an expected 3.1 children in 1960 to 2.2 in 1974. While seemingly small, such a decline is in fact momentous; see U.S. Bureau of the Census, "The Fertility of American Women, June 1980," *Current Population Reports*, Series P-20, no. 375 (Washington, D.C.: U.S. Government Printing Office, 1981), p. 7.

19. E.g., a 1976 national poll of women found that a third of them (32 percent) thought the ideal lifestyle would be as a married woman with children

and a full-time job; 44 percent of those interviewed preferred the traditional female lifestyle of being a full-time wife and mother. Younger women (those under twenty-four) were even more supportive: 45 percent of them wanted to be working mothers, and only 31 percent wanted the traditional role. Furthermore, the perception that the most fulfilling role would be as a worker and a mother was more common among women who had "male" resources. The more education, the higher the social class, and the higher the family income, the more likely a woman was to choose working and a family as a preferred lifestyle; see George Gallup, *The Gallup Poll*, vol. 3 (Wilmington, Del.: Scholarly Resources, Inc., April 1976), pp. 697–99.

20. Ferriss, *Indicators of Trends*, pp. 29–39.

21. Not that there haven't been attempts made to justify such differences of treatment. The Supreme Court held in *Geduldig* v. *Aiello* (417 U.S. 484) that a disability program in California that excluded disabilities arising from pregnancy did not constitute sex discrimination in that the plan did not exclude any persons or groups eligible for coverage, except of course for those persons or groups who became pregnant. In a subsequent case, *General Electric* v. *Gilbert et al.* (429 U.S. 125) the Court upheld this position again.

22. See "Statement of Purpose" (New York: Clergy Consultation Service, 1968).

23. There is a voluminous literature on the American fertility decline of the nineteenth century. See Wilson Grabill et al., *The Fertility of American Women*; Karl Taeuber and Irene Taeuber, *The Changing Population of the United States*; and Warren Thompson and P. K. Whelpton, *Population Trends in the United States* (New York: McGraw-Hill, 1933). For theoretical statements about the general processes of fertility decline and the value of children, see E. A. Wrigley, *Population and History*; and Karen Paige and Jeffrey Paige, *The Politics of Reproductive Ritual*.

24. See J. A. Banks and Olive Banks, *Feminism and Family Planning in Victorian England*; and Sanderson, "Qualitative Aspects of Marriage."

Chapter 6

1. The term *interested publics* is taken from Bardach, *Skill Factor in Politics*.

2. California Supreme Court, *People* v. *Belous*, 71c. 2nd, 954. The court, citing the *Statistical Abstract of the United States*, noted that there were 0.5 maternal deaths per 100,000 population and 29.1 maternal deaths per 100,000 live births. It cited data from Eastern Europe (and the first year of California's new law) to note that mortality from abortion was lower than that of childbirth (*People* v. *Belous*, pp. 963–65).

3. The most recent data suggest that maternal mortality apart from abor-

tion is twelve per 100,000 live births, while abortion-related mortality is 0.8 per 100,000 live births (Tietze, *Induced Abortion*, pp. 84–86). For those who oppose abortion, however, these figures are hardly reassuring because the mortality of the embryo is, by definition, 100 percent.

4. U.S. Supreme Court, *Roe* v. *Wade*, 410 U.S. 113, pp. 158, 159.

5. For amicus briefs in *Roe* v. *Wade*, see Philip Kurland and Gerhard Casper, eds., *Landmark Briefs and Arguments*, vol. 75; for those in the companion case, *Doe* v. *Bolton*, see U.S. Supreme Court Records, 1972 term, 410 U.S.

6. Duffy, "Effects of Changes in the State Abortion Laws."

7. U.S. Supreme Court, *Griswold* v. *Connecticut*, 381 U.S. 479, 14 L. ed. 2nd, 85 S. Ct. (1965).

8. Our content analysis of major California newspapers showed that reaction was mild, and even letters to the editor were infrequent.

9. For a classic exposition of how people are traditionally thought to be recruited to political movements, see James Wilson, *Political Organization*; and Sidney Verba and Norman Nie, *Participation in America*, Chs. 18, 19.

10. The remaining 6 percent is "other," such as the Catholic social worker who became involved when her bishop asked her to "look into" the emerging abortion situation.

11. One-third of the pro-life abortion activists in this study reported what I have called "parental loss"; only 6 percent of the pro-choice activists reported such loss. For confirming data on a larger, nationwide sample, see Donald Granberg, "The Abortion Activists," p. 161.

Chapter 7

1. The classic study is Denis de Rougement, *Love in the Western World*.

2. See WHO Scientific Group, "Biology of Fertility Control by Periodic Abstinence," World Health Organization Technical Report Series, no. 360 (Geneva, 1967). See also Nona Aguilar, *No-Pill, No-Risk Birth Control* (New York: Rawson, Wade, 1980).

3. As natural family planning becomes attractive to a wider audience than just devout Catholics, there are some who argue that the ideal way to practice NFP is by using some form of contraception—such as the condom or the diaphragm—during the fertile period rather than abstinence. For reasons which this chapter should make clear, traditional users of NFP reject this option vociferously: it offends their notions of sexuality, their notions of the meaning and purpose of fertility in that sexuality; and, perhaps most importantly, it makes sex a plentiful—rather than scarce—resource again.

4. Charles Westoff and Larry Bumpass, "The Revolution in Birth Control Practices of U.S Roman Catholics," pp. 41–44.

5. Maurice Moore, *Death of a Dogma?*

6. See J. Marshall, "Cervical Mucus and Basal Body Temperature Methods of Regulating Births: A Field Trial," p. 282; M. E. Wade et al., "A Randomized Prospective Study of the Use-Effectiveness of Two Methods of Natural Family Planning," *American Journal of Obstetrics and Gynecology* 141 (1981):368–76.

7. Joseph Fletcher is considered the "father" of situation ethics. See Joseph Fletcher, *Medicine and Morals*.

8. For a thoughtful exposition of this and other dilemmas associated with the philosophy of utilitarianism, see Amartya Sen and Bernard Williams, eds., *Utilitarianism and Beyond*.

Chapter 8

1. Granberg, "The Abortion Activists," p. 158.

2. Charles Tilly, *The Vendée*.

3. Many of the pro-life people in this study asserted that women have abortions because they do not wish to have stretch marks or because they want to take a European vacation. While I know of no direct data of how women feel who choose abortions, in the course of research for my previous book (*Taking Chances: Abortion and the Decision Not to Contracept* [1975]), I interviewed over 100 women in deep, unstructured verbatim interviews. In subsequent research, I have talked with or interviewed over 500 women who have had abortions. In my own—and possibly biased—experience, few of these women were "casual" about having an abortion. Some were more conflicted about the abortion decision than others, but for all the women I interviewed, the decision to seek an abortion has been serious, thoughtful, and carefully considered.

4. See, e.g., Fuchs, *Who Shall Live?*; Tristam Engelhardt, *Science, Ethics and Medicine*; Crane, *Sanctity of Social Life*; and Paul Ramsey, *Ethics at the Edges of Life*.

5. Westoff and Bumpass, "Revolution in Birth Control Practices," pp. 41–44.

6. There is a long sociological research tradition on the relative power status of husbands and wives and what contributes to their relative power; see Robert Blood and Donald Wolfe, *Husbands and Wives*; Robert Blood and Robert Hamlin, "The Effects of the Wife's Employment on the Family Power Structure," pp. 347–52; Phyllis Hallenbeck, "An Analysis of Power Dynamics in Marriage," *Journal of Marriage and the Family* 27 (1966):200–03; and David Heer, "Measurement and Bases of Family Power: An Overview," *Marrige and Family Living* 25 (1963):133–39. For fundamental critiques of this literature, see Constantina Safilios-Rothchild, "Family Sociology or Wives' Family Sociology? A Cross-Cultural Examination of Decision-Making,"

pp. 290–301; and Dair Gillespie, "Who Has the Power? The Marital Struggle," pp. 445–58.

Chapter 9

1. For the Republican party's stand on abortion, see *New York Times*, Jan. 13, 1980, p. 22. On the constitutionality of the Hyde amendment, see *New York Times*, July 1, 1980, p. 1. For Senate hearings, see U.S. Senate, Senate Judiciary Committee, Subcommittee on Constitutional Amendments, *Hearings to Consider S.J. Res. 119 and S.J. Res. 130* (1974).

2. Gallup, *Gallup Poll*, vol. 1, pt. 3 (1959–1971). For an overview, see Judith Blake, "Abortion and Public Opinion: The 1960–1970 Decade," pp. 541–49.

3. See James Davis, *General Social Surveys*. For an overview, see Donald Granberg and Beth Granberg, "Abortion Attitudes, 1965–1980: Trends and Determinants," pp. 250–61. See also CBS News, *CBS News–New York Times Poll*, reported in the *New York Times*, Aug. 18, 1980, p. 1.

4. For confirming evidence that the movement is predominantly female on the national level, see Granberg, "The Abortion Activists," p. 158.

5. "Issues Important to Voters" (Survey #959-K), *Gallup Poll*, vol. 3 (1976–1977), pp. 879–81.

6. The classic statements of this view are given in Mancur Olson, *The Logic of Collective Action*.

7. See Wilson, *Political Organization*.

8. These documents include pamphlets and ephemera: "Anti-Abortion and the New Right"; "Who Finances the Anti-Abortion Movement?" (National Abortion Rights Action League); "The June 11th Coalition"; Reproductive Rights Task Force (National Organization for Women).

9. Even this figure overstates the case, based as it was on self-report. See U.S. Bureau of the Census, "Voting and Registration in the Nov. 1980 Election," *Current Population Reports*, Series P-20, no. 359, Jan. 1981.

10. Statewide turnout in the 1980 election in New York was 4,929,426 votes, the lowest turnout since 1942. The Right-to-Life (RTL) party polled 130,193 votes, or 2.6 percent of the total. New York state law permits any party polling more than 50,000 votes to be a registered party; thus with the equivalent of less than three voters out of every hundred, the RTL party gained the institutional advantage of being a formal party. (Especially in New York where voting machines are still used, being a formal party gives a group a tactical advantage over write-in groups.) See "Fledgling Right-to-Life Party Unseats Liberals," *New York Times*, Dec. 16, 1980, p. 27.

11. For the first time, *pro-choice* voters may be becoming more willing to

be single-issue voters; see *The Harris Poll*, Survey #63, Aug. 9, 1982, mimeographed.

12. *Gallup Poll*, vol. 3; Blake, "Abortion and Public Opinion," p. 541.

13. Davis, *General Social Surveys*; and Granberg and Granberg, "Abortion Attitudes," p. 252.

14. See Granberg and Granberg, "Abortion Attitudes," p. 252; and Blake, "Abortion and Public Opinion," p. 541. See also C. F. Westoff, E. C. Moore, and N. B. Ryder, "The Structure of Attitudes Toward Abortion."

15. E.g., by 1972, support for abortion when the woman's health was in danger had moved twenty percentage points from 1965 whereas it moved only five points the year after the decision. Similarly, approval of abortion in the case of rape had moved twenty percentage points from 1965 to the year before the decision, and only four points thereafter. See Granberg and Granberg, "Abortion Attitudes," p. 252. For an overview (and a clear tabular presentation that compares these three polls), see Blake, "Abortion and Public Opinion."

16. Davis, *General Social Surveys*; and *Gallup Poll*, vol. 3.

17. Blake, "Abortion and Public Opinion."

18. According to the National Opinion Research Center (NORC), the following percentages of Americans approved of abortion in these circumstances: in 1965, 73 percent approved of abortion when the health of the mother was at risk, 59 percent approved when the pregnancy was the result of rape, and 57 percent approved when there was the likelihood of fetal deformity. In 1972, approval in each of these three conditions was, respectively, 87 percent, 79 percent, and 79 percent. In 1975, approval rates in these three categories had risen to 91 percent, 84 percent, and 83 percent. In 1977, the figures were 90 percent, 84 percent, and 84 percent; in 1980, they were 90 percent, 83 percent, and 83 percent (Granberg and Granberg, "Abortion Attitudes," p. 252).

19. Thomas Bouscaren, *The Ethics of Ecotopic Operations*.

20. This claim is made in the "bible" of the pro-life movement, *The Handbook on Abortion*, by Dr. and Mrs. J. C. Willkie, pp. 38–39. On close examination, Dr. and Mrs. Willkie seem to be saying that women who are treated promptly after a rape (in effect aborted by either a suction curettage or massive doses of DES) rarely become pregnant—which is hardly surprising.

21. U.S. Senate, Senate Judiciary Committee, *Hearings on a Human Life Bill (S. 158 and H.R. 900)*, May–June 1981.

22. There has developed a considerable controversy about exactly when the human embryo implants itself in the wall of the uterus. Like every other "fact" in the abortion debate, as the concrete political implications come to be more obvious, advocates begin to disagree with both the truth and meaning of the other side's facts. For a calm and dispassionate view of when the embryo probably implants, see Ruth Fowler and R. E. Edwards, "The Genetics of

Early Human Development," in Arthur Steinberg and Alexander Bearn, eds., *Progress in Medical Genetics* (New York: Grune and Stratton, 1973), 9:78.

23. By 1980 the NORC polls show 83 percent of all those surveyed supporting abortion in cases of probable deformity; see Granberg and Granberg, "Abortion Attitudes," p. 251.

24. The "search-and-destroy" language is used in Francis Schaeffer and Everett Koop, *What Ever Happened to the Human Race?*; the phrase about genocide is used in *A Speaker's Manual: Love for Life*.

25. Using a different data base, Blake has argued much the same point; see Judith Blake and Jorge del Pinal, "Negativism, Equivocation, and Wobbly Assent: Public 'Support' for the Pro-Choice Platform on Abortion," pp. 309–20.

26. See U.S. Dept. of Labor, Bureau of Labor Statistics, *Perspectives on Working Women*, Table 52: "Median Earnings of Men and Women" (Washington, D.C.: U.S. Government Printing Office, 1980); Fuchs, "Differentials in Hourly Earnings Between Men and Women," pp. 10–14; and U.S. Dept. of Labor, Bureau of Labor Statistics, *Area Wage Surveys*.

27. For data that suggest that these are profound dislocations in American life and that Americans are increasingly less connected to formal institutions, see Joseph Veroff et al., *The Inner American*.

28. See Gusfield, *Symbolic Crusade*.

29. In *Crime and Justice: American Style*, Clarence Shrag writes:

> Before its abandonment in 1933, [Prohibition] may have done more than anything else in American history to corrupt the police and destroy respect for law. . . . One of the things Prohibition tells us is that demands for more strenuous law enforcement are not always in the public interest. Whenever the law reaches too deeply into areas of private morality, the corruption of enforcement procedures seems almost inevitable. Concern over corruption is no doubt one of the elements involved in current revisions of legislation dealing with abortion, gambling, marijuana, and other moral issues. (pp. 127–28)

30. Kai Erikson (*Wayward Puritans*) argues that this is a general social process.

31. See Henry David, "Eastern Europe: Pronatalist Policies and Private Behavior."

Appendix 1

1. These are the "survivors" of the sampling process discussed in this appendix. In some of the chapters of this book, analysis is limited to only women activists. See text.

2. See Blake, "Abortion and Public Opinion," pp. 541–49; see also Granberg and Granberg, "Abortion Attitudes," pp. 250–61.

3. See Granberg, "The Abortion Activists."

4. See ibid.

5. Steinhoff and Diamond, *Abortion Politics*; O'Neil, *Church Lobbying in a Western State*; Jain and Gooch, *Georgia Abortion Act, 1968*; and Jain and Sinding, *North Carolina Abortion Law, 1967*.

Bibliography

"Abortifacient Pastes: Report of the Bureau of Investigation." *Journal of the American Medical Association* 98 (1932):2155.

"Abortion and Leunbach's Paste." Editorial. *Journal of the American Medical Association* 111 (1938):535.

"Abortion Clinic Zoning: The Right to Procreative Freedom and the Zoning Power." *Women's Rights Law Reporter* 5(4) (Summer 1979).

Abrahamson, Milton. "A Study of 2,113 Cases Given Contraception at the Minnesota Birth Control League Clinic." *Journal-Lancet* 56(8) (Aug. 1936):446.

American Friends Service Committee. *Who Shall Live? Man's Control over Life and Death*. New York: Hill & Wang, 1970.

American Law Institute. *Model Penal Code*. Philadelphia: American Law Institute, 1959.

American Medical Association, Council on Medical Education and Hospitals. *Hospital Service in the United States*. Chicago, 1936, pp. ix–xv.

Anderson, Richard. *Abortion Pro and Con: A Debater's Manual*. Los Angeles: Right-to Life League of Southern California, 1980.

Anzia, Joan M. *Marital Intimacy: A Catholic Perspective*. New York: Andrews & McMeel, 1980.

The Apostolic Fathers. Edited by Kirsopp Lake. Cambridge, Mass.: Loeb Classical Library, 1912, 1959.

Ariès, Philippe. *Histoire des populations françaises et leurs attitudes devant la vie depuis le XVIIIe siècle*. Paris: Editions Self, 1948.

Arms, Suzanne. *Immaculate Deception: A New Look at Women and Childbirth in America*. Boston: Houghton Mifflin, 1975.

Arney, W. R., and W. Trescher. "Trends in Attitudes Toward Abortion, 1972–1975." *Family Planning Perspectives* 8(3) (May–June 1976):117–24.

Austin, Robert, *Early American Medical Imprints, 1668–1820*. Washington, D.C.: U.S. Department of Health, Education, and Welfare, National Library of Medicine, 1961.

Ayer, J. Winslow. *The Great Crime of the Nineteenth Century and Perils to Child Life, Physical and Moral*. Grand Rapids, Mich.: Central Publishing Co., 1880.

Ayers' Directory of Publications. Fort Washington, Penn.: I.M.S. Press, 1960–1980.

Baker, Robert, and Frederick Elliston. *Philosophy and Sex*. New York: Prometheus Books, 1975.

Banks, J. A., and Olive Banks. *Feminism and Family Planning in Victorian England*. New York: Schocken Books, 1964.

Bard, Samuel. *A Compendium on the Theory and Practice of Midwifery, Containing Practical Instructions for the Management of Women During Pregnancy, in Labour, and in Child-Bed*. 5th ed. New York: Collins & Co., 1819.

Bardach, Gene. *The Skill Factor in Politics: Repealing the Mental Commitment Laws in California*. Berkeley and Los Angeles: University of California Press, 1971.

Barrett, Donald N. *The Problem of Population: The Cana Conference of Chicago*. Vols. 1–3. Notre Dame, Ind.: University of Notre Dame Press, 1964.

Bates, Jerome, and Edward Zawadzki. *Criminal Abortion: A Study in Medical Sociology*. Springfield, Ill.: Charles C. Thomas, 1964.

Beck, John B. *An Inaugural Dissertation on Infanticide*. New York: John Seymour, 1817.

Beck, Theodoric, and John Beck. *Elements of Medical Jurisprudence*. Vol. 1. Philadelphia: J. B. Lippincott, 1863.

Becker, Gary. *The Economics of Discrimination*. Chicago: University of Chicago Press, 1971.

Bedford, Gunning. *Principles and Practice of Obstetrics*. 3rd ed. New York: William Wood & Co., 1866.

Belkin, Samuel. *Philo and the Oral Law: The Philonic Interpretation of Biblical Law in Relation to the Palestinian Halakah*. Cambridge, Mass.: Harvard University Press, 1940.

Blackstone, William. *Commentaries on the Laws of England*. Vol. 1. Oxford: Clarendon Press, 1765.

Blake, Judith. "Abortion and Public Opinion: The 1960–1970 Decade." *Science* 171 (Feb. 1971):540–49.

Blake, Judith, and Jorge del Pinal. "Negativism, Equivocation, and Wobbly Assent: Public 'Support' for the Pro-Choice Platform on Abortion." *Demography* 18(3) (1981):309–20.

Blood, Robert, and Robert Hamlin. "The Effects of the Wife's Employment on the Family Power Structure." *Social Forces* 36(4) (1958):347–52.

Blood, Robert, and Donald M. Wolfe. *Husbands and Wives: The Dynamics of Family Living*. New York: Free Press, 1960.

Bosk, Charles. *Forgive and Remember: Managing Medical Failure*. Chicago: University of Chicago Press, 1979.

Boulas, Stanley H., et al. "Therapeutic Abortion." *Obstetrics and Gynecology* 19(2) (Feb. 1962):222–27.

Bouscaren, Thomas. *The Ethics of Ectopic Operations*. 2nd ed. Milwaukee: Bruce Publishing Co., 1944.

Bowen, W. G., and T. A. Finegan. *The Economics of Labor Force Participation*. Princeton: Princeton University Press, 1969.

Bradley, J. "A Contribution to the Jurisprudence of Abortion." *Detroit Lancet* 4 (1880–1881):489.

Brieger, Gert H., ed. *Medical America in the Nineteenth Century: Readings from the Literature*. Baltimore: Johns Hopkins University Press, 1972.

Brody, Baruch. *Abortion and the Sanctity of Human Life: A Philosophical View*. Cambridge, Mass.: MIT Press, 1975.

Brunner, Endre, and Louis Newton. "Abortions in Relation to Viable Births in 10,609 Pregnancies." *American Journal of Obstetrics and Gynecology* 38 (July 1939):85.

Buchan, William. *Domestic Medicine, or a Treatise on the Prevention and Cures of Diseases: Adapted to the Climate and Diseases of America*. Philadelphia: J. Dobson, 1797.

Buchler, P. "Mental Indications for Therapeutic Abortion." *Journal of the American Medical Association* 98 (1932).

Burdett, E. W. "Medical Jurisprudence." *New England Medical Gazette* (Boston) 17 (1883):200–14.

Burns, John. *Burns' Obstetrical Works: The Anatomy of the Gravid Uterus: Observations on Abortion and Practical Observations on the Uterine Hemorrhage*. New York: Collins & Perkins, 1809.

Cain, Glenn. *Married Women in the Labor Force*. Chicago: University of Chicago Press, 1966.

Calabresi, Guido, and Phillip Bobbit. *Tragic Choices*. New York: W. W. Norton, 1978.

Calderone, Mary S., ed. *Abortion in the United States: A Conference Sponsored by the Planned Parenthood Federation of America Inc. at Arden House and the New York Academy of Medicine*. New York: Hoeber & Harper, 1958.

Calhoun, Arthur W. *The Social History of the American Family*. Vols. 1–3. New York: Barnes & Noble, 1919.

Calhoun, Daniel. *Professional Lives in America: Structure and Aspiration, 1750–1850*. Cambridge, Mass.: Harvard University Press, 1965.

California State Department of Health, Bureau of Maternal and Child Health. *A Report to the State Legislature on the Implementation of the 1967 Therapeutic Abortion Act*. Berkeley, 1971, 1972, 1973.

Callahan, Daniel. *Abortion: Law, Choice, and Morality*. London: Macmillan, 1970.

Center for Disease Control, Division of Family Planning Evaluation. *Abortion Surveillance Report*. Atlanta, Ga., 1977.

———. *Abortion Surveillance Report*. Atlanta, Ga., 1974.

Cianfrani, Theodore. *A Short History of Obstetrics and Gynecology*. Springfield, Ill.: Charles C. Thomas, 1960.

Clark, Edward H. *A Century of American Medicine, 1776–1876*. Brinklow, Mass.: Old History Bookshop, 1876.

Coale, Ansley J., and Melvin Zelnick. *A New Estimate of Fertility and Population in the United States: A Study of White Births from 1855 to 1960 and of the Completeness of Enumeration of the Censuses of 1880 to 1960*. Princeton: Princeton University Press, 1963.

Coke, Edward. *The Third Part of the Institutes of the Laws of England*. London: W. Rawlins for T. Bassett, 1680.

Connery, John. *Abortion: The Development of the Roman Catholic Perspective*. Chicago: Loyola University Press, 1977.

Copeland, William, et al. "Therapeutic Abortion." *Journal of the American Medical Association* 207(4) (Jan. 1962):713–15.

Cosgrove, S. A., and Patricia Carter. "A Consideration of Therapeutic Abortion." *American Journal of Obstetrics and Gynecology* 48(3) (1944).

Cox, Edward S., et al. "Report of the Special Committee on Criminal Abortion." *Ninth Annual Report of the Secretary of the State Board of Health of the State of Michigan*. Lansing, 1882.

Crane, Diana. *The Sanctity of Social Life*. New York: Russell Sage, 1975.

Cutter, Irving S., and Henry R. Viets. *A Short History of Midwifery*. Philadelphia: W. B. Saunders, 1964.

Dannreuther, W. J. "Therapeutic Abortion in the General Hospital." *American Journal of Obstetrics and Gynecology* 52 (1946):54.

David, Henry P. "Eastern Europe: Pronatalist Policies and Private Behavior." *Population Bulletin* 36 (Feb. 1982).

Davis, G. R. "Abortifacient Drugs Simulating Frequently Observed Diseases." *West Virginia Medical Journal* (Wheeling) 4 (1909–1910):337–39.

Davis, James A. *General Social Surveys*. Chicago: National Opinion Research Center, 1980.

Davis, Katherine. *Factors in the Sex Lives of 2,200 Women*. New York: Harper Brothers, 1929.

De Bracton, Henry. *De Legibus et Consuetudinibus Angliae*. London, 1640.

Degler, Carl. *At Odds: Women and the Family in America from the Revolution to the Present*. New York: Oxford University Press, 1980.

De Laszlo, H., and P. S. Henshaw. *Science* 119 (1954):626.

Derbyshire, Robert C. *Medical Licensure and Discipline in the United States*. Baltimore: Johns Hopkins University Press, 1969.

De Rougement, Denis. *Love in the Western World*. New York: Harcourt Brace, 1940.

De Vaux, Roland. *Ancient Israel*. Vol. 1: *Social Institutions*. New York: McGraw-Hill, 1961.

Devereux, George. *A Study of Abortion in Primitive Societies*. New York: International Universities Press, 1976.

Dewees, William P. *A Compendious System of Midwifery Chiefly Designed to Facilitate the Inquiry of Those Who May Be Pursuing This Branch of Study*. Philadelphia: Blanchard & Lea, 1847.

———. *A Treatise on the Diseases of Females*. 9th ed. Philadelphia: Blanchard & Lea, 1847.

Dixon, E. H. *Woman and Her Diseases: The Cradle to the Grave*. New York: Ring, 1847.

Dixon, Edward. *A Treatise on Diseases of the Sexual Organs*. New York: Burgess, Stenger, & Co., 1845.

Dolger, F. J. "Das Lebensrecht des ungeborenen Kindes und die Fruchtabtreibung in der Bewertung der heidnischen und christlichen Antike." *Antike u. Christentum* 4 (1933):1–61.

Duffy, Edward. "The Effects of Changes in the State Abortion Laws." Washington, D.C.: U.S. Department of Health, Education, and Welfare, Public Health Service, Feb. 1971.

Duster, Troy. *The Legislation of Morality: Law, Drugs, and Moral Judgment*. New York: Free Press, 1970.

Ebaugh, Franklin, and Keith Huser. "Psychiatric Aspects of Therapeutic Abortion." *Postgraduate Medicine* 2 (1947).

Edelstein, Ludwig. "The Hippocratic Oath: Text, Translation, and Interpretation." *Supplement to the Bulletin of the History of Medicine*, no. 1 (1943), pp. 16–38.

Ehrenreich, Barbara, and Deidre English. *For Her Own Good: One Hundred and Fifty Years of the Experts' Advice to Women*. New York: Doubleday, 1978.

Emmet, Thomas A. *The Principles and Practice of Gynecology*. Philadelphia: Henry C. Lea, 1879.

Encyclopedia of Religion and Ethics. Edited by James Hastings. New York: Scribner's, 1961.

Engelhardt, Tristam. *Science, Ethics, and Medicine*. Hastings-on-Hudson, N.Y.: Institute for Society, Ethics, and Natural Sciences, 1976.

Erikson, Kai. *Wayward Puritans: A Study in the Sociology of Deviance*. New York: Wiley, 1966.

Ewell, Thomas. *Letters to Ladies: Detailing Important Information Concerning Themselves and Their Infants*. Philadelphia, 1817.

Farnsworth, Norman K., et al. "Potential Value of Plants as Sources of New Anti-Fertility Agents." *Journal of Pharmaceutical Sciences* 64(4) (April 1975).

Feldman, David. *Birth Control in Jewish Law*. New York: New York University Press, 1968.

Ferriss, Abbott L. *Indicators of Trends in the Status of American Women*. New York: Russell Sage, 1971.

Findley, Palmer. *Priests of Lucina: The Story of Obstetrics*. Boston: Little, Brown, 1939.

Fishbein, Morris. *History of the American Medical Association: 1847–1947*. Philadelphia: W. B. Saunders, 1947.

Flandrin, Jean Louis. *L'église et le contrôle des naissances: Questions d'histoire*. Paris: Flammarion, 1970.

Fletcher, Joseph. *Medicine and Morals*. Princeton: Princeton University Press, 1954.

Flexner, Abraham. *Medical Education in the United States and Canada*. New York: Carnegie Foundation, 1910.

Flexner, Eleanor. *Century of Struggle: The Women's Rights Struggle in the United States*. Cambridge, Mass.: Harvard University Press, 1959.

Ford, C., et al. "Is Abortion a Therapeutic Procedure in Psychiatry?" *Journal of the American Medical Association* 218 (1971):1173–78.

Forster, Colin, and G. S. L. Tucker. *Economic Opportunity and White American Fertility Ratios, 1800–1860*. New Haven: Yale University Press, 1972.

Fowler, Ruth E., and R. E. Edwards. "The Genetics of Early Human Development." In *Progress in Medical Genetics*. Edited by Arthur Steinberg and Alexander Bearn. Vol. 9. New York: Grune & Stratton, 1973.

Freeman, Jo. "The Origins of the Women's Liberation Movement." *American Journal of Sociology* 78(4) (1973):30–49.

———. *Politics of Women's Liberation*. New York: McKay, 1975.

Freidson, Eliot. *The Profession of Medicine: A Study in the Sociology of Applied Knowledge*. New York: Dodd, Mead, 1970.

Fuchs, Victor. "Differentials in Hourly Earnings Between Men and Women." *Monthly Labor Review* 94(5) (May 1971):10–14.

———. *Who Shall Live? Health Economics and Social Choice*. New York: Basic Books, 1974.

Gaillardet, F. *L'aristocratie en Amérique*. Paris, 1883.

Gallup, George. *The Gallup Poll*. Vol. 1, pts. 1–3 (1935–1971). Wilmington, Del.: Scholarly Resources Inc., 1972.

———. *The Gallup Poll*. Vol. 2 (1972–1975). Wilmington, Del.: Scholarly Resources Inc., 1972.

———. *The Gallup Poll*. Vol. 3 (1976–1977). Wilmington, Del.: Scholarly Resources Inc., 1972.

Gamson, William. *The Strategy of Social Protest*. Homewood, Ill.: Dorsey, 1975.

Gardner, Augustus K. *Conjugal Sins Against the Laws of Life and Health*. New York: J. S. Redfield, 1870.

Gebhard, Paul, et al. *Pregnancy, Birth, and Abortion*. New York: Hoeber & Harper, 1958.

Geis, Gilbert. *Not the Law's Business: An Examination of Homosexuality, Abortion, Prostitution, Narcotics, and Gambling*. New York: Schocken Books, 1979.

Gillespie, Dair. "Who Has the Power? The Marital Struggle." *Journal of Marriage and the Family* 33 (1971):445–58.

Gold, Edwin, et al. "Therapeutic Abortions in New York City: A Twenty-Year Review." *American Journal of Public Health* 55(7) (July 1965):964–72.

Gordon, Linda. *Women's Body, Women's Right*. New York: Grossman, 1976.

Grabill, Wilson, et al. *The Fertility of American Women*. New York: Wiley, 1958.

Granberg, Donald. "The Abortion Activists." *Family Planning Perspectives* 13(4) (July-Aug. 1981):158–61.

Granberg, Donald, and Beth Wellman Granberg. "Abortion Attitudes, 1965–1980: Trends and Determinants." *Family Planning Perspectives* 12(5) (Sept.-Oct. 1980):250–61.

Granfield, David. *The Abortion Decision*. New York: Doubleday, 1969.

Grisez, Germain. *Abortion: The Myths, the Realities, and the Arguments*. New York: Corpus Books, 1970.

Gross, Edward. "Plus ça change . . . the Sexual Structure of Occupations over Time." *Social Problems* 16 (Fall 1968):198–208.

Gusfield, Joseph. *Symbolic Crusade*. Urbana: University of Illinois Press, 1966.

Guttmacher, Alan. "Therapeutic Abortions: The Doctor's Dilemma." *Journal of Mt. Sinai Hospital* 111 (1954):17–19.

———. "Therapeutic Abortion in a Large General Hospital." *Surgical Clinics of North America* 37 (1957):459–69.

Hahnel, R. "Der künstliche Abortus im Altertum." *Archiv für Geschichte der Medizin* 29 (1937).

Haire, Doris. *The Cultural Warping of Childbirth*. Hillside, N.J.: International Childbirth Association, 1972.

Hale, Edwin M. *The Great Crime of the Nineteenth Century: Why Is It Committed? Who Are the Criminals? How Shall They Be Detected?* Chicago: C. S. Halsey, 1867.

———. *A Systematic Treatise on Abortion and Sterility*. 2nd ed. Chicago: C. S. Halsey, 1868.

Hale, Matthew. *The History of the Pleas of the Crown*. 1st American ed. Philadelphia: Robert H. Small, 1847.

Hall, Alfred. *Mother's Own Book and Practical Guide to Health*. Rochester, N.Y., 1843.

Hall, R. E. "Therapeutic Abortion, Sterilization, and Contraception," *American Journal of Obstetrics and Gynecology* 91 (1965):518–32.

Haller, Mark. *Eugenics: Hereditarian Thought in America*. New Brunswick, N.J.: Rutgers University Press, 1963.

Hardin, Garrett. *Stalking the Wild Taboo*. Los Altos, Ca.: William Kaufmann, Inc., 1973.

Hart, Thomas. *Living Happily Ever After: Towards a Theology of Christian Marriage*. New York: Paulist Press, 1979.

Haskell, P. S. "Criminal Abortion." *Transactions of the Maine Medical Association* (Portland) 10 (1871–1873):465–73.

Heffernan, Roy, and William Lynch. "What Is the Status of Therapeutic Abortion in Modern Obstetrics?" *American Journal of Obstetrics and Gynecology* 66 (Aug. 1953):335–45.

Hesseltine, H. Close, et al. "Limitation of Human Reproduction–Therapeutic Abortion." *American Journal of Obstetrics and Gynecology* 39 (1940):549.

Hilgers, Thomas, and Dennis Horan. *Abortion and Social Justice*. New York: Sheed & Ward, 1972.

Himes, Norman. *Medical History of Contraception*. New York: Schocken Books, 1970.

Hirschman, Albert. *The Passions and the Interests: Political Arguments for Capitalism Before Its Triumph*. Princeton: Princeton University Press, 1977.

Hodge, Hugh L. *The Principles and Practice of Obstetrics*. Philadelphia: Blanchard & Lea, 1864.

———. *Foeticide, or Criminal Abortion: A Lecture Introductory to the Course on Obstetrics and the Diseases of Women and Children, University of Pennsylvania*. Philadelphia: Lindsay & Blakiston, 1869.

Hole, Judith, and Ellen Levine. *Rebirth of Feminism*. New York: Quadrangle Books, 1971.

Holmes, Samuel J. *The Trend of the Race*. New York: Harcourt Brace, 1921.

Huser, Roger. *The Crime of Abortion in Canon Law*. Washington, D.C.: Catholic University Press, 1942.

Ingram, James. "Interruption of Pregnancy for Psychiatric Indications: A Suggested Method of Control." *Obstetrics and Gynecology* 29 (Jan. 1967):251–55.

Institut National d'Etudes Démographiques. *La prévention des naissances dans la famille: Ses origines dans les temps modernes*. Travaux et Documents. Cahier no. 35. Paris: Presses universitaires de France, 1960.

Iseman, M. S. *Race Suicide*. New York: Cosmopolitan Press, 1912.

Jagger, Allison. "Abortion and a Woman's Right to Decide." *Philosophical Forum* 5(1–2) (Fall–Winter 1973–1974).

Jaffe, Frederick. *Abortion Politics: Private Morality and Public Policy*. New York: McGraw-Hill, 1981.

Jain, Sagar C., and Laurel Gooch. *Georgia Abortion Act, 1968: A Study in Legislative Process*. Chapel Hill: University of North Carolina, School of Public Health, 1972.

Jain, Sagar C., and Steven Hughes. *California Abortion Act, 1967: A Study in Legislative Process*. Chapel Hill: University of North Carolina, Carolina Population Center, 1969.

Jain, Sagar C., and Steven W. Sinding. *North Carolina Abortion Law, 1967: A Study in Legislative Process*. Chapel Hill: University of North Carolina Press, 1968.

Jakobovits, Immanuel. *Jewish Medical Ethics: A Comparative and Historical Study of the Jewish Religious Attitude to Medicine and Its Practice*. New York: Bloch Publishing Co., 1975.

Jeffcoate, T. N. A. "Indications for Therapeutic Abortion." *British Medical Journal* 1 (Feb. 27, 1960).

Jetter, Walter, and Francis Hunter. "Death from Attempted Abortion with a Potassium Permanganate Douche." *New England Journal of Medicine* 240 (1949):794–98.

Jones, Howard, and Georgeanna Jones. *Novak's Textbook of Gynecology*. Baltimore: Williams & Wilkins, 1981.

Jones, W. H. S. *The Doctor's Oath: An Essay in the History of Medicine*. Cambridge: Cambridge University Press, 1924.

———, ed. *Hippocrates*. Vol. 5. Cambridge, Mass.: Harvard University Press, 1923.

Jonsen, Albert, and Michael Garland. *The Ethics of Newborn Intensive Care*. Berkeley: Institute of Governmental Studies, 1977.

Jordan, M. H. "A Case of Artificial Abortion for Relief of Uncontrollable Nausea and Vomiting with Remarks." *Southern Medical Record* 12 (1880):275.

Juvenal (Decimus Junius Juvenalis). Sixth Satire. In *The Sixteen Satires*. Cambridge, Mass.: Loeb Classical Library, 1967.

Kadish, Sanford H. "Legal Norms and Discretion in the Police and Sentencing Process." *Harvard Law Review* 75 (1961):904–31.

Kahne, Hilda, and Andrew Kohen. "Economic Perspectives on the Roles of Women in the American Economy." *Journal of Economic Literature* 14(1) (1975):1249–92.

Kantner, John F., and Melvin Zelnick. "Contraception and Pregnancy: Experience of Young Unmarried Women in the United States." *Family Planning Perspectives* 5 (Winter 1973):21–35.

Kenrick, Francis P. *Theologiae Moralis*. Philadelphia: Eugenium Commiskey, 1841.

Kerr, K. A., ed. *The Politics of Moral Behavior*. Reading, Mass.: Addison-Wesley, 1973.

Kett, Joseph. *The Formation of the American Medical Profession: The Role of Institutions, 1780–1860*. New Haven: Yale University Press, 1968.

Kindregan, Charles P. *The Quality of Life: Reflections on the Moral Values of American Law*. Milwaukee: Bruce Publishing Co., 1969.

Kinney, Abbot. *The Conquest of Death*. New York, 1893.

Kinsey, Alfred, et al. *Sexual Behavior in the Human Male*. Philadelphia: W. B. Saunders, 1948.

———. *Sexual Behavior in the Human Female*. Philadelphia: W. B. Saunders, 1953.

Kopp, Marie E. *Birth Control in Practice: Analysis of Ten Thousand Case Histories of the Birth Control Clinical Research Bureau*. New York: McBride Publishing Co., 1934.

Kretzschmer, Robert, and Albert Norris. "Psychiatric Implications of Therapeutic Abortion." *American Journal of Obstetrics and Gynecology* 98(3) (1967):369.

Kuder, Katherine, and William Finn. "Therapeutic Interruption of Pregnancy." *American Journal of Obstetrics and Gynecology* 49 (Jan. 1945):762.

Kurland, Philip B., and Gerhard Casper, eds. *Landmark Briefs and Arguments of the Supreme Court of the United States*. Constitutional Law Vol.

75 (*Roe* v. *Wade*). Arlington, Va.: University Publications Inc., 1975.

Larson, Magali. *The Rise of Professionalism: A Sociological Analysis*. Berkeley and Los Angeles: University of California Press, 1977.

Leavy, Zad. "Criminal Abortions: Facing the Facts." *Los Angeles Bar Bulletin*, Oct. 1959, pp. 335–83.

Leonardo, Richard H. *The History of Gynecology*. New York: Froben Press, 1944.

Licciardello, A. T., and J. B. Stanbury. "Acute Hemolytic Anemia from Quinine Used as an Abortifacient." *New England Journal of Medicine* 238 (1948):120–21.

Loth, Myrna, and H. Close Hesseltine. "Therapeutic Abortion at the Chicago Lying-In Hospital." *American Journal of Obstetrics and Gynecology* 72(2) (Aug. 1956):304–11.

Lowenberg, Konstantine. "Cerebral Damage in a Case of Fatal Poisoning Due to Compound of Ergot and Apiol." *Journal of the American Medical Association* 110 (1938):573–75.

Luker, Kristin. *Taking Chances: Abortion and the Decision Not to Contracept*. Berkeley and Los Angeles: University of California Press, 1975.

Lurie, Harry J. "Sex Hygiene of Family Life." *Jewish Social Service Quarterly*, December 1926, p. 66.

McDonough, James. "Vaginal Bleeding from Potassium Permanganate as a Abortifacient." *New England Journal of Medicine* 232 (1945):189–90.

Mann, Matthew. *A System of Gynecology*. Vol. 1. Philadelphia: Lea Brothers & Co., 1887.

Marcy, Henry. "Education as a Factor in the Prevention of Criminal Abortion and Illegitimacy." *Journal of the American Medical Association* 47 (1906).

Marshall, J. "Cervical Mucus and Basal Body Temperature Methods of Regulating Births: A Field Trial." *Lancet* 2 (Aug. 1976):282.

Mauriceau, A. M. *The Married Woman's Private Medical Companion. Embracing the Treatment of Menstruation, or Monthly Turns, During Their Stoppage, Irregularity, or Entire Suppression. Pregnancy, and How It May Be Determined, with the Treatment of Various Diseases. Discovery to Prevent Pregnancy, Its Great and Important Necessity Where Malformation or Inability Exists to Give Birth. To Prevent Miscarriage and Abortion. When Proper and Necessary to Effect Miscarriage, When Attended with Entire Safety. Causes and Mode of Cure of Barrenness or Sterility*. New York, 1847.

Maxwell, Mrs. W. H. *A Female Physician to the Ladies of the United States; Being a Familiar and Practical Treatise on Matters of Utmost Im-*

portance Peculiar to Women. Adapted for Every Woman's Own Private Use. Published by the Author at Her Private Hospital. New York, 1860.

Means, Cyril. "The Law of New York Concerning Abortion and the Status of the Foetus, 1664–1968: A Case of Cessation of Constitutionality." *New York Law Forum* 14(3) (1968):441–515.

Meigs, Charles D. *Woman: Her Diseases and Remedies.* Philadelphia: Blanchard & Lea, 1859.

Mincer, Jacob. "Labor Force Participation of Married Women: A Study of Labor Supply." In *Aspects of Labor Economics.* Edited by National Bureau of Economic Research. Princeton: Princeton University Press, 1962, pp. 63–105.

Mohr, James C. *Abortion in America: The Origins and Evolution of National Policy.* New York: Oxford University Press, 1978.

Moïssidés, M. "Contribution à l'étude de l'avortement dans l'antiquité grecque." *Janus: Archives Internationales Pour l'Histoire de la Médicine et la Géographie Médicale* 26 (1922):10–136.

Mommsen, Theodore. *Digest: Corpus Juris Civilis.* Berlin: Weidman, 1892.

———. *Le droit pénal romain.* Translated by J. Dusquene. Paris, 1907.

Money, John, and Anke Ehrhardt. *Man and Woman, Boy and Girl.* Baltimore: Johns Hopkins University Press, 1972.

Moore, Harry, ed. *Medical Care for the American People.* Chicago: University of Chicago Press, 1932.

Moore, J. G., and W. H. Randall. "Trends in Therapeutic Abortion: A Review of 137 Cases." *American Journal of Obstetrics and Gynecology* 63(1) (Jan. 1952):28–40.

Moore, Maurice. *Death of a Dogma? The American Catholic Clergy's View of Contraception.* Chicago: Community and Family Study Center, University of Chicago, 1973.

Moore-Cavar, Emily Campbell. *International Inventory of Information on Induced Abortion.* New York: Division of Social and Administrative Sciences, Columbia University, 1974.

Mortimer, R. C. *Western Canon Law.* Berkeley and Los Angeles: University of California Press, 1953.

Moses, Bessie. *Contraception as a Therapeutic Measure.* Baltimore: Williams & Wilkins, 1936.

Mott, Mrs. *The Ladies' Medical Oracle, or Mrs. Mott's Advice to Young Females, Wives and Mothers. Being a Non-Medical Commentary on the Cause, Prevention, and Cure of the Diseases of the Female Frame.* Boston, 1834.

Musto, David. *The American Disease: Origins of Narcotic Control.* New Haven: Yale University Press, 1973.

Nardi, E. *Procurato Aborto Nel Mundo Graeco-Roman*. Milan: Guiffre, 1971.

National Abortion Rights Actions League. *Legal Abortion: A Speaker's and Debater's Notebook*. Washington, D.C., n.d.

National Committee on Maternal Health. *The Abortion Problem: Proceedings of a Conference at the New York Academy of Medicine, June 1942*. Baltimore: Williams & Wilkins, 1944.

Nebinger, Andrew. *Criminal Abortion: Its Extent and Prevention*. Philadelphia: Collins, 1870.

Needham, James. *A History of Embryology*. 2nd ed. New York: Abelard & Schuman, 1959.

Nichols, Thomas L. *Forty Years of American Life*. London, 1864.

Noonan, John. *Contraception: A History of Its Treatment by Catholic Theologians and Canonists*. Cambridge, Mass.: Harvard University Press, 1965.

———. *A Private Choice: Abortion in America in the Seventies*. New York: Free Press, 1979.

———, ed. *The Morality of Abortion: Legal and Historical Perspectives*. Cambridge, Mass.: Harvard University Press, 1970.

Norwood, William. *Medical Education in the United States Before the Civil War*. Philadelphia: University of Pennsylvania Press, 1944.

Olson, Mancur. *The Logic of Collective Action*. Cambridge, Mass.: Harvard University Press, 1965.

O'Neil, Daniel J. *Church Lobbying in a Western State*. Tucson: University of Arizona Press, 1970.

O'Neill, William. *Everyone Was Brave: A History of Feminism in America*. Chicago: Quadrangle Books, 1971.

Oppenheimer, Valerie K. *The Female Labor Force in the United States: Demographic Factors Affecting Its Change and Growth*. Berkeley, Ca.: Population Monograph Series, no. 5, 1970.

Overstreet, E. W. *Medical Staff Conferences: University of California Hospital* 1 (1948):167.

Overstreet, Edmund, and Herbert Traut. "Indications for Therapeutic Abortion." *Postgraduate Medicine*, 1951, pp. 16–25.

Ovid. *Heroides and Amores*. Edited by Grant Showerman. Cambridge, Mass.: Loeb Classical Library, 1914.

Packer, Herbert, and Ralph Gampell. "Therapeutic Abortion: A Problem in Law and Medicine." *Stanford Law Review* 11 (May 1959).

Paige, Karen, and Jeffrey Paige. *The Politics of Reproductive Ritual*. Berkeley and Los Angeles: University of California Press, 1981.

Pappenfort, Donnell M. *Journey to Labor*. Chicago: University of Chicago Press, 1964.

Perlmutter, Irving K. "Analysis of Therapeutic Abortions, Bellevue Hospital,

1935–1945." *American Journal of Obstetrics and Gynecology* 53 (1947):1008–18.

Pivar, David. *Purity Crusade: Sexual Morality and Social Control, 1868–1900*. Westport, Conn.: Greenwood Press, 1973.

Pliny. *Natural History*. Edited by H. Rackham. Cambridge, Mass.: Loeb Classical Library, 1947.

"Poisoning with Chichester's Pills." *Journal of the American Medical Association* 106 (1936).

Pomeroy, H. S. *Ethics of Marriage*. New York: Funk & Wagnalls, 1888.

Quay, Eugene. "Justifiable Abortion: Medical and Legal Foundations." *Georgetown Law Journal* 49(2–3) (Winter 1960–Spring 1961): 447–520.

Quimby, Isaac M. "Introduction to Medical Jurisprudence." *Journal of the American Medical Association*, Aug. 1887, p. 164.

Ramsey, Paul. *Ethics at the Edges of Life*. New Haven: Yale University Press, 1978.

Rawls, John. *A Theory of Justice*. Cambridge, Mass.: Harvard University Press, 1971.

Reece, Richard. *The Ladies' Medical Guide: Being a Popular Treatise on the Causes, Prevention, and Mode of Treatment of the Diseases to Which Females Are Particularly Subject*. Philadelphia: Carey, Lea, & Blanchard, 1833.

Reese, D. Meredith. "Report on Infant Mortality in Large Cities." *Transactions of the American Medical Association* 12 (1859).

Reiser, Stanley Joel. *Medicine and the Reign of Technology*. Cambridge: Cambridge University Press, 1978.

Requena, Mariano. "Abortion in Latin America." In *Abortion in a Changing World*. Edited by Robert Hall. New York: Columbia University Press, 1970, pp. 338–52.

Ricci, James. *One Hundred Years of Gynecology*. Philadelphia: Blakiston Co., 1945.

Rice, Charles. *The Vanishing Right to Live: An Appeal for a Renewed Reverence for Life*. Garden City, N.Y.: Doubleday, 1969.

Rich, Adrienne. *Of Woman Born: Motherhood as Experience and Institution*. New York: W. W. Norton, 1976.

Risse, Guenther, et al., eds. *Medicine Without Doctors: The History of the Home Health Movement in America*. New York: Science History Publications, 1977.

Robinson, Carolyn. *Seventy Birth Control Clinics: A Survey and Analysis Including the General Effects of Control on Size and Quality of Population*. Baltimore: Williams & Wilkins, 1930.

Robinson, William. *The Law Against Abortion: Its Perniciousness Demon-*

strated and Its Repeal Demanded. New York: Eugenics Publishing Co., 1928.

Rongy, A. J. *Abortion: Legal or Illegal.* New York: Vanguard Press, 1933.

Rosen, Harold, ed. *Therapeutic Abortion: Medical, Psychiatric, Legal, Anthropological, and Religious Considerations.* New York: Julian Press, 1954.

Rosenberg, Charles. "The Therapeutic Revolution: Medicine, Meaning, and Change in Nineteenth-Century America." *Perspectives in Biology and Medicine,* 20(1) (Summer 1977):485–506.

Rothstein, William. *American Physicians in the Nineteenth Century: From Sects to Science.* Baltimore: Johns Hopkins University Press, 1972.

Rovinsky, J. J., and S. B. Gusberg. "Current Trends in the Therapeutic Termination of Pregnancy." *American Journal of Obstetrics and Gynecology* 98 (1967):11–17.

Russell, Keith. "Therapeutic Abortions in California in 1950." *Western Journal of Obstetrics and Gynecology* 60 (1952):497.

———. "Changing Indications for Therapeutic Abortion." *Journal of the American Medical Association* 151 (Jan. 10, 1953):108–11.

Ruzek, Sheryl. *The Women's Health Movement.* New York: Praeger, 1978.

Safilios-Rothchild, Constantina. "Family Sociology or Wives' Family Sociology? A Cross-Cultural Examination of Decision-Making." *Journal of Marriage and the Family* 29 (1969):290–301.

Sanderson, Warren. "Quantitative Aspects of Marriage, Fertility, and Family Limitation in Nineteenth-Century America: Another Application of the Coale Specifications." *Demography* 16(3) (Aug. 1979):339–58.

Sangmeister, Henry J. "A Survey of Abortion Deaths in Philadelphia from 1931 to 1940 Inclusive." *American Journal of Obstetrics and Gynecology* 46 (1943):755–58.

Sarvis, Betty, and Hyman Rodman. *The Abortion Controversy.* New York: Columbia University Press, 1974.

Saur, R. "Attitudes to Abortion in America, 1800–1973." *Population Studies* 28(1) (1974):53–67.

Savel, Lewis, and Irving K. Perlmutter. "Therapeutic Abortion and Sterilization Committee." *American Journal of Obstetrics and Gynecology* 80(60) (Dec. 1960):1194.

Schaeffer, Francis A., and C. Everett Koop. *What Ever Happened to the Human Race?* Old Tappan, N.J.: Revell, 1979.

Scherman, Quinten. "Therapeutic Abortion." *Obstetrics and Gynecology* 11 (1958):323–35.

Schur, Edwin. *Crimes Without Victims.* Englewood Cliffs, N.J.: Prentice-Hall, 1965.

Sen, Amartya, and Bernard Williams, eds. *Utilitarianism and Beyond*. Cambridge: Cambridge University Press, 1982.

Seneca. "Consolation to Helvia." In *Moral Essays*. Vol. 2. Edited by John Basore. Cambridge, Mass.: Loeb Classical Library, 1963.

Shafer, Henry B. *The American Medical Profession, 1783–1850*. New York: Columbia University Press, 1936.

Shattuck, Roger. *The Forbidden Experiment: The Wild Boy of Aveyron*. New York: Farrar, Straus and Giroux, 1980.

Shaw, Nancy Stoller. *Forced Labor: Maternal Care in the United States*. New York: Pergamon Press, 1974.

Shrag, Clarence. *Crime and Justice: American Style*. Washington, D.C.: National Institute for Mental Health, Center for Studies of Crime and Delinquency, 1972.

Shryock, Richard. *The Development of Modern Medicine: An Interpretation of the Social and Scientific Factors Involved*. New York: Alfred A. Knopf, 1947.

———. *The Development of Modern Medicine: An Interpretation of the Social and Scientific Factors Involved*. London: Victor Gollancz, 1948.

———. *Medicine and Society in America, 1660–1860*. Ithaca: Cornell University Press, 1962.

———. *Medical Licensing in America, 1650–1965*. Baltimore: Johns Hopkins University Press, 1967.

Sigerist, Henry E. *American Medicine*. New York: W. W. Norton, 1934.

Sim, Myre. "Abortion and the Psychiatrist." *British Medical Journal* 2 (July 1963):20.

Sinclair, Brevard D. *The Crowning Sin of the Age: The Perversion of Marriage*. Boston: H. L. Hastings, 1892.

Singer, Charles, and E. Ashworth Underwood. *A Short History of Medicine*. 2nd ed. New York: Oxford University Press, 1962.

Skolnick, Jerome K. *Justice Without Trial: Law Enforcement in Democratic Society*. New York: Wiley, 1966.

A Speaker's Manual: Love for Life. Los Angeles: Right-to-Life League of Southern California, 1980.

Speert, Harold. *Obstetric and Gynecological Milestones: Essays in Eponymy*. New York: Macmillan, 1958.

———. *Iconographia Gyniatrica: A Pictorial History of Gynecology and Obstetrics*. Philadelphia: F. A. Davis, 1973.

State of California. State Assembly Interim Committee on Criminal Procedure. *Abortion Hearing AB 2614*. Dec. 17–18, 1962.

———. State Assembly Interim Committee on Criminal Procedure. *Hearings on AB 2310* (*The Humane Abortion Act*). July 1964.

Steinhoff, Patricia G., and Milton Diamond. *Abortion Politics: The Hawaii Experience*. Honolulu: Hawaii University Press, 1977.

Stevens, Rosemary. *American Medicine and the Public Interest*. New Haven: Yale University Press, 1971.

Stix, Regina. "A Study of Pregnancy Wastage." *Milbank Memorial Fund Quarterly* 13(4) (Oct. 1935):347–65.

Stix, Regina, and Dorothy Wiehl. "Abortion and the Public Health." *American Journal of Public Health* 28 (May 1938):621.

Stone, Hannah M., and Henriette Hart. *Maternal Health and Contraception: Part One: Social Data*. Newark, N.J.: New Jersey Birth Control League, 1932.

Storer, Horatio R. *Is It I? A Book for Every Man*. Boston: Lea & Shepard, 1867.

———. *On Criminal Abortion in America*. Philadelphia, 1860.

———. "On the Decrease of the Rate of Increase of Population Now Obtaining in Europe and America." *American Journal of Science and Art* (New Haven), March 1867.

———. *Why Not? A Book for Every Woman*. Boston: Lea & Shepard, 1866.

Storer, Horatio R., and Franklin Fiske Heard. *Criminal Abortion: Its Nature, Its Law, Its Evidence*. Cambridge, Mass., 1868.

Sweet, James A. *Women in the Labor Force*. New York: Seminar Press, 1973.

Taeuber, Karl, and Irene Taeuber. *The Changing Population of the United States*. New York: Wiley, 1958.

Taussig, Frederick. *Abortion: Spontaneous and Induced*. S Louis: C. V. Mosby, 1936.

Taylor, Alfred. *Medical Jurisprudence*. 4th American ed. Edited by Edward Hartshorne, M.D. Philadelphia: Blanchard & Lea, 1856.

Taylor, Howard, ed. *The Abortion Problem: Proceedings of the Conference Held Under the Auspices of the National Committee on Maternal Health at the New York Academy of Medicine*. New York: Williams & Wilkins, 1944.

Tertullian. *Apology*. Edited by T. R. Glover. Cambridge, Mass.: Loeb Classical Library, 1931.

Thomas, T. Gaillard. *A Practical Treatise on the Diseases of Women*. Philadelphia: Henry C. Lea, 1876.

———. *Abortion and Its Treatment: From the Standpoint of Practical Experience*. New York: D. Appleton, 1894.

Thornton, W. N. "Therapeutic Abortion." *Obstetrics and Gynecology* 2 (1953):473.

Tietze, Christopher. "Therapeutic Abortions in New York City, 1943–1947." *American Journal of Obstetrics and Gynecology* 60 (1950):146–52.

———. "Therapeutic Abortions in the United States." *American Journal of Obstetrics and Gynecology* 101(6) (July 13, 1968):784–87.

———. *Induced Abortion: 1979*. New York: Population Council, 1980.

Tilly, Charles. *The Vendée*. Cambridge, Mass.: Harvard University Press, 1964.

Todd, John. *Serpents in the Dove's Nest*. Boston: Lea & Shepard, 1867.

Tolnoi, B. B. "The Abortion Racket." *Forum* 94 (Sept. 1935).

"Two Abortifacients Barred." *Journal of the American Medical Association* 113 (1939):1583.

U.S. Bureau of the Census. "Child Support and Alimony." *Current Population Reports*. Series P-23, no. 112. Washington, D.C.: U.S. Government Printing Office, Sept. 1981.

———. "Fertility Indicators: 1970." *Current Population Reports*. Series P-23, no. 36. Washington, D.C.: U.S. Government Printing Office, 1971.

———. *Historical Statistics of the United States: Colonial Times to 1970*. Part One. Washington, D.C.: U.S. Government Printing Office, 1975.

———. "Voting and Registration in the November 1980 Election." *Current Population Reports*. Series P-20, no. 359. Washington, D.C.: U.S. Government Printing Office, Jan. 1981.

U.S. Department of Labor. Children's Bureau. *Maternal Mortality in Fifteen States*. Bureau Publication no. 223. Washington, D.C.: U.S. Government Printing Office, 1934.

U.S. Department of Labor. Bureau of Labor Statistics. *Area Wage Surveys: Metropolitan Areas, United States, and Regions*. Washington, D.C.: U.S. Government Printing Office, 1979.

U.S. Department of Labor. Women's Bureau. *The Earnings Gap Between Men and Women*. Washington, D.C.: U.S. Government Printing Office, 1979.

U.S. Senate. Senate Judiciary Committee. *Hearings on a Human Life Bill (S. 158 and H.R. 900)*. May-June 1981.

U.S. Senate. Senate Judiciary Committee. Subcommittee on Constitutional Amendments. *Hearings to Consider S.J. Res. 119 and S.J. Res. 130*. 1974.

Van de Warker, Ely. *The Detection of Criminal Abortion and a Study of Foeticidal Drugs*. Boston: James Campbell, 1872.

Velpeau, Alfred. *An Elementary Treatise on Midwifery, or Principles of Tokology and Embryology*. Translated by Charles D. Meigs. Philadelphia: John Griag, 1831.

Verba, Sidney, and Norman Nie. *Participation in America: Political Democracy and Social Equality*. New York: Harper & Row, 1972.

Veroff, Joseph, et al. *The Inner American: A Self-Portrait from 1957 to 1976*. New York: Basic Books, 1981.

Wade, John. "The Second Restatement of Torts Completed." *New York State Bar Journal* 52 (Fall 1980).

Wanamaker, F. D. "The Lay Use of Potassium Permanganate as an Abortifacient." *American Journal of Obstetrics* 69 (1955):259–64.

Ward, David. *Cities and Immigrants: A Geography of Change in Nineteenth-Century America*. New York: Oxford University Press, 1971.

Wertz, Richard, and Dorothy Wertz. *Lying-In: A History of Childbirth in America*. New York: Free Press, 1977.

Westoff, C. F., E. C. Moore, and N. B. Ryder. "The Structure of Attitudes Toward Abortion." *Milbank Memorial Fund Quarterly* 47(11) (1969).

Westoff, Charles, and Larry Bumpass. "The Revolution in Birth Control Practices of U.S. Roman Catholics." *Science* 174 (June 1973):41–44.

Wiehl, Dorothy. "A Summary of Data on Reported Incidence of Abortion." *Milbank Memorial Fund Quarterly* 16 (January 1938).

Wiehl, Dorothy, and Katherine Berry. "Pregnancy Wastage in New York City." *Milbank Memorial Fund Quarterly* 15(3) (July 1937):229–47.

Williamson, Oliver. "Transaction-Cost Economics: The Governance of Contractual Relations." *Journal of Law and Economics* 22(2) (Oct. 1979).

Willkie, Dr., and Mrs. J. C. Willkie. *The Handbook on Abortion*. Cincinnati: Hayes, 1975.

Wilson, David C. "Psychiatric Implications in Abortions." *Virginia Medical Monthly* 79 (1952):448–51.

Wilson, James Q. *Political Organization*. New York: Basic Books, 1975.

Wojitla, Karol (Pope John Paul II). *Fruitful and Responsible Love*. New York: Seabury Press, 1979.

Woodruff, L. "Case of Pregnancy Necessitating Abortion." *Ohio Medical Recorder* 10(5) (1880–1881):470–71.

Wrigley, E. A. *Population and History*. London: Weidenfeld & Nicholson, 1969.

Yasuba, Yasukichi. *Birth Rates of the White Population in the United States, 1800–1860: An Economic Study*. Baltimore: Johns Hopkins University Press, 1962.

Zincke, Foster B. *Last Winter in the United States*. London, 1868.

Index

Designer:	Eric Jungerman
Compositor:	Wilsted & Taylor
Text:	10/12 Times Roman
Display:	Goudy Bold & Times Roman
Printer:	The Murray Printing Co.
Binder:	The Murray Printing Co.